Ultimate Festival & Travel Guide Puglia

Unforgettable Experiences, Unmissable Events, Unique
Destinations, Beaches, Baroque Architecture, & Best
Times to Visit Bari, Lecce, Alberobello & Beyond

Katerina Ferrara

IMMERSION TRAVEL PUBLISHING

ISBN (Paperback): 978-1-966874-03-4

ISBN (Hard Cover): 978-1-966874-04-1

ISBN (eBook): 978-1-966874-02-7

DISCLAIMER

The author is not a travel agent. All opinions, experiences, and views expressed are those of the author based on personal travel experiences. Businesses and websites recommended in this book may change, change ownership, rebrand, or sadly close.

The author has received no compensation or sponsorship for any recommended businesses.

Contents

Explore More and Stay Connected!

T hank you for joining me on this journey through the wonders of Italy.

Unlock the Secrets of Italy with Insider Expertise!

Allow me to be your personal guide, sharing exclusive insider tips, handpicked experiences, and essential travel insights to help you uncover Italy's hidden gems, iconic landmarks, and cultural treasures like never before.

Whether you're dreaming of strolling through ancient ruins, indulging in authentic cuisine, or immersing yourself in Italy's vibrant festivals, I've got you covered! https://katerinaferrara.com/

*KaterinaFerrara.
com*

Sign up for my free monthly newsletter today and receive your FREE downloadable guides, packed with:

- Curated itineraries for unforgettable journeys

- Expert travel advice to maximize your time and budget

- Practical tips for stress-free planning

- Hidden gems and must-visit spots beyond the tourist trail

Join a community of passionate travelers and start planning your next Italian adventure with confidence! Sign up now and get instant access to your exclusive guides:

https://katerinaferrara.com/

Let's make your trip to Italy extraordinary! Sign Up Today!

Travel Italy Book Series

Available now:
Book 1: *Ultimate Festival & Travel Guide Sicily (Available in English, Italian, & Sicily in Celebration Dual-Language)*
Book 2: *Rome 2025 Jubilee Year Travel Guide*
Book 3: *Ultimate Festival & Travel Guide Rome & Beyond*
Book 4: *Ultimate Festival & Travel Guide Puglia*
Arriving in 2025:
Book 5: *Ultimate Festival & Travel Guide Venice & the Veneto*
Arriving in 2026:
Book 6: *Ultimate Festival & Travel Guide Milan & the Lakes*
Book 7: *Ultimate Festival & Travel Guide Tuscany*
Arriving in 2027:
Book 8: *Ultimate Festival & Travel Guide Naples, Amalfi & Beyond*

CHAPTER ONE

The Joy of Festival Travel

Experience Italy in Celebration

Unlock the Magic of Puglia's Timeless Festivals

Picture yourself in a sun-drenched piazza, the scent of freshly baked focaccia mingling with the salty sea breeze. A lively local band begins to play, and suddenly, dancers in traditional attire twirl in a kaleidoscope of color, their movements echoing centuries-old traditions. The warm glow of flickering luminarie, elaborate festival lights, cast intricate patterns across the cobbled streets as the town gathers for its most anticipated celebration of the year. Nearby, a long table is lined with overflowing plates of orecchiette (pasta), local cheeses, and the finest wines from Puglia's sun-kissed vineyards. This is festival travel, where you don't just visit a destination; you experience it.

Welcome to a side of Italy that many travelers overlook: one of ancient traditions and an unforgettable cultural heritage. As someone who has traveled to Italy for over 25 years and immersed myself in its vibrant culture, I have discovered that the best time to visit any town in Italy is during one of its annual festivals.

This is more than a vacation in Italy. This is becoming part of a story that began millennia ago and continues to unfold with each festival, each feast, each celebration. These magical moments define festival travel in Italy: experiences that pierce the veil between past and present, between visitor and local, between watching and belonging. Here, in the festivals and sagre of Puglia, every celebration is a gateway to understanding the soul of a place through its most joyous expressions.

Journey with me through the sun-drenched landscapes of Puglia, where each celebration tells a unique story. From the grand processions in Bari that honor centuries-old traditions to the small-town sagre where the sizzling aroma of bombette (meat filled rolls) on the grill and golden panzerotti just out of the fryer fills the air, you'll discover festivities that transform ordinary moments into extraordinary memories. Each event offers not just a spectacle but an invitation to experience the living essence of Italy's timeless traditions.

Puglia's Adriatic Sea

Finding Festival Culture

I didn't always know about this incredible world of Italian festivals. My husband and I started our international travels on our honeymoon in 1997, and we have made it a priority to return to Italy each year. Our journey began like that of many travelers, exploring Italy's famous landmarks and savoring its cuisine. But it was during a visit to a small town in Sicily that everything changed.

As I stood in the town square, surrounded by vibrant colors, the rhythmic drumbeats of the tamburi echoing off the baroque architecture, and the enticing aromas of festival specialties in the air, I felt something shift. The locals welcomed me with such warmth and pride in their traditions that I couldn't help but be drawn in. That moment sparked my love for Festival Travel: a way of engaging with Italy that goes beyond sightseeing to truly becoming part of its living traditions.

Each festival since has only deepened this connection. I'll never forget the scent of fresh focaccia drifting through a whitewashed alley in a coastal town, or the sight of a dazzling tarantella performance bringing a piazza to life under the stars. These experiences aren't just memories: they're windows into the heart and soul of Puglia, revealing the genuine spirit of its people. They've inspired me to create the *Travel Italy Book Series,* which will eventually grow to include 20 Festival and Travel Guides covering all of Italy's diverse regions and both major islands.

Festivals as a Gateway to Puglia's Culture

This book springs from my experiences at these extraordinary events. It's more than a travel guide, it's your gateway to discovering the living spirit of Italy. While it includes all the essential travel information you need (top sights, walking tours, restaurant and hotel recommendations), it offers something unique that you won't find anywhere else: an invitation to become part of Puglia's living traditions, it's festivals.

Puglia's rich tapestry of culture, woven over millennia, reveals itself in every sun-drenched town and coastal village. The trulli of Alberobello, with their cone-shaped stone roofs, stand as a testament to centuries of ingenuity, while the whitewashed cliffs of Polignano a Mare perch dramatically over turquoise waters, echoing with the poetry of Domenico Modugno's famous song Volare. In Lecce, baroque facades glow golden in the afternoon light, showcasing the artistry of local stone carvers. Along the coast, castles built by Frederick II guard the horizon, and the ruins of Egnazia tell of Roman roads that once connected this land to the empire.

But Puglia is more than just its monuments and beaches; it's a place where the past and present come together, preserving a rich cultural heritage. My husband and I especially loved how alive it still feels with everyday life. Puglia hasn't been overtaken by mass tourism, many towns haven't turned into rows of Airbnbs, but remain places where local families still gather every day for lunch, children return home from school, and life follows a beautiful, familiar rhythm. In some towns we visited, there weren't any other tourists at all, just the two of us, double-checking my walking tours for this book and making sure each site was worth the mention.

The region's vibrant traditions and festivals infuse every piazza and fishing port with infectious energy, transforming historic settings into stages for modern celebrations. Here, history isn't confined to museums: it lives in the processions of Holy Week, in the tarantella rhythms of folk festivals, in the sagre that celebrate fresh seafood and handmade pasta, and in the daily rhythms of life that echo through time.

Trulli of Puglia

Understanding Feste and Sagre

What Sets a Festa Apart from a Sagra?

As you explore this guide, you'll naturally pick up some Italian along the way, starting with two essential festival terms: "festa" and "sagra."

A festa (plural: feste) often grows from Roman Catholic traditions, like Bari's Festival of Saint Nicholas, which draws pilgrims from around the world to honor the beloved patron saint, or Ostuni's Festa di Sant'Oronzo, a spectacular event featuring costumed riders on horseback. Yet not all feste are religious: Puglia also hosts vibrant cultural festivals, from the Notte della Taranta in Melpignano, celebrating the hypnotic rhythms of pizzica music, to the Disfada di Barletta, a historic fair and knightly duel that dates back centuries. Among the most visually stunning is Putignano's Carnival, where entire streets become dazzling tunnels of light thanks to elaborate light displays and giant papier-mâché floats rule the roads.

While two thousand years of Catholic traditions shape many Italian festivals, these celebrations welcome everyone, regardless of faith. They're joyful expressions of history, tradition, and community spirit, offering moments where all can create lasting memories.

A sagra (plural: sagre), by contrast, springs from ancient harvest celebrations. The word itself derives from sacro, meaning "sacred" in Latin. Originally held in temple yards to thank Roman gods for bountiful harvests, these annual events live on in Puglia's small towns and villages as community fundraisers for local projects, powered entirely by volunteers.

While feste celebrate various aspects of culture, sagre focus specifically on local cuisine. From Turi's Sagra della Ciliegia Ferrovia, where the region's famous deep-red cherries take center stage, to Bitonto's Sagra delle Olive, honoring Puglia's prized olive oil, each festival is a feast for the senses. Some celebrate handmade pasta, like Cisternino's Sagra delle Orecchiette, while others highlight iconic local specialties, such as Acquaviva delle Fonti's Sagra del Calzone, featuring the town's famous onion-filled calzone. Whether it's cheeses like caciocavallo, crispy focaccia, or bold wines from the region, Puglia's sagre offer an unforgettable culinary journey.

Bari's Famous Focaccia

Here's my essential sagra tip: arrive hungry. Purchase your meal ticket at the event booth for 12 to 15 euros, you will enjoy an exceptional zero kilometro meal with local wine. (Zero kilometro refers to food produced within roughly 150 kilometers, ensuring peak freshness and supporting local farmers.)

For feste, I recommend staying two to three nights minimum, as celebrations often continue into the late evening. (You'll find specific accommodation recommendations in each chapter.) Sagre, however, work perfectly as day trips, since they often occur in tiny villages that may not even have hotels. Many visitors base themselves in larger nearby towns and venture out to experience these local food festivals.

Whether you're traveling solo, with family, or planning a multi-generational trip, these festivals offer rich experiences for everyone. Photographers, influencers, and creatives discover endless possibilities, from vibrant processions to intimate cultural moments. Music festivals showcase Italy's performing arts, while markets built around the festivals highlight local artisans creating unique treasures. Many festivals also offer hands-on experiences with traditional crafts or cooking techniques.

Families particularly appreciate the child-friendly atmosphere, complete with puppet shows, costumes, parades, and special treats. Importantly, these events support sustainable tourism and directly benefit local communities, helping to preserve these cherished traditions for future generations.

Consider this guide your personal festival planner for creating authentic experiences beyond the typical tourist path.

An Insider's Perspective

Because of my love for Italy and our goal to move there one day, I started studying Italian in 2020 when our son Augustus left for university. I don't do anything halfway, so when I decided to learn Italian, I really committed myself to it and became fluent quickly (somewhat thanks to lockdowns). What began as a personal challenge soon opened up a whole extra dimension of Italian culture to me.

Every morning, I tune into Di Buon Mattino on TV2000. What started as a simple language immersion exercise blossomed into a genuine passion. The show, broadcasting from Rome, goes beyond typical news coverage: it journeys across Italy, discovering festivals, traditions, and local specialties. Between watching Italian TV series, chatting with Italian friends, reading Italian newspapers, and my daily dose of Di Buon Mattino, I kept discovering one fascinating festival after another. Even now, each day the show transports me to a new celebration somewhere in Italy, revealing another region's unique culture. It's a daily way to learn about new cities, regions, saints, or celebrated foods.

As I explored deeper, I realized these festivals truly embody Italian culture: they're living celebrations of community, history, folklore, and tradition. This sparked an idea: why not experience these festivals firsthand? When I began planning our travels around them several years ago, I was thrilled that my husband, son, cousins, and friends were just as excited to join the adventure.

While we have cultural festivals in the U.S., they're different. Italian festivals are lifelong commitments, drawing people back year after year, even from far away. These aren't just celebrations: they're cherished reunions with family and friends.

A huge part of what makes these festivals special is the food: dishes and desserts you can only find during these celebrations, flavors that stay hidden from restaurant menus the rest of the year. As I researched these festivals for our trips, the cuisine emerged as a crucial part of the story, deeply woven into local traditions and memorable experiences.

I'll never forget hunting down the Testa del Turco at the Festa della Madonna delle Milizie in Scicli, Sicily. Following the enticing aromas through the centro storico, my anticipation grew with each step. Never before had I tasted such a thing: delicate, crisp pastry filled with a rich, creamy delight. It wasn't just delicious; it was a gateway into the festival's spirit, a flavor that captured the essence of celebration and tradition. Don't worry: I've included all these special festival foods in the chapters!

My friend Annalisa's story perfectly captures this Italian attitude toward festivals. Like many Italians, she moved to Rome for work but returns to her hometown every year for her patron saint's festival. When I asked to join her one year, she laughed and said, "Katerina, you wouldn't be able to keep up! I run all over town just to see the procession of Sant'Ambogio at every important viewpoint!" Her enthusiasm showed me how deeply these festivals are woven into Italian life.

Why Festival Travel?

- Experience cities at their most alive and authentic, when streets pulse with music, color, and celebration.

- Join in centuries-old traditions that most tourists never witness, from solemn processions to joyous feasts.

- Savor once-a-year delicacies and festival-specific dishes that rarely appear on restaurant menus.

- Discover the fascinating stories and cultural significance behind each celebration, passed down through generations.

- Connect meaningfully with local communities as they welcome visitors into their cherished traditions.

- Capture extraordinary moments, from elaborate costumes to breathtaking ceremonial displays.

- Share in activities that delight all ages, making these festivals perfect for family memories.

- Support and help preserve local traditions while contributing directly to community economies.

What to Expect in This Book

In the chapters that follow, we'll delve deep into Puglia's most captivating festivals, exploring their origins, significance, and the best ways to experience them. Whether you're planning a trip or simply armchair traveling, this book will be your guide to the heart of Apulian culture through its vibrant celebrations.

Bari's Norman Fortress, one of 10+ in Puglia

Maximize Your Festival Experience with FestaFusion

Why see just one festival when you can experience several during your visit?

I've coined the term FestaFusion to help you discover the magic of timing your visit to catch multiple celebrations. With so many festivals throughout Puglia, experiencing several in one trip is not only possible but incredibly rewarding. For example:

- Join FestaFusion Taranto, a combination of Taranto's Palio and the Festival of San Cataldo.

- Experience FestaFusion Fasano, where history and devotion unite in a spectacular celebration. This unique event blends La Scamiciata, commemorating Fasano's victory over Turkish invaders on June 2, 1678, with the Festival of the Patron Saints, creating an unforgettable fusion of tradition, pageantry, and local pride.

- Plan a Sant'Oronzo journey, visiting Lecce, Ostuni, and other towns that celebrate the patron saint with processions, fireworks, and lively street performances.

- Celebrate Carnival season with Putignano's historic Carnival, one of Italy's oldest, followed by the Carnival of Massafra or Gallipoli for even more masked parades and vibrant floats.

- During harvest season, savor multiple sagre, from olive and wine festivals to sagre celebrating cheeses, pasta, and traditional Pugliese breads.

Mix and match festivals across chapters. They are all within easy reach, making it possible to experience multiple celebrations in a single trip.

These festival combinations offer more than convenience; they're transformative. Each celebration adds new layers to your understanding of Apulian culture, revealing hidden connections in traditions, foods, and customs. With some planning, this guide makes it easy to experience several events in one trip, exactly what my husband and I plan to do in our retirement: Una festa ogni settimana-A festival every week!

Worried about crowds?

Don't be. While major events like Holy Week in Taranto, Easter celebrations across Puglia, the Carnevale di Putignano, and Lecce's Festa di Sant'Oronzo draw large numbers, most festivals in this book are intimate affairs, primarily attended by locals. These relaxed, laid-back celebrations let you soak in the culture without the tourist rush. Yes, I hope to inspire more travelers to become Festival Followers, but you won't find yourself lost in crowds. In fact, many of these festivals are far less crowded than a summer afternoon in Polignano a Mare, offering a more authentic and personal experience. At many events, we've been the only tourists present, making each discovery feel special.

This guide to Puglia's festivals marks just the beginning of our journey through Italy's rich cultural landscape. As the fourth book in the Travel Italy series, it joins my personal mission to explore the festivals and traditions of all 20 Italian regions. Each book delves deep into a different region, uncovering its unique celebrations, local customs, and hidden gems.

Festival Travel transforms ordinary tourism into extraordinary experiences. Instead of viewing Puglia through the lens of a guidebook, you'll experience it through the joy of its celebrations, the warmth of its communities, and the depth of its traditions.

Join me in discovering the real Italy: one festival at a time. Let's embark on this journey together, where every cobblestone street echoes with history, every local dish tells a story, and every celebration invites you to become part of Europe's living heritage.

How to Use This Book

Italy, with its rich tapestry of history, culture, and natural beauty, offers an abundance of treasures for travelers. Recognizing that most visitors have limited vacation time, this guide is designed to help you make the most of your Italian adventure, focusing especially on **Festival Travel**. This book introduces a distinctive way to experience Italy: through its vibrant sagre and feste. By timing your visit with local celebrations, you'll gain unparalleled insights into the culture, traditions, and community life.

The chapters in this book are organized chronologically by festival date, providing a year-round journey through Italy's celebratory calendar. This framework simplifies finding festivals during your travel schedule. A comprehensive festival calendar is included to further assist your planning, offering a quick overview of events throughout the year. At the end of the book, there are two chapters: **Calendar of Events** and **Alphabetical Index of Locations** to help guide you. Discover festivals in your planned destinations, or find festivals of interest and incorporate their towns into your trip.

To use this guide effectively, start by considering your travel dates. Consult the festival calendar to see which events coincide with your visit. Once you've identified festivals of interest, you can turn to the relevant chapters for detailed information about each celebration and its location. Each chapter provides not only festival details but also detailed descriptions of the host cities, including must-see attractions, local customs, and authentic experiences beyond the tourist track.

The guide offers more than just festival information. It provides historical context for each event, explaining their origins and why they remain crucial to Italian identity today. You'll find practical advice on transportation, restaurant recommendations, accommodation suggestions during peak festival periods, and nearby sites, cities, and towns for day trips.

Embrace the spontaneity of Italian travel, particularly during festive seasons. While this guide offers well-researched information, the dynamic nature of festivals means schedules can evolve. To enhance your experience, I've included a variety of options and activities for each destination. This way, you're guaranteed an enriching adventure, with plenty of room for delightful surprises along the way.

Italian festivals fall into two categories: fixed-date celebrations that occur annually on specific dates, and moveable feasts that align with weekends, harvests, or religious calendars. Each festival listing includes timing details to help you plan effectively.

My website offers sample itineraries that show how to combine festival experiences with broader regional exploration, making it easier to create your perfect Italian journey. https://katerinaferrara.com/

Walking Tours

While other travel guides simply list attractions and leave you to puzzle out the logistics, I've designed this book differently. Each town features carefully crafted walking tours that present sites in a logical, walkable sequence, complete with practical details to help you plan efficiently.

Though festivals are our focus, this guide serves equally well as a companion for general travel. You'll find detailed city guides, walking tours, cultural context, and practical advice valuable for any visit to the region.

Consider this guide your key to unlocking Italy's vibrant spirit. Whether you're here for the festivals or seeking to explore the region's rich tapestry of experiences, you'll discover everything needed to create a memorable adventure.

Allow yourself to be swept up in the warmth of Italian hospitality, savor the flavors of local cuisine, and immerse yourself in the country's millennia-old traditions. With this book as your companion, you're well-equipped to venture beyond the typical tourist path and create lasting memories in one of Europe's most captivating countries.

Festival Chapters—What's Included

Each Festival Chapter unfolds like a story, featuring:

1. **The Essentials**: Where, When, Festival Website, and Seasonal Temperatures

2. **Town Portrait**: A Vivid Snapshot and History for Each Town

3. **Festival Details**: Origins, Traditions, Events, and Those Special Festival-Only Treats

4. **Walking Discovery**: Top Sights to See in Walkable Order with Detail

5. **Year-Round Magic**: Celebrations for every Season

6. **Beyond the Festival**: Nearby Sites, Cities, and Towns

7. **Making It Happen**:

   - Getting There and Around

   - Where to Eat Like a Local

   - Where to Stay and for How Long

Immersion Experiences: Beyond the Festivals

While festivals are the heart of this book, I've discovered that Italy's magic extends far beyond its celebrations. That's why I've included special Immersion Experience chapters. Think of these as your guide to authentic adventures near each festival location: experiences that let you dive deeper into local life, whether you're between festivals or creating your own unique journey.

These year-round experiences invite you to:

- Get Your Hands Dirty: Learn to cook alongside local nonnas (grandmothers) or watch master artisans at work in their centuries-old crafts.

- Embrace Nature's Drama: Trek the areas hilly landscapes, explore hidden swimming spots, or sail along rugged coastlines.

- Live the History: Watch classical dramas in ancient theaters or discover secret historical sites tourists rarely see.

- Go Behind the Scenes: Visit family vineyards, learn the secrets of olive oil making, or try your hand at traditional cheese crafting.

Immersion Experience - Swim in the Sea Caves

Each Immersion Experience chapter is your insider guide, packed with:

- The Full Story: What makes this experience special and what to expect.

- Making It Happen: Booking tips, packing essentials, perfect timing, and how to get there.

- Insider Secrets: Little-known tips to make your experience even better.

A Word About Tours

While I've crafted over 30 self-guided walking adventures for you, there's something special about exploring with a local guide. If your budget allows, I recommend booking through Tours By Locals or With Locals, especially in smaller towns where local knowledge is invaluable. Their stories and insights can transform a simple walk into an unforgettable journey.

Planning Your Festival Travel

Want to make the most of your festival experience? Arrive the evening before. This golden rule has served me well: it gives you time to discover the town's rhythm, wander its streets without rushing, and scout the perfect spots for tomorrow's celebrations. My first stop is always finding the main piazza and central church (whether it's called a cattedrale, duomo, or chiesa madre). These are the heart of most festivals, and knowing their location helps you navigate the festivities like a local.

How Long to Stay

Puglia is a fairly spread-out region, with its treasures scattered from coast to countryside. To truly settle in, explore its main cities, and experience the local rhythm, I recommend spending at least a week to ten days. If you have more time, even better, Puglia rewards those who linger. For major festivals, I recommend two to three nights minimum. Don't let accommodation costs worry you: outside major cities, Italian hotels are surprisingly affordable. (One of my favorite stays was right in Piazza Duomo in Ragusa for just $100 a night!) Longer stays let you fully immerse yourself in evening events, especially during those magical summer festivals, without worrying about late night drives. Plus, festival schedules can be delightfully unpredictable: having extra time lets you go with the flow.

For food festivals (sagre), you can often make it a day trip or enjoy the town for a night or two.

Early Bird Benefits

Arrived with time to spare? Perfect! Use these precious hours to:

- Follow my walking tour to uncover the town's hidden gems.

- Sample regional specialties at local restaurants.

- Stop by cafes to chat with locals—they often share insider festival tips and stories that you won't find in any guide.

As the festival draws near, keep an eye out for event programs. In my experience, they're usually posted on cathedral doors and other prominent spots around town.

**Festival events and dates are subject to change due to weather conditions, local circumstances, or other unforeseen factors. To ensure you have the most up-to-date information, I recommend checking local flyers, the official festival website provided in this guide, or the comune's website both before booking and upon arrival.

The Art of Festival Immersion

Once the festival begins, let yourself be swept up in the experience. Join in the activities, savor those once-a-year festival treats, and connect with the community.

Not Just Festivals: A Complete Guide to Top Cities and Experiences

Beyond Festivals: Your Complete Guide to Puglia's Treasures

While the festivals of Italy ignite its cities with vibrant life, this guide unveils much more than just celebrations. Think of it as your key to unlocking everything from Puglia's ancient quarters to Locorotondo's white washed streets, from coastal gems to hidden hilltop towns.

Whether you're timing your visit to join in centuries-old celebrations or creating your own path through this enchanting region, you'll find the insights here to make every moment count.

What This Guide Offers:

- **City Highlights:** Discover what makes each place unique, from Bari's eternal majesty to Lecce's southern charm. Each city profile reveals the character that only locals usually know.

- **Living History:** Uncover how Greek, Roman, and medieval influences weave through daily life here. These aren't just facts, they're the stories that bring these places to life.

- **Natural Wonders:** Journey from the vine-covered hills to pristine beaches and secret nature reserves. I'll show you where to find the views that postcards miss.

- **Local Life:** Find those authentic moments that make travel meaningful: from morning markets where locals shop for dinner to quiet piazzas, where time seems to stand still.

- **Food Finds:** Through countless meals and recommendations from our local friends, we've curated a list of restaurants that serve authentic regional specialties at honest prices.

- **Festival Focus:** While this guide covers all aspects of Puglia, I've highlighted the celebrations that transform ordinary places into extraordinary experiences, helping you time your visit for maximum magic.

Experience the Joy of Puglia's Festivals

Puglia's sun-drenched landscapes, whitewashed villages, and turquoise coastlines are only part of its allure, the region's heart beats strongest in its festivals. Imagine yourself here: standing beneath a canopy of dazzling luminarie as a town erupts in music and celebration, following a centuries-old procession winding through ancient olive groves, or savoring local wine at a lively sagra in a hilltop village. These are the moments that reveal the soul of Puglia, experiences that most travelers never uncover.

This guide isn't just about where and when these festivals happen, it's about how to immerse yourself in them. I'll take you beyond the main squares to hidden courtyards where the real celebrations unfold, introduce you to artisans who keep Puglia's traditions alive, and show you the best places to taste the festival foods perfected over generations.

No matter where you're traveling in Puglia, there's always a festival or sagra nearby, it's just a matter of knowing where to look. Whether it's the vibrant celebration of Novoli's Festa di Sant'Antonio, the awe-inspiring procession of Monte Sant'Angelo's Festa di San Michele, or the spiritual atmosphere of San Giovanni Rotondo's festival, Puglia's festas will transform your journey into an unforgettable experience.

Welcome to Festival Travel— your most extraordinary Italian adventures are about to begin.

CHAPTER TWO

Discover Puglia, A Tapestry of Civilizations

Five Thousand Years of History, Culture & Transformation

P uglia: Layers of History, Timeless Beauty

Bordered by the Adriatic and Ionian Seas, Puglia occupies a prime position on Italy's southeastern coast, a crossroads of history for millennia. From the arrival of the ancient Greeks to the Roman Empire's eastern ports, each era has left its mark on the region's landscapes, traditions, and architecture.

During our Puglia travels from the northern coast down to the southern tip of the Salento, one thing has become strikingly clear: olive trees are the lifeblood of this land. We drove for hours through groves of all kinds, towering and short, ancient and newly planted. Some hugged the hillsides; others framed our path along the coast. We learned Puglia produces around 40% of all Italian olives, and once we saw the endless groves, it made perfect sense. The trees, with their twisted trunks and silver-green leaves, seemed to carry the weight of centuries.

One day, we spotted the white city of Ostuni from afar, shimmering in the sunlight like a vision from a dream. Later, while working on one of my walking tours for this book, we turned a corner and found ourselves face-to-face with a Roman column, quietly standing guard in a town piazza, blending seamlessly into daily life. Those were the moments that made Puglia unforgettable, not just its famous architecture or landscapes, but the way the past and present live side by side.

Ostuni, the white city

Today's Puglia emerges from this rich tapestry of history as a land of contrasts. Whitewashed hill towns crown ancient olive groves, Baroque splendor rises from medieval streets, and fishermen still cast their nets as their ancestors did millennia ago. From the rocky Gargano peninsula in the north to the fertile plains of the Salento in the south, each corner of Puglia tells its own story.

In this land where time seems to flow differently, ancient olive trees twist their gnarled trunks toward the sun as they have for over a thousand years, while church bells echo across valleys dotted with cone-roofed trulli houses, each stone a testament to centuries of human ingenuity and tradition.

Ancient Origins

Long before Rome's rise to power, Puglia's fertile soil and strategic position attracted waves of settlers. The Messapii people established prosperous settlements across the Salento peninsula, while Greek colonists founded wealthy city-states like Taras (modern-day Taranto), bringing their sophisticated culture and traditions. These early inhabitants left behind a legacy of art, architecture, and cultural practices that still influence the region today, from the Greek-derived Griko dialect still spoken in some villages to the ancient olive cultivation techniques that produce Puglia's liquid gold.

The Roman Empire

Under Roman rule, Puglia became a crucial gateway to the East. The Via Appia, Rome's most important highway, ended at Brindisi's natural harbor, making the city a bustling port for trade and diplomacy with Greece and the Orient. Roman engineers transformed the landscape with aqueducts and roads, while wealthy patricians built luxurious villas along the coast. The remnants of this golden age can still be seen in sites like the ancient amphitheater of Lecce and the Via Traiana that connected Benevento to Brindisi.

Fall of Rome

As the Roman Empire crumbled, Puglia's strategic position made it both valuable and vulnerable. Byzantine rulers fortified coastal cities, while Lombard duchies controlled inland territories. The region became a crossroads of cultures, with Greek Orthodox monasteries flourishing alongside Latin churches. Arab raids led to the construction of coastal watchtowers, many of which still stand sentinel along Puglia's shoreline, while Norman conquerors left their mark on the distinctive Romanesque cathedrals that dot the landscape.

Medieval and Crusader Age

I'd be happy to expand on the medieval period in your historical overview of Puglia. Here's an enhanced version that provides more depth about this fascinating era:

Medieval and Crusader Age

During the Middle Ages, Puglia rose to extraordinary prominence as a vital gateway between Western Europe and the East. From the 11th to 13th centuries, the region became a dazzling mosaic of cultural influences under successive Byzantine, Norman, Swabian, Angevin, and Aragonese rulers, each leaving indelible marks on the landscape.

The Norman conquest, beginning in 1071, transformed Puglia's architectural identity. Under leaders like Robert Guiscard and his successors, magnificent Romanesque cathedrals arose in Trani, Bari, and Otranto, their facades adorned with intricate stone carvings depicting biblical scenes and mythical creatures. These churches combined Northern European structural elements with Byzantine artistic motifs and Islamic decorative influences, creating Puglia's distinctive architectural fusion.

Trani Cathedral, started in 1099
under Norman rule

Emperor Frederick II of Hohenstaufen, called "Stupor Mundi" (Wonder of the World), made Puglia his beloved homeland during the 13th century. His crowning achievement, the octagonal Castel del Monte near Andria, stands as one of medieval Europe's most mysterious and mathematically perfect structures. Frederick's cosmopolitan court brought together Christian, Jewish, and Muslim scholars, fostering an intellectual renaissance centuries before Florence's flourishing.

Puglia's position made it crucial during the Crusades, with ports such as Bari, Brindisi, and Otranto serving as bustling embarkation points for knights, pilgrims, and merchants bound for the Holy Land. The Via Francigena, an ancient pilgrim road, brought travelers from across Europe to Monte Sant'Angelo's Sanctuary of Saint Michael the Archangel, a sacred grotto believed to have been consecrated by the archangel himself and one of Christendom's most important medieval pilgrimage sites.

This period also saw the rise of powerful maritime republics like Amalfi, Venice, and Genoa establishing trading outposts along Puglia's coast. Their influence brought further wealth and artistic patronage, funding the construction of merchant palaces, loggias, and defensive structures. The Knights Templar and Knights Hospitaller established commanderies throughout the region, providing protection for pilgrims and developing sophisticated agricultural techniques that transformed the landscape.

The medieval era's tumultuous history is recorded in Puglia's fortified towns, where massive walls, watchtowers, and castles stand as testaments to centuries of invasion and conflict. Cities like Gallipoli, Otranto, and Barletta developed distinctive urban layouts designed for defense, with narrow, winding streets leading to fortified central areas where inhabitants could shelter during attacks.

Renaissance and Baroque

While Florence and Rome experienced the height of Renaissance glory, Puglia developed its own artistic identity. The real flowering came in the Baroque period, when Lecce's soft limestone allowed craftsmen to create some of Italy's most exuberant architectural decorations. Wealthy merchants and nobles competed to build ever more elaborate churches and palaces, giving birth to the distinctive style known as "Barocco Leccese." Meanwhile, in rural areas, the construction of trulli houses reached its peak, creating the otherworldly landscapes we see today.

Lecce's Baroque Cathedral Facade

Modern Era

From the unification of Italy to the present day, Puglia has transformed while maintaining its essential character. Traditional agriculture has modernized, making the region Italy's largest producer of olive oil and a significant wine exporter. Historic centers have been carefully preserved and revitalized, while coastal areas have developed thoughtfully to welcome visitors seeking authentic experiences. Today, Puglia stands as a model of how a region can embrace progress while honoring its past, where ancient traditions live on in daily life and historic sites serve not just as monuments, but as living spaces where community and culture continue to thrive.

The Regions of Puglia

Gargano Peninsula & Northern Coast

The wild, forested promontory of Gargano juts dramatically into the Adriatic, offering a landscape unlike anywhere else in Puglia. Ancient beech forests of the Foresta Umbra give way to limestone cliffs where whitewashed fishing villages cling to rocky coves. Vieste and Peschici charm with their maze-like old towns, while Monte Sant'Angelo's sacred cave has drawn pilgrims for centuries. This is Puglia at its most rugged and spiritual.

Tavoliere delle Puglie

The "tableland of Puglia" stretches inland as Italy's second-largest plain, a patchwork of wheat fields that once served as Rome's breadbasket. Foggia anchors this agricultural heartland, where seasonal festivals celebrate harvests and ancient transhumance routes. Less visited by tourists, this region offers authentic glimpses into rural Puglian life and hearty inland cuisine.

Terra di Bari

Centered on the vibrant capital of Bari, this coastal strip balances urban energy with medieval charm. Polignano a Mare's dramatic sea caves and Trani's seafront cathedral exemplify the region's stunning coastal architecture. Inland, discover the Norman-Swabian Castle of Castel del Monte, a UNESCO marvel of medieval geometry, while towns like Ruvo di Puglia showcase the area's ancient Peucetian heritage through exceptional museum collections.

Valle d'Itria

Perhaps Puglia's most enchanting landscape, this gentle valley of rolling hills, is distinguished by its concentration of trulli, the iconic cone-roofed dwellings that create a fairy-tale atmosphere. Alberobello's trulli-lined streets draw visitors, but the real magic lies in whitewashed towns like Locorotondo, Cisternino, and Martina Franca, where baroque elegance meets rural simplicity. The valley's microclimate produces exceptional wines and the region's distinctive cucina povera.

Salento Peninsula

The sun-baked "heel" of Italy's boot, Salento, is where distinct Greek influences still flavor the culture, cuisine, and even language. Lecce, the "Florence of the South," dazzles with its ornate baroque architecture and golden stone. The peninsula is embraced by two seas, the Adriatic to the east and Ionian to the west—creating a coastline of remarkable diversity, from the dramatic cliffs of Otranto to the Caribbean-like beaches of Porto Cesareo. This is the spiritual home of pizzica music and dance, celebrated during summer's La Notte della Taranta festival.

Murgia

The limestone plateau of Alta Murgia offers Puglia's most dramatic inland scenery, a stark, beautiful landscape of rocky outcrops, cave dwellings, and ancient sheep paths. Towns like Altamura, famous for its DOP-protected bread, and Gravina in Puglia, with its spectacular ravine, showcase the region's deep connection to the land. This less-traveled corner reveals Puglia's prehistoric heritage through remarkable cave systems and archaeological sites.

The Tremiti Islands

San Domino, San Nicola, and Capraia float offshore like precious stones scattered in azure waters, offering world-class diving among Roman shipwrecks and vibrant marine life. Inland towns such as San Giovanni Rotondo, Padre Pio's hometown, and Vico del Gargano, famed for its Valentine's Day celebrations, authentically preserve Gargano's culture.

Note on Historical Terms:

Because I want to keep the history sections concise and get you to the festivals and travel information as quickly as possible, I have included many historical terms in the **Glossary of Key Terms** section. If you come across a ruling family, architectural style, or historical reference that is not fully covered in the history section, please refer to the glossary for additional details.

CHAPTER THREE

Arrive and Explore

A Quick Guide to Transportation and Accommodation

Puglia's Pathways: Getting Around the Region

For more detailed information, see the **Transportation Details Chapter** towards the end of the book.

Picture this: you're standing in Puglia, surrounded by olive groves, whitewashed villages, and stunning coastline, ready for adventure. But how do you navigate this sun-drenched paradise? Don't worry, I've got you covered!

The Big Picture

Airports: Puglia has two main international airports in Bari and Brindisi, connecting travelers to Italy and beyond.

Trains: A solid network links major cities like Bari, Lecce, Taranto, and Foggia, with regional trains reaching charming coastal and inland towns.

Buses: Cover areas not serviced by trains, making them essential for reaching smaller villages and hidden gems.

Ferries: Connect Puglia to destinations across the Adriatic, including Croatia, Greece, and Albania.

Taxis and Private Drivers: Great for day trips, wine tours, or reaching off-the-beaten-path locations.

Car Rentals: Ideal for flexibility, but narrow roads and ZTL (limited traffic or pedestrian only) zones in historic centers require careful navigation.

In my travels, I've found that a combination of trains, buses, taxis, and private drivers works best. It takes the stress out of parking and navigating winding roads while letting you soak in Puglia's beauty. That said, we've always chosen to rent a car in Puglia, as it's often the best way to road trip through areas like the Valle d'Itria, Gargano Peninsula, or Salento, especially where public transportation is limited. When possible, though, we prefer traveling by train to avoid the hassle of parking, so we often plan our stays around towns with good rail connections and use trains whenever it makes sense.

Travel planning websites can help you map your trip and find bus, ferry, or train routes. These include Rome2Rio, Omio, or Moovit.

Bari's charming historic center

Where to Stay: Puglia's Diverse Accommodation Options

Find more information in the **Accommodation Details Chapter** toward the end of the book.

For accommodations, I've found a strategy that balances comfort and exploration:

- Stay put for 3-5 nights before moving on. This allows for a mix of "stay days" (local exploration) and "go days" (Immersion Experiences and day trips). Choose a town with a train station within a walkable distance.

- Alternate between hotels and Airbnbs with washing machines. This gives you hotel comforts and the practicality of doing laundry and packing light.

- Search for accommodation within a half-mile radius of the historic center. In most Puglian towns, this puts you within walking distance of key sites, charming piazzas, and local dining spots. If you can see the town's main cathedral or piazza from your balcony, you've struck gold! I provide accommodation ideas in each festival chapter.

Beautiful Polignano a Mare is our favorite, central with train station

Types of Accommodation in Puglia

See the **Accommodation Detail** toward the end of the book for websites and more information.

Hotels. Rated from one-star (basic) to five-star (luxury with full services), hotels are a great option for travelers looking for comfort and convenience.

Private Rooms and B&Bs. These offer a more personal touch and often provide insights into local life. You'll find everything from small family-run guesthouses to boutique B&Bs in historic buildings.

Holiday Apartments. Ideal for longer stays or for travelers who prefer independence. Self-catering apartments are especially great for families or groups looking for extra space.

Rural Accommodations

Masseria: These traditional farmhouses-turned-hotels offer an authentic taste of rural Puglia, often with homegrown meals, olive groves, and vineyard views.

Trulli Stays: In Alberobello and the Itria Valley, you can sleep inside the region's famous white stone trulli houses, an unforgettable experience!

Wineries: Some vineyards offer on-site accommodations, allowing you to fully immerse yourself in Puglia's wine culture while staying in a scenic setting.

Budget-Friendly Options

Hostels. Puglia has a handful of hostels, mostly in larger cities like Bari and Lecce. They provide budget-friendly stays with communal spaces, great for solo travelers.

Campsites. Outdoor lovers can find campsites along Puglia's coast and countryside, ranging from basic tent spots to well-equipped sites with bungalows, pools, and restaurants.

Booking Accommodations for Festivals in Puglia

Remember, accommodation availability can vary by season in Puglia, and this is especially true during festival periods. For the best experience, keep these tips in mind:

- **Book Early:** If you're planning to attend a festival, aim to book your accommodation at least 6 months in advance when possible. This is crucial for securing the best locations and rates, especially in popular destinations like Lecce, Alberobello, or Polignano a Mare.

- **Flexible Bookings:** Look for options with free cancellation policies that allow you to modify your plans if needed. Many accommodations offer free cancellations up to a certain date.

- **Festival Periods:** Plan to stay for more than one night if possible. Summer festivals, Holy Week events, and major food sagre attract large crowds, so securing accommodations well in advance is highly recommended.

- **Local Insights**: Some B&Bs, masserie, and boutique hotels may offer special festival packages or exclusive local insights for attendees. Don't hesitate to reach out directly and ask if they provide any festival-related perks or tips.

By planning ahead and securing your accommodation early, you'll be well-prepared to fully enjoy Puglia's vibrant festival culture without the stress of last-minute booking scrambles.

Andiamo!

Enough with the basics, it's time to dive into the heart of Puglia and explore its vibrant traditions. Let's uncover the festivals, sagre, and unforgettable events that bring this region to life throughout the year. Ready? Andiamo! (Let's Go!)

CHAPTER FOUR

Map of Must-See Celebrations

Explore Puglia's Festivals and Sagre with Our Interactive Map

Festival & Sagra Map: Your Essential Guide

Immerse yourself in Puglia's most cherished traditions. Our detailed festival map pinpoints every vibrant celebration across the region, from ancient religious processions to mouthwatering food sagre. Each marker reveals event dates and locations, making it easy to weave these authentic Italian experiences into your journey. Find the map here:

https://katerinaferrara.com

Interactive Google Map: Plan Your Adventure

Take your exploration further with our comprehensive Google Map. This dynamic tool brings Puglia's festival cities to life, helping you visualize your route, estimate travel times, and preview each destination through local photos. From North to South, plan your journey here: https://maps.app.goo.gl/5nJxmnyVKGxC8WxX9

Puglia Region highlighted, the heel of the boot of Italy

Puglia Festival Map. The Puglia Festival Map is also available in color on the book's page.

https://katerinaferrara.com/

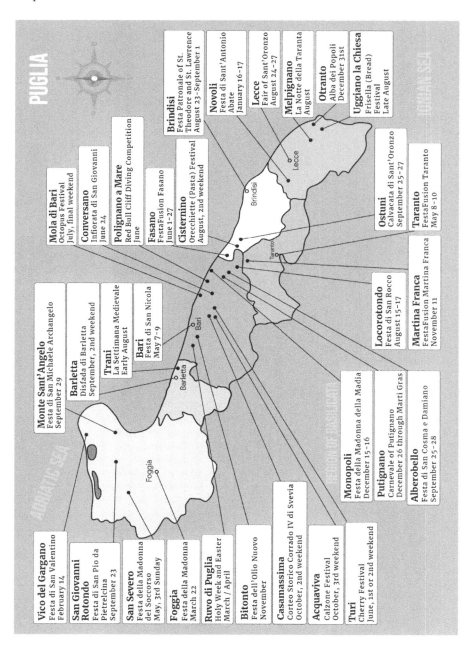

Summer Celebrations

May through August

CHAPTER FIVE

Bari's Beacon of Faith

The Festa di San Nicola and Its Timeless Traditions

Festa di San Nicola

Where: Bari

When: May 7-9 (primary festival) and December 6.

Average Festival Temperatures: High 22°C (72°F). Low 13°C (55°F).

Bari Vecchia: Timeless Charm in the Heart of History

Bari Vecchia, the historic core of Bari, stands as a living testament to centuries of history, from its Bronze Age origins to its medieval grandeur and Renaissance transformations. On a peninsula between two bustling ports, this quarter has long been a crossroads of trade, conquest, and cultural fusion. While the 19th century saw the rise of Bari's New Town to the south, Bari Vecchia remained untouched, its medieval streets preserving the echoes of its storied past.

Ancient Bari, known as Barium to the Romans, thrived as a strategic port on the Adriatic, connecting Italy to the Eastern Mediterranean. Under the Byzantines, it became the capital of the Catepanate of Italy, a critical stronghold against

Norman invaders. By the 11th century, the Normans seized control, fortifying the city with the imposing Norman-Swabian Castle, which still dominates the skyline today. The Middle Ages saw Bari flourish as a center of religious devotion, drawing pilgrims to the Basilica of San Nicola, built to house the relics of Saint Nicholas, and the Metropolitan Cathedral of San Sabino, a masterpiece of Romanesque architecture.

Bari's Norman-Swabian Castello

The Renaissance brought renewed prosperity as Bari became a duchy under Isabella of Aragon and later, Bona Sforza. The city expanded, yet Bari Vecchia retained its dense, labyrinthine layout, a defensive legacy of its medieval past. Even today, its triangular plan, chaotic alleyways, and hidden courtyards reveal a city designed for both protection and mystery.

At its heart lie Piazza Mercantile and Piazza Ferrarese, once vibrant commercial hubs and gathering places for merchants and sailors. These squares, along with the palm-lined Corso Vittorio Emanuele II, form a natural bridge between the old and new, connecting Bari Vecchia's historic charm with the modern city beyond.

Today, Bari Vecchia remains a thriving district within a city of over 320,000 residents. While exact population figures for the historic quarter are elusive, its presence is unmistakable. By day, the streets hum with local life, vendors selling fresh orecchiette, friendly residents chatting from doorways, and tourists exploring its 40 churches and 120 votive shrines. At night, the district transforms into a lively social hub, where history and modernity coexist in a way only Bari can offer.

Feast of St. Nicholas

The Festa di San Nicola in May transforms Bari into a mesmerizing tapestry of faith, history, and celebration. As the city's grandest festival honoring its cherished patron saint, this spectacular event draws pilgrims and visitors from across the globe, turning the coastal streets into a living testament of devotion and joy.

History of the Festa di San Nicola

Picture yourself in 1087, when brave sailors from Bari embarked on a fateful journey to Myra in what is now Turkey. Their mission? To rescue the precious relics of Saint Nicholas from the shadows of political upheaval that threatened their sanctity. Upon their triumphant return, they enshrined these sacred remains within the magnificent Basilica di San Nicola, destined to become one of Europe's most revered pilgrimage destinations.

Through the centuries, this profound moment has blossomed into an annual celebration that marks the relics' arrival on May 9, 1087. What began as a solemn commemoration has evolved into a captivating festival where sacred traditions dance with cultural festivities, creating an unforgettable tapestry of experience.

12th century Romanesque Basilica di San Nicola

Who is San Nicola?

San Nicola, or Saint Nicholas as he's known throughout the Christian world, stands as a beacon of compassion whose influence reaches far beyond Bari's shores, even inspiring the beloved figure of Santa Claus. Born around 270 AD in the ancient city of Patara, near Lycia in modern-day Turkey, Nicholas would rise to become the Bishop of Myra, leaving an indelible mark on history through his extraordinary acts of kindness and miraculous deeds.

His most celebrated miracle tells of a father and his three daughters, teetering on the edge of despair. In the dark of night, Nicholas secretly delivered bags of gold for their dowries, saving them from a fate of slavery. Tales of his divine intervention spread far and wide: from calming tempestuous seas to bring three children back from death's embrace.

When his relics found their new home in Bari in 1087, they transformed this coastal city into a beacon of faith, drawing pilgrims from distant lands. Today, sailors still look to Saint Nicholas as their guardian, seeking his blessing for safe passage across the seas.

San Nicola

San Nicola's Two Celebrations

May 9

The 1087 transfer of sacred remains ignited a flame of devotion that would spread throughout Western Europe. Today, Bari erupts in joyous celebration, with colorfully costumed performers bringing history to life in grand processions.

Perhaps most remarkably, pilgrims gather to witness the collection of "manna," a mysterious liquid said to form within the saint's tomb, connecting present-day devotees to centuries of faith.

December 6

As winter nights grow long, millions around the world commemorate St. Nicholas's death with traditions that sparkle with wonder. On December 5th, children across Europe place their shoes by the door with hearts full of hope, dreaming of the treasures morning might bring. In the Netherlands, this magical evening transforms into Sinterklaas, a beloved celebration that would later shape how we experience Christmas itself. Churches fill with song and prayer, families gather in warm embrace, and charitable acts flourish in every corner, living tributes to a saint who once slipped gold through windows in the dark of night to help those in need.

Across the vast tapestry of Christianity, Saint Nicholas stands as a bridge between traditions. Catholics, Orthodox faithful, and Protestants alike find common ground in his story. Orthodox Christians tell tales of his miraculous powers, while Western churches draw inspiration from his legendary generosity. Yet all unite in remembering a man who dedicated his life to protecting society's most vulnerable, the children who needed guidance, the sailors who sought safe harbor, and the poor who required compassion's gentle touch.

May Festival Events

May 7th: The Sacred Preparation

As dawn breaks over San Giorgio Bay, an electric anticipation fills the air. Skilled artisans and devoted locals gather to prepare the treasured painting of Saint Nicholas for its maritime journey. The chosen fishing vessel transforms into a floating sanctuary, its weathered deck blooming with vibrant flowers and shimmering religious banners. Locals, their faces etched with pride, consider it a profound honor to be chosen as guardians of the sacred image. This modern ceremony mirrors the historic 1087 voyage when the saint's relics first crossed these waters, creating a living bridge between past and present.

6:00 p.m.

The Grand Procession

As the sun begins its descent, Molo San Nicola erupts into a spectacular maritime festival. The painting's journey becomes a floating parade of light and sound, with vessels of every size joining the sacred procession. Small fishing boats dance alongside elegant yachts, their hulls twinkling with countless lights, while colorful flags snap in the sea breeze. The air fills with a heavenly chorus as musicians aboard various craft perform ancient hymns, their melodies carried across the waves.

As the sun sets, boats dramatically and respectfully send water high into the air, briefly making rainbows. The flotilla's approach to the old port draws thousands of onlookers who line every inch of the waterfront, their collective presence transforming the harbor into an amphitheater of faith and festivity. The scene captures a perfect balance between joyous celebration and deep spiritual reverence, as the community comes together to honor their beloved patron saint.

8:30 p.m.

The Medieval Pageant Awakens

As night settles over Bari, the Norman-Swabian Castle's ancient walls come alive with an extraordinary spectacle. Hundreds of performers emerge in a breathtaking display of medieval splendor, each costume a masterpiece of historical recreation. Proud sailors in rough-spun tunics march alongside nobles draped in rich velvets and gleaming brocades. Clergy members glide past in elaborate period vestments, while citizens dressed in authentic 11th-century attire complete this living tapestry of Bari's golden age.

The air vibrates with the haunting sounds of medieval instruments - lutes, drums, and pipes blend with ancient chants that echo through time. Torch bearers weave through the procession, their flames painting the limestone walls of Bari Vecchia with flickering shadows that seem to summon the spirits of centuries past, transforming narrow alleyways into corridors of living history.

10:00 p.m.

The Sacred Culmination

The procession's arrival at the Basilica creates a moment of true beauty. Massive bronze doors, worn smooth by centuries of faithful hands, swing open with a resonant boom that seems to make the very air tremble. Church bells erupt in joyous celebration, their deep sounds cascading across rooftops to every corner of the sleeping city. Inside the basilica's hallowed walls, the atmosphere transforms into one of profound reverence.

Prayers ascend like fragrant incense, a multilingual chorus of Italian, Greek, Russian, English, and more, uniting in a global hymn of faith. The evening reaches its spiritual zenith with the blessing, followed by soul-stirring hymns in Latin and Greek. These ancient songs, passed down through generations, fill the vaulted space with their timeless melody, embodying Saint Nicholas's eternal role as a bridge between East and West, old and new, heaven and earth.

May 8th: Saint Nicholas Goes to Sea

5:00 a.m.

The Sacred Dawn

In the hushed moments before sunrise, the Basilica of San Nicola's lower church becomes a sanctuary of whispered prayers and flickering candlelight.

10:00 a.m.

Procession of Saint Nicholas

As morning light bathes Bari's limestone streets, the city erupts in a spectacular display of devotion. The chosen portatori, their faces beaming with barely contained pride, shoulder their precious burden, a magnificent silver statue of Saint Nicholas. The saint gleams in the sunlight, adorned with sparkling jewels and crowned with fresh flowers, seeming almost alive atop his ornate platform.

Religious confraternities sweep past in their distinctive robes, their colors creating a moving tapestry against the ancient walls. The air becomes thick with incense and alive with music as traditional bands fill the narrow streets with triumphant melodies.

The Maritime Tribute

At San Nicola Pier, the ceremony reaches its most poignant moment. The statue's transfer to its chosen vessel becomes a dance of precision and reverence, symbolizing the saint's eternal connection to the sea. A decorated fishing boat, chosen after much deliberation, is transformed into a floating shrine, its deck a sacred space. As it leads a constellation of smaller vessels along Bari's coast, the flotilla creates a moving testament to Saint Nicholas's role as guardian of those who brave the seas. The sight of dozens of boats, their wakes creating intricate patterns on the azure Mediterranean, offers a powerful reminder of how a 4th-century saint continues to unite faith, tradition, and community in the modern world.

4:00 p.m.

Thunder in the Heavens

The afternoon sky erupts in a display of national pride as the legendary Frecce Tricolori command the heavens above Bari's seafront. Italy's elite air force demonstration team transforms the Mediterranean canvas with breathtaking precision. Jets slice through the air in perfect formation, their vapor trails painting massive Italian flags across the azure sky. Each maneuver tells a story of skill, courage, and devotion.

8:00 p.m.

The Sacred Return

As dusk embraces the city, Piazza del Ferrarese undergoes a magical transformation. Thousands of lights and candles pierce the gathering darkness, turning the ancient square into a glittering constellation. Church bells toll across Bari, their deep voices calling the faithful to witness the saint's return.

The statue processes through this sea of light as traditional hymns float on the evening air. Historic palazzos and churches, their weathered stones bathed in golden light, stand as silent sentinels to this timeless ceremony. The square becomes a vast cathedral under the stars, where the boundaries between heaven and earth seem to dissolve in the flickering candlelight.

10:00 p.m.

Fireworks Display

The festival reaches its crescendo at Molo Sant'Antonio with a pyrotechnic spectacle that marries ancient tradition with modern artistry. Each burst of color reflects in the Adriatic's dark waters, creating mirror images that double the display's magnificence. This dazzling finale unites heaven and earth, past and present, in a celebration that honors both the saint's ancient legacy and his living presence in the hearts of the faithful.

May 9th: The Relics and the Feast of the Bari People

6:00 p.m.

The Sacred Homecoming

As evening shadows lengthen across Bari's ancient stones, the Basilica becomes a sanctuary of intimate devotion. The 6:00 p.m. Mass unfolds as a deeply personal communion between Saint Nicholas and his adopted city. In the mystical depths of the basilica's crypt, where centuries of prayers have seeped into the very walls, the Dominican fathers perform their sacred duty with measured grace. Their collection of the manna, that mysterious, healing liquid, becomes a bridge between heaven and earth, each crystalline drop a testament to the saint's enduring presence.

The historic religious confraternities process with dignified pride, their presence adding layers of living history to the ceremony. Their traditional robes sweep across ancient stones as they bear their precious standards - each banner and symbol telling its own story of faith and community. Through the hushed basilica, traditional Barese hymns to San Nicola rise with particular poignancy, their familiar melodies carrying the emotions of generations. Local families sing words taught by grandparents to grandchildren, creating an unbroken chain of devotion that stretches back through time.

As precious drops of manna are carefully distributed, priority given to the city's residents, each small vessel becomes a treasure chest of faith and tradition.

10:00 p.m.

A City's Luminous Farewell

As the clock strikes ten, Molo Sant'Antonio becomes the stage for Bari's most intimate moment with its beloved patron saint. This final fireworks display weaves a uniquely local story across the night sky, transforming ancient traditions into bursts of contemporary joy. Traditional Barese melodies float across the harbor, their rhythms perfectly matched by cascading lights that dance between sea and sky. Each explosion seems to carry whispered stories of the city's soul - here a burst of red and white mirrors the colors of San Nicola's cathedral, there a shower of golden sparks recalls the gleam of olive oil on local orecchiette pasta.

Bari Walking Tour

#1. Castello Normanno-Svevo (Norman-Swabian Castle)

The Castello Normanno-Svevo stands as a magnificent example of medieval military architecture, its imposing walls rising from the heart of Bari's historic center. Originally constructed in 1132 by Norman King Roger II, the fortress gained its current form during Emperor Frederick II's ambitious renovation in the 13th century. The emperor transformed the military stronghold into a sophisticated royal residence while maintaining its formidable defensive capabilities.

The castle's architecture reflects its dual military and courtly roles. The outer walls, reinforced by massive corner towers, encompass an inner courtyard where medieval life once flourished. Frederick II's renovation added the distinctive trapezoidal layout and introduced elements of Swabian architectural style, including the ornate portal and the sophisticated system of arrow slits and machicolations.

In our opinion walking around the exterior is adequate. We paid to enter, but there is not much to see inside.

#2. Basilica di San Nicola (Basilica of Saint Nicholas)

The Basilica di San Nicola represents one of the finest examples of Romanesque architecture in Puglia and serves as a crucial bridge between Western and Eastern Christianity. The church's construction began immediately after Bari sailors brought Saint Nicholas's relics from Myra in 1087, marking the beginning of the city's golden age as a major pilgrimage destination.

The basilica's architectural design masterfully combines elements of Norman, Byzantine, and local Puglian styles. Its façade features twin towers, elegant arched windows, and intricate stone carvings, while the interior showcases soaring vaulted ceilings supported by granite columns. The silver altar in the crypt, where Saint Nicholas's relics rest, demonstrates the extraordinary craftsmanship of medieval silversmiths.

The church continues to draw pilgrims from both Catholic and Orthodox traditions, particularly during the Festa di San Nicola, when thousands gather to witness the extraction of the saint's miraculous manna. The basilica also houses an important collection of medieval art, including stunning 12th-century floor mosaics and carved stone capitals.

#3. Cattedrale di San Sabino (Cathedral of Saint Sabinus)

The Cathedral of San Sabino exemplifies the pure Romanesque style that flourished in medieval Puglia. Built in the late 12th century atop the ruins of an earlier Byzantine cathedral destroyed by William the Bad, the cathedral's clean lines and harmonious proportions create an atmosphere of sublime spiritual tranquility.

Cathedral di San Sabino

The cathedral's interior features a magnificent central nave flanked by double aisles, a rare architectural feature for its time. The crypt, supported by 28 marble columns, houses the relics of Saint Sabinus and contains fragments of an exceptional 11th-century floor mosaic depicting scenes from the medieval epic "Alexander Romance."

The cathedral museum preserves precious religious artifacts, including the exquisitely carved throne of Bishop Elias and illuminated medieval manuscripts. The adjacent Archbishop's Palace houses a valuable collection of historic documents that chronicle Bari's ecclesiastical history and its role as a crossroads of Mediterranean culture.

#4. Piazza Mercantile

This bustling square has been a center of Bari's commercial life since the Middle Ages. Dominating the piazza is the Palazzo della Dogana, a 16th-century customs house, and the Colonna della Giustizia, a marble column once used to punish debtors. The square is surrounded by cafes and restaurants, making it a great spot to pause and soak in the atmosphere.

#5. Piazza del Ferrarese

Next to Piazza Mercantile, this lively square serves as a gateway to the old town. It's named after a merchant from Ferrara who lived here in the 17th century. The square features remnants of an ancient Roman road and is a popular meeting point for locals and tourists.

#6. Strada delle Orecchiette (Orecchiette Street)

Fresh Orecchiette

Step into one of Bari's most charming living traditions. Along this narrow, sun-washed alley near the old city gates, local women known as le signore delle orecchiette sit outside their doorways, skillfully hand-shaping Puglia's beloved pasta. Their fingers move with incredible speed, turning tiny bits of dough into perfect "little ears" on wooden boards. You can watch the time-honored process unfold before your eyes, chat with the artisans, and even buy fresh or dried pasta to take home.

We couldn't resist purchasing a batch of the fresh orecchiette right from the street vendors. Back at our Airbnb, we combined them with simple, local ingredients, fresh tomatoes, fragrant basil, golden olive oil, and a touch of salt and pepper, creating an incredibly delicious dinner that captured the essence of Puglia. A word of advice: if you buy the fresh pasta and aren't cooking it the same day, make sure to refrigerate it immediately. I learned this lesson the hard way when our first batch didn't keep well at room temperature! The experience of eating handmade pasta just hours after watching it being crafted made for one of our most memorable meals in Bari.

#7. Chiesa di San Marco dei Veneziani (Church of Saint Mark of the Venetians)

Tucked away in the historic center, this modest yet fascinating Romanesque church was built in the 11th century by Venetian merchants. As Bari grew into a vital Adriatic port, strong ties with Venice developed, especially through trade and commerce. Dedicated to Venice's patron saint, San Marco, the church reflects a time when Bari was a key link between East and West. Its simple stone façade and understated interior speak to the practical faith of seafarers who sought divine protection for their voyages, adding another layer to Bari's rich maritime history.

#8. Lungomare Nazario Sauro (Bari Seafront Promenade)

End your tour with a stroll along Bari's beautiful seafront promenade, built in the 1920s. The walkway offers stunning views of the Adriatic Sea and is lined with elegant lampposts and Art nouveau buildings. It's the perfect place to relax after your tour and enjoy a refreshing sea breeze.

Bari's Seaside Promenade

Bari's Festivals Throughout the Year

Bari International Film Festival

March

Bari International Film Festival is a prominent film festival that attracts celebrities and filmmakers from around the world. The event features film screenings, retrospectives, workshops, and discussions, aiming to promote cinematic culture and showcase both Italian and international films.

Festa di San Giuseppe

March 19

The Feast of Saint Joseph is marked by incense-filled church services and the irresistible preparation of zeppole di San Giuseppe, delicate cream-filled pastries dusted with powdered sugar and topped with amarena cherries, made following centuries-old recipes passed down through generations of Barese families.

Easter Holy Week

March/April

Bari's Holy Week celebrations feature haunting processions through the cobblestone streets of the old town, particularly notable on Holy Thursday and Good Friday. Local confraternities, wearing traditional hooded robes, carry ornate wooden statues depicting scenes from the Passion of Christ, while mournful ancient hymns and the rhythmic beat of drums echo off medieval stone walls.

Sagra delle Orecchiette

Summer

This food festival celebrates Bari's famous ear-shaped pasta. Skilled local women, known as "le signore delle orecchiette," demonstrate their lightning-fast pasta-making techniques in the narrow streets of Bari Vecchia, their fingers dancing across wooden boards as they transform simple semolina dough into perfect shells. Restaurants offer special menus featuring various pasta preparations, from classic ragù to innovative seafood variations.

Bari in Jazz

July

This summer jazz festival transforms the city into a melodic haven, bringing international and local musicians together for soul-stirring performances. Concerts take place in atmospheric venues across the city, from candlelit baroque churches to star-lit palazzo courtyards, with the sound of improvised solos drifting through warm Mediterranean nights.

Bari Pride

Usually takes place in early July

Bari Pride is one of the prominent LGBTQ+ events in Puglia's capital city. The parade and associated festivities celebrate diversity and advocate for LGBTQ+ rights. The event has grown over the years, featuring performances, speeches, and a vibrant march through the city's streets.

Fiera del Levante

September

Established in 1929, the Fiera del Levante is one of the most important trade fairs in southern Italy. This bustling marketplace spans over 280,000 square meters, featuring cutting-edge commercial exhibitions, vibrant cultural events, and forward-thinking conferences. The fair attracts exhibitors and visitors from various sectors worldwide, serving as a crucial bridge between European and Middle Eastern markets.

European Jazz Conference

Late September

Bari hosts the European Jazz Conference, a significant event gathering over 400 delegates from 40 countries, including promoters, cultural managers, agents, and artists. The conference features performances, discussions, and showcases, highlighting the vibrant jazz scene in Europe. https://www.europejazz.net/press-release/11th-european-jazz-conference-puglia-september-2025

Festa di Santa Cecilia

November 22nd

This festival honors the patron saint of music with a harmonious blend of sacred and traditional sounds. It features spellbinding concerts throughout Bari's churches and concert halls, with particular focus on Puglian musical heritage. Ancient Gregorian chants mix with the haunting melodies of traditional folk instruments, creating an unforgettable acoustic journey through time.

Festa dell'Immacolata & Christmas Markets

December 8

The Feast of the Immaculate Conception of Mary marks the official beginning of the Christmas season in Bari. The day is celebrated with religious processions, special masses, and community gatherings. Families traditionally gather for festive meals, and the city's principal streets are illuminated with dazzling lights. Around this time, Bari's Christmas markets come to life, especially in Piazza del Ferrarese and Piazza Mercantile, where visitors can stroll among stalls selling local crafts, holiday treats, and traditional decorations. The spirit of the season fills the air as sacred devotion and festive celebration blend seamlessly throughout the city.

Nearby Sites, Cities, and Towns

Matera. 65 kilometers (40 miles), approximately 1.5 hours by car from Bari. A UNESCO World Heritage Site, Matera is renowned for its Sassi, ancient cave dwellings carved into limestone cliffs. These extraordinary structures date back to prehistoric times and were inhabited until the mid-20th century, making Matera one of the world's oldest continuously inhabited cities.

Among the top sights is the Sassi di Matera, where visitors can explore a labyrinth of cave houses, rock-hewn churches, and ancient cisterns in the districts of Sasso Caveoso and Sasso Barisano. Another highlight is the Casa Grotta di Vico Solitario, a restored cave house that offers an authentic glimpse into how families once lived in these remarkable dwellings.

Giovinazzo (Medieval Seaside Gem). 18 kilometers (11 miles) northwest. Nestled along the Adriatic coast, Giovinazzo is a charming seaside town with medieval roots, narrow stone streets, and a picturesque port where fishing boats bob in the turquoise waters. Originally an ancient Roman settlement, it flourished in the Middle Ages under the Normans and Swabians. Today, it remains a captivating mix of history and coastal beauty.

Start your visit at the Piazza Vittorio Emanuele II, the heart of town, where you'll find the elegant Fontana dei Tritoni, a 20th-century fountain inspired by classical mythology. From there, stroll through the Arco di Traiano, a historic gateway leading into the old town, where white limestone buildings gleam under the southern sun.

A must-see is the Cattedrale di Santa Maria Assunta, a stunning 12th-century Romanesque cathedral with an elegant rose window and intricate stone carvings. Inside, the crypt holds relics from the early Christian period. Walk along the Mura di Giovinazzo, the medieval walls offering sweeping sea views, and explore the Torrione Aragonese, a fortified watchtower once guarding against pirate invasions.

Logistics

Train: Bari Centrale Station is in Bari. Rome direct in 4-5 hours. Naples 3.5 hours. Regional trains cover the coastline.

Bus: Regional Operated by AMTAB, Bari's municipal bus company. Tickets are available at newsstands, tabaccherias, and via the AMTAB app.

Car: Bari can be congested, especially during peak hours. The centro storico is not car-friendly because of its narrow streets.

Parking: Private garages are available near the city center, such as Park & Ride Pane e Pomodoro. Free Parking: Limited spots exist on the outskirts of the city.

Restaurant Recommandations

Le Nicchie. Address: Vico Corsioli, 11b

Tucked away in the winding alleys of Bari Vecchia, Le Nicchie offers a memorable dining experience with authentic local flavors and warm hospitality. We enjoyed a delicious three-course dinner here on a rainy evening, comfortably seated under the large umbrellas of their charming outdoor patio. My husband savored a generous portion of fresh mussels, while I opted for the local sausage as my main dish, flavorful, rustic, and perfectly cooked. The atmosphere was relaxed, the service attentive, and the quality of the food stood out in every bite. A delightful stop for those seeking a true taste of Puglia in the heart of Bari's historic center.

Antò Cucina e Sapori Tipici. Address: Strada Palazzo di Città, 14

A family-run trattoria near the Church of San Nicola. Antò offers a menu that caters to all tastes, emphasizing simplicity and substance. Popular dishes include generously garnished focaccias, orecchiette with turnip tops or meat sauce, potatoes, rice and mussels, spaghetti with seafood or all'assassina, meatballs with sauce, and stuffed mussels. House wine is available to complement the meals.

Panificio Fiore. Address: Strada Palazzo di Città, 38

One of the longest-running bakeries in the city, Panificio Fiore is set in an old church and has been operated by the Fiore family for over a century. The wood-fired oven is always on, ready to bake their amazing focaccia, known as the 'hot wheel,' crispy on the base and soft on top. Customers may need to wait patiently, but the wait is worth it. The bakery also offers pasta, taralli in several variations, freselle, bread, and pastries.

La Uascezze. Address: Corte S. Agostino, 2/3/4

A rustic osteria located in the heart of Bari Vecchia, La Uascezze specializes in authentic Apulian cuisine served in a tapas-style format. The menu features a variety of local dishes, including Parmigiana, meats and cheese boards, focaccia, potato pizza, and involtini. The establishment offers a selection of local wines at reasonable prices and provides a cozy and romantic ambiance.

Accommodation

For either Festa di San Nicola, I recommend three to four nights in town.

JR Hotels Bari Grande Albergo delle Nazioni. Address: Lungomare Nazario Sauro, 7

This is where we stayed in Bari. It is not in Bari's historic center, but a simple walk from there. Bari's most iconic seafront accommodations, perfectly positioned along the Lungomare with stunning views of the Adriatic Sea. The rooms were pleasant and there is a rooftop pool, spa services, and an on-site restaurant.

JR Hotels Bari Oriente. Address: Corso Cavour 32

This elegant 4-star hotel is housed in a historic building near the Petruzzelli Theatre, close to Bari Vecchia. It features stylish rooms with modern furnishings and a rooftop terrace with city views.

Palace Hotel Bari. Address: Via Francesco Lombardi 13

On the edge of Bari Vecchia, this 4-star hotel provides easy access to the historic center. It boasts spacious rooms with classic décor, a fitness center, and a rooftop restaurant, Terrazza Murat, offering panoramic views of the city and the Adriatic Sea.

CHAPTER SIX

Immersion Experience: Grotte di Castellana

Beneath the Surface: Unveiling the Wonders of the Castellana Caves

Castellana Grotte: The Gateway to Underground Wonders

Nestled in the heart of Puglia, in the Metropolitan City of Bari, lies a town that guards one of Italy's most spectacular secrets beneath its streets. Castellana Grotte, with its world-renowned karst cave system, beckons visitors into a realm where nature's artistry has been quietly at work for millions of years. While the caves may be the crown jewel, this charming town offers far more than just its underground wonders, it's a place where time seems to slow down, where ancient traditions blend seamlessly with modern life, and where the essence of authentic Puglia comes alive.

The story of Castellana Grotte begins in the tumultuous medieval period, when people sought refuge from invasions in fortified settlements. The town's very name echoes its defensive origins, derived from the Castellan, the guardian of the castle who once watched over this strategic outpost. But perhaps the most pivotal moment in the town's history came in 1691, when the Madonna della Vetrana reportedly saved the population from a devastating plague. Today, this miracle is celebrated in the enchanting Festa delle Fanòve, where the town comes alive with the warm glow of traditional bonfires, marking a centuries-old testament to survival and community spirit.

Perched atop the Murgia plateau at 290 meters (951 feet) above sea level, Castellana Grotte commands breathtaking views of the surrounding countryside. The landscape is a masterpiece of nature's design, rolling hills dotted with ancient olive groves, verdant vineyards, and traditional masserie (Puglian farmhouses) that tell stories of generations past. This elevation not only provides spectacular vistas but also conceals the natural wonder that would transform the town's destiny.

Castellana Grotte is well-connected to nearby cities, including Bari (40 kilometers/25 miles away) and Alberobello (15 kilometers/9 miles away), making it an accessible and popular destination.

The Underground Marvel: Grotte di Castellana

The year 1938 marked a turning point in Castellana's history when speleologist Franco Anelli made a discovery that would capture the world's imagination. Descending into what appeared to be just another sinkhole, Anelli unveiled a vast underground network that would become known as the Grotte di Castellana, one of Europe's most magnificent cave systems.

Stretching over three kilometers beneath the Earth's surface, these caves tell a story 90 million years in the making. During the Cretaceous period, when much of Puglia lay beneath a shallow sea, nature began its patient work. Acidic water slowly carved through limestone, creating an intricate labyrinth of passages and chambers that would eventually become one of Italy's most cherished natural treasures.

The journey begins at La Grave, where natural light pours through an immense opening, creating a dramatic gateway between our world and the mysterious realm below. As visitors venture deeper, they enter the Corridor of Wonders, where every turn reveals formations that seem plucked from the pages of a fantasy novel. Stalactites and stalagmites, shaped by countless millennia of dripping water, create an otherworldly landscape that challenges the imagination.

The culmination of this underground odyssey is the renowned Grotta Bianca (White Cave), often hailed as the world's brightest cave. Here, pure alabaster walls gleam with an almost ethereal radiance, creating a natural cathedral that leaves visitors in awe.

Cavern of the Castellana Caves

Planning Your Visit

For the best experience, consider visiting in the morning when the caves are less crowded, allowing you to fully absorb the serene beauty of these natural formations. Wear comfortable, non-slip shoes, as the cave floors can be damp, and bring a light jacket, the constant cool temperature can be surprising, especially during summer months.

Website for tickets and information: https://www.grottedicastellana.it/en/

CHAPTER SEVEN

Festa Fusion Taranto

Sails, Saints, and Spectacle: A FestaFusion of Taranto's Palio and San Cataldo

FestaFusion Taranto

Where: Taranto

When: May 8-10

Average Festival Temperatures: High 23°C (74°F). Low 14.8°C (58.6°F).

#1. Festival of San Cataldo. Ancient celebration honoring Taranto's patron saint with religious processions, maritime traditions, and citywide festivities.

#2. Palio di Taranto. Historic rowing regatta featuring traditional wooden boats competing between city neighborhoods in a spectacular display of maritime heritage and local pride.

#FestaFusion means two or more festivals happen at around the same time in the same town, so visitors can enjoy multiple events during their visit.

Taranto Unveiled: The City of Two Seas and Endless Stories

Nestled on the southeastern coast of Italy, Taranto is a captivating blend of ancient history, stunning landscapes, and modern charm. Often referred to as the "City of Two Seas," Taranto straddles the Ionian Sea and its two inner bays, the Mar Grande and Mar Piccolo. With its strategic position in the Puglia region, Taranto has served as a crossroads for civilizations for over 2,800 years, leaving an indelible mark on its culture and identity. Today, it is a thriving port city, balancing its rich heritage with the vibrant life of a contemporary Mediterranean hub.

Taranto's history stretches back to 706 BC, when it was founded as a Spartan colony known as Taras. Unique among Spartan settlements, Taras was established by a group of exiled Partheniae, or illegitimate children of Spartan women, who ventured across the seas to create a new home. The city quickly grew into one of the most powerful and prosperous colonies of Magna Graecia, renowned for its art, philosophy, and naval strength.

During the Roman era, Taranto was absorbed into the Republic in 272 BC after a series of conflicts and became an important hub for trade and culture. In the Middle Ages, it was conquered by the Byzantines, Lombards, Normans, and later the Aragonese, each leaving behind traces of their rule in its architecture and traditions. In the 19th and 20th centuries, Taranto played a pivotal role in Italy's naval defense, earning the moniker "The Capital of the Italian Navy."

Despite periods of economic hardship and environmental challenges because of industrialization in the 20th century, Taranto has undergone significant revitalization efforts, with its historical center, waterfront, and cultural institutions drawing visitors from across the globe.

Taranto's unique geography defines its identity as a city shaped by water. The city is on the Gulf of Taranto, part of the Ionian Sea, and is divided into two distinct areas: the mainland and the small island that forms its historic center.

Aragonese Fortress, Taranto

As of recent estimates, Taranto has a population of 190,000 residents. This makes it one of the largest cities in the Puglia region.

#1 The Feast of San Cataldo

In the heart of Taranto, where ancient streets wind their way to sun-dappled waters, a centuries-old celebration brings the city to life each year.

Who is San Cataldo?

The story of San Cataldo begins far from the warm Mediterranean waters he would come to protect. Born in the small village of Rachau, Ireland, in the 7th century, Cataldo's journey from Irish bishop to beloved Italian saint reads like an epic tale of divine providence. As a bishop in Lismore, he was renowned for his wisdom and devotion, but it was a mysterious vision that would forever change his path, and the future of a city he had yet to know.

Following this divine call, Cataldo embarked on a pilgrimage to the Holy Land. Yet it was his return journey that would prove most fateful. As his ship battled Mediterranean storms, fate, or perhaps divine intervention, drove him to the shores of Taranto. What might have seemed a disaster became destiny, as Cataldo recognized in this shipwreck the hand of providence guiding him to his true calling.

In Taranto, Cataldo found not just refuge but purpose. The city's streets and squares became the stage for remarkable events that would cement his place in local legend. Perhaps most famous was the miracle of the spring, where Cataldo struck the ground with his staff, causing fresh water to burst forth near the Mar Piccolo. This spring, believed to possess healing properties, became a symbol of his divine connection and his commitment to the welfare of his adopted home.

San Cataldo

But it was his role as guardian of the seas that truly captured the hearts of Taranto's people. Sailors and fishermen came to view him as their celestial protector, praying for his intercession before venturing into treacherous waters. When plagues threatened the city, stories tell of his miraculous interventions, sparing Taranto from devastation. These acts of divine protection transformed Cataldo from a foreign visitor into the city's most beloved patron.

The Evolution of the Festival

The festival honoring San Cataldo has strengthened like the city itself, each era adding new layers to its rich traditions. What began as simple religious processions in medieval times has grown into a magnificent celebration that captures the essence of Taranto's identity.

In the Middle Ages, the rediscovery of Cataldo's relics in 1071 during cathedral renovations sparked a renaissance of devotion. Pilgrims began flooding into Taranto, their prayers and presence transforming the city into a center of spiritual significance. The processions of this era were solemn affairs, with the saint's relics carried through narrow streets as blessings for the city's protection.

As Taranto's maritime power grew through the 16th to 18th centuries, the festival took on a distinctly nautical character. The addition of the sea procession became a defining moment, the saint's statue, adorned with flowers and lights, floating majestically across the waters accompanied by a flotilla of decorated vessels. This tradition perfectly embodied the fusion of spiritual devotion with maritime culture that characterized Taranto's identity.

The 19th century brought additional dimensions to the celebration as Taranto emerged as a naval powerhouse. Military displays and patriotic elements joined the traditional religious observances, while the addition of fireworks and public feasts transformed the festival into a grand civic celebration that united all segments of society.

A Modern Celebration

Today, the Festival of San Cataldo stands as a testament to Taranto's ability to preserve its sacred traditions while embracing the present. The highlight of the modern festival is the Palio di Taranto, a spirited rowing competition that transforms the city's waters into an arena of neighborhood pride and friendly rivalry. This addition bridges the ancient and the modern, honoring both the city's maritime heritage and its contemporary community spirit.

As the sun sets over the Gulf of Taranto during the festival, and the waters reflect the glow of countless lights, one can almost imagine San Cataldo himself looking out over his adopted city with pride. In the mingling of prayers and cheers, in the splash of oars and the boom of fireworks, his legacy lives on, a testament to the enduring power of faith, community, and the mystical connection between a city and its patron saint.

Festival Events

May 8th

Morning: Religious Ceremonies

As dawn breaks over Taranto, the ancient Cathedral of San Cataldo comes alive with the melodious sounds of choir hymns and the warm glow of candlelight. Devotees from across Puglia gather within its hallowed walls for a solemn Mass, their prayers echoing through the same space where the faithful have worshipped for centuries.

Afternoon: Matrimonio di Maria d'Enghien (Marriage of Maria d'Enghien)

This event reenacts the 1407 marriage between Maria d'Enghien, the Countess of Lecce and Princess of Taranto, and King Ladislaus of Naples. Taranto and Naples saw their relationship strengthened by the politically significant union. The reenactment features a historical procession with participants in period costumes parading through Taranto's streets. The procession visits key historical sites, including the Aragonese Castle, where festivities such as medieval banquets, music, and theatrical performances are held, immersing attendees in the 15th-century atmosphere.

Special Festival Food
Mustazzueli

Mustazzueli (also sometimes written as Mustazzoli or Mustaccioli) are traditional spiced cookies or biscuits that are particularly associated with religious festivals in Puglia, including the Festival of San Cataldo in Taranto. Their origin appears to trace back to medieval times, reflecting the Arab influence on southern Italian cuisine.

Key characteristics of Mustazzueli di San Cataldo:

Ingredients and Preparation:

- The base is typically made with flour, honey, and almonds.

- They're flavored with spices that would have been precious in medieval times - typically including cinnamon, nutmeg, and sometimes cloves.

- The dough is traditionally kneaded until firm and shaped into small diamond or rhombus shapes.

- They have a firm, slightly chewy texture with a glossy surface from honey glazing.

Medieval trade between Taranto and the East is evidenced by the use of spices and honey. Arab-influenced sweet traditions, prevalent in southern Italy, likely gave rise to the recipe.

Evening: Sea Procession

As the sun begins its descent, the gilded statue of Saint Cataldo embarks on its magical journey across Taranto's waters. Adorned with flowers and lights, the saint's vessel leads a mesmerizing flotilla of boats through the Mar Piccolo into the Mar Grande, their reflections dancing on the twilight waters. The celebration reaches its crescendo with a breathtaking fireworks display, illuminating the Aragonese Castle and ancient bastions in a cascade of light and color that mirrors in both seas.

May 9th: Cultural Activities

Open-Air Concerts

The city's squares and historic corners transform into natural amphitheaters, where the sounds of traditional pizzica mix with contemporary melodies. Local musicians fill the air with songs that tell stories of Taranto's rich maritime heritage and vibrant culture.

Street Food Festival

Aromas of freshly caught fish and centuries-old recipes waft through the streets as local chefs showcase their culinary artistry. From sizzling fritture di paranza to delicate cozze tarantine, each stall offers a taste of Taranto's maritime bounty and culinary traditions.

Additional Culinary Delights:

Food stalls line the streets, offering a taste of Taranto's culinary heritage. Popular dishes include:

- **Cozze alla Tarantina:** Mussels cooked with tomatoes, garlic, and parsley.

- **Frittura di Pesce:** Crispy fried seafood.

- **Cartellate:** Sweet, honey-drizzled pastries, often associated with festive occasions.

#2. The Palio di Taranto

As the morning sun glints off the waters of Taranto's twin seas, an ancient tradition springs to life. The Palio di Taranto, born in the mid-20th century, stands as a living bridge between the city's rich maritime past and its vibrant present. Here, in the dancing waters between the Mar Piccolo and Mar Grande, the spirit of ten historic neighborhoods clash in a spectacular display of skill, tradition, and pride.

The Heart of the Race: Lance a Remi

The true stars of the Palio are the lance a remi, masterpieces of maritime engineering that seem to whisper tales of centuries past. These magnificent vessels, stretching 10 meters (32 feet) from bow to stern, are more than mere boats; they are floating testaments to Tarantine craftsmanship. In the skilled hands of local artisans, native timber transforms into sleek racing vessels, each one a unique canvas painted in the proud colors of its rione. As eight rowers and their helmsman take their positions, these boats become living embodiments of their neighborhoods' hopes and dreams.

The Challenge: A Test of Skill and Spirit

Picture the scene: the iconic Ponte Girevole stands sentinel as crews prepare for the challenge ahead. The 2000-meter (1.25 mile) course that awaits them is no mere straight shot to glory. Instead, it's a demanding dance through both the Mar Piccolo and Mar Grande, where every turn around historical markers and every sweep past ancient buoys tests not just raw strength, but the very essence of seamanship. Here, in these waters, where countless generations of local sailors learned their trade, modern crews prove their worth.

A Spectacle of Color and Tradition

The visual feast begins before the first oar touches water as each team emerges in meticulously crafted medieval costumes, their colors and symbols telling stories of neighborhood pride that stretch back centuries. The helmsmen, crowned with their distinctive caps, stand as proud flag-bearers of their rioni's heritage. In the opening parade, these contemporary athletes transform into living links to Taranto's medieval past, their ceremonial rowing uniforms bridging the gap between historical authenticity and competitive necessity.

The Neighborhoods: Keepers of the Flame

At the heart of the Palio beat the pulse of Taranto's historic rioni; Borgo Antico, Tre Carrare, Solito, Corvisea, and Paolo VI among them. Within each neighborhood, training facilities serve as sacred spaces where the art of rowing passes from one generation to the next.

The Ceremonies: Where Past Meets Present

Dawn breaks over the Cathedral as ancient traditions unfold. The blessing of the boats, a solemn reminder of the sea's sacred role in Tarantine life, gives way to the rhythmic thunder of traditional drums as teams process to the water's edge. The boom of a cannon from the Aragonese Castle splits the air, while centuries-old maritime flags flutter their silent commands across the waters.

Victory and Celebration: A Community United

When the waters calm, and victory is claimed, the proper celebration begins. The winning team's triumph is marked not just by the presentation of the historic palio banner, but by a deeply spiritual moment as their neighborhood church hosts a special Mass of thanksgiving. The feast that follows is a symphony of local seafood and communal joy, while their victorious vessel stands proud in the neighborhood, a year-round reminder of glory earned on the waves.

The Schedule: A Two-Act Drama

May 10th

Morning: Rowing Regatta

The waters come alive with the traditional rowing regatta, as crews in medieval garb battle for neighborhood glory.

Evening: Final Procession

The day crescendos with the Final Procession, where Saint Cataldo's statue, adorned with flowers, leads a grand parade of clergy, officials, and faithful through Taranto's ancient streets.

June or July: The Ultimate Phase

Summer brings the competition to its peak, as elite teams face off in the Mar Grande, their struggles set against the backdrop of Taranto's stunning coastline and historic architecture.

Beyond Competition: The Heart of Taranto

The Palio transcends mere sport. It stands as a living testament to:

- The fierce pride and unity of Taranto's neighborhoods.

- A maritime heritage that has shaped the city's soul for centuries.

- A developing tradition that welcomes all while honoring its past.

In the Palio di Taranto and the Festival of Saint Cataldo, visitors witness more than just a race or a religious celebration. They see the very essence of Taranto, a city where faith, history, and community spirit dance an eternal dance on the waters that have always been its lifeblood.

Taranto Walking Tour

#1. Castello Aragonese (Aragonese Castle)

The castle's construction began in 1481 under Ferdinand I of Aragon, built atop earlier fortifications dating back to the Byzantine era. Southern Italy was shocked by the Ottoman sack of Otranto in 1480; this led to the decision to build such a massive fortress. The castle's design was entrusted to Francesco di Giorgio Martini, one of the most renowned military architects of the Renaissance.

The fortress's architectural design is a masterpiece of military engineering. Its pentagonal shape was revolutionary for its time, with five massive circular towers connected by thick curtain walls. Rising 20 meters (65 feet) above sea level, the Torre Maestra is the most impressive of these. The walls, reaching up to 4 meters in thickness, were designed to withstand the most powerful artillery of the period.

The moat, which originally surrounded the castle, could be filled with seawater from both the Mar Grande and Mar Piccolo.

Castello Aragonese

Inside, the castle contains several notable features. Dating from 1492, the Chapel of San Leonardo displays remnants of original frescoes. The castle's internal courtyard, known as the Piazza d'Armi, served as a gathering place for troops and today hosts cultural events. The sophisticated system of underground tunnels and chambers includes ammunition stores, emergency exits, and a complex water collection system.

The castle underwent significant modifications during the Spanish period in the 16th century, including the addition of new gun ports and the strengthening of its defenses against increasingly powerful artillery. The Spanish also added the distinctive coat of arms of Charles V above the main entrance, which remains visible today.

Throughout the centuries, the castle served multiple purposes. Beyond its military function, it housed the Royal Navy College in the 19th century. During World War II, it served as a strategic defensive position and suffered some damage from Allied bombing. Today, while still partially used by the Italian Navy, much of the castle is open to the public through guided tours.

The restoration work carried out in recent decades has revealed several archaeological finds, including Greek and Roman artifacts, demonstrating the site's continuous occupation since ancient times. The castle's museum now houses many of these discoveries, along with a collection of medieval and Renaissance weapons and armor.

The guided tours offer access to several remarkable areas. Visitors can explore the Renaissance ramparts, which provide stunning views across the Gulf of Taranto. The tour includes the castle's deep cisterns, carved into the bedrock, which were crucial for surviving long sieges. The former officers' quarters now house exhibitions on the castle's history and the various military orders that occupied it.

Swing Bridge, Taranto

#3. Cathedral of San Cataldo

The Cathedral of San Cataldo, with its commanding presence in Taranto's old town, represents over a millennium of architectural evolution and spiritual devotion. Originally consecrated in 1071, it stands on the site of an earlier Greek temple dedicated to Poseidon, connecting the city's ancient pagan past to its Christian present. The cathedral's façade, rebuilt in the 17th century, combines Baroque grandeur with elements of the original Romanesque design, while its bell tower maintains distinctive Byzantine influences.

The interior showcases remarkable artistic treasures spanning several centuries. Within: Accessed through an ornate marble portal, the Cappella del Tesoro houses the cathedral's most precious relics, including the silver bust containing the remains of San Cataldo.. The chapel's ceiling features elaborate frescoes depicting scenes from the saint's life, painted by Paolo De Matteis in 1713. 18th-century Neapolitan majolica tiles, depicting maritime miracles linked to the saint, decorate the walls.

Perhaps the cathedral's most striking feature is its marble floor, which incorporates fragments of ancient Roman and medieval mosaics. The main altar, crafted from polychrome marble, dates from the 18th century and is crowned by a magnificent baldachin. Behind it, the choir stalls showcase intricate wooden carvings depicting biblical scenes, created by local artisans in the 16th century. During the Festival of San Cataldo, the cathedral becomes the focal point of celebrations, with its bronze doors thrown open to welcome thousands of pilgrims who come to honor their patron saint.

#4. Piazza Fontana

Piazza Fontana is a lively square that serves as a hub for locals and visitors alike. Named after its central fountain, this charming piazza is surrounded by cafés and shops where you can enjoy a quick espresso or browse for souvenirs. The vibrant atmosphere makes it the perfect spot to soak in Taranto's daily life.

#5. Museo Archeologico Nazionale di Taranto (MArTA)

A 10-minute walk from Piazza Fontana leads to one of Taranto's crown jewels: the MArTA. This world-class archaeological museum is a treasure trove of artifacts from Taranto's ancient Greek past. Admire the famous gold jewelry, intricately crafted ceramics, and the hauntingly beautiful statues that tell the story of Taranto's role in Magna Graecia. Each exhibit is a step back in time to the city's days as a powerful Spartan colony.

#6. Palazzo Pantaleo

Tucked away in the old city, Palazzo Pantaleo offers a glimpse into 18th-century aristocratic life. This elegant residence, now a cultural center, showcases period furnishings, art, and breathtaking views of the Mar Piccolo from its terrace. A visit here feels like stepping into a bygone era of refinement and grandeur. https://www.museoetnograficomajorano.it/

#7. Isola del Borgo Antico (Historic Center)

Wander through the narrow streets of the Borgo Antico, the historic heart of Taranto. This island is a living museum, with its maze of alleyways, crumbling facades, and hidden courtyards telling the stories of centuries past. Look out for artisans crafting traditional goods and vibrant street art that juxtaposes the old with the new.

#8. Lungomare Vittorio Emanuele III (Seafront Promenade)

End your tour with a leisurely walk along the Lungomare Vittorio Emanuele III, a picturesque seafront promenade. The fresh sea breeze, glittering waters, and views of the Mar Grande make this a perfect place to relax and reflect on your day. Stop at one of the seaside restaurants to enjoy local seafood specialties, like cozze alla tarantina, paired with a glass of crisp Puglian wine.

The total walking distance for this tour is around 4–5 kilometers (2.5–3 miles), which should take about 3-4 hours of walking.

Taranto Festivals and Sagre Throughout the Year

Settimana Santa (Holy Week)

The week leading up to Easter Sunday (March or April, dates vary annually)

The Holy Week processions in Taranto stand as some of Italy's most ancient and evocative religious traditions, with documented history stretching back to 1703. The celebrations began when Don Diego Calò, driven by profound religious devotion, commissioned two masterful statues from Neapolitan artisans: the Madonna Addolorata and the Dead Christ. These sacred works of art, still central to today's ceremonies, embody the deep spiritual connection between the city and its Easter traditions.

The Procession of the Madonna Addolorata begins on Holy Thursday evening, creating one of the week's most moving spectacles. Mary's painful search for her son is reenacted as the statue of Our Lady of Sorrows is paraded through the ancient streets. The slow, deliberate pace of the procession, accompanied by the mournful notes of traditional music, creates an atmosphere of deep contemplation and empathy with the Virgin's suffering.

The Procession of the Mysteries commences in the pre-dawn hours of Good Friday, when the city's streets are still shrouded in darkness. This extended procession features multiple statues depicting scenes from Christ's Passion, each carried with solemn dignity through Taranto's narrow alleys and broad avenues. The participants, maintaining strict adherence to tradition, move barefoot through the streets regardless of weather conditions, their hooded attire and measured steps adding to the profound sense of penitence and reflection that characterizes this sacred event.

Taranto Pride

Typically held in early July

Taranto Pride is an annual event that brings together the LGBTQ+ community and allies in the city of Taranto. Organized by local groups, the pride parade and related activities aim to foster acceptance and highlight the ongoing struggles and achievements of LGBTQ+ individuals in the region.

Festa di San Rocco (St. Roch)

August 16th annually

Saint Rocco, a revered figure in southern Italy, is known as a protector against plagues and a helper of the sick. His devotion spread across Italy in the Middle Ages, following accounts of miraculous healings attributed to him. Taranto's veneration of Saint Rocco stems from this tradition, particularly during times of epidemic.

Sagra del Mare (Festival of the Sea)

Late August (exact dates vary)

The Festival of the Sea in Taranto celebrates the profound relationship between the city and its maritime heritage, embodying centuries of fishing traditions that have shaped local culture and cuisine. What began as a humble celebration among fishing families has evolved into one of the region's most anticipated cultural events, drawing visitors from across Italy to experience Taranto's renowned seafood and maritime customs. The city's famous mussels, cultivated in the Mar Piccolo using techniques passed down through generations, receive special attention during the festivities.

Festa dell'Immacolata Concezione (Feast of the Immaculate Conception)

December 8th

The Festival of the Immaculate Conception in Taranto represents one of the city's most cherished religious traditions, celebrated with devoted fervor since the 18th century. This celebration honors the Catholic doctrine of the Immaculate Conception of the Virgin Mary, which holds that Mary was conceived without original sin. Though the doctrine was formally declared by Pope Pius IX in 1854, the belief had been deeply rooted in Italian religious culture for centuries before, particularly in southern regions like Puglia.

Christmas in Taranto (Natale a Taranto)

December 8 – January 6

Christmas celebrations in Taranto reflect a mix of religious devotion and local traditions, dating back centuries. The city's maritime heritage also influences its holiday customs.

Day Trip Options: Nearby Sites, Cities, and Towns

Pulsano Beaches. 20 kilometers (12 miles) from Taranto. Escape to the pristine beaches of Pulsano, a slice of paradise along the Ionian coast. Renowned for their crystal-clear waters and powdery white sand, these beaches are perfect for a day of relaxation or water sports. The vibrant hues of the sea contrast beautifully with the lush Mediterranean vegetation that frames the shore.

Grottaglie. Distance from Tarantois 25 kilometers (16 miles). Discover the artistic soul of Grottaglie, a town celebrated for its centuries-old tradition of ceramics. Stroll through the Quartiere delle Ceramiche (Ceramics District), where artisans work in family-run workshops, creating exquisite hand-painted pottery that ranges from decorative plates to stunning tiles.

Logistics

Train: Taranto is well-connected by train, making it a convenient option for travelers coming from major cities in Puglia and beyond. Bari to Taranto is 1.5–2 hours on a regional train.

Bus: Long-distance and regional buses provide another efficient option for reaching Taranto. Marozzi, Flixbus, and local services are offered.

Car: Driving to Taranto offers flexibility, especially if you plan to visit nearby towns, beaches, or countryside locations. From Bari take the SS100, approximately 1.5 hours.

Parking: Parking is very limited in the old city. It's recommended to park outside the historic center and walk or use local transportation. Park and Ride Facilities, which are on the outskirts of the city, such as near the train station or the Mar Grande area, with shuttle services to the center.

Restaurant Recommendations

Ristorante La Paranza Address: Via Cariati, 68

A charming waterfront restaurant specializing in fresh fish and shellfish, offering stunning views of the sea and a welcoming ambiance. Their mixed seafood platter is a local favorite.

Al Gatto Rosso Address: Via Camillo Benso Conte di Cavour, 2

A classic seafood restaurant with over 50 years of history, offering fresh, locally-sourced seafood dishes in a cozy, traditional setting. Known for its excellent pasta with mussels and octopus specialties.

Accommodation

For the festival, I recommend three to four nights in town.

Hotel Akropolis. Address: Vico I° Seminario, 3

Four-star hotel in the heart of Taranto's historic center. This elegant boutique hotel offers stylish rooms and a rooftop terrace with panoramic views of the city. Perfect for history enthusiasts exploring the old town.

Hotel Europa. Address: Via Roma, 2

A refined four-star hotel with modern amenities and spacious rooms, conveniently between the historic center and the newer part of the city. Known for its excellent breakfast and attentive service.

Albergo del Sole. Address: Piazza Fontana, 45

A charming three-star hotel located right in the historic Piazza Fontana. Offers comfortable, well-furnished rooms with a blend of modern and traditional decor.

CHAPTER EIGHT

San Severo's Fiery Tribute

The Dazzling Festa della Madonna del Soccorso

Festa della Madonna del Soccorso

Where: San Severo

When: Third Sunday of May and the following Monday (plus activities throughout the month of May, the month of Mary).

Average Festival Temperatures: High 23°C (73°F). Low 12°C (54°F).

Festival Website: https://lafestadelsoccorso.weebly.com/

San Severo: A Historic Crossroads of Tradition and Resilience

Nestled in the northern reaches of Puglia, San Severo is a town rich in history, culture, and deep-rooted traditions. In the province of Foggia, this charming destination is known for its blend of medieval heritage and Baroque architecture, as well as its long-standing role as a regional agricultural and commercial center.

History: A Town Shaped by Time and Tradition

Standing on the fertile plains of the Tavoliere delle Puglie, San Severo tells a story that stretches back to the footsteps of the ancient Dauni people. Long before the first grape vines took root in its soil, these early settlers recognized the potential of this strategic location, but it was the Romans who would truly capitalize on it, transforming the settlement into a bustling waypoint along the Via Traiana, a vital artery connecting Benevento to Brindisi.

Like rings in an ancient olive tree, each era has left its mark on San Severo. The town weathered storms of invasion as Lombards, Byzantines, and Saracens swept through its streets, each adding their own cultural flavors to the growing settlement. Under Frederick II's watchful eye during the Norman and Swabian periods, the town flourished, its walls strengthened and its urban character beginning to take the shape we see today.

By the time the Renaissance gave way to the Baroque period, San Severo had blossomed into one of Puglia's jewels. Its markets overflowed with golden wheat, precious olive oil, and wines that would eventually earn fame beyond Italy's borders. Yet nature had other plans, in 1627, the earth itself shook the town to its foundations. But from this devastation emerged opportunity, as the rebuilding efforts filled San Severo's streets with the sweeping curves and ornate details of Baroque and Rococo architecture that still catch the eye of visitors today.

Modern San Severo, home to 50,000, sits at a crossroads of geography and culture.

Feast of Our Lady of Help

The Festa della Madonna del Soccorso in San Severo is one of the most spectacular and deeply rooted religious celebrations in Puglia, blending centuries-old devotion with dramatic firework displays known as batterie. The festival has been celebrated for hundreds of years, strengthening from a simple religious observance into a grand event that draws visitors from all over Italy.

Origins: A Miraculous Intervention

In the shadows of 16th century San Severo, when disease stalked the streets and hunger gnawed at hope, a remarkable story of faith and salvation began to unfold. It was during these darkest hours that the townspeople first turned their eyes heavenward, their prayers rising like incense to the Madonna del Soccorso, Our Lady of Succor, the mother who never abandons her children.

The streets that had once echoed with the sounds of daily life fell quiet under the weight of plague and famine. But within homes and churches, voices joined in desperate supplication to Mary, begging for her protection and intervention.

Then, as spring follows winter, salvation came. The plague retreated, the granaries filled, and the people of San Severo found themselves standing in the light of what they believed to be a profound miracle, the end of the plague. Their gratitude overflowed into celebration, and from this wellspring of joy and relief emerged a tradition that would echo through the centuries, the yearly festival of the Madonna del Soccorso.

The Evolution of the Festival: From Solemn Devotion to Spectacular Celebration

Initially, the Festa della Madonna del Soccorso was primarily a religious event, centered on prayers, processions, and masses. The faithful would carry a statue of the Madonna through the streets, expressing gratitude for her continued protection.

By the 18th and 19th centuries, the festival had grown into a larger public event, incorporating music, lights, and traditional festivities. Over time, one of its most distinctive features emerged: the tradition of the batterie, intense and continuous firework displays set off during the procession. These rows of deafening firecrackers symbolized devotion, purification, and the triumph of faith over darkness.

Despite wars, economic hardships, and social changes, the festival has remained a cornerstone of San Severo's identity. In the 20th century, the celebration expanded even further, with more elaborate fireworks, folk performances, and cultural events added to the mix.

Festa della Madonna del Soccorso

Today, the Festa della Madonna del Soccorso is recognized as one of Puglia's most exhilarating religious celebrations. Every May, thousands of visitors flock to San Severo to witness the stunning processions, the breathtaking batterie, and the unwavering devotion of the townspeople.

While deeply tied to Catholic tradition, the festival also serves as a symbol of community strength, resilience, and cultural pride, ensuring that the legacy of Our Lady of Succor continues to be honored for generations to come.

Festival Events

Friday: The Celebrations Begin

8:00 a.m. - 12:00 p.m.

Dawn Fireworks ("Bombe alla Diana")

The festival begins with the traditional dawn-breaking fireworks, a centuries-old custom that awakens the city with thunderous explosions marking the start of the celebrations. These distinctive morning fireworks, known as "bombe alla diana," create a powerful atmosphere of anticipation throughout San Severo.

6:00 p.m.

Band Parade & Historic Procession

A dual spectacle unfolds as the city band parades through the historic streets while the magnificent Carlo V Historic Procession recreates the pageantry of the 16th century. The procession culminates in a solemn Mass at the Cathedral, blending historical reenactment with sacred tradition.

9:00 p.m.

Musical Entertainment

Piazza Allegato comes alive with music, bringing a contemporary festive atmosphere to the historic square.

11:30 p.m.

Grand Fireworks Finale

The night sky erupts in a spectacular display featuring the traditional "Batteria alla Bolognese," a unique pyrotechnic show that combines synchronized explosions with intricate light patterns, creating a magnificent end to the opening day.

Saturday, The Vigil of the Feast Day

8:00 a.m. - 12:00 p.m.

Dawn Fireworks

The second day begins with another round of the traditional "bombe alla diana," their thunderous reports echoing through the morning air.

8:30 a.m. - 1:00 p.m.

Sacred Celebrations and Band Concert

The morning unfolds with Holy Masses in the Cathedral, while the traditional band concert fills the town squares with music, creating a festive atmosphere throughout the historic center.

6:00 p.m.

Procession of Maria SS. del Soccorso

The revered statue of the Madonna del Soccorso processes through the streets, accompanied by the prestigious "N. Franconi - Città di San Severo" Band, their music adding solemnity to this sacred moment.

7:00 p.m.

Solemn Pontifical Mass

The bishop presides over a grand outdoor mass in Piazza Allegato, uniting the community in prayer and celebration.

9:30 p.m.

First Festival of Fujente

A spectacular fireworks competition showcases the artistry of pyrotechnics, with master fireworkers displaying their skills in a dazzling performance.

11:30 p.m.

Grand Fireworks Display

The evening culminates in another magnificent "Batteria alla Bolognese," illuminating the night sky with choreographed explosions and cascading lights.

Feast of Our Lady of Help (Third Sunday in May, Principal Feast Day)

8:00 a.m. - 12:00 p.m.

Dawn Fireworks

Again the city awakens to the heart-pounding "bombe alla diana," as thunderous explosions roll across San Severo like drums of ancient warriors, heralding the magnificent celebrations to come. The morning air crackles with excitement and anticipation.

10:00 a.m.

Procession of the Archangels

In a breathtaking display of celestial splendor, the Archangels and Guardian Angel glide through the streets, their gilded wings catching the morning light. This ethereal procession transforms the path to the Cathedral into a bridge between heaven and earth.

10:30 a.m.

Grand Procession

In the day's most awe-inspiring moment, Maria SS. del Soccorso emerges in radiant glory, accompanied by San Severo Vescovo and San Severino Abate. The air fills with incense and prayer as these sacred figures process through streets steeped in centuries of devotion, while thousands of faithful onlookers stand in reverent wonder.

12:45 p.m.

Festival of Fujente Finale

The afternoon sky erupts with the legendary "Batteria alla Sanseverese," a pyrotechnic symphony unique to San Severo. This dazzling display showcases the city's mastery of fire and light, as explosions paint the heavens in patterns passed down through generations.

8:00 p.m. - 8:30 p.m.

Evening Musical Performances

As twilight embraces the city, Piazza Carmine and Piazza Municipio become enchanted amphitheaters. The air vibrates with sublime melodies as local musicians and celebrated tenors weave a tapestry of sound that echoes off ancient stones.

11:30 p.m.

Spectacular Finale

The night reaches its crescendo with an extraordinary fireworks display. The "Batteria alla Sanseverese" returns in full glory, transforming the dark canvas of night into a kaleidoscope of color and thunder, as centuries of tradition culminate in a pyrotechnic masterpiece.

Monday, The Procession

8:00 a.m. - 12:00 p.m.

Dawn Fireworks

The master artisans of Pirotecnica San Pio unleash their thunderous "bombe alla diana," their explosive artistry echoing through narrow streets and across piazzas, awakening the city to its final day of celebration.

9:15 a.m.

Return of the Archangels

In a moment of profound spirituality, the Archangels make their solemn journey back to their Sanctuary, their passage marking a sacred threshold between festival and eternity.

10:15 a.m.

Grand Final Procession

A moving tapestry of faith unfolds through San Severo's historic heart as Maria SS. del Soccorso, San Severo Vescovo, and San Severino Abate process amid clouds of incense and waves of devotion. The journey becomes a spiritual odyssey, punctuated by Maestro Luca Modola's soul-stirring violin performance of Ave Maria, the heavenly voices of the "Laudate Dominum" choir, and a deeply touching moment at Masselli-Mascia Hospital where the Virgin's presence brings hope and healing.

10:30 a.m.

XX Palio delle Batterie

The morning air crackles with excitement as master pyrotechnicians compete in a spectacular display of their art, each seeking to outdo the other in a dazzling competition that pushes the boundaries of pyrotechnic possibility.

7:30 p.m.

Flag-Bearers Spectacle

The "Sbandieratori e Musici Florentinum" transform the streets into a medieval pageant, their flags painting the air with swirling colors while ancient rhythms pulse through the gathering dusk.

9:00 p.m.

Il Festakkione del Soccorso

The ancient and modern collide as DJ's transform the historic street into a contemporary celebration of joy and life.

11:15 p.m.

Fire-Dance in the Night

The festival culminates in an extraordinary fusion of flame and movement, as dancers weave through curtains of fire before the night explodes in the grand finale of Pirotecnica San Pio's "Batteria alla Bolognese", a symphonic display of light, music, and pyrotechnic mastery that brings the celebrations to a triumphant close.

Tuesday, The Day of Thanksgiving

8:30 a.m.

Morning Mass

The day begins with a thanksgiving Mass in the Sanctuary, offering prayers of gratitude for the successful festa.

7:30 p.m.

Solemn Eucharistic Celebration

The parish priest celebrates the mass with the participation of the Brothers and Sisters of the Archconfraternity of Maria SS. del Soccorso.

9:00 p.m.

Spectacular Batteria alla Sanseverese

The local tradition continues with a magnificent fireworks display in the distinctive Sanseverese style.

9:30 p.m.

Grand Concert

A spectacular concert brings contemporary entertainment to the historic festivities, followed by an innovative drone light show.

11:30 p.m.

Palio dei Fuochi Pirotecnici

The festa concludes with the traditional fireworks competition, bringing together the region's finest pyrotechnicians for one final spectacular display.

San Severo Walking Tour

#1. Cattedrale di Santa Maria Assunta (Holy Mary Assumption)

The Cathedral of San Severo, dedicated to Santa Maria Assunta, is the town's most important religious landmark. Originally built in the 13th century, it underwent significant Baroque renovations in the 18th century. Inside, visitors can admire stunning frescoes, intricate stucco decorations, and a beautifully sculpted high altar. The cathedral also houses an important relic of San Severo Vescovo, the town's patron saint.

#2. Santuario di Maria Santissima del Soccorso (Sanctuary of St. Mary of Help)

The Sanctuary of Maria Santissima del Soccorso is central to the spiritual aspects of San Severo's Festa della Madonna del Soccorso. This historic church, built in the 16th century, is where the beloved statue of the Madonna is kept. The sanctuary's elegant façade and richly decorated interior, with its grand altarpiece and Marian artwork, make it a must-visit for those exploring the town's religious heritage.

#3. Chiesa di San Severino Abate (Saint Severus Abbot)

One of the oldest churches in San Severo, this Romanesque-Baroque church, is dedicated to San Severino Abate, an important figure in the town's history. Its simple yet charming exterior contrasts with its ornate interior, which features beautiful frescoes, and an altar dedicated to the saint. It plays a central role in the annual processions during the Festa della Madonna del Soccorso.

#4. Piazza Municipio & Palazzo Celestini

The heart of San Severo's historic center, Piazza Municipio, is surrounded by elegant buildings and lively cafés. Overlooking the square is Palazzo Celestini, a 17th-century palace that once housed a monastery and later became the San Severo Town Hall. Its grand Baroque-style façade and historical significance make it a key stop on any walking tour.

#5. Museo dell'Alto Tavoliere

In a former convent, the Museo dell'Alto Tavoliere offers a fascinating look into the history of San Severo and the Tavoliere delle Puglie region. The museum houses archaeological artifacts, medieval relics, and a collection of contemporary art, including works by the famous painter Luigi Schingo, a native of San Severo. http://www.museoaltotavoliere.it/

#6. Porta San Marco

A remnant of San Severo's medieval past, Porta San Marco is one of the town's historic city gates. It once served as an entrance to the fortified town, protecting its residents from invaders. Today, the well-preserved archway stands as a symbol of San Severo's rich history and serves as a picturesque gateway to the old town.

#7. Teatro Comunale Giuseppe Verdi

Built in the 19th century, the Giuseppe Verdi Municipal Theater is a beautifully preserved example of Italian neoclassical theater architecture. Its lavish red and gold interior, elegant balconies, and grand stage make it a cultural landmark in San Severo. If visiting during opera or concert season, it's worth checking the schedule for performances.

#8. Villa Comunale

The Villa Comunale is the town's largest public park, offering a tranquil escape from the bustling streets. Lined with century-old trees, fountains, and walking paths, it's a perfect spot for a relaxing break. The park is also home to several historical monuments and statues honoring prominent figures from San Severo's past.

San Severo Festivals and Sagre Throughout the Year

Festa di Sant'Antonio Abate (St. Anthony Abbot)

The Sunday following January 17

This festival honors Saint Anthony the Abbot, the patron saint of animals. The day begins with a procession of the saint's statue through the streets, accompanied by a parade of decorated horses and other animals, culminating in the blessing of the animals. It reflects the town's agricultural heritage and devotion to St. Anthony.

Venerdì Santo (Good Friday)

Good Friday

Good Friday in San Severo features two solemn processions. The first takes place at dawn, with the statue of Christ Flagellated meeting the Addolorata (Our Lady of Sorrows) in Piazza Castello, symbolizing the encounter of Mary and Jesus on the way to Calvary. The second procession occurs in the evening, where the statue of the Dead Christ and Our Lady of Sorrows are carried through the streets, accompanied by moving hymns and prayers.

Festa del Soccorso

May 17-19

The Festa del Soccorso in San Severo is one of Puglia's most dramatic and thrilling religious festivals. Honoring the Madonna del Soccorso, the celebration features solemn processions where the statue of the Madonna is carried through the streets accompanied by marching bands and devoted followers. What makes this festival especially famous are the batterie, intense sequences of daytime and nighttime fireworks that are launched along the streets and even accompany the procession itself, creating a deafening, thrilling spectacle that draws thousands of spectators. The combination of faith, tradition, and the adrenaline-pumping pyrotechnics has made this festival a beloved and unforgettable event for both locals and visitors.

La Festa del Carmine

July 16

This celebration honors the Madonna del Carmine, a devotion deeply rooted in San Severo. The festival includes a solemn procession of the Madonna's statue and a spectacular fireworks display, known as the "incendio del campanile" (burning of the bell tower). It is one of the most visually stunning events in the town.

La Festa delle Grazia (Feast of Our Lady of Grace)

Early July

Dedicated to the Madonna delle Grazie, this festival celebrates one of the oldest Marian devotions in San Severo. While historically celebrated on July 2, the modern-day festivities include a procession and efforts to revive the traditional celebration with cultural and religious events.

La Festa del Rosario (Madonna of the Rosary)

Third Sunday of October

One of the town's oldest devotions, this festival honors the Madonna del Rosario. The highlight is the morning procession of a wooden Neapolitan statue of the Virgin, accompanied by the statues of Saint Dominic and Saint Rose. It reflects San Severo's rich religious history.

Day Trips: Nearby Sites, Cities, and Towns

Lesina. 25 kilometers (15.5 miles) from San Severo. Lesina is a quaint town on the shores of Lake Lesina, a coastal lagoon famous for its eel fishing and natural beauty. Visitors can explore the lake by boat or enjoy the tranquility of the surrounding wetlands, home to diverse bird species.

Rodi Garganico/Tremiti Islands. 90 kilometers (56 miles) from San Severo. A colorful coastal town, Rodi Garganico is a gateway to the Gargano Peninsula. Known for its citrus groves and old-world charm, it features sandy beaches like Lido del Sole, perfect for relaxing. The town is also a hub for ferries to the Tremiti Islands.

Marina di Lesina (Beach). 30 kilometers (18.6 miles) from San Severo. One of the nearest beaches to San Severo, Marina di Lesina offers golden sands and shallow, calm waters, making it ideal for families. The beach is along the Lesina Lagoon, offering a unique mix of seaside relaxation and scenic beauty.

Lucera. 40 kilometers (25 miles) from San Severo. A historic town with roots in the Roman and medieval periods, Lucera is home to impressive sites such as the Lucera Cathedral and the Angevin Castle, which offers panoramic views of the surrounding countryside.

Logistics

Train: San Severo is served by the San Severo Railway Station, a key stop on the Adriatic Railway Line connecting Bologna to Lecce. Trains operated by Trenitalia and other regional services provide frequent connections to major cities like Foggia, Bari, and Termoli, as well as smaller towns in Puglia.

Bus: San Severo is a hub for regional bus services, offering connections to nearby towns and cities, including Foggia, Lesina, and Gargano National Park.

Car: San Severo exit. San Severo is well-connected by road, Bologna–Taranto highway. From the A14, take the A14 Autostrada to access the town.

Parking: Parking in San Severo is available in several locations, including street parking and public parking lots near the town center.

Restaurant Recommendations

Il Giardino dei Sapori. Address: Via Solferino 25

A charming restaurant known for its delicious local cuisine and cozy atmosphere.

Ristorante L'Esca. Address: Largo Carmine 11

This restaurant offers a variety of traditional Puglian dishes in a lovely setting. It's a brilliant spot to enjoy a meal with family or friends.

Officina del Gusto. Address: Via Don Felice Canelli 61

Known for its creative and flavorful dishes, this restaurant is a favorite among locals and visitors alike.

Accommodation

For the festival, I recommend three or four nights in town with visits to nearby towns during the days.

Hotel Palazzo Giancola. Address: Piazza della Costituzione 3

This stately 3-star hotel occupies a beautifully restored historic palazzo in the pulsing heart of San Severo. With its imposing façade and elegant lobby featuring vaulted ceilings and local marble, Hotel Palazzo Giancola offers a perfect blend of traditional Puglian architecture and modern comforts. The spacious rooms are tastefully furnished with antique-inspired décor, premium bedding, and updated bathrooms. The hotel's central location places you just steps from San Severo's magnificent Baroque cathedral, the bustling Piazza Municipio, and many authentic trattorias.

Palazzo Ducale. Address: Via Calabria 42

This enchanting 4-star bed-and-breakfast occupies a meticulously restored 18th-century ducal residence that showcases the aristocratic heritage of San Severo. The property features six uniquely designed guest rooms and suites, each named after notable figures from the town's history and decorated with a harmonious blend of period antiques and contemporary Italian design.

Tenuta Inagro. Address: SP 142, KM 49,100

This sophisticated 4-star hotel is nestled among olive groves and vineyards just outside San Severo's historic center. Tenuta Inagro represents the perfect marriage of contemporary design and rural tranquility. The property features 24 spacious, elegantly appointed rooms with floor-to-ceiling windows that frame panoramic views of the estate's meticulously maintained grounds.

CHAPTER NINE

FestaFusion Fasano

Heroic Triumph and Sacred Celebration

FestaFusion Fasano

Where: Fasano

When: La Scamiciata is June 1-27. Festa Patronale is the third Sunday in June.

Average Festival Temperatures: High 28-30°C (82-86°F). Low 18-20°C (64-68°F).

Event Website: https://www.lascamiciata.it/

#1. La Scamiciata. The festival commemorates Fasano's victory over Turkish invaders on June 2, 1678.

#2. Festa Patronale di Fasano. Dedicated to two patron saints: St. John the Baptist and Our Lady of the Well, this festival is a blend of religious devotion and cultural celebration.

#FestaFusion means two or more festivals happen at around the same time in the same town, so visitors can enjoy multiple events during their visit.

Fasano Through the Ages

Nestled between the rolling hills of the Murgia and the azure expanse of the Adriatic Sea, Fasano is a town in Italy's Apulia region that boasts a rich tapestry of history and geography. Its story is one of resilience, adaptation, and a deep connection to the land and sea.

Fasano's beginnings are deeply connected to the ancient city of Egnatia, near present-day Fasano. Established by the Messapii tribe in the 8th century BC, Egnatia thrived as a significant port along the Via Traiana, the Roman road connecting Benevento to Brindisi. The city's strategic coastal position made it a bustling hub for trade and cultural exchange during Roman times. However, with the decline of the Roman Empire, Egnatia faced repeated invasions and was eventually abandoned.

Seeking refuge from coastal raids by Saracens and other invaders, the inhabitants of Egnatia moved inland in the 11th century, founding the settlement of Casale di Santa Maria de Fajano in 1088. This new community, which would grow into present-day Fasano, was strategically situated away from the vulnerable coastline, offering better protection. In the 14th century, Fasano became a fiefdom of the Knights of Malta, leading to significant developments, including the construction of the Mother Church (Chiesa Matrice) dedicated to St. John the Baptist.

A pivotal event in Fasano's history occurred on June 2, 1678, when the townspeople repelled an attack by Turkish pirates. Legend holds that the Madonna appeared in the sky to lead the defense, a miraculous intervention that is commemorated annually with the "Scamiciata," a historical reenactment celebrating this victory.

Geographically, Fasano marks the transition between the Salento peninsula and the Metropolitan City of Bari. The coastal areas, including the fishing village of Savelletri and the seaside resort of Torre Canne, are renowned for their natural beauty and have been awarded the Blue Flag (see glossary for Blue Flag definition) for their pristine beaches.

Fasano has a population of 38,665 residents, reflecting its status as one of the more populated towns in the Province of Brindisi.

#1. La Scamiciata (Historical Reenactment)

It began on a warm June night in 1678, in the sleeping coastal town of Fasano, Italy. The Mediterranean air is still, broken only by the gentle rustling of olive trees. But something sinister lurks in the darkness, Ottoman pirates creeping silently toward the unsuspecting town, their weapons gleaming in the moonlight. What happens next would become the stuff of legend.

The citizens of Fasano, rudely awakened from their slumber, faced a heart-stopping choice: surrender to the raiders or fight in whatever clothes they wore to bed. In a display of raw courage that still echoes through time, they chose to fight. Men and women stripped off their shirts, transforming from peaceful villagers into fierce defenders in mere moments. Their battle cry pierced the night air as they charged toward the invaders, their bare skin gleaming like armor in the moonlight.

According to town lore, something miraculous happened during that desperate battle. The townspeople swear they saw the Madonna di Pozzo Faceto herself, their beloved patron saint, appearing as a divine warrior queen above the fray. Whether divine intervention or sheer human determination, the outcome was extraordinary: the mighty Ottoman raiders were driven back into the sea by a town of "shirtless" civilians.

Today, this astounding victory lives on in one of Italy's most unique festivals. Every June 2nd, the streets of Fasano explode with energy as the town transforms into a living time capsule. Local participants don meticulously crafted period costumes (though nowadays, thankfully, they keep their shirts on!) to recreate the legendary battle. The air fills with the clash of prop weapons, the thunder of drums, and the cheers of spectators as the town relives its finest hour.

What makes La Scamiciata truly special is how it weaves together so many threads of Italian culture: the pageantry of Baroque celebrations, the deep connection to Catholic faith, the pride in local history, and the unifying power of shared tradition. As actors recreate the desperate midnight battle, elderly townspeople tell wide-eyed children how their ancestors fought for the very streets they now play in.

La Scamiciata remains deeply authentic. When you attend, you're not just watching a show, you're stepping into a living piece of history, feeling the same surge of community pride that has animated this celebration for over 300 years.

Festival Events

First Friday in June: Innalzare lo Stendardo (Raising the Standard)

5:30 p.m.

Unveiling of the Banner

In the historic Piazza Ciaia, witness the breathtaking moment as the banner of the Protector is unveiled against the twilight sky. Costumed participants in meticulously crafted period attire gather in the square, their presence transforming the piazza into a living tableau of the past as they officially inaugurate the festival.

7:30 p.m.

Event at Chiesa Sant'Antonio Abate

Within the magnificent Chiesa Sant'Antonio Abate, immerse yourself in an enlightening cultural presentation that unveils the rich tapestry of Baroque art in Fasano.

Second Sunday in June

8:00 p.m.

Pilgrimage of the Historical Parade

Journey with the historical parade to the ancient Sanctuary of Maria SS. di Pozzo Faceto, where participants in period dress undertake a moving pilgrimage to honor the Madonna. As twilight descends, this deeply spiritual procession connects modern-day participants with centuries of tradition.

Third Thursday in June

8:00 p.m.

Aspettando la Festa (Waiting for the Celebration)

Piazza Ciaia comes alive with an enchanting evening of revelry, where traditional craftsmanship meets contemporary celebration. In partnership with the Patronal Feast Committee, visitors can savor local delicacies, enjoy spirited musical performances, and witness artisans at work. #FestaFusion Event

Third Friday in June

6:00 p.m.

Festa dei Cortei Storici d'Italia (Festival of Italy's Historical Parades)

The grand Piazza Ciaia in Fasano transforms into a living museum as historical reenactment groups from across Italy converge, each bringing their unique regional traditions and spectacular costumes.

6:30 p.m.

Consegna delle Chiavi (Key Ceremony)

In a gesture steeped in centuries of tradition, witness the solemn ceremony in Piazza Ciaia as the city keys change hands, symbolizing the transfer of leadership and protection of Fasano's heritage.

8:00 p.m.

Intronizzazione delle Sacre Immagini (Enthronement of the Sacred Images)

Experience a moment of profound spiritual significance as the sacred icons of the town's patrons are ceremonially enthroned, blending ancient ritual with contemporary devotion. #FestaFusion Event

Third Saturday in June

6:30 p.m.

Corteo Storico Rievocativo: La Scamiciata (Historical Reenactment Parade)

The historic procession begins in the heart of the town center, where you can join the magnificent parade as it winds through ancient streets. Watch as participants in elaborate period costumes bring history to life with every step through Fasano's timeless corridors.

9:00 p.m.

The grand procession arrives at Piazza Ciaia, where the atmosphere crackles with anticipation as hundreds of spectators gather to witness this climactic moment of the festival.

9:30 p.m.

The evening culminates in a spectacular celebration of Mediterranean Rhythms and music that transforms Piazza Ciaia into an open-air theater, where traditional melodies blend with contemporary performances to create an unforgettable display of cultural fusion.

Third Sunday in June: Patron Festival Events

Festivities in Honor of Madonna SS. di Pozzo Faceto and San Giovanni Battista

Two days of joyous celebration fill the streets of Fasano with religious processions, enticing food stalls, and warmhearted community gatherings that honor the town's beloved patron saints. #FestaFusion Event

Last Thursday in June

9:00 p.m.

La vittoria sui Turchi (Victory Over the Turks)

At the stunning Il Minareto in Selva di Fasano, experience the festival's grand finale - a powerful five-act cantata that brings to life the town's historic triumph over Turkish invaders through dramatic performance and stirring music.

#2 Patron Saints Festival Fasano

The Festa Patronale di Fasano is an annual celebration held on the third Sunday of June, honoring the town's patron saints: St. John the Baptist and Our Lady of the Well (Madonna di Pozzo Faceto). This festival is deeply rooted in Fasano's history, blending religious devotion with cultural festivities. The tradition of celebrating patron saints dates back centuries in Italian culture, serving both religious and communal purposes. In Fasano, the veneration of St. John the Baptist and the Madonna di Pozzo Faceto has been integral to the town's identity. The festival has evolved over time, incorporating various events that reflect the community's devotion and cultural heritage.

Who is St. John the Baptist?

St. John the Baptist was a significant Jewish prophet known for his role in foretelling the coming of Jesus Christ. Born to Zechariah and Elizabeth, he is recognized for preaching about God's final judgment and baptizing repentant followers, including Jesus himself. His feast day is celebrated on June 24th.

Who is the Madonna di Pozzo Faceto?

Our Lady of the Well, known in Italian as Madonna di Pozzo Faceto, is a revered Marian figure and one of the patron saints of Fasano. The title "Madonna di Pozzo Faceto" translates to "Our Lady of the Well of Faceto," referencing the location associated with her veneration.

Legend of the Discovery

According to local tradition, during the construction or cleaning of a well in the area now known as Pozzo Faceto, workers unearthed a cave or cavity. Inside, they discovered an ancient image of the Virgin Mary painted on a rock. Recognizing its significance, they carefully extracted the stone and built a chapel on the site to house the sacred image. This event is believed to have occurred between the 11th and 12th centuries.

The Sanctuary

The original chapel has since evolved into the Sanctuary of Santa Maria di Pozzo Faceto, which remains a significant pilgrimage site. The sanctuary features a Latin cross layout and a simple gabled façade, harmoniously blending architectural elements. Notably, the well where the image was found is still present and accessible to visitors near the entrance of the sanctuary.

Patronage and Veneration

In 1784, the citizens of Fasano officially declared the Madonna di Pozzo Faceto as their patroness, alongside St. John the Baptist. Her feast day is celebrated with great devotion, featuring religious processions, cultural events, and community gatherings. The Madonna di Pozzo Faceto holds a special place in the hearts of the local community, symbolizing faith, protection, and historical continuity.

The enduring veneration of the Madonna di Pozzo Faceto highlights the deep-rooted religious traditions of Fasano and the surrounding regions.

The Festa Patronale di Fasano not only honors these revered figures but also strengthens the communal bonds among residents and offers visitors a glimpse into the town's rich traditions.

Festival Events

Sunday one week before Patron Saint Festival

Morning

Religious Services

Throughout Fasano's historic churches, reverent masses are held in honor of the patron saints, with each sacred space resonating with prayers and hymns that have echoed through these halls for centuries.

Evening

Procession of the Patron Saints

In a display of profound devotion, the sacred images of Fasano's patron saints are carried with dignity through the town's ancient streets. Local clergy, distinguished town officials, and faithful residents walk together in this solemn procession, their footsteps tracing paths walked by generations before them.

Night

Musical Concerts

The majestic Piazza Ciaia comes alive as local talents and acclaimed guest artists fill the evening air with enchanting melodies, their performances echoing off the historic facades that surround this grand square.

Patron Saint Festival (Third Sunday in June)

8:30 a.m.

Traditional Morning Fireworks

The dawn sky above Fasano erupts with the spectacular "bombe alla Diana," traditional daytime fireworks that announce the day's festivities with thunderous glory, awakening the town to continue its celebrations.

9:00 a.m.

City Tour by Concert Bands

Musical ensembles weave through Fasano's charming streets and alleyways, their festive melodies floating through windows and drawing residents to their balconies in delighted appreciation.

10:00 a.m.

Morning Musical Performance

The historic Piazza Mercato Vecchio resonates with harmonious sounds as musicians gather in this centuries-old marketplace to present a morning concert that bridges past and present.

7:00 p.m.

Evening Mass

The beautiful Chiesa dell'Assunta welcomes worshippers for a special evening mass, its baroque interior creating a perfect setting for this moment of spiritual reflection.

8:00 p.m.

Return of the Sacred Images

In a solemn procession from Piazza Ciaia to the Mother Church, the sacred images of the patron saints make their ceremonial journey home, accompanied by devoted followers through lamp-lit streets to their traditional place of veneration.

10:00 p.m.

Grand Finale Concert and Fireworks

The festival reaches its magnificent conclusion as the night sky above Fasano explodes with color and light, while concert performances below create a symphony of sight and sound that marks a spectacular end to the celebrations.

Fasano Walking Tour

#1. Piazza Ciaia

Start your adventure in the lively Piazza Ciaia, the center of Fasano's historic district. Here, the majestic Palazzo Municipale stands as a testament to the city's rich heritage, its walls holding centuries of stories since its days as a 16th-century Jesuit monastery. The square's iconic Clock Tower rises above the daily bustle, its face watching over countless festivals and celebrations that have brought the community together through generations. As you stand in this historic square, you'll feel the authentic rhythm of daily Italian life, from morning coffee rituals to evening passeggiatas (strolls).

#2. Chiesa Matrice di San Giovanni Battista (Mother Church of St. John the Baptist)

Just steps away, the Chiesa Matrice di San Giovanni Battista rises in breathtaking splendor, embodying the spiritual soul of Fasano. This architectural masterpiece, with its roots in the 16th century, showcases the evolution of Italian religious art through its stunning Baroque enhancements. Step inside to be mesmerized by the intricate wooden coffered ceiling that seems to float above, while the richly decorated altar draws you into centuries of devotion.

Church of St. John the Baptist

#3. Arco del Balì and the Old City Streets

Venture deeper into Fasano's medieval quarter through the Arco del Balì, an enchanting gateway that transports you to a world where time seems to stand still. This beautifully preserved archway marks the entrance to what was once the noble quarter, leading you into a maze of whitewashed buildings and intimate alleyways. As you wander down Via degli Archi, perhaps the most photogenic street in all of Fasano, you'll discover a perfectly preserved slice of medieval Italy.

Small balconies adorned with flowering plants hang over the narrow cobblestone path, while ancient homes tell silent stories of the countless generations who have called this remarkable street home.

#4. Museo della Casa alla Fasanese (Fasano House Museum)

Step into living history at the Museo della Casa alla Fasanese. As you move through rooms furnished exactly as they would have been centuries ago, you can almost hear the echoes of family gatherings and daily life. Each carefully preserved artifact tells its own story, from well-worn cooking implements to handcrafted furniture that bears the patina of generations. Here, you'll discover not just how Fasanese families lived, but how they transformed simple spaces into warm, vibrant homes that reflected the region's rich cultural heritage.

#5. Chiesa di San Nicola di Bari (St. Nicolas of Bari)

The Chiesa di San Nicola di Bari rises like a neoclassical dream against the Fasanese sky, its elegant façade drawing visitors into a sanctuary of peace and artistic beauty. Inside, the veritable treasures await: a magnificent 16th-century organ still fills the space with celestial music during special occasions, while overhead, breathtaking frescoes tell timeless stories in vivid color. The play of light through ancient windows creates an atmosphere of tranquil reflection, making this church not just a monument to faith, but a haven of serenity in the bustling historic center.

#6. Via del Mercato Vecchio (Old Market Street)

Wander down Via del Mercato Vecchio, where the spirit of ancient commerce lives on in a delightful blend of traditional craftsmanship and modern enterprise. This historic thoroughfare pulses with the energy of local artisans continuing centuries-old traditions, while the aroma of freshly baked Fasanese focaccia wafts from family-run bakeries. Stop for a perfectly crafted espresso in one of the intimate piazzas, where the unhurried pace of life invites you to linger and observe the daily rhythms of this enchanting street.

#7. Piazza Mercato Vecchio (Old Market Square)

Your journey leads you to Piazza Mercato Vecchio, where centuries of trading have left an indelible mark on Fasano's character. Though the market stalls of old have given way to charming outdoor cafés, the square retains its role as a gathering place for both locals and visitors.

Beyond Fasano's Historic Walls: Sacred Sanctuaries and Seaside Splendor

Sanctuary of Mary of the Well

Journey just beyond the city's ancient stones to discover the mystical Santuario di Maria SS. di Pozzo Faceto, a sanctuary whose story is woven deeply into Fasano's legendary victory over Ottoman raiders. Standing proudly about 2.5 kilometers(a mile) from the city center, this sacred site draws pilgrims and history lovers alike. The sanctuary's name, "Pozzo Faceto" or "Pleasant Well," hints at its origins, a place where divine grace is said to flow as freely as water. Here, amidst the quiet countryside, you can explore the very grounds where, according to local lore, the Madonna appeared during that fateful battle in 1678, turning the tide of history. The sanctuary's peaceful atmosphere and architectural beauty make it worth the short journey by taxi or bicycle through the picturesque Apulian landscape.

Fasano Festivals and Sagre Throughout the Year

Processione dei Misteri (Procession of the Mysteries)

Good Friday

This solemn procession is a significant part of Fasano's Holy Week observances. Participants carry statues depicting scenes from the Passion of Christ through the town's streets, reflecting deep-rooted religious traditions.

Sagra delle Olive (Olive Festival)

December (specific dates may vary)

Celebrating the olive harvest, a staple of the local economy, this festival offers tastings of various olive-based products, including extra virgin olive oil. Visitors can enjoy local culinary delights and take part in demonstrations of traditional olive harvesting methods.

Day Trips: Nearby Sites, Cities, and Towns

Ceglie Messapica. 28 kilometers (17 miles) from Fasano. This ancient settlement, one of Puglia's oldest, traces its roots to the mysterious Messapian civilization that flourished here before Rome's rise. As you wander through its maze-like streets, the whitewashed walls seem to glow in the Mediterranean sun, leading you to unexpected discoveries around every corner. The imposing

Castello Ducale stands as a testament to Norman might, its 15th-century expansions telling stories of medieval power and intrigue.

Altamura. Venture 95 kilometers (59 miles) from Fasano to discover Altamura, where the aroma of centuries-old bread-making traditions fills the air. This is no ordinary bread – the famous Pane di Altamura DOP has been crafted here since ancient times, its recipe passed down through generations of master bakers. The city's soul was shaped by Frederick II of Swabia, whose vision transformed it in the 13th century. His greatest legacy stands in the form of the Cattedrale di Santa Maria Assunta, a masterpiece of Gothic architecture that dominates the skyline.

Gravina in Puglia. A 97-kilometer (60 mile) journey from Fasano brings you to Gravina in Puglia, a city that seems to defy gravity as it clings to the edges of its namesake ravine. Since the Bronze Age, civilizations have been drawn to this dramatic location, carving homes and churches into the living rock. The magnificent Ponte Acquedotto spans the gorge like a stone rainbow, offering views that will take your breath away. Below the surface, a hidden world awaits in Gravina Sotterranea, where centuries of inhabitants have carved out elaborate underground networks.

Logistics

Train: Fasano has a train station on the Bari-Lecce railway line. Trains run frequently between Bari, Brindisi, Lecce, and Fasano.

Bus: Marozzi, Ferrovie del Sud Est, and STP Brindisi operate bus routes to Fasano from nearby cities. Buses are useful for connections between Fasano and Ostuni, Alberobello, Ceglie Messapica, and Cisternino.

Car: The SS16 highway (E55) runs along the coast, with exits for Fasano. The SS172 road connects Fasano with inland towns like Alberobello, Locorotondo, and Martina Franca.

Parking: Free and paid parking areas are available, especially near the historic center and main piazzas.

Restaurant Recommendations

Ardecuore - Trattoria Contemporanea. Address: Corso Vittorio Emanuele, 109

A delightful trattoria offering contemporary twists on classic Italian and Mediterranean dishes, set in an elegant yet relaxed ambiance.

Pizzeria Gambrinus. Address: Via Piave, 24

A cozy spot specializing in delicious, traditional Italian pizzas with a variety of toppings and a friendly atmosphere.

Trimalchione. Corso Vittorio Emanuele, 153

Celebrated for its authentic Apulian cuisine, this restaurant combines local flavors with a warm, welcoming environment.

Accommodation

For this festa fusion event, I recommend three or four nights in town.

Park Hotel Sant'Elia. Address: Via dello Zoosafari

This elegant 4-star retreat sits just minutes from the popular Zoo Safari Fasano, offering the perfect balance of convenience and tranquility. The hotel's crowning feature is its stunning panoramic terrace where guests can enjoy breakfast or evening aperitivos while taking in sweeping views of the Adriatic Sea. Rooms combine contemporary comfort with traditional Puglian design elements, featuring locally-crafted furniture and modern amenities.

Al Palazzo La Dimora by Apulia Hospitality. Address: Via Roma 87

Housed in a meticulously restored historic palazzo in the heart of town, this sophisticated 4-star hotel seamlessly blends centuries-old architecture with contemporary luxury. The thoughtfully appointed rooms feature high ceilings, designer furnishings, and large windows offering enchanting views across the city's terracotta rooftops and church spires.

CHAPTER TEN

Polignano a Mare Takes the Plunge

Red Bull Cliff Diving Thrills

Red Bull Cliff Diving World Series

Where: Polignano a Mare

When: June

Average Festival Temperatures: High 29°C (85°F). Low 20°C (68°F).

Event Website:

https://www.redbull.com/int-en/events/red-bull-cliff-diving-polignano-a-mare-italy

Polignano a Mare: A Coastal Gem in Southern Italy

Polignano a Mare is a picturesque town along the Adriatic Sea. Known for its stunning cliffs, charming old town, and beautiful beaches, it's a popular destination for tourists seeking a mix of history, culture, and natural beauty.

The history of Polignano a Mare dates back to prehistoric times, with archaeological evidence suggesting settlements as early as the Neolithic period. It is believed to be the site of the ancient Greek city of Neapolis of Apulia, which was founded around the 4th century BC by Dionysius II of Syracuse. The town later became an important trading center under the Romans and saw further development under various foreign dominations, including the Byzantines, Normans, and Aragonese.

View of Polignano a Mare from the sea

The area is also known for its natural caves and hidden cove beaches, such as the famous Lama Monachile. Polignano a Mare has a population of 17,000 people.

Red Bull Cliff Diving World Series

The Red Bull Cliff Diving World Series transforms the peaceful coastal town of Polignano a Mare into an arena of breathtaking athleticism and spectacle.

Since its inception in 2009, the World Series has elevated cliff diving from a daring feat to a prestigious sport demanding exceptional precision, courage, and artistry. Among all the locations on the international tour, Polignano a Mare stands out as a crown jewel. The town's unique architecture, where ancient buildings seem to emerge directly from the clifftops, creates an unparalleled setting where human achievement meets natural grandeur.

The competition itself is a masterpiece of athletic prowess. Male divers launch themselves from platforms 27 meters (88 feet) high, nearly the height of a nine-story building, while female athletes dive from equally impressive 21-meter (69 foot) platforms. These diving boards, often ingeniously integrated into the town's rooftops and cliff edges, add an architectural element to the natural drama. World-class athletes execute complex acrobatic maneuvers during their three-second journey through the air, each dive scrutinized by judges for technical perfection, artistic impression, and sheer difficulty.

The event transforms Polignano into a vibrant festival of sport and culture. Thousands of spectators create an electric atmosphere as they gather along the cliffs, crowd onto boats in the Adriatic, or find vantage points among the town's winding streets and terraces. The local community embraces this transformation, enriching the experience with food markets, musical performances, and cultural exhibitions that showcase the region's rich heritage.

Beyond the spectacular athletics, the World Series has profoundly affected Polignano a Mare's identity and economy. The global broadcast reaches millions, putting this once-quiet fishing town firmly on the international stage. Tourism has flourished, with visitors drawn by both the competition and the town's natural allure. For locals, the event has become a source of immense pride, highlighting their home's unique combination of historical charm, natural beauty, and modern sporting excellence.

Cliff Diving Platform is set up on the Stone Building on the right

As each edition of the Red Bull Cliff Diving World Series unfolds in Polignano a Mare, it reinforces the town's reputation as a premier destination for both adventure sports and cultural tourism. This remarkable event has become more than just a competition. It's a celebration of human courage, natural beauty, and the enduring appeal of a small Italian town that opens its arms to the world.

Polignano A Mare Walking Tour

#1. Piazza Vittorio Emanuele II

Begin your tour in this central square, the heart of Polignano a Mare. Surrounded by cafes and shops, the square is a popular meeting point for locals and visitors. It features the town's clock tower, which dates back to the 19th century. Historically, this piazza has been the center of public life, hosting markets and community gatherings.

#2. Chiesa Matrice di Santa Maria Assunta

The Chiesa Matrice di Santa Maria Assunta stands as a testament to Polignano a Mare's rich religious heritage, its limestone façade weathered by centuries of sea breezes. Originally constructed in the 13th century on the foundations of an earlier religious structure, the church showcases the evolution of architectural styles that shaped Puglia's sacred buildings. The current façade, with its rose window and pointed arch portal, demonstrates the transition from Romanesque to Gothic styles that characterized this period of church building in southern Italy.

The church's interior reveals layers of historical modifications, with its original Romanesque structure enhanced by later Gothic and Baroque additions. Robust columns and a series of pointed arches divide the nave into three aisles, focusing the eye on the main altar. Cross-vaulting, a hallmark of its era, is a prominent ceiling feature; original frescoes are faintly visible under later additions.

Among the church's most precious artifacts is the wooden statue of San Vito, Polignano's patron saint, dating from the 16th century. Annually paraded during the town's festa, the statue boasts exceptional craftsmanship and emotional depth in its carving. The church also houses several significant paintings, including a 17th-century canvas depicting the Assumption of the Virgin Mary and a collection of ex-votos that tell stories of local devotion through the centuries.

The bell tower, added in the 15th century, rises above the town's historic center and served historically as both a religious marker and a watchtower against coastal raiders. Its bells still ring out daily, marking time as they have for generations of Polignano's residents. Because of its location near Piazza Vittorio Emanuele II, the church served not only as a religious center but also as a hub for community life, hosting religious festivals and gatherings for centuries.

#3. Balconata Santo Stefano

This panoramic terrace offers one of the best views of the cliffs and the Adriatic Sea. Named after the nearby Abbazia di Santo Stefano (Abbey of Saint Stephen), a medieval monastery, the balconata is a must-visit spot to appreciate the dramatic natural beauty of Polignano. Historically, this area symbolized the town's connection to the sea and its maritime heritage.

#4. Lama Monachile (Cala Porto)

Walk down to this iconic pebble beach nestled between two towering cliffs. Lama Monachile, also known as Cala Porto, was once an ancient Roman bridge crossing point and a key trading route. Today, it's a favorite spot for visitors to swim or simply admire the striking cliffs. The beach's historical significance as a gateway to the town highlights Polignano's role in regional trade.

#5. Ponte Borbonico (Bourbon Bridge)

Just above Lama Monachile, this 18th-century bridge offers stunning views of the inlet below. Built during the Bourbon era, it replaced the original Roman bridge and played a crucial role in connecting Polignano to nearby towns. The bridge showcases Polignano's historical importance as a transportation hub.

#6. Statue of Domenico Modugno

Head to this bronze statue of Domenico Modugno, the famous Italian singer and songwriter born in Polignano a Mare. Modugno is best known for his hit song "Volare", which became an international sensation. The statue, with open arms, overlooks the sea, symbolizing freedom and the joy of his music. It's a beloved landmark for both locals and fans of Italian music.

#7. Grotta Palazzese (External Viewpoint)

Stroll towards a viewpoint to admire the Grotta Palazzese, a natural sea cave carved into the cliffs. Historically, the cave was used as a banquet hall for nobility during the 18th century. Today, it's home to one of the most famous restaurants in the world, offering a unique dining experience within the cave. The grotto highlights Polignano's geological wonders and cultural history.

Polignano Festivals Throughout the Year

Kite Festival

May

This family-friendly event fills the skies above Polignano with colorful kites. Participants of all ages gather to fly kites, turning the seafront into a vibrant display and offering a joyful experience for both locals and visitors.

Festa di San Vito (Feast of Saint Vito)

June 14-16

This festival honors San Vito, the town's patron saint. Festivities begin with a procession where the saint's effigy is transported by sea from the small port of San Vito to Cala Paura. From there, the statue is carried on shoulders to Piazza Vittorio Emanuele, where a symbolic ceremony of handing over the town keys takes place. The celebration includes religious ceremonies, music, and fireworks.

Il Libro Possibile (The Book Festival)

Summer

As a significant cultural event, this literature festival transforms the historic center of Polignano a Mare into an open-air stage. Writers, journalists, and public figures engage in discussions, book presentations, and debates, fostering a dynamic exchange between authors and readers.

Mareviglioso Festival

July

Celebrating the sea and the town's maritime traditions, this festival features various activities, including boat tours, seafood tastings, and cultural performances, highlighting Polignano's connection to the Adriatic.

Festival dei Balcone Fioriti

Early October

In Polignano a Mare, residents adorn their balconies with vibrant flowers, transforming the town into a floral spectacle. The event includes guided tours, workshops, and competitions.

Nearby Sites, Cities, and Towns

Abbazia di San Vito. 5 kilometers (3 miles) from Polignano. Just a short drive or bike ride north of Polignano a Mare lies the picturesque coastal hamlet of San Vito, home to the elegant Abbazia di San Vito. From the small harbor next to the abbey, you can embark on a boat tour of Polignano's sea caves, an unforgettable experience that reveals the dramatic cliffs, hidden grottos, and turquoise waters that have made this coastline famous.

Caves under Polignano

Local captains navigate into the caves, some of which are only accessible by sea, offering views of natural rock formations, secret coves, and even the famous Grotta Palazzese from below. Many tours also include a swim stop, and some offer prosecco tastings on board. Tours typically last about 1–2 hours and run regularly during spring, summer, and early fall.

Whether you're seeking photography, adventure, or pure relaxation, this boat tour offers a fresh perspective of the coastline that complements any visit to Polignano.

Corato/Castel del Monte. 47 kilometers (29 miles) west of Polignano. Nestled in the Murge plateau, Corato is a charming town known for its medieval streets, excellent wine production, and proximity to Castel del Monte, the legendary octagonal fortress built by Emperor Frederick II. With its deep-rooted agricultural traditions, Corato is a perfect day trip for travelers interested in history, wine, and the rugged beauty of inland Puglia. Start your visit in the Centro Storico, where narrow alleys lead to the Chiesa Matrice di Santa Maria Maggiore, a 12th-century church blending Romanesque and Gothic influences. Nearby, the Torre dell'Orologio stands as a symbol of the town's medieval past.

Logistics

Train: Polignano has a train station and is 25 minutes from Bari Centrale.

Bus: Local Buses are operated by companies like STP. They connect Polignano to neighboring towns like Monopoli and Conversano.

Car: From Bari take the SS16 (Adriatic Highway) southbound. The drive takes approximately 30–40 minutes. Polignano is a small town, and the centro storico (historic center) is pedestrian-only, so plan to park and walk into the old town.

Parking: Parcheggio Polignano a Mare is near the train station, a 10-minute walk to the old town. Via Martiri di Dogali Parking is close to the town center, ideal for quick visits.

Restaurant Recommendations

Ristorante Antiche Mura. Address: Via Roma, 11

Nestled in the heart of the historic center, Ristorante Antiche Mura offers a romantic ambiance, with its rustic interior featuring rough-hewn whitewashed walls and high vaulted ceilings adorned with chandeliers.

Pescaria. Address: Piazza Aldo Moro, 6/8

Near the historic center, Pescaria is renowned for its innovative approach to seafood, offering a variety of seafood sandwiches and dishes in a fast-casual setting. The menu features items like the octopus sandwich and tuna tartare, emphasizing fresh, high-quality ingredients.

Grotta Palazzese and Hotel. Address: Via Narciso, 59

Set within a natural limestone cave overlooking the Adriatic Sea, Grotta Palazzese offers a unique and luxurious dining experience. The restaurant serves refined Italian cuisine with an emphasis on seafood, providing an unforgettable ambiance that has made it one of the most famous dining spots in the region.

Accommodation

For this event, I recommend two or three nights in town. During our recent trip, 5 nights flew by, and we wanted more time there.

Covo dei Saraceni. Address: Via Conversano, 1/A

This 4-star hotel is perched on a cliff overlooking the Adriatic Sea, offering panoramic views and direct access to the beach.

San Tommaso Hotel. Address: Contrada Bagiolaro, S.C. 62

Housed in a historic building, this 4-star hotel exudes old-world charm and elegance. It features luxurious guest rooms and suites equipped with modern amenities and breathtaking views of the Mediterranean Sea from its terraced gardens.

Suite Dimora Merlata a picco sul mare. We stayed at this stunning vacation rental, and the balcony you see in the photos from this chapter is part of that very suite. I booked directly with the owner and receive no compensation for including it here, I simply loved the experience. If you're interested, send me a message through my website, and I'll be happy to pass along their contact information.

CHAPTER ELEVEN

Turi's Tempting Treasures

A Celebration of the Sweetest Cherries in Puglia

Sagra della Ciliegia Ferrovia

Where: Turi

When: 1st or 2nd weekend in June.

Average Festival Temperatures: High 27°C (80.6°F). Low 18°C (64.4°F).

Event Website: https://www.sagraciliegiaferrovia.it/

Ancient Roots to Modern Culture: Discovering Turi

Amid the sun-drenched hills of southern Italy's Puglia region lies Turi, a town where ancient stones whisper tales of civilizations past. Archaeological treasures scattered throughout the area reveal that this fertile land first drew settlers in pre-Roman times, when the mysterious Messapic people made these hills their home.

As Rome's power grew, Turi became a vital trade hub, its strategic position between the ports of Bari and Taranto made it indispensable to the empire's commercial network. Roman artifacts discovered in the area, from ancient coins to pottery fragments, paint a picture of a prosperous settlement where merchants and traders gathered to exchange goods from across the Mediterranean.

The Middle Ages brought waves of conquest and cultural transformation, as Lombards, Normans, and Swabians each left their mark on Turi's landscape. Perhaps no ruler had a greater impact than Frederick II of Swabia, the brilliant 13th-century Holy Roman Emperor known as "Stupor Mundi" (Wonder of the World).

Under his enlightened policies, Turi flourished as an agricultural center, its fields and orchards feeding the growing population. Later, the powerful Carafa family would govern these lands for centuries, their influence shaping the town's development through the Renaissance and Baroque eras.

Today's Turi, home to roughly 12,000 inhabitants, sits proudly in the Metropolitan City of Bari, about 30 kilometers (18 miles) southeast of the regional capital. Perched 250 meters (850 feet) above sea level on the fertile Murgia plateau, the town enjoys a privileged position between the sparkling Adriatic Sea to the east and the enchanting Valle d'Itria to the south.

The modern town has gained recognition beyond its ancient walls for an unexpected reason: within the stark confines of its Fascist-era prison, the brilliant Italian philosopher Antonio Gramsci penned his influential "Prison Notebooks" during his incarceration in the 1920s and 1930s. These writings, born in captivity, would go on to shape political thought across the globe.

Today, Turi's economy remains rooted in the land, with vineyards and olive groves carpeting the surrounding countryside. The town offers visitors an authentic slice of Puglian life, far from the tourist crowds that flock to better-known destinations.

The Railway Cherry Festival

The Ferrovia cherry's journey to becoming Turi's crowning glory begins with an intriguing tale from the early 1900s. Near the town's railway tracks stood a remarkable cherry tree, its branches heavy with fruit that caught the local farmers' attention. These cherries were different - larger, deeper red, and remarkably sweet. The tree's proximity to the railroad gave this exceptional variety its name: "Ferrovia" (Railway).

What started as one extraordinary tree transformed Turi into one of Italy's premier cherry-producing regions. By the early 1990s, the town launched the Sagra della Ciliegia Ferrovia to celebrate their prized fruit. From modest beginnings, this festival has blossomed into one of Puglia's most anticipated summer events, drawing thousands who come to experience both the cherries and the vibrant local culture.

Today's festival is a feast for all senses. Beyond sampling the famous dark red fruits, visitors immerse themselves in Puglian traditions through folk music that echoes through medieval streets, artisan markets showcasing local crafts, and stalls offering regional specialties. Local chefs demonstrate creative ways to incorporate cherries into traditional dishes, while farmers proudly display their finest specimens, sharing cultivation secrets passed down through generations.

What sets this festival apart is its authenticity. Unlike many tourist-oriented events, the Sagra remains true to its agricultural roots, offering visitors a genuine glimpse into Puglia's rural heritage. Each June, as cherry trees heavy with fruit paint the countryside red, Turi transforms into a living celebration of its agricultural legacy, inviting all to taste the sweetness of tradition.

Sagra Events

Saturday

6:30 p.m.

Piazza Silvio Orlandi: Opening of exhibition spaces by local cherry producers.

Launch of the food and wine showcase, "Eccellenze di Puglia" (Excellence of Puglia).

7:00 p.m.

Inaugural ceremony and performance with the presence of civil and military authorities.

Mobile performance by the Young Marching Band.

8:30 p.m.

Lighting of an artistic luminary installation and performance of Cazacu's Dancing Fountains in Largo San Giovanni.

9:00 p.m.

Live music and dancing.

Sunday

10:00 a.m.

Opening of cherry producer exhibition spaces.

Continuation of the enogastronomic showcase, "Eccellenze di Puglia".

9:30 a.m.

Free guided tours of the historic center, cultural sites, and attractions.

Throughout the Event

Cherry Tasting and Sales: Local producers showcase and sell the renowned Ferrovia cherries.

Culinary Stands and Food Trucks: Visitors can enjoy a variety of local dishes and cherry-based delicacies.

Live Music and Folk Performances: Evenings are enlivened with traditional Puglian music and dances.

Artisan Markets: Stalls offering handcrafted goods and local products.

Turi Walking Tour

#1. Piazza Silvio Orlandi and the Chiesa Madre (Main Church)

Begin your tour at Piazza Silvio Orlandi, where centuries of daily life have worn smooth the limestone pavers beneath your feet. This vibrant square comes alive each morning as locals gather at historic cafes like Bar Centrale, which has served espresso to generations of Turesi since 1952. During the famed Sagra della Ciliegia Ferrovia in June, the plaza transforms into a celebration of Turi's prized cherry, with the sweet scent of fruit filling the air.

The commanding presence of the Chiesa Madre di San Giovanni Battista dominates the square's eastern edge. Built in 1741 on the site of an earlier medieval church, this Baroque masterpiece showcases the work of local stone carvers who left their mark in the intricate façade. Inside, your eyes are drawn to the ceiling's trompe l'oeil frescoes, painted by Vito Calò in 1778, creating an illusion of infinite heavens above.

The church's bell tower, added in 1832, still marks time with its original bronze bells, their deep tones echoing through Turi's streets just as they have for nearly two centuries.

#2. Palazzo Marchesale

Following the gentle slope of Via XX Settembre, you'll reach the imposing Palazzo Marchesale, whose honey-colored limestone walls tell stories of 16th-century nobility. Originally built for the Moles family in 1568, the palace features unique architectural elements that blend Venetian and local Pugliese styles. Look for the distinctive carved masks above the windows.

Local legend says they were modeled after actual family members. The palace's courtyard, accessible through massive wooden doors studded with hand-forged iron, contains a hidden gem: a Renaissance well with relief carvings of mythological scenes.

#3. Grotta di Sant'Oronzo

Descending the ancient steps to the Grotta di Sant'Oronzo, you enter a world where history and faith intertwine. This natural limestone cave, formed over millions of years, served as a refuge for Saint Oronzo in the 1st century AD. The cave's walls still bear traces of early Christian symbols, barely visible in the flickering light of votive candles.

A remarkable, living-rock altar, carved in the 17th century, is found within the small chapel. Throughout the year, the cave stays at a cool 17°C (63°F), perfect for summer respite.

#4. Borgo Antico

Returning to the Borgo Antico, you'll find yourself in a maze of narrow streets where time seems to stand still. These winding pathways, some barely wide enough for a Vespa to pass, are lined with houses whose whitewashed walls have been refreshed every spring for centuries. Look for the distinctive "gattoni", carved stone rain spouts shaped like cats, that peer down from rooftops.

The Torre dell'Orologio, built in 1883, stands as the district's sentinel. Its clock mechanism, still wound by hand every week, was crafted by the renowned Milanese clockmaker Giuseppe Fagnani. The tower's evening bell still signals to farmers in the surrounding cherry orchards that it's time to head home, continuing a tradition that dates back to medieval times.

#5. Local Artisan Shops

Explore local artisan shops and sample regional delicacies, including olive oil, wine, and Ferrovia cherries (if in season). Stop at a café for an espresso or gelato.

#6. Parco di Sant'Oronzo

End your tour at the Parco di Sant'Oronzo, a quiet green space located just outside the town center (7-minute walk from the Borgo Antico). It's a perfect spot to relax and enjoy views of the surrounding countryside.

Optional Extension: Cherry Orchards (Seasonal)

If visiting during the cherry season (May-June), arrange for a short guided visit to the nearby cherry orchards. Some local producers offer tours where you can see the Ferrovia cherry trees and even pick your own cherries.

Turi Festivals and Sagre Throughout the Year

Holy Week Celebrations

March or April

During Holy Week, Turi's medieval streets echo with centuries-old traditions as the town transforms into a living theater of faith. The most dramatic moment occurs on Good Friday when the haunting sounds of the "troccola" (wooden rattle) replace church bells, signaling the start of the Processione dei Misteri.

Life-sized statues, some dating back to the 18th century and masterfully carved by local artisans, are carried through torch-lit streets on the shoulders of the confraternities, each member wearing distinctive robes passed down through generations.

The procession follows an ancient route, stopping at seven churches, a tradition dating to medieval pilgrimages in Rome. Local women maintain the custom of preparing "scarcelle," distinctive Easter breads shaped like doves and decorated with hard-boiled eggs, following recipes preserved in family chronicles since the 1700s.

Festa del Passa Passa (& Liberation Day National Holiday)

April 25

The Festa del Passa Passa in Turi is a unique blend of religious devotion and local tradition. The festival centers on a grand procession in honor of the Annunciation, during which participants carry large, elaborately decorated wooden structures known as Passa Passa through the streets of the historic center. These structures, adorned with flowers, ribbons, and religious symbols, are passed from shoulder to shoulder among the faithful as a sign of communal participation and spiritual offering. The event is accompanied by music, church bells, and the gathering of families who line the streets to witness this vibrant expression of faith and cultural pride. The festival also features local food stalls offering traditional Puglian dishes, creating a festive atmosphere that draws both residents and visitors.

Festa Patronale di Sant'Oronzo (Patron Saint Festival)

August 24–28

The festival honoring Sant'Oronzo transforms Turi into a kaleidoscope of light, color, and tradition. The highlight is the processional cart, known locally as "u traìne," pulled by mules adorned with intricate brass bells and handwoven tapestries. This massive wooden structure, standing over 20 feet tall, carries musicians playing traditional instruments, including the "ciaramella," a medieval double-reed instrument unique to this region. The cart's decorations, featuring thousands of hand-tied wheat stalks and fresh flowers, take local artisans months to prepare using techniques passed down since the 17th century.

Each evening, the town's historic center blazes with "luminarie", elaborate archways of lights depicting scenes from Sant'Oronzo's life, created by master craftsmen using wooden frames and thousands of colored bulbs. The festival culminates in the "Cavalcata Storica," where riders in medieval costume recreate Sant'Oronzo's legendary arrival in Turi, their horses' hooves striking sparks from the ancient cobblestones.

Primitivo Wine Festival

October

As autumn paints the surrounding vineyards in gold and crimson, Turi celebrates its renowned Primitivo wine in the historic courtyards of Palazzo Marchesale. Local vintners, whose families have tended these vines for generations, share not just their wines but the stories behind each vintage. Visitors can explore the town's ancient "palmenti" – underground wine-pressing chambers carved from solid rock, some dating to the 15th century.

Master coopers demonstrate the traditional art of barrel-making, while local chefs prepare dishes based on recipes found in the town's 18th-century agricultural archives. The festival features the unique "Cantina Itinerante," where residents open their historic private cellars to the public, many of which still contain wine-making equipment from the early 1900s.

Christmas Festivities

December 8 through January 6

During the Christmas season, Turi becomes a wonderland of light and tradition. The highlight is the living nativity scene in the Grotta di Sant'Oronzo, where local artisans recreate medieval crafts in the cave's ancient chambers. The town's famous "presepe vivente" features over 100 participants in period costume, using authentic tools and techniques to demonstrate traditional crafts like bread-making, blacksmithing, and wool-spinning.

The Christmas market in Piazza Silvio Orlandi showcases local artisans working with cartapesta (papier-mâché), a craft brought to Turi by traveling artists in the 1800s. Each evening, the sound of zampognari (bagpipers) fills the narrow streets, playing pastoral Christmas songs on instruments crafted in the traditional way using local goatskin.

The celebration culminates on January 6 with the arrival of La Befana, featuring a unique local tradition where the witch figure descends from the bell tower of the Chiesa Madre, distributing sweets and small gifts to children gathered below.

Day Trip Options: Nearby, Sites, Cities, and Towns

Egnazia Archaeological Park (Archaeological Site). About 45 kilometers (28 miles) southeast. Between Monopoli and Savelletri, the Egnazia Archaeological Park showcases ruins from an ancient Messapian city, including remnants of defensive walls, tombs, and Roman structures. The on-site museum provides deeper insights into the area's rich history.

Torre Guaceto Beach Nature Reserve. Roughly 80 kilometers (50 miles) southeast. This protected coastal area boasts unspoiled beaches with clear waters, making it perfect for swimming and snorkeling. The reserve also offers walking trails through Mediterranean scrubland and wetlands, providing opportunities for birdwatching and appreciating diverse ecosystems.

Logistics

Train: Turi is served by the Ferrovie del Sud Est (FSE) railway line, connecting it to Bari and neighboring towns. From Bari Centrale: Direct trains take 35–45 minutes. The Turi train station is a short 10-minute walk to the town center.

Bus: Several regional bus lines connect Turi to Bari and other nearby towns. The FSE bus service is a reliable option. Schedules vary, so check online or at local terminals.

Car: From Bari: Turi is about 30 kilometers (18.6 miles) southeast of Bari. Drive via the SP122 or SP215, which takes approximately 40 minutes.

Parking: Parcheggio Largo Pozzi at Largo Pozzi, 70010 Turi

Restaurant Recommendations

Ristorante Al Buco. Address: Via XX Settembre, 25

Known for its authentic Puglian dishes, this restaurant offers handmade orecchiette, grilled meats, and fresh local produce. Try the orecchiette con cime di rapa (pasta with turnip greens) or their Primitivo wine pairing.

Pizzeria da Peppino. Address: Via Giuseppe Verdi, 17

A local favorite for pizza lovers, with wood-fired pizzas featuring fresh ingredients. They also serve hearty antipasti and desserts like tiramisu.

Accommodation

It is unnecessary to stay overnight for a sagra but if you choose to do so, two nights in town would be perfect.

Relais Il Santissimo. Address: S.S. 172 Turi - Putignano, 121

A luxurious 4-star hotel offering elegantly furnished suites, a spa, and an on-site restaurant serving gourmet cuisine. Guests appreciate its serene atmosphere and attentive service.

Albergo Diffuso Dimora Rossi Suite B&B. Address: Via Maggiore Orlandi, 16

A charming 3-star bed and breakfast located in the heart of Turi, featuring well-appointed rooms that blend modern amenities with traditional architecture. Guests enjoy its central location and warm hospitality.

Masseria Gravelle. Address: Strada Provinciale Turi Castellana, 13

A delightful agriturismo located just outside Turi, offering rustic yet comfortable accommodations amidst olive groves and vineyards. Guests can enjoy authentic Puglian cuisine made from farm-fresh ingredients.

CHAPTER TWELVE

The Artistry of Conversano's Infiorata

A Floral Tribute to San Giovanni

I nfiorata di San Giovanni

Where: Conversano

When: June 24

Average Festival Temperatures: High 26°C (79°F). Low 20°C (68°F).

Conversano: A Timeless Treasure of Puglia

Perched on the gentle hills of Puglia, Conversano is a town where history unfolds in layers, from ancient times to the vibrant present. Located just 30 kilometers (18.6 miles) southeast of Bari, this enchanting town boasts a rich tapestry of civilizations that have shaped its identity. With a population of around 25,000 residents, Conversano is a cultural and artistic hub, where its past and present intertwine seamlessly.

Conversano's history dates back to the Iron Age, when it was known as Norba, a thriving Peucetian settlement that flourished before being absorbed into the

Roman world. The strategic location, nestled between the Murge Plateau and the Adriatic Sea, made it a crucial stronghold for trade and defense. Though much of the ancient city remains hidden beneath its medieval structures, artifacts and remnants from the era continue to surface, offering glimpses into its distant past.

During the Middle Ages, Conversano rose to prominence under the Normans, becoming an important feudal center ruled by the powerful Counts of Conversano. The Castello di Conversano, a formidable fortress with its origins in the 11th century, stands as a testament to this period. Expanded by the Acquaviva d'Aragona family in later centuries, the castle remains one of the town's most iconic landmarks, its sturdy towers and elegant Renaissance additions narrating the passage of time. The medieval core of Conversano, with its narrow streets, stone-paved piazzas, and beautifully preserved churches, evokes an era when knights and nobles shaped the town's destiny.

Norman Tower of the Castle

The Renaissance ushered in a period of artistic and architectural splendor. The Monastery of San Benedetto, with its stunning cloisters and intricate frescoes, is a highlight of this era, reflecting the deep influence of the Benedictine order. Conversano's cathedral, rebuilt in the 14th century but showcasing Baroque embellishments, is home to the Madonna della Fonte, a revered icon and symbol of the town's enduring faith. Under the rule of Giangirolamo II Acquaviva, also known as the "Guercio delle Puglie," Conversano became a flourishing center of culture, attracting artists, poets, and intellectuals.

Infiorata (Flower Art) Festival

The Infiorata di Conversano is a vibrant festival that transforms the town's streets into stunning floral tapestries. While the exact origins of this event in Conversano are not well-documented, the tradition of creating intricate designs with flower petals, known as "infiorata," dates back to the early 17th century in Italy. It began in Rome, where artists used flower petals to craft elaborate decorations on church floors during religious celebrations. This custom spread to various parts of Italy, evolving into annual festivals that celebrate religious events, local culture, and the arrival of spring.

Local artists and volunteers collaborate to design and assemble intricate floral carpets along the town's historic streets, depicting religious themes, historical scenes, or abstract patterns. The festival not only showcases the artistic talents of the community but also fosters a sense of unity and pride among residents and attracts visitors to experience Conversano's rich cultural heritage.

Art of the Infiorata

Festival Events

Besides the breathtaking flower art of the Infiorata, the festival transforms Conversano into a vibrant celebration of culture and community.

Market stalls line the surrounding streets, offering local handicrafts, regional specialties, and floral-inspired souvenirs.

Food vendors tempt visitors with traditional Puglian delicacies, from orecchiette pasta and focaccia barese to sweet pasticciotti and mandorle atterrate (sugar-coated almonds).

Throughout the day, local bands and musicians create a festive atmosphere, performing folk music that has echoed through the narrow streets of this Apulian town for generations. The joyful melodies, enticing aromas, and colorful displays come together to create a multisensory experience that celebrates both artistic tradition and local heritage.

Conversano Walking Tour

#1. Castello di Conversano (Conversano Castle)

Begin your journey through Conversano at its most iconic landmark, the Castello di Conversano, a powerful medieval fortress that has stood watch over the town for centuries. Built by the Normans in the 11th century as part of their defensive network across Puglia, the castle was later transformed by the Acquaviva d'Aragona family, one of the region's most influential noble dynasties.

During the rule of Count Giangirolamo II Acquaviva, known as the "Guercio di Puglia" (the Squinter of Puglia), the castle underwent significant expansions, becoming not just a military stronghold but a refined noble residence. Giangirolamo II was a controversial figure, both feared and admired for his ruthless governance and patronage of the arts.

Today, the castle's massive square towers and imposing walls dominate the historic center, offering visitors a glimpse into Conversano's feudal past. Inside, the castle houses art exhibitions, historical collections, and relics from the Acquaviva era, including portraits and artifacts tied to the family's rule.

The Pinacoteca Civica, within the castle, features a collection of large-scale canvases depicting the life of Saint Benedict, painted by the Neapolitan artist Paolo Finoglio in the 17th century. From the castle's elevated position, you can enjoy sweeping views over the town and surrounding countryside, making it the perfect introduction to Conversano's layered history.

#2. Cattedrale di Santa Maria Assunta

A quick stroll from the castle leads to the majestic Cattedrale di Santa Maria Assunta, one of the finest examples of Apulian Romanesque architecture. Constructed in the 11th century, the cathedral reflects the medieval prosperity of Conversano, which thrived under Norman and later Swabian rule.

Bell Tower of the Cathedral

Its grand facade is marked by a beautiful rose window, symbolizing divine light, and an elaborately carved portal that welcomes visitors into a space where centuries of history intertwine. Inside, the cathedral's high vaulted ceilings, stone columns, and minimalistic Romanesque design create an atmosphere of solemn grandeur. The interior, however, also bears traces of Baroque modifications, including ornate chapels and decorative altars added in later centuries.

One of the most revered treasures inside the cathedral is the statue of the Madonna della Fonte, the patron saint of Conversano. This wooden sculpture, believed to date back to Byzantine times, is closely linked to local religious traditions and is carried in procession during the town's annual celebrations.

#3. Monastero di San Benedetto

A short walk from the castle and cathedral brings you to the Monastero di San Benedetto, a religious institution that played a pivotal role in the spiritual and political landscape of medieval Puglia. Founded in the 6th century, this Benedictine monastery flourished under the Normans and later became one of the most powerful monastic centers in southern Italy.

What makes this monastery unique is its history as a female Benedictine convent, known as a "badessa mitrata" monastery, where the abbesses wielded nearly the same authority as bishops. These women had remarkable power, governing extensive landholdings, influencing local politics, and even issuing official decrees. Their prominence set this monastery apart from many other female religious institutions of the time. The architectural complex includes an impressive Romanesque bell tower, elegant cloisters, and remnants of medieval frescoes.

#4. Porta Tarantina and the Ancient City Walls

Head towards Porta Tarantina, one of the ancient entrances to the city. You can see remnants of the medieval city walls, offering a glimpse into the defensive structures that protected Conversano from invaders.

#5. Chiesa e Convento di San Cosma e Damiano

A small but charming church dedicated to the twin saints, Cosma and Damiano. This site is an example of the deep religious devotion in Conversano and features beautiful altarpieces and sacred art.

#6. Largo della Corte and Piazza XX Settembre

End your walk in Conversano's lively central square. This area is full of cafés, restaurants, and gelaterias where you can relax and soak in the town's atmosphere. It's a glorious spot to taste local specialties like sgagliozze (fried polenta) or panzerotti.

Conversano Festivals and Sagre Throughout the Year

Sant'Antonio Abate

January 17

Celebrated in the Sacro Cuore parish, this feast honors Saint Anthony Abbot, traditionally the protector of animals. After a mass and the blessing of animals (from farm animals to pet rabbits), festivities include an enormous bonfire, amusement park rides, a charity raffle, and stalls offering homemade local food specialties.

Holy Week Celebrations

March or April (dates vary based on Easter).

One of the most deeply felt traditions in Conversano, Holy Week features the decoration of the "Sepolcri" (altars of repose) in churches on Holy Thursday. On Good Friday, the ancient "Black Christ" crucifix is carried in a solemn dawn procession from the Monastery of Santa Maria dell'Isola to the city center, where it meets the statue of the Virgin of Sorrows. The Procession of the Mysteries, accompanied by the Latin chant of the "Miserere," takes place in the afternoon, winding through the historic center in a moving display of faith.

Madonna della Fonte (Patronal Feast)

First Saturday and Fourth Sunday in May.

The most important festival in Conversano, dedicated to its patroness, the Madonna della Fonte. The town comes alive with religious processions, illuminations, fireworks, sports tournaments, concerts, and cultural events.

Cherry Festival (Sagra della Ciliegia)

June (exact date varies).

A tribute to Conversano's famous cherry production, this sagra features food stands offering tastings of different cherry varieties, local desserts, and other regional specialties.

Sant'Antonio di Padova

June 13

Held at the Church of San Francesco, this feast includes a novena, a procession, and the distribution of "Pane di Sant'Antonio" (Saint Anthony's bread). Children also create small decorative altars in the streets.

Festival of Saints Peter and Paul

June 29

This festival includes a traditional market fair, where vendors sell goods ranging from clothing to local crafts and food.

Madonna del Carmine

July 16

Hosted by the former Carmelite convent, this festival honors Our Lady of Mount Carmel with a procession featuring both the Madonna and Saint Elijah, alongside fireworks, music, and illuminations.

Maris Stella Festival

First Sunday in August.

A parish festival featuring the Sagra del Bocconotto, where visitors can taste this delicious traditional pastry while enjoying folk music and local performances.

San Rocco Festival

August 16

This medieval-inspired event features the "Cavalcata", a parade of decorated horses ridden by children and young people in traditional costumes. The festival is organized by the medieval Church of San Rocco.

Festival of SS. Medici and Santa Rita

First Sunday in October.

Celebrated at the Church of San Cosma, this religious festival honors Saints Cosmas and Damian and Saint Rita, former patrons of Conversano. The statues are carried in a procession alongside a display of precious ex-votos—devotional offerings such as jewelry, medals, or tokens left in gratitude for answered prayers or miracles. The secular celebrations include fireworks, illuminations, an amusement park, and a musical program.

Novello sotto il Castello (New Wine under the Castle)

Mid-November

This food and wine festival, whose name means "New Wine under the Castle," celebrates the arrival of novello wine, Italy's young wine similar to Beaujolais nouveau. For three evenings, the streets around Conversano's medieval castle fill with wineries offering tastings of novello and other local wines, alongside stands featuring olive oil, cheeses, and traditional autumn dishes. The festival also includes live music and art performances. Supported by the town and local cultural associations, this well-organized event has become a highlight of Puglia's fall, blending enogastronomy with the charm of Conversano's historic center.

San Flaviano Festival

November 24

Honoring San Flaviano, Conversano's co-patron saint, the festival includes a procession of the saint's statue from the Cathedral Basilica and a traditional market fair, where vendors sell livestock, textiles, and artisanal goods.

Immaculate Conception Festival

December 8

Hosted at the Church of San Francesco, this event marks the start of the Christmas season with a novena, a grand procession, and the Sagra della Pettola, a food festival celebrating pettola, a traditional fried dough.

Santa Lucia Festival

December 13

Organized by the Rettoria della Passione, the festival includes a novena, a candlelit procession, an artistic nativity scene, and musical performances, along with food stalls selling traditional delicacies.

Christmas Celebrations

December 8 to January 6

Conversano's historic center comes alive with nativity scenes, concerts, and street performances. Artisanal presepi (nativity displays) are set up in churches and public spaces, while local vendors offer Christmas sweets and crafts.

Day Trips: Nearby Sites, Cities, and Towns

San Vito. 10 kilometers (6.2 miles) northeast of Conversano. San Vito is a small fishing village just outside Polignano a Mare, known for its Benedictine Abbey of San Vito overlooking the sea. The abbey dates back to the 10th century and features a charming cloister. The small harbor, colorful fishing boats, and rocky coastline make it a peaceful escape. While it's not a full-day destination, it's great for a half-day trip combined with Polignano a Mare.

Rutigliano. 15 kilometers (9.3 miles) west of Conversano. Rutigliano is famous for its terracotta craftsmanship, especially handmade whistles (fischietti), which have a centuries-old tradition. The Museo del Fischietto showcases these artistic clay whistles. The town is also known for its grape festival in September and historic center, with the Torre Normanna and the Chiesa Matrice di Santa Maria della Colonna e San Nicola.

Logistics

Train: The train station is within the town and part of the Ferrovie del Sud Est (FSE) network. This regional train line connects Conversano to Bari (about 40 minutes) and other nearby towns, making train travel a convenient option.

Bus: Several bus operators provide services to and from Conversano, mainly Ferrovie del Sud Est (FSE) and Miccolis. Buses connect Conversano with Bari, Polignano a Mare, Monopoli, and Putignano, offering an alternative for travelers who prefer not to drive. Schedules can vary, so checking the latest timetables in advance is recommended.

Car: Conversano is easily accessible by car from Bari via the SP240 provincial road, with a drive time of approximately 35–40 minutes. If coming from further away, take the SS16 coastal highway and exit at Polignano a Mare or Monopoli, then follow signs to Conversano.

Parking: Parking in Conversano is convenient, with free and paid parking options available. The historic center has ZTL (Limited Traffic Zones), so visitors should park outside this area. Some recommended parking spots include Piazza della Repubblica (near the train station) and Via Matteotti, both of which are within walking distance of the principal attractions.

Restaurant Recommendations

Pashà. Address: Via Morgantini, 2

A Michelin-starred restaurant offering contemporary Apulian cuisine in an elegant setting. Chef Maria Cicorella crafts innovative dishes that honor regional traditions, providing a memorable culinary experience.

Vita Pugliese. Address: Via Ospedale, 15

A charming restaurant nestled in a quaint alley, known for its authentic Puglian dishes. Guests appreciate the warm atmosphere and specialties like orecchiette pasta paired with a curated selection of local wines.

Goffredo Ristorante - Osteria in Terrazza. Address: Vico Goffredo Altavilla, 8

On the terrace of the Corte Altavilla hotel, this restaurant offers panoramic views of the historic center. The menu features a blend of traditional and modern Italian cuisine, with an emphasis on fresh, local ingredients.

Accommodation

Corte Altavilla Relais & Charme. Address: Vico Goffredo Altavilla, 8

Housed in a historic building, this upscale hotel offers a blend of medieval charm and modern amenities. Guests can enjoy the on-site spa, rooftop terrace with panoramic views, and the Goffredo Ristorante, which serves traditional Apulian cuisine.

Hotel Palazzo d'Erchia. Address: Via Acquaviva d'Aragona, 116

Set in a historic palace, this hotel provides an intimate atmosphere with individually decorated rooms featuring antique furnishings. Its central location allows easy access to Conversano's principal attractions.

D'Aragona Hotel. Address: Via San Donato, 5

Near the historic center, D'Aragona Hotel offers modern accommodations with amenities like an outdoor pool and on-site restaurant. It's a short walk from Conversano's historic sites and offers convenient access to explore the town.

CHAPTER THIRTEEN

Mola's Maritime Tradition

Honoring Local Octopus

Sagra del Polpo

Where: Mola di Bari

When: Last weekend of July.

Average Festival Temperatures: High 29°C (84.2°F). Low 22.8°C (73°F).

Sagra Website: https://visitabari.com/eventi/

Mola's Maritime Tradition: A Crossroads of History and Culture

Nestled along the Adriatic coast of Puglia, Mola di Bari has stood for millennia as a vital hub of trade, defense, and maritime tradition. Known simply as Mola to locals, this coastal town has witnessed the passage of ancient civilizations, medieval conquerors, and Renaissance prosperity, all shaping its unique identity.

Mola's origins stretch back to pre-Roman times, with evidence suggesting settlements of the Peucetians, an ancient Italic tribe that inhabited Puglia before Greek and Roman influence took hold. The town's strategic position along the Adriatic made it an important stop for maritime trade, connecting southern Italy with Greece and the eastern Mediterranean. Under Roman rule, Mola flourished as a port town, supporting the movement of goods and people along the empire's expansive trade networks.

The Middle Ages brought waves of invasions, from Byzantine forces to Norman and Saracen raids. To protect the town, Holy Roman Emperor Frederick II and later the Angevins (House of Anjou) reinforced Mola's coastal defenses. The Castello Angioino, built in the 13th century, stands as a testament to this era, constructed to repel Saracen pirates and secure the town's strategic position along the Adriatic. In the 15th century, under Aragonese rule, the castle was further fortified, marking Mola as a stronghold against Ottoman threats and rival maritime powers.

During the Renaissance, Mola flourished as a fishing and trading port, benefiting from its proximity to Bari (just 20 km southeast). The town's economy became increasingly linked to the sea, as local merchants expanded their reach across the Adriatic. The era also saw the growth of religious and civic architecture, with churches, noble palaces, and town squares reflecting the wealth and artistic influences of the time.

Mola di Bari sits on a coastline that blends rugged cliffs with sandy shores, framed by olive groves and vineyards stretching inland toward the Murge plateau. Its Mediterranean climate, with warm summers and mild winters, has long supported a lifestyle centered on agriculture and maritime traditions.

Today, Mola is home to around 25,000 residents, though this number swells in summer as visitors are drawn to its historic charm, bustling piazzas, and vibrant local traditions. The town's dialect, a unique variation of Apulian Italian, echoes through lively markets and festivals celebrating centuries-old heritage.

The Octopus Festival

Picture this: On a balmy July evening, the ancient stones of Mola di Bari come alive with the sparkle of festival lights and the mouthwatering aroma of simmering octopus. Yes, octapus!

As the Mediterranean sun sets, the town's waterfront transforms into a bustling carnival of flavors. Local fishermen, whose families have worked these waters for generations, proudly display their prized catch. The air fills with the sizzle of grills and the gentle bubbling of copper pots where tender octopus slowly stews to perfection. Locals share age old cooking secrets while young chefs add contemporary twists to traditional recipes, serving everything from classic octopus stew to innovative street food creations.

Sagra Events

For three days, the waterfront and historic center of Mola di Bari transform into an open-air spectacle, where visitors can enjoy dazzling lights, traditional music, and local delicacies. The star of the show? Freshly caught Mediterranean octopus, prepared in various ways, from grilled perfection to stewed specialties.

Festival Highlights

Culinary Delights: Indulge in expertly prepared octopus dishes, paired with regional wines and street food specialties.

Live Music & Dancing: Traditional Puglian folk music and dance performances bring the town to life.

Vibrant Atmosphere: The streets light up with festive decorations, artisanal markets, and a strong sense of community.

Whether it's your first time or you're returning for another unforgettable experience, the Sagra del Polpo is a must-visit summer festival that captures the heart of Puglia's maritime traditions.

Mola di Bari Walking Tour

#1. Piazza XX Settembre

This vibrant square pulses with energy from dawn to dusk, as locals gather at historic cafés like the century-old Caffè dell'Angolo, where the art of espresso-making has been perfected over generations. The elegant Palazzo Roberti, its 18th-century façade glowing golden in the afternoon sun, watches over the scene like a noble guardian. Its intricate stone balconies, adorned with hand-carved flora motifs, tell tales of aristocratic life from centuries past.

#2. Chiesa Matrice di San Nicola (Mother Church of St. Nicholas)

At the heart of Mola di Bari's old town stands the Chiesa Matrice di San Nicola, a sacred landmark that has watched over the community since the 12th century. Built in the Apulian Romanesque style, its façade is a striking blend of simplicity and elegance, featuring rounded arches, sturdy columns, and finely sculpted stonework. Over the centuries, additions in the Baroque period softened its austere medieval lines, introducing intricate decorations and a more ornate interior.

As you step inside, the dimly lit nave stretches toward the high altar, where a magnificent 18th-century wooden statue of San Nicola, Mola's patron saint, presides over the faithful. The play of light through stained glass windows creates an ethereal atmosphere, illuminating centuries-old frescoes that narrate biblical stories in rich, vivid tones. The church's wooden coffered ceiling, a masterpiece from the Renaissance era, adds warmth to the sacred space, while the worn stone floors whisper of generations who have walked this path in prayer.

One of the church's most intriguing features is its crypt, where remnants of older religious structures suggest that this site has been a place of worship since the early medieval period. During religious celebrations, particularly on the Feast of San Nicola (December 6), the church becomes the heart of Mola's spiritual life, filled with music, candlelight, and the voices of the community carrying on traditions that have endured for nearly a thousand years.

#3. Teatro Van Westerhout

This intimate 19th-century gem, named for Mola's celebrated native composer, may be modest in size but possesses the grandeur of Europe's splendid opera houses in miniature. Its perfectly proportioned interior, with its velvet seats and gilded details, creates an atmosphere of timeless elegance. When the house lights dim and music fills the air, the theater transforms into a magical space where past and present merge in perfect harmony. Even today, local performers and international artists alike grace its stage, their voices soaring to the same rafters that once resonated with Van Westerhout's own compositions.

#4. Castello Angioino-Aragonese

Standing proudly at the water's edge, the Castello Angioino-Aragonese rises from the Adriatic shoreline like a stone sentinel. This formidable 15th-century fortress, built in an age when pirates prowled these waters, still commands respect with its imposing presence. As you walk along its massive walls, imagine the watchmen of centuries past scanning the horizon for approaching sails, ready to sound the alarm at any sign of danger.

Each of its weather-worn towers tells tales of siege and survival, while the castle's strategic position offers breathtaking views across the very waters it was built to defend. Today, rather than repelling invaders, the castle welcomes visitors to explore its robust architecture and discover the stories hidden within its ancient stones. During sunset, when the fortress is bathed in golden light, you might catch a glimpse of what the pirates saw, a formidable guardian protecting one of Puglia's most charming coastal towns.

#5. Lungomare Dalmazia (Seafront Promenade)

Follow the whispers of the Adriatic as you stroll along Lungomare Dalmazia, where the ancient relationship between Mola and the sea unfolds before you. This beloved promenade, paved with limestone worn smooth by countless footsteps, transforms throughout the day: at dawn, it buzzes with fishermen preparing their nets, while sunset brings families and couples for their traditional passeggiata.

#6. Porto di Mola di Bari, Traditional Fishing Harbor

Each morning around 4:00 a.m., the port springs to life as the fleet returns laden with the day's catch. Watch as weathered hands sort through glistening nets full of orata, spigola, and the prized red Mola shrimp, a local delicacy. Many of these vessels bear names of saints or beloved family members, their wooden hulls showing proud battle scars from years of challenging the Adriatic's moods. Listen for the melodic calls of fishmongers at the dockside market, where the ancient practice of contrattazione (price negotiation) continues just as it has for hundreds of years. The harbor's stone walls, built in the 1800s using local limestone, still bear carved initials of fishermen from generations past.

#7. Monumento ai Caduti del Mare (Monument of the Fallen Soldier)

Created in 1956 by local sculptor Antonio Bassi, the monument features three bronze figures, a fisherman, a sailor, and a grieving woman, each telling part of Mola's maritime story. The base, crafted from the same stone used in the town's ancient walls, bears the names of over 200 local mariners lost since 1908. Each name has its own story, passed down through families who still cast flowers into the sea on All Souls' Day. The monument becomes particularly poignant during the Festa della Madonna a Mare in July, when it serves as a focal point for the maritime procession, its bronze figures illuminated by hundreds of floating lanterns released onto the water in memory of the fallen.

Mola Festivals Throughout the Year

Festa della Madonna d'Altomare (Feast of our Lady of the Sea)

First Sunday of July.

When the Madonna d'Altomare festival begins, Mola di Bari's seafaring soul truly comes alive. This intimate celebration honors the protector of those who brave the Mediterranean waters. Fishing boats, adorned with lights and flowers, create a floating procession in the harbor, their reflections dancing on the twilight waters. Fishermen share tales of the Madonna's protection during storms, while their families gather to give thanks for safe returns. The festival weaves together maritime tradition and spiritual devotion, creating a profound reminder of the town's eternal relationship with the sea that sustains it.

Palio dei Capatosta

Mid-July

The Palio dei Capatosta is one of Puglia's most vibrant and spirited local festivals. The name "Capatosta" translates roughly to "hard-headed" or "stubborn," reflecting the determined character of Mola's residents. This colorful event transforms the town into a medieval spectacle where the four historic districts (quartieri) compete in traditional games and challenges that test strength, skill, and teamwork. Local participants dress in elaborate medieval costumes, parading through streets adorned with banners and coats of arms representing each district, while drummers and flag-throwers create an atmosphere that transports visitors back in time.

The festival typically culminates in a grand finale where representatives from each quarter battle for supremacy in challenges that often include tug-of-war contests, sack races, and the iconic "palo della cuccagna" (greasy pole) competition where contestants attempt to climb a slippery pole to claim prizes.

Festa Patronale di Maria Santissima Addolorata (Festa Grande) Feast of Our Lady of Sorrows (Main Festival)

Second Sunday of September.

As autumn breezes sweep through Mola di Bari, the town transforms for its grandest celebration of the year. The Festa Grande brings the community together in a spectacular display of faith and tradition. Ancient stone streets echo with sacred hymns as the revered statue of Maria SS. Addolorata processes through candlelit pathways. Local families gather on flower-adorned balconies, while the evening air fills with the melody of orchestras performing in historic piazzas. For four magical days, the town becomes a tapestry of lights, music, and devotion, where centuries-old religious customs blend seamlessly with joyous celebration.

Day Trip Options: Nearby Sites, Cities, and Towns

San Giorgio. 10 kilometers (6.2 miles) northwest. Just beyond Bari's bustling center lies San Giorgio, where the authentic pulse of coastal Italian life beats strong and true. This hidden gem of the Adriatic offers a pristine rocky coastline where local families gather on sun-warmed stones to swim in crystal-clear coves.

Torre a Mare. 7 kilometers (4.3 miles) northwest. What began as a humble fishing village has blossomed into a cherished local escape, without losing its maritime soul. Torre a Mare's marina still echoes with the calls of fishermen selling their morning catch, while the evening air fills with the aromas of grilled seafood from family-run restaurants tucked into ancient stone buildings along the waterfront. The village's medieval watchtower stands sentinel over the harbor, a reminder of its historical role in protecting the coastline, now serving as a romantic backdrop for the evening passeggiata.

Beaches: The coastline around Torre a Mare is predominantly rocky, with clear waters ideal for swimming and snorkeling. There is a small beach area near the village that offers access to the sea. While not extensive, it provides a convenient spot for a quick dip.

Logistics

Train: Mola di Bari has a train station on the Bari-Lecce railway line, served by Trenitalia regional trains.

Bus: Local buses connect Mola di Bari with nearby towns like Conversano, Rutigliano, and Polignano a Mare. Buses also run to Bari's main bus station for intercity connections.

Car: 20 kilometers (12.5 miles) north of Bari. Take the SS16 southbound from Bari, following signs for Mola di Bari. Exit at Mola di Bari and follow local signs into town.

Parking: Via Lungara Porto, near the port and seafront, ideal for visiting the marina and restaurants.

Restaurant Recommendations

La Cantina dei Briganti. Address: Vico Morgese 1

La Cantina dei Briganti offers an authentic dining experience reminiscent of the early 20th century. The menu features traditional dishes such as stewed donkey roulades, handmade stuffed pasta with Mediterranean fish, and classic Italian favorites like amatriciana and cacio e pepe. The restaurant boasts a selection of over 60 Italian wines, carefully curated by an expert sommelier.

Accommodation

For sagre a day trip is fine, but if you have time, you could easily spend three to four nights here, enjoying nearby sites and beaches.

Hotel Gabbiano. Address: Viale Pesce P. D., 24

A charming 3-star hotel near the town center and the beach, Hotel Gabbiano offers a terrace and complimentary bicycles for guests. Guests have praised its friendly and attentive staff, as well as its convenient location just a 3-minute walk from the main piazza.

Le Carasse Boutique Hotel. Address: Via Giovanni Bovio, 90

This 4-star boutique hotel features a garden, shared lounge, and bar, providing a comfortable and stylish stay. Guests have lauded its exquisite design, attentive staff, and excellent continental breakfast. The property also boasts a modern spa carved into limestone, offering a unique relaxation experience. Its central location allows easy access to local attractions, making it a highly recommended choice for visitors to Mola di Bari.

Tenuta Pinto. Address: SC Chiancarelle, 13

A luxurious 5-star farmhouse hotel outside of the town center, Tenuta Pinto offers a beautiful garden and pool, providing a unique and relaxing experience. Set amidst olive groves and vineyards, this agriturismo combines rustic charm with modern comforts, allowing guests to immerse themselves in the tranquil Puglian countryside while still being within reach of Mola di Bari's coastal attractions.

CHAPTER FOURTEEN

Trani's Medieval Splendor Unveiled

Knights, Traditions, and History

La Settimana Medievale

Where: Trani

When: Early August.

Average Festival Temperatures: High 28°C (83°F). Low 20°C (68°F).

Festival Website: https://www.tranitradizioni.com/

Trani: The Pearl of the Adriatic

Trani, often called the "Pearl of the Adriatic," is a picturesque coastal town in the Puglia region of southern Italy. Its origins date back to Roman times, although the town rose to prominence during the Middle Ages, becoming a significant trading hub along the Adriatic Sea. By the 11th century, Trani was flourishing as a maritime power, playing a pivotal role in Mediterranean trade, particularly with the Byzantine Empire and the Middle East.

One of the most notable contributions of Trani's medieval era is the Ordinamenta Maris, a maritime code established in 1063, which is one of the oldest known compilations of maritime laws. This document reflects the town's importance as a maritime and legal center during the Middle Ages.

The Normans, Swabians, and later the Angevins all left their mark on Trani's architecture and culture, contributing to its stunning array of Romanesque and Gothic structures. A historic synagogue, still important today, attests to the town's once-prominent Jewish community.

Castello Svevo

Trani is on the Adriatic coast of Puglia, approximately 40 kilometers (25 miles) northwest of Bari. Its natural harbor, framed by crystal-clear waters, has been a central feature of the town's history and charm. The town's coastline offers a blend of scenic beauty and cultural landmarks, with the historic center situated just steps from the sea.

The gently rolling countryside around Trani is dotted with olive groves, vineyards, and Murgia stone quarries, sources of building materials for centuries. Its strategic position along the coast has made it a gateway to trade and cultural exchange throughout its history.

Trani is home to 55,000 residents. The local economy thrives on a mix of tourism, agriculture, and small-scale fishing, making it a quintessential example of Puglia's coastal charm.

The Medieval Festival

The Settimana Medievale di Trani (Medieval Weekend of Trani) is an annual event that immerses the city in its rich medieval heritage. Organized by the Associazione Culturale Trani Tradizioni, the festival was first held in 2004 and has since become a significant cultural celebration.

The festival was conceived to commemorate and reenact pivotal historical events from Trani's medieval past, particularly the marriage of King Manfredi of Sicily to Princess Elena Comneno of Epirus, which took place in Trani in 1259. This union is a cornerstone of the city's history, symbolizing its importance during the medieval period.

Trani's medieval significance, highlighted by landmarks such as the Castello Svevo built by Emperor Frederick II and its role as a major Adriatic port during the Crusades, makes it an ideal location for such a festival. The Settimana Medievale not only celebrates these historical milestones, but also aims to preserve and promote the city's cultural heritage, allowing residents and visitors to experience the traditions, customs, and daily life of the Middle Ages.

Over the years, the festival has grown, featuring reenactments, parades, and various events that bring medieval history to life, reinforcing Trani's identity and pride in its historical legacy.

Day 1: NOX TEMPLARIORUM, The Night of the Templars

As darkness descends upon Trani, the city steps back to an age of mystery and crusading knights. This dramatic evening recreates the powerful presence of the Knights Templar in medieval Trani, when the city served as a crucial departure point for crusaders heading to the Holy Land. Through a series of theatrical performances, from solemn processions to dramatic confrontations, the night brings to life the complex world of these warrior monks, complete with tales of valor, episodes of medieval justice, and mysterious rituals that defined this fascinating period of history.

7:30 p.m.

Templar Gathering

In the atmospheric Piazza Mazzini, the crimson-crossed Knights Templar assemble for their solemn procession, their armor gleaming in the fading light of dusk. The gathered crowd falls silent as these legendary warriors prepare for their march through the ancient streets.

7:45 p.m.

Tales of the Templars

At Piazza Duomo, a masterful storyteller captivates the audience with dramatic tales of the Templar knights, weaving histories of their crusades, bravery, and mysterious traditions. The stories build anticipation for the warriors' arrival as darkness begins to settle over the city.

Piazza Duomo from the Castello

8:00 p.m.

Arrival of the Templars

The Knights Templar make their grand entrance into Piazza Duomo, their red crosses stark against their white mantles, creating a powerful testament to the city's role in the Crusades.

8:30 p.m.

Bandit Attack

The peaceful evening erupts into chaos as brigands emerge from the shadows to threaten local merchants, recreating the dangerous times of medieval commerce. The dramatic clash between order and lawlessness unfolds before the crowd.

8:45 p.m.

The Witch's Curse

A haunting performance brings to life medieval superstitions as a witch's curse threatens the peace of the city, creating an eerie atmosphere that transports viewers back to an age of mystery and magic.

9:20 p.m.

Justice of King Frederick

Under royal decree, the captured bandits face their punishment, demonstrating the swift justice of medieval law. The scene provides a glimpse into the strict social order of the 13th century.

9:40 p.m.

The Exorcism Ritual

A dramatic exorcism ceremony unfolds, combining medieval religious traditions with theatrical elements to showcase the period's spiritual beliefs and practices.

10:00 p.m.

Tribute to King Frederick

The evening's events culminate in a formal tribute to King Frederick, celebrating his role in establishing order and justice in medieval Trani.

10:30 p.m.

Dragons of Fire

The night reaches its spectacular conclusion with an enchanting fire show by the Dragons of Trani Traditions, illuminating the ancient stones of Piazza Duomo with their mesmerizing performance of flame and skill.

Day 2: L'incontro di Re Manfredi e Elena Comneno- The Meeting of King Manfredi and Elena Comneno

On this enchanted evening, Trani recreates one of its most significant historical moments - the first meeting between King Manfredi and his future bride, Elena Comneno of Epirus. The carefully choreographed sequence of events follows the historical protocols of medieval royal encounters, building from separate court processions to a grand unified celebration.

7:30 p.m.

Madonna Marianna's Royal Tale

A traditional storyteller, dressed in period attire, weaves the romantic tale of how King Manfredi, son of Frederick II, met and fell in love with Elena Comneno, the beautiful princess from Epirus. The story is told in both medieval Italian and the local Tranese dialect.

8:00 p.m.

King Manfredi's Court Procession

From the majestic Castello Svevo, King Manfredi and his court emerge in a spectacular display of medieval pageantry, with knights, nobles, and courtiers in full regalia accompanying their sovereign.

8:10 p.m.

Elena Comneno's Court Procession

Princess Elena's procession departs from Castello Svevo, creating a separate but equally magnificent spectacle as her retinue displays the splendor of the Byzantine court of Epirus.

8:50 p.m.

Royal Arrival

The royal parties converge on Piazza Re Manfredi in a carefully choreographed ceremony that demonstrates the grand protocol of medieval court life.

9:00 p.m.

Meeting of the Royals

In Piazza Libertà, the two courts finally meet in a formal ceremony that recreates the historic first encounter between King Manfredi and his future bride.

9:10 p.m.

Investiture of Knights

A solemn ceremony where new knights are dubbed into service, following ancient protocols and traditions of medieval chivalry.

9:30 p.m.

Royal Entertainment

The evening reaches its peak with spectacular performances including medieval court dances, elegant ladies' presentations, thrilling displays by the fire-eating Dragons of Trani Traditions, and the mesmerizing Green Clouds show, all performed in honor of the royal couple.

Day 3: Le Nozze di Re Manfredi e La Principessa Elena Comneno -The Wedding of King Manfredi and Elena Comneno

The pinnacle of Trani's Medieval Week recreates the historic 1259 royal wedding that united the Kingdom of Sicily with the Despotate of Epirus. This evening transforms Piazza Re Manfredi into a scene of magnificent medieval pageantry, culminating in the recreation of one of the most significant ceremonies in the city's history. From the thundering drums of the opening ceremony to the spectacular castle illumination, every moment brings to life the splendor and romance of this royal union.

7:45 p.m.

Opening Ceremony with Timpanists and Flag-bearers

The evening begins with Trani's renowned sbandieratori (flag-wavers) performing intricate choreographies accompanied by thundering medieval drums. These highly skilled performers execute complex flag-tossing routines in authentic 13th-century costumes, their flags bearing the heraldic symbols of Trani and the House of Hohenstaufen.

8:00 p.m.

Madonna Marianna's Royal Tale

A traditional storyteller, dressed in period attire, weaves the romantic tale of King Manfredi and Elena Comneno, setting the stage for the grand wedding ceremony to follow.

8:10 p.m.

Royal Wedding Ceremony

A magnificent spectacle unfolds as over 100 costumed performers bring a historic wedding reenactment to life. Authentic period instruments playing medieval music, traditional 13th-century wedding rituals and customs, and nobles and knights in historically accurate attire bring the ceremony to life.

8:40 p.m.

Official Thanks and Greetings

Local authorities and dignitaries offer their formal congratulations to the royal couple, following the strict protocols and etiquette of medieval court life.

9:00 p.m.

Castle Fire Display

A spectacular pyrotechnic display transforms the Castello Svevo into a cascade of light, creating the illusion of the castle being bathed in flames as part of the royal celebration.

9:30 p.m.

Triumphal Medieval Procession

A grand parade winds through Trani's medieval streets, showcasing the full splendor of the royal wedding celebration with nobles, knights, musicians, and performers.

10:00 p.m.

Evening Festivities

The night concludes with medieval music and dancing in Piazza Re Manfredi. Performers teach traditional 13th-century dances to visitors while musicians play authentic medieval instruments, including lutes and mandolins, percussion instruments, reed pipes, and early stringed instruments. The evening continues well into the night with medieval feasting and entertainment.

Incendio al Castello: The Final Act

The festival concludes with "Incendio al Castello Svevo," a dramatic performance at the castle. Best viewing spots include the cathedral steps and harbor promenade. Costume rentals are available for visitors wanting to participate fully in the medieval atmosphere.

Other Key Events:

Medieval Market and Crafts: Artisans demonstrate period techniques including coin minting, armor forging, manuscript illumination, and herbal medicine preparation. Visitors can take part in workshops learning medieval crafts and period dances.

Traditional Feasts: Local taverns transform into medieval inns serving historically inspired dishes like hypocras (spiced wine), traditional Pugliese orecchiette, and recipes from medieval cookbooks.

Interactive Entertainment: Street performers present mystery plays and commedia dell'arte in piazzas. Children can join "knight training" sessions with foam weapons and heraldry workshops. Visitors can try archery under expert guidance.

Locations & Events:

- Piazza Manfredi: Central stage for the grand wedding reenactment of King Manfredi and Princess Elena Comneno, featuring period-accurate costumes and ceremonies.

- Castello Svevo: Hosts medieval banquets, combat demonstrations, and the dramatic "Incendio al Castello Svevo" closing ceremony.

- Porto di Trani: Medieval marketplace and setting for the opening "Nox Templariorum" featuring Templar knights.

- Piazza della Repubblica: Artisan demonstrations of coin minting, manuscript illumination, and armor forging.

Trani Walking Tour

#1. Trani Cathedral (Cattedrale di San Nicola Pellegrino)

Begin your journey through Trani at its most iconic landmark, the Cattedrale di San Nicola Pellegrino. Standing majestically on a limestone promontory overlooking the Adriatic Sea, this cathedral is one of the finest examples of Apulian Romanesque architecture. Built between the 11th and 13th centuries, it honors Saint Nicholas the Pilgrim, a Greek-born wanderer who arrived in Trani and died there in 1094. His reputation for miracles led to his rapid canonization, forever tying his name to the spiritual heart of the city.

Trani Peninsula

What sets Trani Cathedral apart is its unique three-tiered structure, an architectural marvel rarely seen elsewhere. Beneath the main sanctuary lies the crypt of Santa Maria della Scala, a 6th-century chapel adorned with ancient columns and medieval frescoes, remnants of early Christian worship. Just above, the crypt of San Nicola Pellegrino houses 28 grand columns of marble and granite, repurposed from ancient Roman ruins, their varied styles hinting at centuries of layered history. The upper church, with its vast, airy nave, is crowned by a soaring 59-meter transept, drawing the eye upward to its magnificent bronze doors, crafted in 1175 by Barisano da Trani. These intricately detailed doors feature 32 panels depicting religious scenes, a stunning testament to medieval artistry.

Step outside, and the cathedral's white limestone façade gleams in the southern sun, an architectural masterpiece adorned with delicate carvings and intricate reliefs. Among its most striking elements are:

- A breathtaking rose window, its finely carved tracery radiating out like a lacework of stone.

- Three grand portal doors, each adorned with sculpted biblical scenes and medieval symbols.

- A slender, 59-meter (193-foot) bell tower, rising in elegant tiers above the Adriatic.

- Twin spiral staircases leading to the upper church, adding a sense of grandeur to the entrance.

With its seaside location, the Cathedral of Trani appears almost to float above the water, creating one of the most photographed views in Puglia. Whether you admire its Romanesque grandeur, its centuries-old relics, or its spectacular coastal setting, this cathedral remains a timeless symbol of Trani's rich history and enduring faith.

#2. Castello Svevo di Trani (Swabian Castle)

Walk a short distance from the cathedral, and you'll find yourself before the Castello Svevo, an imposing fortress built in 1233 by Emperor Frederick II. Designed as both a defensive stronghold and a symbol of imperial power, the castle exemplifies medieval military architecture at its finest. Its rectangular layout and strategic coastal position made it a key fortification along the Adriatic, protecting Trani from maritime threats while asserting Frederick's dominance over the region. Unlike many castles of the era, this one was commissioned and overseen by the emperor himself, reflecting his innovative military vision and refined architectural taste.

The castle's massive stone walls, once surrounded by a deep moat carved into solid rock, give it an unyielding presence. Each corner tower, fortified with arrow slits, allowed defenders to repel invaders with deadly precision. Of particular strategic importance was the west tower, uniquely positioned to guard the port, ensuring Trani's maritime security. Inside, the castle's internal courtyard reveals a sophisticated rainwater collection system, an impressive feat of medieval engineering that ensured the fortress could withstand long sieges. Secret passages and underground chambers once provided both defensive and logistical advantages, while the structure's double walls and drawbridges offered multiple layers of protection against enemy assaults.

Over the centuries, the Castello Svevo strengthened to serve a variety of functions. Initially, a royal residence for the Hohenstaufen dynasty, it later became a maritime customs house controlling Trani's bustling trade routes. During the 19th and 20th centuries, the fortress took on a darker role as a prison, housing inmates from 1844 to 1974 before being restored and repurposed as a modern cultural center.

Today, its grand halls and restored chambers host exhibitions, historical displays, and cultural events, offering visitors a glimpse into its layered past. From the castle's ramparts, breathtaking views of the Adriatic and Trani's historic port complete the experience, showcasing the enduring legacy of Frederick II's architectural genius, a perfect blend of military might and aesthetic beauty that continues to captivate all who visit.

#3. Trani Harbor (Porto di Trani)

From the castle, stroll toward the picturesque Trani Harbor, lined with colorful fishing boats and bustling restaurants. This historic port has been central to Trani's maritime activities for centuries. Take a moment to enjoy a coffee or gelato at one of the waterfront cafes while soaking in the lively atmosphere.

Trani Harbor

#4. Jewish Quarter and Synagogue Scolanova

Head to the historic Jewish Quarter, a testament to Trani's multicultural past during the Middle Ages. Visit the Synagogue Scolanova, a 13th-century synagogue that was converted into a church and later restored to its original purpose. Its simple yet significant design reflects the town's vibrant Jewish history.

#5. Piazza della Repubblica and Palazzo Caccetta

Walk to Piazza della Repubblica, a central square surrounded by charming buildings and cafes. Nearby is the Palazzo Caccetta, a 15th-century Gothic-style palace that once housed Trani's nobility. Its elegant facade with pointed arches is a highlight of late medieval architecture.

#6. San Francesco Church and Monastery

End your tour at San Francesco Church, near the waterfront. This 13th-century complex represents one of Trani's most significant religious monuments, commissioned by the Franciscan order shortly after St. Francis himself visited the city in 1222.

The church showcases a fascinating blend of Gothic and Romanesque architectural styles, with its striking rose window featuring intricate stone tracery and pointed Gothic arches contrasting with Romanesque rounded portals. Built from local limestone, the church takes on a mesmerizing golden hue at sunset. Original medieval frescoes, though partially damaged over time, still adorn the side chapels, while the bell tower serves as both religious symbol and maritime reference point.

The monastery complex centers on a peaceful cloister garden with an ancient well, surrounded by elegant stone columns. Its chapter house contains remarkable remnants of 14th-century frescoes depicting Franciscan saints. The original scriptorium, where monks once created illuminated manuscripts (handwritten books decorated with gold leaf and vibrant colors), connects to dormitory cells now converted into museum spaces displaying religious artifacts. A medieval herb garden, traditionally used for medicinal purposes, adds to the site's historical authenticity.

Throughout its history, the complex served multiple crucial roles in Trani's development. It functioned as a center of learning and manuscript production, provided a refuge for pilgrims traveling to the Holy Land, and served as a meeting place for medieval merchants because of its proximity to the port. During various plague outbreaks, it transformed into a hospital, while continuously acting as a cultural center preserving local traditions and documents.

Today, while part of the monastery still houses a small community of Franciscan friars, portions are open to visitors, offering a glimpse into medieval monastic life and showcasing an impressive collection of religious art and artifacts from the 13th to 18th centuries. The waterfront location provides stunning views of the Adriatic and creates a serene atmosphere, particularly in the early morning or at sunset when the limestone walls reflect the changing light.

Trani Feste and Sagre Throughout the Year

Festa del Corcifisso dei Colonna

May 3

The Festa del Crocifisso di Colonna commemorates a 1480 legend in which a wooden crucifix, stolen and mutilated by Turkish pirates, miraculously returned to Trani's shore. The celebration features a sea procession carrying the crucifix from the Monastero di Santa Maria di Colonna to the port, followed by a solemn procession through the city streets. Fireworks, music, and religious ceremonies mark this deeply rooted expression of local faith and tradition.

Festa di San Nicola il Pellegrino (Saint Nicholas the Pilgrim)

June 2

Trani celebrates its patron saint, San Nicola il Pellegrino (Saint Nicholas the Pilgrim), with an annual festival that blends deep religious devotion and lively cultural events. Born in 1075 in Greece, San Nicola journeyed as a pilgrim through southern Italy, arriving in Trani in 1094 where he passed away shortly after. Canonized in 1098, he became the city's beloved protector, and the magnificent Trani Cathedral was built to house his relics. His feast day is officially June 2, but the main Festa Patronale takes place over three days, usually from Saturday to Monday in the first week of August. The celebrations include solemn masses, religious processions featuring the silver bust and relics of the saint, and the much-loved maritime procession where his statue is brought ashore before being carried through the streets.

I Dialoghi di Trani (Trani Dialogues)

Mid-September (Dates vary annually)

An intellectual festival that brings together philosophers, writers, scientists, and artists to discuss contemporary issues. The event includes lectures, debates, and workshops held in various historic venues across Trani and neighboring towns.

Festival delle Bande Musicali (Festival of Musical Bands)

Late December to Early January (Specific dates vary)

This festival celebrates Puglia's musical traditions by featuring performances from various wind orchestras and bands. Concerts are held in different venues, aiming to engage both locals and tourists during the festive season.

Natale nel Borgo Antico (Christmas in the Old Village)

December 6 to January 6

During the Christmas season, Trani's old town is adorned with festive decorations, hosting markets, nativity scenes, and cultural events. Visitors can enjoy local crafts, foods, and traditional music, immersing themselves in the holiday spirit.

Day Trips, Nearby Sites, Cities, and Towns

Molfetta. 12 kilometers (7.5 miles) north of Trani. This atmospheric port city traces its origins to ancient Greek settlements, later growing into a significant medieval maritime center. During the Crusades, Molfetta served as a crucial departure point for the Holy Land, leading to the construction of its masterpiece - the Duomo Vecchio (Old Cathedral) of San Corrado. Built between the 12th and 13th centuries, this rare example of Romanesque architecture features twin domed cupolas and stands as one of Puglia's most distinctive churches.

The compact historic center is a maze of narrow medieval streets leading to unexpected piazzas and churches. The Duomo Nuovo (New Cathedral), built in the late 17th century, houses the remains of San Corrado, the city's patron saint. Don't miss the 16th-century Torrione Passari, part of the ancient defensive walls, or the Church of Santo Stefano with its remarkable 12th-century frescoes. The bustling fishing port offers excellent seafood restaurants where you can sample local specialties.

Logistics

Train: Trani has a station. Trani is 30 minutes from Bari and 10 minutes from Bartletta.

Bus: Several bus companies operate in Trani, offering convenient connections across Puglia and beyond. MarinoBus provides routes to cities like Bari, Naples, and Rome, with tickets available online or at local ticket offices. Itabus connects Trani to destinations such as Milan and Bologna, and tickets can be purchased on their website or at authorized vendors. For regional travel, STP (Società Trasporti Provinciale) operates routes within Puglia, including services to Gravina in Puglia, with tickets available directly from the driver or at sales points.

Car: From Bari you take the A14 (Autostrada Adriatica) northbound, exit at Trani.

Parking: Limited near the historic center and port. Some areas have paid parking (blue lines). Free spots are available farther from the center. Piazzale Stazione is near the train station and offers paid parking.

Restaurant Recommendations

Diavoletto Epicureo. Address: Via Fra' Diego Alvarez 17

A la carte restaurant near the Castle and the Cathedral, offering an intimate and magical atmosphere with Mediterranean cuisine and a modern twist. The chef combines traditional Apulian flavors with sophisticated cooking techniques.

Pepoi Caffe. Address: Via S. Marittimi, 66

A cozy café offering a variety of dishes and drinks. It's a brilliant spot to relax and enjoy a meal in the heart of Trani.

Locanda Trani. Address: Via Zanardelli, 10

A family-run restaurant since 1999, Locanda Trani blends traditional flavors of the region with products from all over Italy. Each dish tells a story of the family's passion for cooking.

Accommodation

For this event I recommend four or five nights in town. There are sights to see and nearby towns to visit.

San Paolo Al Convento Hotel. Address: Via Statuti Marittimi, 111

We stayed at this hotel during one of our visits and, as always, we do not receive any payment or compensation for including businesses in our guides. This 4-star hotel is housed in a beautifully renovated former monastery, complete with an ancient chapel and sweeping views of Trani's picturesque harbor. The location is ideal, right on the waterfront and just a short, scenic walk along the promenade to the cathedral and castle. It offers a truly unique and immersive stay that blends history, charm, and convenience. Breakfast was included, extensive, and delicious.

ibis Styles Trani. Address: Corso Matteo Renato Imbriani 137

A 3-star hotel located just a few steps from the station and close to the historic center and the port of Trani. It offers modern, elegant, and functional rooms with a vintage touch.

CHAPTER FIFTEEN

Melpignano's Midnight Magic

FestaFusion August: La Notte della Taranta

FestaFusion Melpignano

Where: Traveling Festival throughout the Salento Region ending in Melpignano.

When: August 15 and throughout August.

Average Festival Temperatures: High 29°C (84°F). Low 20°C (68°F).

Festival Website: https://lanottedellataranta.it/it/

#1. La Notte della Taranta across Puglia. Italy's largest folk music festival, this electrifying summer event celebrates the hypnotic rhythms of pizzica with concerts, dance performances, and cultural events across Puglia, culminating in a grand finale in Melpignano.

#2. Ferragosto. A beloved Italian holiday on August 15, Ferragosto blends ancient Roman traditions with the Feast of the Assumption, bringing lively beach parties, festivals, and fireworks as Italians take a well-deserved summer break.

#FestaFusion means two or more festivals happen at around the same time in the same town, so visitors can enjoy multiple events during their visit.

Melpignano: A Crossroads of Civilizations and Sound

In the heart of Grecìa Salentina, the small town of Melpignano stands as a testament to over two millennia of history, shaped by ancient settlers, Greek colonists, Byzantine rulers, and Norman conquerors. With just over 2,000 residents, this town, rising 89 meters (292 feet) above the Salentine plains, carries a rich cultural heritage that continues to thrive today.

Melpignano's history dates back to prehistoric times. During the era of Magna Graecia, Greek settlers arrived, leaving behind a lasting imprint on the region's language, traditions, and architecture. Even today, Griko, an ancient Greek dialect, is still spoken by some residents, serving as a living bridge to the town's distant past.

During the Byzantine era (6th–11th century), Melpignano became an important religious and cultural center, deeply influenced by Greek Orthodox traditions. Byzantine monks established churches and monasteries, many adorned with frescoes and religious icons that still survive in fragments. The town's Byzantine influence persisted even after the arrival of the Normans in the 11th century, when Latin Catholic traditions took hold, blending with the Greek legacy.

By the 16th and 17th centuries, Melpignano flourished as a center of trade and noble estates, benefiting from the economic expansion of the Salento region. Wealthy families and religious orders commissioned the construction of grand palaces and churches, many featuring the intricate Baroque architecture typical of southern Puglia. Among them, the Palazzo Marchesale and the Chiesa Madre di San Giorgio stand out, showcasing elaborate stone carvings and ornate facades that reflect the town's Renaissance prosperity.

Surrounded by centuries-old olive groves and the rolling landscapes of southern Puglia, Melpignano enjoys a Mediterranean climate, with warm summers and mild winters that have long supported olive oil production and viticulture (wine production). Whether wandering its narrow streets, admiring its timeless architecture, or experiencing its cultural heartbeat, visitors will find that

Melpignano remains a melodic bridge between civilizations, where the ancient world still sings in harmony with the modern era.

La Notte della Taranta Festival

Imagine a warm August night in Puglia's Salento, where the air vibrates with the thunderous beat of tambourines and the passionate cries of ancient folk songs. This is La Notte della Taranta. Here in Melpignano, the historic squares and streets transform into a swirling celebration as tens of thousands of visitors flood in to experience one of Europe's largest and most vibrant folk music festivals.

Born in 1998, this extraordinary festival has transformed from a local celebration into one of Europe's most spellbinding musical spectacles. But don't mistake this for just another music festival. La Notte is a journey through time, where centuries-old pizzica rhythms, a traditional folk dance and music style from Salento, once used in healing rituals, collide with modern beats, creating something entirely magical.

Think of it as a musical caravan of joy, traveling from village to village throughout August. Each stop brings its own unique flavor to the celebration, as ancient town squares become open-air concert halls and narrow medieval streets pulse with the energy of dancing feet. One night you might find yourself in a tiny village where jazz musicians improvise over traditional tamburello rhythms, a style rooted in the sounds of the tamburello, a southern Italian hand drum similar to a tambourine. The next night, in a baroque piazza, classical orchestras might blend with folk melodies.

The magic reaches its crescendo in Melpignano, where the final concert draws over 100,000 people from around the world. Picture this: the majestic backdrop of a historic monastery, a sea of swaying bodies, and music that seems to rise from the very stones of Salento. Here, world-renowned musicians share the stage with local masters, creating a sound that's both deeply rooted and daringly new.

The pizzica, originally a ritual dance believed to cure the mythical tarantula's bite, has evolved into a powerful symbol of Salento's cultural resilience. Each performance, whether traditional or experimental, carries echoes of the countless generations who have danced these same steps on these same streets.

As the festival moves from town to town, it weaves together the threads of Salento's communities into a tapestry of shared pride and joy. In an age of global homogenization, La Notte della Taranta stands as a testament to how traditional culture can remain vibrantly alive, not by staying frozen in time, but by dancing boldly into the future.

La Notte della Taranta is a traveling music festival that takes place across multiple cities in the Salento region of Apulia (Puglia), Italy throughout August, with a grand finale in Melpignano.

How It Works:

The festival spans several weeks in August, with concerts held in various towns and villages throughout Salento, such as Lecce, Galatina, Nardò, Otranto, and Zollino.

Each night features live performances of pizzica music, a form of traditional Apulian folk music known for its energetic tambourine rhythms and hypnotic dance.

The last event takes place in Melpignano, a small town near Lecce, usually on the last Saturday of August.

The grand concert in Melpignano attracts over 100,000 spectators and features collaborations between local folk musicians and international artists, blending pizzica with contemporary music styles.

This festival celebrates the cultural heritage of Apulia and has gained international recognition as one of Europe's largest folk music festivals.

La Notte della Taranta Festival Schedule

This festival program gives you an idea of how this event travels, but you need to check the website above for year-to-year specifics.

First Week of August

First Saturday of August

Town: Corigliano d'Otranto

7:00 p.m.

Parade: Departure from the mezzanine of the Flying Castle with arrival at Piazza Falcone e Borsellino.

The festivities begin at 7:00 p.m. with a departure from the mezzanine of the iconic Flying Castle. This ancient fortress, dating back to the Middle Ages, stands majestically with its unique blend of medieval and Renaissance architecture. The mezzanine, an elevated and intimate space within the castle, serves as the perfect starting point for the evening's celebrations.

As the sun sets over the picturesque landscape, the parade sets off from the mezzanine, weaving through the charming cobblestone streets of Corigliano d'Otranto. The air is filled with the sounds of traditional music and the rhythmic beats of the pizzica, a lively folk dance. The town comes alive with energy and excitement as various folk orchestras and dance troupes perform, showcasing the rich cultural heritage of the Salento region.

9:15 p.m.

Following the parade, the festival continues with a Workshop of Pizzica conducted by the renowned Taranta Dance Corps. This workshop offers a hands-on experience where participants can learn the traditional dance steps and rhythms of pizzica. It's an excellent opportunity for everyone, from beginners to experienced dancers, to engage with the heart and soul of Salento's cultural heritage.

First Sunday of August

Town: Calimera

9:15 p.m.

The festival in Calimera features a special performance by a talented folk music group from the region. That evening, the market area is transformed into a vibrant stage for the event. The group will perform traditional Salento music, captivating the audience with their energetic and soulful tunes. Following the performance, there will be a workshop of pizzica led by skilled dancers.

NOTE From this point I will just name the towns as the celebrations repeat what we have above until the Finale at Melipignano. Each evening begins at 9:15 p.m.

Monday

Town: Sogliano

9:15 p.m.

The "La Notte della Taranta" festival continues its journey in Sogliano Cavour on Monday, in the vibrant Piazza Falcone e Borsellino.

Tuesday

Town: Cursi

9:15 p.m.

The "La Notte della Taranta" festival continues its journey in Cursi on Tuesday.

Wednesday

Town: Zollino

9:15 p.m.

The evening's festivities begin in the vibrant Largo Villa Comunale.

Thursday

Town: Nardò

9:15 p.m.

A captivating performance by a talented music group. The rhythms and melodies fill the air, captivating the audience and creating an exhilarating atmosphere.

Friday

Town: Ugento

9:15 p.m.

Orchestera Performance: "The Night of the Taranta".

Second Week of August

Second Saturday

Town: Sant'Andrea Marina di Melendugno

Second Sunday

Town: Sternatia

Monday

Town: Carpignano Salentino

Tuesday

Town: Galatone

Wednesday

Town: Lecce

Third Friday

Town: Soleto

Third Week of August

Third Saturday

Town: Galatina

Third Sunday

Town: Cutrofiano

Monday

Town: Alessano

The Grand Finale: When 100,000 Souls Dance Under the Stars

Last Saturday in August

Town: Melpignano

8:00 p.m.

As the sun sets behind Melpignano's ancient Augustinian monastery, Piazza Falcone e Borsellino transforms into a pulsating arena where tradition and innovation collide. Over 100,000 people gather for La Notte della Taranta's grand finale, the air electric with anticipation as the Popular Orchestra takes the stage.

Dancers spin and weave through space, their revolutionary choreographies telling stories of love, loss, and celebration. Traditional Salentine love songs and work chants blend with modern arrangements, while the hypnotic rhythm of tambourines drives the crowd forward. Ancient dialect lyrics carry messages that feel startlingly relevant today.

As the night deepens, the distinction between performers and audience dissolves. The piazza becomes one massive dance floor where tourists and locals, young and old, move as one under the Pugliese stars. In this extraordinary moment, Melpignano becomes the epicenter of a cultural earthquake, showing how tradition stays alive by daring to evolve.

Melpignano Walking Tour

#1. Piazza San Giorgio

This charming piazza features Palazzo Marchesale, a noble residence from the 16th century with an elegant courtyard. Admire the Baroque-style facade before continuing. Look for the Porta Terra, an ancient gateway to the town.

#2. Chiesa Madre di San Giorgio

Chiesa Madre di San Giorgio is a masterpiece of 16th-century Salentine Baroque architecture. Its imposing limestone facade features intricate carvings of saints and biblical scenes, crowned by an elaborate rose window. Inside, the church reveals a Latin cross plan adorned with twelve richly decorated altars, each showcasing the region's finest marble work and gilding.

#3. Ex Convento degli Agostiniani

The Ex Convento degli Agostiniani stands as a magnificent testament to 17th-century monastic architecture and has evolved into a vibrant cultural symbol of Melpignano. The former Augustinian convent's impressive baroque facade features local pietra leccese limestone, with its warm golden hues catching the Mediterranean light.

The serene cloister is surrounded by elegant arched porticoes and decorated with carefully preserved frescoes depicting scenes from Augustinian history. You know I love a cloister!

#4. Porta del Sole

One of the last remnants of Melpignano's medieval fortifications, Porta del Sole (Gate of the Sun) offers a glimpse into the town's history and its defensive past.

#5. Palazzo Palmieri

Palazzo Palmieri stands as one of Melpignano's most elegant aristocratic residences, built in the 17th century during the town's period of noble prosperity. The palace's commanding facade showcases the finest elements of baroque residential architecture, featuring ornate wrought-iron balconies, decorative stone cornices, and imposing portal adorned with the Palmieri family coat of arms.

Melpignano Festivals and Sagre Throughout the Year

Festa di San Giorgio

April 23

This festival honors Saint George, the patron saint of Melpignano. The celebration includes religious processions, traditional music, and local food stalls, providing insight into the town's rich cultural heritage.

Festa della Madonna del Carmine

July 16

Dedicated to Our Lady of Mount Carmel, this event features a solemn procession through the town's streets, accompanied by musical performances and communal feasting, reflecting the deep-rooted religious traditions of the community.

SEI Festival (Sud Est Indipendente Festival)

Mid-August

Organized by the Cool Club cooperative, the SEI Festival showcases independent music acts from Italy and beyond. Concerts are held in various venues around Melpignano, including the picturesque Piazza San Giorgio.

Day Trip: Nearby Sites, Cities, and Towns

Sternatia. 15 kilometers (9 miles) southwest. Visitors can explore several remarkable sites, including a fascinating 15th-century underground oil mill, the Chiesa Parrocchiale di Maria Santissima Assunta, an impressive Baroque church built in the 18th century, the Chiesa dei Domenicani, another Baroque church featuring interesting works of art, and the Castello de' Monti, which stands as one of the best-maintained castles in the Salento region.

Galatone. 20 kilometers (12 miles) southwest. Galatone is a small town with a rich cultural heritage, known for its historical sites and beautiful landscapes. Visitors can explore several notable attractions, including the Church of San Pietro Apostolo with its stunning architecture, the impressive historical Palazzo Ducale, and the vibrant local markets where one can experience the authentic culture and cuisine of the region.

Logistics

Train: Melpignano has a small train station on the Ferrovie Sud Est (FSE) railway network. Trains from Lecce run daily, taking ~45 minutes with stops in Zollino and Maglie.

Bus: From Lecce take Ferrovie Sud Est (FSE) buses, which connect Lecce to Melpignano in about 50 minutes.

Car: Arrive in Melpignano from Lecce via SS16 and SP48.

Parking: There are free parking areas near the town center, particularly around Piazza San Giorgio and near the Ex Convento degli Agostiniani. During large events like the Notte della Taranta, temporary parking lots are set up on the outskirts, with shuttle services into town.

Restaurant Recommendations

Vizio Pizzeria. Address: Parco Rimembranza, 3

A casual pizzeria known for its wood-fired pizzas and local flavors. Great for a relaxed meal with a friendly atmosphere.

Portico San Giorgio. Address: Via Giuseppe Verdi 33

A well-regarded restaurant offering traditional Pugliese dishes in a charming setting. Known for high-quality ingredients and an inviting ambiance.

Accommodation

For this event I recommend four or five nights in town moving between events of the festival in the area.

Domus Liventa. Address: 7 Via Ghetto, Cursi

A highly-rated hotel with clean, quiet rooms, wonderful breakfast, and friendly staff.

B&B San Giorgio. Address: Via Benedetto Croce, 86

A spacious and clean B&B with friendly and helpful hosts. The breakfast is abundant and tasty, and the rooms are well-maintained.

CHAPTER SIXTEEN

Cisternino's Pasta Passion

A Mid-August Festival of Food, Music, and Tradition

S agra delle Orecchiette

Where: Cisternino

When: Second weekend of August.

Average Festival Temperatures: High 31°C (87°F). Low 23°C (74°F).

Cisternino: A Timeless Jewel in the Heart of Puglia

Perched at 394 meters (1,292 feet) above sea level, Cisternino is one of Italy's "Most Beautiful Villages," where history, architecture, and traditions have stood the test of time. Overlooking the Valle d'Itria, this enchanting hilltop town blends ancient roots, medieval influences, and Baroque elegance, creating a setting where the past and present coexist in perfect harmony.

Cisternino's history dates back to the Messapians, an ancient Italic people who inhabited Puglia long before the arrival of the Romans. The town's strategic hilltop location made it a desirable settlement for subsequent rulers, including the Normans and Swabians, who shaped much of its medieval character. Under

Swabian rule, Emperor Frederick II reinforced Cisternino's defenses, integrating it into his network of strongholds across southern Italy. The town's medieval labyrinthine streets, whitewashed houses, and fortified gates still reflect these historical influences today.

By the Renaissance and Baroque periods, Cisternino had strengthened into a prosperous agricultural center, known for its olive oil, vineyards, and artisanal craftsmanship. Wealthy families and religious orders contributed to the town's architectural expansion, constructing elegant churches and noble palaces that continue to define its historic center. Among them, the Chiesa Madre di San Nicola, with its Romanesque and Baroque elements, stands as a testament to Cisternino's artistic and spiritual heritage.

Today, Cisternino remains a vibrant town with a population of around 11,000 residents, many of whom continue to uphold centuries-old traditions. The town is renowned for its fornelli pronti, a unique culinary tradition where local butchers grill meats to order in small, open-air eateries, a practice that turns Cisternino's historic streets into a living dining experience every evening.

Sagra delle Orecchiette: A Celebration of Puglia's Most Beloved Pasta

The rhythmic tap-tap-tap of wooden rolling pins against marble echoes through Cisternino's medieval alleys. Dozens of practiced hands dance across tables, transforming simple flour and water into edible art. This is the Sagra delle Orecchiette, where for one magical August weekend, this whitewashed town becomes the epicenter of pasta-making artistry. Typically held during the second weekend of August, the festival unfolds across three lively days, with events beginning Friday evening and continuing until Sunday night.

These "little ears" of pasta, shaped by the swift, practiced thumb-press of local women, carry centuries of culinary wisdom. Each dimpled piece tells a story of Pugliese kitchens, where generations of nonne have perfected this craft. The pasta's subtle roughness isn't a flaw, it's genius, designed to embrace rich sauces like bitter cime di rapa or slow-cooked Sunday ragù with an almost magnetic devotion. Festival-goers can witness this artistry firsthand in the cooking workshops held on Saturday morning, where expert pasta-makers reveal the secrets behind shaping the perfect orecchiette.

Street corners transform into impromptu cooking theaters, where pasta artisans create orecchiette with hypnotic speed, their fingers moving as fast as the staccato rhythm of Pizzica dancers, whose performances electrify the piazzas every evening. Communal tables stretch through torch-lit streets, inviting strangers to become friends over steaming plates of orecchiette al pomodoro, crisp taralli, and glasses of full-bodied local wines.

Wandering the festival's maze-like paths reveals treasures at every turn. Local vendors display mountains of freshly made orecchiette, their golden hues glistening like precious gems in the late summer light. Bottles of fragrant olive oil, jars of handcrafted preserves, and blocks of aged pecorino tempt passersby, while the air thickens with the perfume of simmering sauces and freshly baked bread. On Sunday afternoon, history comes to life with the medieval court procession, where costumed performers and flag-throwers bring a sense of pageantry to the festivities.

Festival Events

Friday Evening

The festival traditionally kicks off with an opening ceremony in the town's main square, featuring speeches by local officials and a performance by a folk music ensemble.

Saturday

Morning: Visitors can participate in cooking workshops, where local chefs and nonnas (grandmothers) demonstrate the art of making orecchiette by hand, it is a beautiful sight!

Afternoon: The streets come alive with a medieval court procession, complete with participants in period costumes, flag throwers, and traditional musicians.

Evening: The main piazza hosts a concert featuring traditional Pizzica music, encouraging attendees to dance and immerse themselves in the local culture.

Sunday

Morning: A local artisan market is set up, showcasing handcrafted goods, local produce, and souvenirs.

Afternoon: The festival often features a jousting tournament, reenacting historical competitions with skilled riders.

Evening: The festival concludes with a grand feast, where attendees can savor various orecchiette dishes paired with local wines, accompanied by live music performances.

A plethora of orecchiette variations, from traditional to inventive local chef creations, are available at the festival's many food stalls.

Cisternino Walking Tour

#1. Piazza Vittorio Emanuele II

Begin your journey in Piazza Vittorio Emanuele II. This elegant square unfolds like a medieval theater, its limestone-paved expanse framed by noble palazzi whose weathered facades tell stories of centuries past. The commanding Torre dell'Orologio (Clock Tower), added in 1850, rises above the square with its distinctive green copper dome and original mechanical workings still keeping time for the town.

At dawn, watch as morning light gradually illuminates the square's graceful arched porticos, where vendors once sheltered their goods. Today, these spaces house charming cafés where locals gather for their morning caffè and cornetto.

#2. Chiesa Matrice di San Nicola di Bari

Following the gently sloping Via San Quirico, you'll reach this architectural masterpiece dating to 1420. The church's façade presents a harmonious blend of styles: Romanesque solidity in its base, Gothic aspirations in its rose window, and Baroque flourishes in later additions. The asymmetrical placement of its portal speaks to medieval building techniques, while the weathered stone carries the patina of six centuries.

Step inside to discover a forest of ancient columns, their capitals each uniquely carved. The most remarkable are four granite columns, their polished surfaces betraying their Roman origins, possibly from a temple that once stood nearby. Look up to admire the church's unique wooden ceiling, its deep browns contrasting with the luminous white stone walls. The 16th-century statue of San Nicola, carved from a single piece of walnut, shows remarkable detail in the saint's facial expression and flowing robes. The baroque altar, completed in 1767, dazzles with intricate gold leaf work and lapis lazuli inlays.

#3. Torre Normanno-Sveva

Climb the medieval streets to reach this 11th-century sentinel, its massive limestone blocks still bearing mason's marks from Norman craftsmen. The tower's strategic position, 498 meters (1633 feet) above sea level, created a vital link in a network of coastal warning systems. When Saracen ships were spotted, signals would be relayed from tower to tower, allowing inland towns precious time to prepare.

The tower's military architecture reveals its dual heritage: Norman ingenuity in its base construction and Swabian military refinements in its upper sections, added during Frederick II's reign (1220-1250). Climb the recently restored spiral staircase to reach the observation platform, where each direction offers a different vista.

#4. Porta Grande (Arco di San Nicola)

Once the main entrance to Cisternino's fortified old town, Porta Grande is a striking stone archway that still retains its defensive character. Above it sits a sculpture of San Nicola, a symbol of divine protection for the town. Walking through this gate feels like stepping back in time, as it leads into the oldest and most atmospheric part of Cisternino.

#5. Centro Storico (Historic Center & Whitewashed Alleys)

This is Cisternino's soul, a labyrinth of narrow streets, sunlit courtyards, and secret passageways. The town's whitewashed houses, many dating back to the Middle Ages, are adorned with flower-filled balconies and wrought-iron lanterns. Unlike other towns, Cisternino lacks grand monuments, but that's precisely its charm, the town itself is the attraction.

#6. Chiesa di San Quirico e Giulitta

Dedicated to the early Christian martyrs San Quirico and Giulitta, this Baroque church stands out for its lavish interiors and intricate stuccoes. The church houses an ancient crypt, believed to be one of the oldest in the region, possibly dating back to the 8th century.

Festa di San Quirico e Giuletta

#7. Belvedere di Cisternino (Viewpoint)

Cisternino's most breathtaking scenic viewpoint, the Belvedere, offers a sweeping panorama of the Valle d'Itria. The rolling landscape is dotted with trulli houses, traditional white stone dwellings with conical roofs unique to this region, along with olive groves and vineyards, creating a timeless Puglian postcard view.

#8. Fornello Pronto District (Cisternino's Famous Butcher-Restaurants)

End your walking tour where history meets food, Cisternino's famous fornelli pronti (butcher-restaurants). This tradition dates back generations: visitors select their cut of meat directly from a butcher, which is then grilled over open flames and served at communal tables. The experience is unpretentious, delicious, and deeply rooted in local culture.

Cisternino Festivals and Sagre Throughout the Year

Festa di San Biagio

February 3

The Festa di San Biagio in Cisternino is one of the town's most cherished religious celebrations, dedicated to Saint Blaise, the protector against throat ailments. The day begins with a solemn Mass at the church of San Biagio, followed by the traditional benedizione della gola (blessing of the throat), where priests cross two candles over the faithful's necks while invoking the saint's protection. A statue of San Biagio is carried through the streets in a devotional procession, accompanied by local confraternities and bands. The celebration also includes music, fireworks, and community gatherings.

Pasquarèdde (Easter Monday Festival)

Easter Monday (date varies annually)

On Easter Monday, locals gather at the Sanctuary of the Madonna d'Ibernia to celebrate Pasquarèdde. Participants bring traditional sweets, such as "u churrüchele," symbolizing prosperity and fertility. The festival honors the Madonna of Ibernia, associated with life and abundance.

Gnummeredd Festival (Sausage Festival)

June (specific date varies)

This festival celebrates gnummeredd, traditional sausages made from lamb or goat entrails. Visitors can savor these local delicacies, reflecting Cisternino's rich culinary heritage.

Festa di San Quirico e Giulitta (Feast of Saints Quirico and Giulitta)

First weekend of August

Dedicated to Cisternino's patron saints, this festival features illuminations (special light installations over the streets in the town center), religious processions, musical performances, and fireworks. The town comes alive with cultural events, including band concerts and craft markets, celebrating the legacy of Saints Quirico and Giulitta.

Sagra della Castagna (Chestnut Festival)

Mid-October

As autumn sets in, Cisternino hosts the Chestnut Festival, celebrating the seasonal harvest. Attendees can enjoy roasted chestnuts, local pastries, and mulled wine, all set against the backdrop of the town's picturesque streets.

Day Trips: Nearby Sites, Cities, and Towns

Marina di Ostuni. 22 kilometers (13 miles) from Cisternino. Twenty-two kilometers from Cisternino, where the white city descends to meet the Adriatic, lies Marina di Ostuni. Along this stretch of the celebrated "Blue Flag Coast," nature has painted a masterpiece of crystal-clear waters and golden sands. Here, the Parco Naturale Regionale Dune Costiere unfolds like a living tapestry, ancient olive groves bow to sea breezes, while coastal dunes shelter rare orchids and provide sanctuary for migratory birds.

Gioia del Colle. 40 kilometers (24 miles) from Cisternino, Gioia del Colle rises from the Murge plateau, its medieval streets echoing with tales of emperors and artisans. The magnificent Castello Normanno-Svevo, beloved by Frederick II, commands the town's highest point, its honey-colored stones glowing at sunset. Below its walls, master cheese makers practice their ancient craft, creating clouds of mozzarella and burrata that have made the town's name synonymous with dairy excellence.

Logistics

Train: Cisternino has a train station, but it is not in the town center, it is about 10 kilometers (7 miles) away in the valley, requiring a bus or taxi to reach the historic center. One hour from Bari via train.

Bus: Ferrovie del Sud Est (FSE): Operates regional buses connecting Cisternino to Martina Franca, Ostuni, and Fasano.

Car: From Bari 1 hour via SS16 Adriatica and SP3. From Brindisi 45 minutes via SS379 and SP17.

Parking: Several convenient parking options await visitors just outside the old town. The most recommended choice is Parcheggio Via San Quirico, which offers easy access to the historic center while providing ample space for vehicles.

Restaurant Recommendations

Osteria Bell'Italia. Address: Via Duca D'Aosta, 29

The restaurant prides itself on using seasonal ingredients and fresh fish sourced directly from local ports. The elegant yet simple interior reflects the travels and experiences of the owners, Luano and Erika, who warmly welcome each guest.

Trattoria Bère Vecchie. Address: Via Regina Elena, 8

The menu features local specialties like "bombette" (pork rolls filled with various ingredients) and handmade orecchiette pasta. The friendly atmosphere and commitment to organic ingredients make it a must-visit spot.

Al Vecchio Fornello. Address: Via Basiliani, 18

Al Vecchio Fornello offers a unique dining experience where guests can select their preferred cuts of meat from the adjoining butcher shop, which are then grilled to perfection.

Accommodation

Staying overnight for a sagra is not necessary, but if you want to stay in town, I recommend two nights.

Borgo Canonica. Address: Contrada Minetta 20

Set amidst olive groves, this 3.5-star establishment offers a serene environment with traditional trulli accommodations. Guests can enjoy a seasonal outdoor swimming pool, free private parking, and an on-site restaurant.

Hotel Lo Smeraldo. Address: Contrada Don Peppe Sole 7

In the hills of the Itria Valley, this 3-star hotel features an outdoor pool, restaurant, and panoramic views of the surrounding countryside. The hotel offers comfortable rooms with modern amenities.

Relais Masseria Villa Cenci. Address: SS 581

This 4-star hotel is set in a historic masseria (farmhouse) and offers elegant rooms, an outdoor pool, and extensive gardens. Guests can experience authentic Puglian hospitality in a tranquil setting.

CHAPTER SEVENTEEN

Celebrating San Rocco in Locorotondo

FestaFusion August

FestaFusion Locorotondo

Where: Locorotondo

When: August 15-17

Average Festival Temperatures: High 30°C (86°F). Low 20°C (68°F).

#1. Festa di San Rocco. Locorotondo's most important religious festival, held every August 16, honoring Saint Rocco with a grand procession, fireworks, and traditional music, transforming the town into a vibrant celebration of faith and heritage.

#2. Ferragosto. A beloved Italian holiday on August 15, Ferragosto blends ancient Roman traditions with the Feast of the Assumption, bringing lively beach parties, festivals, and fireworks as Italians take a well-deserved summer break.

#FestaFusion means two or more festivals happen at around the same time in the same town, so visitors can enjoy multiple events during their visit.

Locorotondo: A Perfectly Round Jewel in Puglia

Locorotondo, whose name translates to "round place," owes its name to the circular layout of its historic center, a unique feature that has captured the imagination of visitors for centuries. The town's origins date back to the 11th century, when it was established as a rural settlement under the rule of the Counts of Conversano. Over time, Locorotondo grew into a thriving agricultural community, with its fertile lands producing wine, olive oil, and grains.

By the Middle Ages, the town was fortified with walls, and its central layout became a distinctive feature. During the Renaissance and Baroque periods, many of the churches and noble palazzi that still stand today were constructed, giving Locorotondo its architectural elegance. Its deep-rooted agricultural traditions remain central to its identity, particularly its production of white wine, which has earned Locorotondo a place on Italy's list of Città del Vino (Wine Cities).

Locorotondo is located in the heart of the Valle d'Itria, one of Puglia's most picturesque regions, known for its rolling hills, olive groves, vineyards, and scattered trulli (traditional conical stone houses). The town sits at an elevation of 410 meters (1,345 feet) above sea level, offering panoramic views of the surrounding countryside.

Its central location in Puglia makes it a perfect base for exploring nearby towns like Alberobello, Martina Franca, and Cisternino. The town's natural beauty, combined with its charming architecture, has made it a popular destination for travelers seeking a mix of culture, history, and relaxation.

Locorotondo is home to 14,000 residents, many of whom are engaged in agriculture, winemaking, and tourism-related industries. Despite its growing popularity among visitors, the town has retained its authentic charm and slow-paced way of life.

The Feast of St. Roch: A Celebration of Faith and Community

The Festa di San Rocco stands as Locorotondo's cherished tradition honoring their patron saint, chosen as protector during times of plague. The festival's origins trace to the late 16th or early 17th century, when devotion to San Rocco spread across Europe in response to the Black Death.

Locorotondo adopted San Rocco after witnessing his miraculous protection of the town. What began as religious observances of prayers and processions evolved into a vibrant communal celebration incorporating music and fireworks.

Who is Saint Roch?

Born to wealth in 14th century Montpellier, France, San Rocco gave away his inheritance after his parents' death to devote himself to God. During a pilgrimage to Rome, he healed many plague victims through prayers and the sign of the cross.

After contracting the plague himself, he retreated to a forest, surviving on stream water and bread brought by a dog, now a symbol of loyalty in religious art depicting the saint. Following his recovery, San Rocco continued healing until his death in obscurity. His later canonization established him as a venerated figure throughout Catholic Europe, particularly as a protector against epidemics.

The people of Locorotondo maintain a profound connection to their patron saint, turning to him in times of crisis. Their feast day celebrations blend reverence with festivity, embodying both the town's faith and communal spirit.

Festival Events

August 15th: Ferragosto

Ferragosto, a national Italian holiday celebrating the Feast of the Assumption of the Virgin Mary, marks the beginning of the festival. The day sets the festive tone with preparations for San Rocco's feast.

The town is decorated with illuminated arches and streets adorned in lights, creating a magical atmosphere as day transitions into night.

August 16th: Feast Day of San Rocco

Morning Solemn Mass

The day begins with a solemn Mass held at the Chiesa Madre di San Giorgio (Mother Church of Saint George). This Mass is attended by town officials, religious leaders, and the faithful who gather to honor the saint.

The Processions

12:00 p.m.

The statue of San Rocco is carried through the historic center's streets, accompanied by local clergy, officials, and devotees. This procession reflects the community's deep-rooted faith and longstanding traditions.

8:00 p.m.

In the evening, the grand procession is the highlight of the day. The statue of San Rocco, carried on a beautifully decorated float, is paraded through the streets of Locorotondo.

Accompanied by marching bands and faithful devotees, the statue makes its way through the town, symbolizing the saint's protection over the community.

Many locals follow barefoot as an act of devotion, while others offer prayers and candles along the route.

Pyrotechnic Displays

The evening concludes with an awe-inspiring fireworks show, lighting up the skies over the Valle d'Itria. This tradition is not only a visual spectacle but also a symbolic gesture of joy and thanksgiving.

August 17th: Community Celebrations

The final day of the festival focuses on the local community, featuring more relaxed and communal activities.

Concerts and Performances: Live performances from local and national artists take place in Piazza Vittorio Emanuele, drawing crowds of all ages.

Cultural Events: The town organizes cultural exhibitions, showcasing Locorotondo's rich history, crafts, and culinary traditions.

Farewell Fireworks: A second round of fireworks marks the official end of the celebrations, bidding farewell to San Rocco until the following year.

Festival Traditions

Food Stalls: Throughout the festival, stalls line the streets offering traditional Puglian dishes, from orecchiette to panzerotti, and sweet treats like cartellate and pasticciotti.

Local Markets: Artisan vendors display handmade crafts, jewelry, and souvenirs, reflecting the region's rich culture.

Illuminations: The decorative lights remain a centerpiece of the festival, creating a breathtaking backdrop for all the events.

A Testament to Faith and Unity

The Festa di San Rocco is more than just a celebration; it is a profound expression of faith, gratitude, and community. For centuries, it has been a cornerstone of Locorotondo's identity, bringing together generations to honor their patron saint. Whether through solemn prayers or joyful celebrations, the festival encapsulates the enduring spirit of this picturesque Puglian town.

Locorotondo Walking Tour

#1. Chiesa Madre di San Giorgio (Mother Church of Saint George)

This baroque-style church, built between 1790 and 1825, is dedicated to Saint George, the town's original patron saint. In the heart of Locorotondo, the church stands on the site of an earlier medieval structure.

Its grand facade features Corinthian columns and intricate decorations, while the interior houses impressive frescoes, a beautiful organ, and statues of Saint George slaying the dragon.

Interior of the Chiesa Madre

#2. Chiesa di San Rocco

This church, first mentioned in 1568, began as a small chapel located outside the town walls. It was later rebuilt and expanded, especially after the town was spared from the plague in 1690–1691, an event attributed to the intercession of San Rocco. The current structure reflects architectural elements similar to the Chiesa Madre, indicating a reconstruction in the 18th century.

#3. Villa Comunale (Town Park)

On the edge of the historic center, the Villa Comunale is a serene public park with well-maintained gardens, shaded paths, and benches. The park offers panoramic views of the Valle d'Itria, including its famous trulli and vineyards. The Villa Comunale is the perfect spot to relax and enjoy breathtaking views of the surrounding countryside. It's a great place to take a break during your walking tour while soaking in the natural beauty of the region.

#4. Porta Napoli (Naples Gate)

This historical gateway marks one of the main entrances to Locorotondo's old town. Dating back to the 18th century, the gate served as part of the town's defensive walls. It is named after its role as a key passage on the road connecting Locorotondo to Naples. Walking through the Porta Napoli is like stepping back in time. Its historic significance and connection to the town's past make it a great starting point for exploring Locorotondo's charming streets.

#5. Chiesa della Madonna della Greca (Church of Our Lady of the Greek)

This small yet significant church is one of the oldest buildings in Locorotondo, dating back to the 12th century. It reflects a mix of Romanesque and Gothic architectural styles and is believed to have been built by Greek Orthodox settlers. The interior features simple but elegant frescoes and a serene atmosphere.

Its historical importance and unique architectural style make this church a fascinating stop on your walking tour. It's also a peaceful retreat for reflection.

#6. Piazza Vittorio Emanuele II

The central square of Locorotondo, Piazza Vittorio Emanuele II, is surrounded by elegant whitewashed buildings and features a charming fountain at its center. The square has long been a meeting point for locals and visitors alike. This lively square is the heart of Locorotondo's social life. It's a great place to enjoy a coffee at one of the nearby cafes while admiring the town's quintessential architecture and soaking in the local atmosphere.

Torre dell'Orologio

#7. Palazzo Morelli

One of the finest examples of baroque architecture in Locorotondo, Palazzo Morelli stands as a testament to 18th-century aristocratic grandeur. Its ornate facade showcases the height of baroque craftsmanship, featuring delicate stone carvings of floral motifs, mythological figures, and an elaborate family crest positioned prominently above the main entrance. The windows are framed by decorative cornices and elegant balconies with intricate wrought-iron railings.

The palazzo was commissioned by the noble Morelli family, who played a significant role in Locorotondo's social and economic development. Its symmetrical form, imposing size, and detailed ornamentation all point to the building's reflection of its period's architectural style. Typical of local Puglian architecture, the structure's limestone exhibits warm, honey-colored tones.

Though the interior remains private, the palazzo's exterior continues to be a highlight for architecture enthusiasts and photographers, particularly during the golden hour when the sun's rays emphasize the detailed stonework. Its location along one of Locorotondo's main historical streets makes it an unmissable stop on any architectural tour of the town's centro storico.

Facade Palazzo Morelli

#7. Lungomare del Balcone (The Balcony Over the Valle d'Itria)

Often referred to as Locorotondo's "balcony," this panoramic walkway runs along the edge of the historic center, offering sweeping views of the Valle d'Itria. The walkway is lined with beautiful flowers and overlooks the iconic trulli and vineyards below.

The views from the Lungomare del Balcone are nothing short of spectacular, making it one of the most photographed spots in Locorotondo. It's a peaceful and scenic end to your walking tour.

Locorotondo Festivals Throughout the Year

Festa di San Giorgio (Feast of Saint George)

April 23rd

The celebration begins at dawn with the ringing of church bells throughout Locorotondo's pristine white streets. The main procession starts from the Chiesa Madre San Giorgio Martire, where a centuries-old statue of Saint George is carried through the town's narrow alleyways. Local families decorate their balconies with intricate tapestries and fresh flowers in red and white, Saint George's colors.

Traditional activities include the "Corteo Storico" - a historical parade featuring locals dressed in medieval costumes depicting Saint George's legendary battle with the dragon. A special mass is conducted in the Pugliese dialect, preserving local linguistic traditions. During "La Tavola di San Giorgio," families share communal feasts of traditional dishes like orecchiette alla cima di rapa and local Locorotondo DOC white wine.

Evening performances of pizzica, the traditional folk dance of Puglia, fill the streets with the sounds of tambourines and accordions. Artisan markets showcase local crafts, particularly handmade lace and ceramics. The day concludes with a spectacular fireworks display over the valley at midnight.

Locus Festival

Late June to mid-August.

This contemporary cultural festival has grown from a small local event to an internationally recognized celebration of music and arts. The festival utilizes multiple performance spaces throughout Locorotondo, with the Villa Comunale's amphitheater serving as the main stage. Intimate concerts take place in historic trulli houses, while late-night DJ sets transform converted masserie (traditional farmhouses) into vibrant music venues. Pop-up stages throughout the historic center create an immersive musical experience that winds through the town's characteristic circular layout.

The festival extends beyond music to embrace broader cultural expressions. The "Locus Focus" program presents photography exhibitions featuring both local and international artists, while "Locus Words" hosts literary discussions and book presentations with Italian authors. Culinary traditions are celebrated through "Locus Kitchen," offering workshops that explore Pugliese cuisine. A dedicated children's program, "Locus Kids," ensures the festival remains accessible to all ages through interactive music workshops.

Environmental consciousness is woven into the festival's organization. The event partners with local organic farms to supply food vendors, implements a reusable cup system to minimize waste, and provides free shuttle services from nearby towns to reduce traffic impact. Solar-powered stages at smaller venues demonstrate the festival's commitment to sustainability.

The festival typically hosts over 30,000 visitors across its six-week run, with performances scheduled to take advantage of the cooler evening temperatures. Past headliners have included international artists like Bonobo, Gregory Porter, and Robert Glasper, alongside emerging Italian talent. This blend of global and local artistry has established Locus Festival as a cultural cornerstone of the Pugliese summer, while maintaining the intimate atmosphere that makes Locorotondo special.

Festa dell'Uva (Wine Festival)

Late September/October

Every autumn, as the late summer sun ripens the last of the season's grapes, the narrow cobblestone streets of Locorotondo fill with the infectious energy of celebration. Children's laughter echoes off ancient walls as they participate in grape-stomping competitions, their feet purple-stained and faces beaming with delight - just as their grandparents did before them. The air becomes heavy with the irresistible aroma of frittelle, cheese-stuffed turnovers that sizzle in deep pots of oil, their golden crusts a testament to generations of culinary expertise.

Day Trips: Nearby Sites, Cities, and Towns

Craco. 90 kilometers (56 miles) from Locorotondo. Craco is known as the "ghost town" and captivates visitors with its haunting beauty. This abandoned medieval village was evacuated in the 1960s due to devastating landslides. Today, Craco stands as a dramatic and poignant reminder of Basilicata's history, its crumbling towers and churches set against a rugged, breathtaking landscape. The town has become a favorite destination for photographers and filmmakers drawn to its evocative atmosphere.

Visitors can explore the eerie ruins of the historic center, wandering through the remnants of homes, stairways, and squares that once bustled with life. At the heart of the village stands the Chiesa Madre di San Nicola, a strikingly preserved church that adds a solemn grandeur to the site. Craco has also gained fame as a film location, most notably featured in *The Passion of the Christ*, further enhancing its allure for those seeking both history and cinematic intrigue.

Castelmezzano and Pietrapertosa. Located 130 kilometers (81 miles) from Locorotondo. High in the rugged peaks of the Dolomiti Lucane, two ancient villages cling to the mountainsides like eagles' nests, their stone houses seemingly carved from the very cliffs that cradle them. Castelmezzano and Pietrapertosa have watched over these valleys since medieval times, their narrow streets winding between rocks and sky in a testament to human perseverance and architectural ingenuity.

But it's what connects these two sentinel villages that captures the imagination of modern adventurers. The Volo dell'Angelo, the Flight of the Angel, stretches across the dizzying void between them, a steel cable along which brave souls can soar like birds of prey. Suspended hundreds of meters above the valley floor, riders experience the same sweeping views that hawks and eagles have enjoyed for millennia, their hearts racing as they glide between these twin pearls of the Lucanian mountains.

Each village holds its own ancient secrets. In Castelmezzano, weathered steps lead to the haunting remnants of a Norman castle, where crumbling walls still whisper tales of medieval knights and long-forgotten battles. Across the valley, Pietrapertosa crowns its peak with an Arab fortress, a reminder of the many cultures that have left their mark on this dramatic landscape. From its heights, visitors can gaze out over a panorama of saw-toothed peaks and deep valleys that seem to stretch to the very edge of the world.

Logistics

Train: Locorotondo has a train station and is 2.5 hours from Bari, 10 minutes from Alberobello.

Bus: Operated by Ferrovie del Sud Est (FSE) and other regional companies.

Car: Driving is one of the most convenient ways to visit Locorotondo, especially if you're exploring other towns in the Valle d'Itria or nearby regions. From Bari, it is about 75 kilometers (43 miles) via SS16 and SP134; the drive takes about 1 hour.

Parking: Parking can be challenging near the historic center, especially during peak tourist seasons or festivals. Via Nardelli Parking Lot, near the old town with paid parking. Ideal for accessing the Lungomare del Balcone and other central sites. Or Piazza Marconi Parking, which is a convenient location for visitors arriving by car, just a short walk from the center.

Restaurant Recommendations

Bina Ristorante di Puglia. Address: Via Vincenzo Recchia Dottor 44/50

Nestled in the historic center, Bina Ristorante di Puglia seamlessly blends the past and present within a structure dating back to the 1700s. The ambiance is characterized by cross vaults and subtle lighting, creating a warm and elegant atmosphere. The menu offers a modern take on traditional Puglian cuisine, featuring dishes that highlight local ingredients and culinary traditions.

Quanto Basta Pizzeria. Address: Via Morelli 12

In the heart of Locorotondo's old town, Quanto Basta Pizzeria offers a charming setting with tables in a tiny street adorned with hanging plants and lights, providing a warm and romantic atmosphere. The menu features a variety of pizzas made with different types of flour, including spelt, and generous portions of antipasti. It's an ideal spot for both lunch and dinner, offering a delightful dining experience.

Ai Tre Santi. Address: Via Dottor Guarnieri, 51

In the historic center, Ai Tre Santi provides a lovely setting for a romantic date or a small group gathering. The restaurant is known for its typical local cuisine and offers the opportunity to pair meals with delicious regional wines. Guests have praised the authenticity and taste of the dishes, making it a must-visit spot for those seeking an authentic Puglian dining experience.

Accommodation

For the festival, I recommend a minimum of two nights in Locorotondo.

Masseria Grofoleo. Address: Contrada Grofoleo 24

A charming 4-star hotel featuring a garden, terrace, bar, and free Wi-Fi. Guests can enjoy a buffet, continental, or Italian breakfast. The hotel also offers a 24-hour front desk, airport transfers, and room service, making it a comfortable and convenient base for exploring Locorotondo.

Ottolire Resort. Address: 59 Contrada Papariello Serafino

This elegant 4-star resort boasts an outdoor swimming pool, fitness center, and garden. Guests can dine on Italian and Mediterranean cuisine at the on-site restaurant and airport transfers. Ideal for relaxation and indulgence amidst the beauty of Puglia.

Il Palmento Hotel Relais. Address: Contrada Cupa

Offering luxurious accommodations in traditional Apulian trulli, this 5-star resort features an outdoor swimming pool and restaurant. It provides a unique opportunity to immerse yourself in the charm of the Itria Valley while enjoying top-tier amenities.

CHAPTER EIGHTEEN

Brindisi's Celebration of Saints

Where Saints and Sea Unite

F esta Patronale dei Santi Teodoro d'Amasea e Lorenzo da Brindisi

Where: Brindisi

When: August 23-September 1

Average Festival Temperatures: High 29.5°C (85.1°F). Low 24.5°C (76.1°F).

Brindisi: Where the Appia Meets the Sea

Brindisi, a captivating port city where the whispers of ancient mariners still echo along its shores, stands as a living testament to centuries of Mediterranean history. Perched on the Adriatic Sea, this maritime sentinel has served as a crucial crossroads of culture and commerce since antiquity, its natural harbor welcoming vessels from distant shores while sheltering their precious cargo.

Nestled in Puglia's southeastern embrace, Brindisi cradles one of nature's finest harbors, a protected inlet that reaches like gentle fingers into the mainland from the azure Adriatic. The city unfolds across a landscape that epitomizes Puglia's timeless beauty: rolling plains where silver-leafed olive groves, centuries old, stand sentinel over orderly vineyards. The coastline alternates between dramatic limestone cliffs and gentle beaches, each telling its own story of the sea's eternal dialogue with the land.

Today, 87,000 proud Brindisini call this city home, their daily lives weaving new threads into a social fabric colored by countless cultural influences. As the provincial capital, Brindisi pulses with administrative energy while maintaining the warm, unhurried rhythm of a Mediterranean port town.

The city's story begins in the mists of the Bronze Age, when its naturally forked harbor, shaped like the antlers of a stag, inspired the Messapians to name it "Brentesion." This remarkable port would later become the jewel in Rome's maritime crown, marking the terminus of the mighty Via Appia. The Roman Columns, standing like ancient sentinels, still mark where this "queen of roads" met the sea, silent witnesses to countless journeys begun and ended.

Through the ebb and flow of empires, Brindisi adapted and endured. Byzantine merchants haggled in its marketplaces, Lombard warriors patrolled its walls, and Norman nobles shaped its medieval character. During the Crusades, Brindisi emerged as a vital stopover town for warriors and pilgrims from France, England, and other European kingdoms. Its strategic harbor provided a crucial embarkation point for Crusaders journeying from Western Europe to the Holy Land, its quays teeming with knights and pilgrims, their prayers mixing with the cries of sailors and the creaking of ship timbers as they prepared for the arduous voyage across the Mediterranean.

Even in modern times, Brindisi's strategic significance has persisted. During World War II's darkest days, it served as Italy's temporary capital, providing a haven of governance when Rome fell under occupation.

The Festival of Saint Theodore and Saint Lawrence

The Festa Patronale dei Santi Teodoro d'Amasea e Lorenzo da Brindisi is the annual celebration in the city of Brindisi dedicated to its patron saints, St. Theodore of Amasea and St. Lawrence of Brindisi. The festival traditionally takes place between late August and early September, with the major celebrations occurring on August 31 and September 1.

Who is St. Theodore of Amasea?

St. Theodore was a young soldier (hence the title *Tiro*, meaning "recruit") in the Roman army during the early 4th century, around the time of the persecutions of Christians under Emperor Maximian or Galerius. He was stationed in Amasea, a city in what is now modern-day Turkey (then in the Roman province of Pontus).

According to tradition, Theodore boldly declared his Christian faith and refused to participate in pagan rituals. As an act of defiance, he reportedly set fire to a temple dedicated to the goddess Cybele. For this, he was arrested, tortured, and eventually burned alive around 306 AD. His cult spread quickly throughout the Christian world. By the 5th century, he was widely venerated in the Eastern Roman Empire (Byzantium), and many churches were dedicated to him. One of the most famous is the Church of San Teodoro in Rome, which reflects the blending of his veneration between Eastern and Western Christianity.

The exact origins of the festival are not precisely documented, but the veneration of St. Theodore of Amasea dates back to at least the 13th century. According to a popular legend, around 1225, a Venetian ship being pursued by the Turks abandoned an urn containing the relics of St. Theodore off the coast of Brindisi. Local fishermen recovered the urn and handed it over to Archbishop Gerardo, who placed it in the city's cathedral. This event is commemorated through the "Palio dell'Arca", a rowing competition that re-enacts the retrieval of the urn.

Who is St. Lawrence of Brindisi?

Born Giulio Cesare Russo in 1559 in Brindisi, St. Lawrence was a brilliant Capuchin friar known for his deep faith, humility, and incredible language skills, he spoke Hebrew, Greek, Latin, German, Spanish, and more.

During the Counter-Reformation, he served as a papal diplomat, working to keep peace among Christian rulers and standing firm against the Ottoman Empire. In 1601, he famously led Christian troops into battle in Hungary holding only a crucifix, inspiring them to victory.

Despite his high rank, he stayed true to a simple, humble life. He died in 1619 on a mission to defend the rights of oppressed Neapolitans in Lisbon, leaving behind a legacy of courage, compassion, and service.

Festival Events

August 23: The Sacred Beginning

6:30 p.m

Opening Mass

As evening shadows lengthen across the ancient stones of the Pontifical Basilica Cathedral, a profound silence falls over the gathered faithful. The ordination ceremony marks not just the beginning of the festival, but the continuation of a spiritual lineage that stretches back through centuries. Incense fills the air as new clergy take their vows beneath soaring vaults that have witnessed countless such ceremonies.

August 24: The Procession

Dawn breaks over the Sanctuary of Santa Maria degli Angeli as preparations begin for one of the festival's most moving moments. The wooden statue of San Lorenzo da Brindisi, worn smooth by generations of reverent touches, begins its solemn journey alongside precious relics. The procession winds through streets where time seems to stand still, each step marking the path to the Basilica Cathedral in a tradition that echoes through the ages.

As the statue moves forward, the streets fill with the sound of local marching bands, their music lending a ceremonial grandeur to the solemn ritual. Participants, some dressed in traditional attire recalling Brindisi's rich past, accompany the saint's image with candles and flowers. Residents and visitors alike line the streets, joining in prayers and songs that rise into the morning air. The procession becomes not only a religious act but a living expression of the community's cultural identity and enduring devotion to San Lorenzo.

August 27: A Night of Divine Contemplation

As stars twinkle over the Scalinata Virgilio, hundreds of candles create a river of light as the faithful gather for Eucharistic Adoration in the cathedral. Local religious associations lead to an evening where the modern world falls away, replaced by the timeless practice of prayer and reflection. The ancient steps, worn by countless feet, become a temporary sanctuary under the summer sky.

Candlelit procession

This solemn event involves participants carrying candles through the city's historic center, creating a serene and reflective atmosphere. The procession usually begins in the evening, following a Mass held in the Basilica Cattedrale, and proceeds through designated streets, allowing the faithful to express their devotion in a communal setting.

August 30: The Grand Culmination

The festival reaches its crescendo with an evening that begins in sacred solemnity and builds to spectacular celebration. Within the hallowed walls of the Basilica Cathedral, voices rise in prayer during the solemn Mass, their hymns floating through the same space where centuries of faithful have gathered before.

As night falls, the city holds its breath for the procession's pinnacle moment. The majestic equestrian statue of San Teodoro, its bronze catching the last rays of sunset, and the beloved figure of San Lorenzo da Brindisi emerge from the Cathedral's embrace. Their journey to the city's central intersection becomes a river of faith and tradition, as thousands of onlookers line the route, many holding candles that create a flickering pathway through the darkness.

When the statues reach their destination signals more than just the official start of festivities, it marks the transformation of Brindisi itself. As decorative lights suddenly illuminate the city in a blaze of glory, the air fills with gasps of wonder and the sounds of celebration. These illuminations, known locally as luminarie, turn the city's ancient architecture into a canvas of light, creating an ethereal backdrop for the days of celebration to come.

August 31: A Night on the Waters

7:00 p.m.

Maritime Procession

As the sun begins its descent at 7:00 p.m., Brindisi's ancient harbor comes alive with one of the festival's most enchanting traditions. The Maritime Procession begins at the tourist port, where adorned vessels carry the sacred statues across waters that have witnessed two millennia of faith and commerce. The gentle lap of waves against boat hulls creates a natural hymn as the procession weaves through the inner harbor, its path illuminated by hundreds of flickering lights reflected in the darkening waters.

8:30 p.m.

Landing Ceremony

Anticipation builds at the historic Scalinata Virgilio, where crowds gather for the Landing Ceremony. In a moment that bridges centuries of tradition, the statues emerge from their maritime journey to be welcomed by the faithful.

9:00 p.m.

Fireworks Display

September 1: The Grand Finale

8:00 p.m.

The festival reaches its spiritual apex when Piazza Duomo transforms into an open-air cathedral for the Solemn Pontifical Mass. Under the stars, the Archbishop leads the city's most significant liturgical celebration, where the voices of clergy and faithful blend in ancient prayers that have echoed through Brindisi's streets for centuries.

Brindisi Walking Tour

#1. Basilica Cattedrale della Visitazione e San Giovanni Battista (Cathedral of St. John the Baptist)

Basilica Cattedrale della Visitazione e San Giovanni Battista stands as a magnificent testament to Brindisi's historical importance, weaving together Romanesque foundations and Baroque grandeur. Originally constructed in the 11th century and consecrated by Pope Urban II in 1089, this cathedral served as a spiritual beacon for crusaders departing from Brindisi's port. The devastating earthquake of 1743 led to its resurrection in a harmonious blend of styles, the original Romanesque structure enriched with Baroque embellishments.

Basilica Cattedrale of Brindisi

The cathedral's interior showcases spectacular frescoes, including the masterful Assumption of the Virgin Mary adorning the central dome. Among its precious artifacts are a fragment of the True Cross in an ornate silver reliquary and a rare 12th-century mosaic floor fragment that whispers tales of its Norman origins.

The building's commanding presence is anchored by its octagonal Romanesque bell tower, which once guided ships into harbor and continues to define Brindisi's skyline. Piazza Duomo, the cathedral's home, remains the beating heart of Brindisi's religious quarter, surrounded by the Archbishop's Palace and historic noble residences that chronicle the city's architectural evolution.

#2. Roman Columns

The Roman Columns stand as silent sentinels of Brindisi's ancient glory, marking the end of the legendary Via Appia where Rome reached toward the East. These 2nd-century AD monuments once formed a magnificent pair until the 16th century, when one succumbed to time's passage.

The surviving column rises 18.74 meters (61 feet) skyward, its marble shaft crowned with an elegant Corinthian capital, marking the point where countless travelers first glimpsed the Eastern horizon. Its fallen twin, now carefully preserved nearby, completes the story of this ancient gateway where Roman power met Eastern promise. Together, they represent not just the end of a road, but the beginning of countless journeys that shaped the ancient world.

#3. Scalinata Virgiliana (Virgil's Steps)

These scenic steps lead from the waterfront up to the Roman Columns. Tradition links them to the Roman poet Virgil, who reportedly died in Brindisi in 19 BC. The steps provide breathtaking views of the inner harbor and serve as a link between the city's maritime and Roman heritage. The staircase is flanked by lush greenery and opens to panoramic views of the harbor, making it a peaceful yet historical spot.

#4. Palazzo Granafei-Nervegna

This Renaissance palace dates back to the 16th century and has served various roles, including as a noble residence and civic building. It now houses cultural exhibits, including the original capital of one of the Roman Columns, and provides insights into the city's aristocratic past. The palace combines Renaissance and Baroque elements with elegant arches and courtyards. Its cultural displays are well-curated and worth exploring.

#5. Chiesa di San Giovanni al Sepolcro (St. John at the Sepulchre)

Built in the 11th century, this small round church was linked to the Crusades and served as a resting point for pilgrims traveling to the Holy Land. The church is an architectural gem with intricate carvings, frescoes, and a unique circular layout inspired by Jerusalem's Church of the Holy Sepulchre. Medieval frescoes and a captivating ambiance are found within, while the portal showcases detailed Biblical carvings.

The church's unique octagonal design reflects the sacred geometry popular in medieval religious architecture, with eight pillars supporting the central dome. Inside, traces of original frescoes depict scenes from the life of Christ and various saints, though many were damaged during the church's varied history. Of particular interest is the ancient crypt beneath the church, which contains several medieval tombs and was used by the Knights Templar during the Crusades. Archaeological excavations have revealed evidence of an earlier structure on the site, possibly dating to the 6th century, suggesting the location's long-standing religious significance in Brindisi's history.

San Giovanni al Sepolcro

#6. Port of Brindisi

Brindisi's natural harbor has been a strategic maritime hub since antiquity, used by Greeks, Romans, and later by Crusaders embarking for the East. A walk along the waterfront offers views of the harbor's historic significance and modern vitality. The harbor is flanked by historic buildings, docks, and views of the Aragonese Castle and the Monument to Italian Sailors.

Honorable Mention: Castello Svevo (Swabian Castle)

We walked to the castle but I don't necessarily want to incude it in the walking tour because it is an active military base and you cannot enter. While historically important, I'll include it with a cautionary note.

Built by Emperor Frederick II in the 13th century, this fortress served as a defensive stronghold and a royal residence. It is a striking example of medieval military architecture, though its interiors are only partially open to visitors because of military use. The castle features thick walls, enormous towers, and a moat. Its exterior exudes historical strength and dominance.

Castello Svevo

The castle's strategic location at the entrance to Brindisi's inner harbor made it a crucial part of the city's maritime defense system. Frederick II, known as "Stupor Mundi" (Wonder of the World), incorporated innovative military architectural features, including an advanced system of arrow slits and defensive positions that could protect the harbor from both land and sea attacks. The fortress represents the height of Hohenstaufen military engineering, with walls up to four meters thick and towers positioned to maximize defensive coverage.

Brindisi Festivals Throughout the Year

Processione del Cavallo Parato (Corpus Christi)

Late May or June (dependent on the liturgical calendar).

This unique religious procession takes place in late May or June, depending on the liturgical calendar. The local archbishop rides a white horse through the city, carrying the Eucharist. The procession includes blessings at the harbor and Victory Square. Dating back to the 13th century, the tradition commemorates King Louis IX of France, who supposedly left the Eucharist as a pledge while traveling.

Negroamaro Wine Festival

Early to mid-June.

Held in early to mid-June, this festival celebrates the renowned Negroamaro wine. The event takes place in Brindisi's historic center, featuring wine tasting stations, street food, and live music. The festival creates a lively atmosphere with unique flavors and an unforgettable experience.

Salento Pride

Typically held in July or August.

Salento Pride, also known as Puglia Pride, is a vibrant celebration of LGBTQ+ rights and culture in the Salento region. Since its inception in 2015, the event has been hosted in various cities, including Gallipoli, Brindisi, and Lecce. Organized by local LGBTQ+ organizations such as Rainbow Network and Arcigay Salento, Salento Pride aims to promote inclusivity and visibility for the LGBTQ+ community in southern Italy.

Nativity Scenes and Christmas Markets

December 8 to January 6.

A festive atmosphere takes over Brindisi with traditional nativity scenes, Christmas lights, and holiday markets.

Day Trips: Nearby sites, cities, and towns

Latiano. 28 kilometers (17 miles) west of Brindisi. Latiano offers a blend of history and local tradition, highlighted by the impressive Palazzo Imperiali, a baronial residence that now hosts cultural exhibitions and events. Visitors can stroll through the historic center, where narrow streets lead to the Church of Santa Maria della Neve and the Museum of Rural Civilization, which showcases the agricultural heritage of the region. Latiano's authentic atmosphere and deep connection to the land make it an appealing stop for those seeking a quieter, culturally rich experience.

Mesagne. 17 kilometers (11 miles) west of Brindisi. Mesagne enchants visitors with its beautifully preserved old town, where whitewashed houses and winding alleys lead to the impressive Norman-Swabian Castle and the Baroque-style Mother Church. The Porta Grande marks the historic entrance to the center, now a lively area with cafés and artisan shops. Mesagne's welcoming atmosphere, historical landmarks, and vibrant cultural life make it a perfect choice for a half-day or full-day excursion.

Logistics

Train: Brindisi is well-connected by train, with its central train station at Piazza Crispi, just a short walk from the historic center. Trenitalia operates frequent regional and intercity trains to nearby cities like Lecce, Bari, and Taranto, as well as high-speed trains to major hubs like Rome and Milan.

Bus: The city's public transportation is operated by STP Brindisi, which provides an extensive bus network throughout the city and surrounding areas. Long-distance buses by companies like FlixBus and MarinoBus connect Brindisi to other Italian regions.

Car: Brindisi is conveniently on the Adriatic coast and easily accessible by car. From Bari, take the SS16 (Strada Statale 16) southbound for approximately 115 km (71 miles).

Parking: Parking options in Brindisi include public lots,street parking, and private garages. Piazzale Spalato is a convenient lot near the port and the city center. Paid parking is available with hourly or daily rates. Via del Mare, this parking area provides easy access to the waterfront and principal attractions.

Restaurant Recommendations

La Locanda del Porto. Address: Via Montenegro, 20

Near the waterfront, this cozy restaurant offers a mix of traditional Puglian and Mediterranean cuisine. Known for its fresh seafood, handmade pastas, and friendly service, it's a favorite among both locals and tourists.

Brunda Pizzeria. Address: Piazza Dante Alighieri, 8

Famous for its wood-fired pizzas, Brunda also serves a variety of Italian classics. Its central location and casual atmosphere make it an excellent spot for a relaxed meal after exploring the historic center.

Trattoria Pantagruele. Address: Salita di Ripalta, 1

This charming trattoria specializes in regional dishes made with seasonal ingredients. The warm ambiance and thoughtfully curated wine list provide a perfect setting for an authentic Puglian dining experience.

Accommodation

For the festival, I recommend three to four nights in town.

Grande Albergo Internazionale. Address: Viale Regina Margherita, 23

This elegant 4-star hotel offers stunning views of the harbor and a prime location near Brindisi's chief attractions. The historic building features classic décor, comfortable rooms, and a restaurant serving local and international cuisine.

Hotel Palazzo Virgilio. Address: Corso Umberto I, 141

A modern 4-star hotel conveniently near the train station and the historic center. Palazzo Virgilio provides stylish accommodations, a contemporary restaurant, and excellent service for both leisure and business travelers.

Hotel Orientale. Address: Corso Giuseppe Garibaldi, 40

A charming 3-star hotel in the heart of the historic center. Hotel Orientale features well-appointed rooms, a welcoming atmosphere, and easy access to the city's top sites, making it ideal for exploring Brindisi on foot.

CHAPTER NINETEEN

Radiant Lecce, the Baroque City's Devotion

Honoring Sant'Oronzo Through the Ages

F **iera di Sant'Oronzo**

Where: Lecce

When: August 24-27

Average Festival Temperatures: High 30-33°C (86-91°F). Low 20-23°C (68-73°F).

Lecce: The Baroque Jewel of Salento

Lecce, the "Florence of the South," where master artisans transformed soft limestone into intricate facades that seem to dance in the Mediterranean sun. For over two millennia, this jewel of Puglia has been collecting stories within its honey-colored walls.

Long before Rome cast its shadow across Italy, the ancient Messapians made this land their home. But it was under Roman rule that the city, then called Lupiae, truly began to shine. Merchants and travelers bustling along the Via Traiana brought goods, ideas, and cultures that would shape Lecce's destiny.

The Middle Ages brought a parade of rulers, Byzantine emperors, fierce Lombard warriors, and Norman knights, each leaving their mark. The Normans, with their eye for defense, gave Lecce its mighty walls, but it was during the Renaissance and Baroque periods that the city discovered its true artistic voice.

The secret behind Lecce's architectural magic? A unique, butter-soft limestone called pietra leccese. In the hands of local artisans, this malleable stone became a canvas for their wildest artistic dreams. Walk through the historic center today, and you'll find yourself surrounded by their masterpieces. Cherubs seem to float off church facades, while intricate floral patterns climb up palazzo walls. The Basilica di Santa Croce stands as their crowning achievement, its facade so detailed it looks more like embroidered lace than carved stone.

Carved Pietra Lecesse (local limestone) of the Basilica

In the shadow of baroque churches, 95,000 residents go about their daily lives. University students crowd into cafes in elegant piazzas, while artisans keep traditional crafts alive in their workshops, including the distinctive art of papier-mâché. The surrounding countryside tells its own story through endless olive groves and vineyards, providing the foundation for the region's renowned oils and wines.

Perfectly positioned between two seas, just 12 kilometers (7 miles) from the Adriatic and 40 (25) from the Ionian, Lecce continues to be what it has always been: a crossroads where history, art, and daily life merge into something extraordinary.

Fair of Saint Oronzo

This festival is one of the most important religious and cultural celebrations in the Salento region, honoring the city's patron saint, Sant'Oronzo. The festival dates back several centuries, originating as a way for the people of Lecce to express gratitude to their protector saint, particularly in times of crisis.

Who Was Saint Oronzo?

Saint Oronzo was a 1st-century bishop and martyr, believed to have been the first bishop of Lecce. According to tradition, he was converted to Christianity by Saint Paul while the Apostle was passing through Italy on his way to Rome. Oronzo quickly became a devoted evangelizer, spreading the Christian faith throughout the region.

However, during the reign of Emperor Nero (54-68 AD), Christianity was still considered a threat to the Roman Empire, and Oronzo faced persecution. He was eventually captured and executed, making him one of the earliest Christian martyrs in Italy. His feast day, August 26, marks his martyrdom and has been celebrated in Lecce for centuries.

The Miracle of Saint Oronzo

The festival in its current form was officially instituted in the 17th century, following a miraculous event that saved Lecce from the plague of 1656. During this devastating epidemic, much of southern Italy suffered immense losses, but Lecce was largely spared. The people of Lecce attributed this divine protection to Saint Oronzo's intercession, and in gratitude, they vowed to honor him with an annual festival.

Since then, the Festa di Sant'Oronzo has grown into a major event featuring religious processions, traditional music, illuminated streets, and public celebrations. While it remains a deeply religious occasion, the festival has also strengthened into a vibrant cultural spectacle that attracts visitors from across Puglia and beyond.

Festival Events

August 24: Opening Ceremony

10:00 a.m.

Opening Ceremony (Piazza Sant'Oronzo)

Experience the grandeur of tradition as the city comes alive with the official opening of our beloved festival. Watch as the historic square fills with color, music, and ceremonial splendor.

11:00 a.m.

Youth Confirmation Mass

A moving celebration of faith as our young community members affirm their spiritual journey, presided over by Monsignor Arcivescovo (Archbishop).

7:00 p.m.

Band Performance

Let the renowned local bands fill the evening air with their masterful blend of traditional and contemporary pieces, bringing the city's musical heritage to life.

8:00 p.m.

Theatrical Performance

Watch a spellbinding theatrical production that weaves together music, drama, and local folklore in the stunning baroque setting of Teatro dei Teatini.

10:30 p.m.

Traditional Pugliese folk music comes to life in the piazza.

August 25: City Celebrations

10:00 a.m.

City Band of Lecce Performance (Piazza Sant'Oronzo)

Start your morning in the heart of Lecce as the prestigious city band fills the historic piazza with melodic harmonies, performing a repertoire that spans from beloved classical pieces to contemporary favorites.

6:30 p.m.

Solemn Procession of the Patron Saints

Witness one of Lecce's most cherished traditions as the sacred simulacra of our patron saints process through candlelit streets. This deeply moving spectacle brings together faith, tradition, and community in a magnificent display. The renowned Tamburellisti of Torrepaduli (drummers) add their rhythmic expertise to this unique presentation.

August 26: The Vigil of the Feast Day

7:00 a.m.

Solemn Pontifical Mass

Begin this special day with a majestic celebration in the stunning cathedral, as the Archbishop leads this time-honored tradition.

Join in this ancient tradition celebrating our agricultural heritage, where local farmers gather to honor old customs and share in community festivities.

8:00 p.m.

Evening Concerts and Events

August 27: Feast of Sant'Oronzo

6:30 p.m.

Exhibition of Original Artworks and Crafts

Wander through an impressive showcase of local talent, where traditional craftsmanship meets contemporary creativity in this carefully curated exhibition.

7:00 p.m.

Thanksgiving Mass

Join the local archbishop for this heartfelt service of gratitude, reflecting on the festival's blessings and community spirit.

8:00 p.m.

Garden Concert and Dance Lessons

Experience the magic of music under the stars in the conservatory's beautiful gardens, where classical melodies mingle with the evening breeze. Learn the steps of Puglia's most beloved traditional dances from expert instructors in this interactive and joyful workshop.

10:30 p.m.

Street Performances

Follow the sound of music and laughter as artists, musicians, and performers transform our historic streets into stages of wonder and delight.

11:00 p.m.

Grand Finale Fireworks

Bid farewell to this year's festival with an awe-inspiring display of pyrotechnic artistry, illuminating the night sky in a spectacular tribute to Sant'Oronzo.

Lecce Walking Tour

#1. Porta Napoli

Porta Napoli stands as a majestic testament to Lecce's golden age, its limestone façade gleaming like honey in the Pugliese sun. Built in 1548 as a tribute to Charles V, this triumphal arch replaced a medieval gateway and transformed the city's entrance into a statement of baroque grandeur.

Its classical design features robust Doric columns and elaborate carvings that showcase the masterful work of local stone craftsmen. The arch's architectural elements, including decorative friezes, the Habsburg eagle, and commemorative inscriptions, tell the story of Lecce's prominence within the Spanish Kingdom of Naples. Rising above the ancient Via Appia, Porta Napoli continues to serve its original purpose as the city's ceremonial gateway, welcoming visitors through the same passage that has witnessed nearly five centuries of history.

#2. Obelisk of Lecce

Just outside Porta Napoli, this obelisk was erected in 1822 to commemorate Ferdinand I of the Kingdom of the Two Sicilies. Decorated with intricate symbols representing different cities in the region, it stands as a tribute to the unification efforts of the time.

#3. Basilica di Santa Croce

Basilica di Santa Croce reigns as the crowning achievement of Lecce's Baroque artistry, its façade a mesmerizing symphony carved in local pietra leccese limestone. Completed in 1695 after nearly two centuries of construction, the basilica showcases the virtuosity of master craftsmen who transformed stone into a theatrical display of religious symbolism and artistic imagination. The extraordinary façade rises in three tiers of increasing complexity, where fantastical creatures, writhing vegetation, cherubs, and grotesque figures emerge from the honey-colored stone.

A massive rose window, framed by an explosion of sculptural detail, dominates the upper level, while below, classical columns and intricate cornices frame scenes from Christian mythology. Inside, the basilica's Latin cross plan unfolds beneath soaring vaulted ceilings, with twelve chapels housing magnificent baroque altars. The play of natural light through the rose window illuminates the interior's rich ornamentation, including Giuseppe Zimbalo's masterful sculptural work and precious artworks that span centuries of religious devotion.

#4. Palazzo dei Celestini

Next to the Basilica di Santa Croce, this 17th-century former convent of the Celestine monks now houses government offices. Its facade is a prime example of Lecce's elaborate Baroque style, featuring detailed stonework and grand windows.

#5. Piazza Sant'Oronzo

This main square is the vibrant heart of Lecce, surrounded by historical buildings and modern cafes. A column topped with a statue of Saint Oronzo, the city's patron saint, dominates the piazza. The remains of a Roman amphitheater (1st-2nd century AD), discovered in the early 20th century, provide a fascinating glimpse into Lecce's ancient past.

#6. Roman Amphitheater

The Roman Amphitheater emerges from Lecce's Piazza Sant'Oronzo as a dramatic reminder of the city's ancient past, its massive limestone blocks telling tales of gladiatorial spectacle. Built in the 2nd century AD, this elliptical arena could hold up to 25,000 spectators, with its tiered seating arrangement reflecting the strict social hierarchy of Roman society. Though only half-visible today, with modern Lecce built atop its northern section, the excavated portion reveals sophisticated engineering features including underground chambers, drainage systems, and the original arena floor.

The surviving architectural elements showcase both practical Roman design and decorative touches, from the carefully carved seating tiers to fragments of marble that once adorned the imperial box. The amphitheater's strategic location at the intersection of ancient Roman roads underscores Lecce's importance as a major cultural center in Roman Puglia, while its partial burial beneath the modern piazza creates a striking dialogue between ancient and contemporary urban layers.

Buildings follow the curve of the Roman Amphitheater

#7. Chiesa di San Matteo

The Church of St. Matthew stands as one of Lecce's most architecturally innovative religious monuments, distinguished by its dynamic baroque facade that seems to ripple with waves of stone. Built in 1667, its unique design features an undulating surface of concave and convex curves, breaking from the traditional flat church facades of the period. The masterful manipulation of pietra leccese limestone creates a play of light and shadow that changes throughout the day, while ornate decorative elements, including elaborate cornices, statues, and floral motifs, enhance the facade's theatrical effect.

#8. Piazza del Duomo and Duomo (Chiesa Cattedrale) di Lecce

One of the most breathtaking squares in Italy, Piazza del Duomo is a baroque masterpiece, an enclosed space that exudes elegance and grandeur. Surrounded by magnificent buildings, including the Campanile (bell tower), the Bishop's Palace, and the Seminary Palace, the piazza is a harmonious blend of religious and civic architecture that reflects Lecce's rich history.

Duomo di Lecce

At its heart stands the Duomo di Lecce (Cathedral of Santa Maria Assunta), a stunning example of Lecce Baroque. Originally built in 1144, the cathedral was extensively redesigned in 1659 by Giuseppe Zimbalo, one of the most influential Baroque architects of southern Italy. The result is an architectural masterpiece, where the cathedral's ornate façade, intricate sculptures, and dramatic use of light and shadow embody the extravagance of the Baroque era.

The main façade, which faces the square, is relatively simple, while the side façade, visible upon entering the piazza, is far more elaborate, adorned with statues of saints, intricate reliefs, and decorative pilasters. Inside, the cathedral's opulent Baroque interior is adorned with majestic columns, gilded stucco decorations, and an intricately carved wooden ceiling. It houses twelve richly decorated chapels, each dedicated to a different saint, with the most notable being the Chapel of Saint Orontius (Sant'Oronzo), the patron saint of Lecce.

Stunning 16th- and 17th-century paintings, including works by Giuseppe da Brindisi and Oronzo Tiso, line the cathedral walls, enriching the sacred atmosphere. The high altar, framed by massive Corinthian columns, is a triumph of Baroque artistry. But beneath this grandeur lies a more somber and intimate space: the crypt, a vast chamber supported by 92 stone columns, dimly lit and cloaked in silence.

Once used as a burial site for bishops and nobles, the crypt offers a powerful contrast to the ornate world above. Here, you'll find visible tomb markers and burial niches, and in some areas, fragments of human remains or skeletal bones are respectfully preserved as a quiet testimony to Lecce's spiritual past. The air is cooler, the ceiling lower, and the atmosphere charged with reverence, an invitation to reflect on mortality, faith, and the continuity of devotion across the centuries.

The bell tower, added in 1661, rises 72 meters (236 feet). It has elevator access, offering panoramic views across the rooftops of Lecce to the Adriatic Sea. On a clear day, it's one of the most rewarding experiences in the city.

#9. Castello di Carlo V

The Castello di Carlo V rises as a formidable testament to 16th-century military architecture, its massive star-shaped fortifications dominating Lecce's urban landscape. Commissioned by Emperor Charles V to defend against Ottoman incursions, the castle brilliantly combines medieval robustness with Renaissance innovation. Its imposing structure features four corner bastions, a deep moat, and walls up to 12 meters thick, while the interior reveals a more refined character with elegant courtyards and vaulted halls adorned with period frescoes.

The castle's sophisticated defense systems, including advanced artillery positions and underground passages, showcase the era's military engineering expertise. Though it never faced a major siege, the fortress served as both a military garrison and a symbol of Spanish authority. Today, its restored chambers host cultural exhibitions and events, while the castle's architectural details, from gun ports to decorative cornices, tell the story of a time when Lecce stood as a strategic frontier between East and West.

Castello di Carlo V Courtyard

Lecce Festivals and Sagre Throughout the Year

Lecce European Film Festival

April (specific dates vary annually).

Established in 2000, this annual festival celebrates European cinema, aiming to promote dialogue between different European cultures and languages. The event features film screenings, meetings with directors and actors, photographic exhibitions, and theatrical performances. It is held at the Multisala Massimo cinema in Lecce.

Lecce Cortili Aperti

May (specific dates vary annually).

Organized by the Associazione Dimore Storiche d'Italia, this event opens the private courtyards of Lecce's historic palaces to the public. Visitors can admire Baroque architecture and enjoy concerts, shows, and artistic performances held within these usually inaccessible spaces.

Festa di Santa Irene

May 2-5

The Festa di Santa Irene in Lecce is celebrated annually on May 5, honoring the city's former patron saint who held this role until 1656. The celebrations center on the magnificent Chiesa di Sant'Irene in Lecce's historic center and typically span several days with a solemn triduum beginning on May 2.

Devotees gather for evening rosaries and special Masses, culminating in a vigil Mass led by the archbishop on May 4 and a solemn feast day Mass on May 5. While more intimate than the city's grand Festa di Sant'Oronzo, the Festa di Santa Irene reflects Lecce's deep spiritual traditions and often includes classical music performances, offering a reverent and culturally rich experience for both locals and visitors.

Festival del Cinema

August (specific dates vary annually).

The Lecce Film Festival, established in 2000, is a cultural gem that showcases Italian and international films. Attendees can experience screenings, meet directors and actors, and immerse themselves in the artistic energy of this Baroque city.

Panorama Festival

Mid-August for one week.

An immersive electronic music festival combining sound and scenery. Set in the heart of Puglia, it offers a blend of electronic music performances against breathtaking backdrops.

Christmas in Lecce

December 8 to January 6.

Christmas in Lecce transforms the baroque city into a festive wonderland, with twinkling lights illuminating its golden stone facades and lively events filling the streets. The heart of the celebrations is Piazza Sant'Oronzo, where a traditional Christmas market features wooden chalets selling artisan crafts, festive decorations, local delicacies, and seasonal sweets like cartellate and purceddhruzzi.

Nearby, Piazza Mazzini also hosts a market with a modern flair, offering gifts, food, and entertainment for all ages. Throughout December, nativity scenes (presepi) are displayed in churches and public spaces, including elaborate mechanical nativity scenes crafted by local artisans. Concerts, street performances, and special events add to the joyful atmosphere, making Lecce's Christmas season a blend of history, art, and warm southern Italian holiday traditions.

Day Trip Options: Nearby Sites, Cities, and Towns

Acaya. 12 kilometers (7.5 miles) from Lecce. A beautifully preserved walled medieval town, Acaya is one of the few remaining examples of Renaissance military architecture in southern Italy. Built in the 16th century, the town features the Castello di Acaya, an imposing fortress with impressive bastions and a moat. Walking through its quiet streets feels like stepping back in time. Acaya is also a gateway to the Cesine Nature Reserve, a protected wetland perfect for nature lovers.

Galatina. The distance from Lecce is 22 kilometers, or 13.7 miles. A hidden gem of the Salento region, Galatina is famous for its stunning Baroque architecture and the Basilica di Santa Caterina d'Alessandria, a 14th-century church with some of the most breathtaking Gothic frescoes in southern Italy, often compared to those in Assisi.

Nardò. 25 kilometers (15.5 miles) from Lecce. A charming town with a strong Baroque influence, Nardò boasts an elegant Piazza Salandra, considered one of the most beautiful squares in Puglia. Its cathedral, built in the 11th century, preserves an impressive Byzantine-style Crucifixion fresco. The town is close to the Porto Selvaggio Natural Park, a scenic coastal reserve with hidden coves, forests, and ancient watchtowers.

Logistics

Train: Lecce is well-connected by train, serving as a key railway hub in southern Puglia. Main Train Station: Lecce Centrale (Piazzale Oronzo Massari, Lecce).

Bus: Lecce's central bus station near the train station on Via Don Bosco serves as a major transport hub, with Marozzi and FlixBus operating long-distance routes to cities like Rome and Naples, while STP Lecce and FSE provide frequent regional connections throughout Puglia, including popular destinations like Otranto (1 hour), Gallipoli (1.5 hour), and Brindisi (40 minutes).

Car: Driving to Lecce is a convenient option, but parking in the historic center can be difficult because of the ZTL (Limited Traffic Zone) restrictions. SS16 (Brindisi-Lecce highway, ~30 minutes from Brindisi). SS101 (Lecce-Gallipoli highway, ~40 minutes). SS613 (Lecce-Bari, ~1.5 hours).

Parking: For visitors arriving by car, it's best to park outside the historic center and walk in. Here are safe parking options: Parcheggio Ex Foro Boario (Piazzale Carmelo Bene, ~10 min walk to centro storico) offers paid parking. Or Parcheggio Via Adua (Via Adua, ~15 min walk), offers free parking.

Restaurant Recommendations

La Rusticana. Address: Via Vittorio Emanuele II, 31

Tucked just steps from Lecce's majestic cathedral, La Rusticana offers a casual yet flavorful dining experience that blends quick bites with traditional southern hospitality. Whether you're grabbing a meal on the go or sitting down for a relaxed lunch, the menu delivers hearty Pugliese classics made fresh.

The panzerotti here are a must, crispy on the outside, soft and savory within. They were so good I had a second! Alongside these irresistible stuffed pastries, La Rusticana serves everything from pizzas and pasta to sandwiches and local snacks, with both fast food and full restaurant-style service available. Ideal for a quick break during your walking tour or a satisfying, affordable meal near the Duomo.

Alle Due Corti. Address: Corte dei Giugni, 1

Specializing in traditional Salento cuisine, Alle Due Corti offers a genuine taste of the region. The menu features a variety of local dishes, including vegetarian options. The restaurant's interior exudes a homely atmosphere, reflecting the warmth of Lecce's culinary heritage.

Osteria degli Spiriti. Address: Via Cesare Battisti

Osteria degli Spiriti is known for its elegant setting and a menu that balances traditional Apulian dishes with innovative twists. The restaurant prides itself on using fresh, local ingredients to create flavorful and artfully presented meals. The extensive wine list complements the culinary offerings, ensuring a memorable dining experience.

Accommodation

For the Festival of Sant'Oronzo, I recommend three or four nights in town.

Patria Palace Lecce. Address: Piazzetta Riccardi, 13

In the heart of Lecce's historic center, Patria Palace Lecce is a 5-star luxury hotel housed in an 18th-century palazzo. Directly opposite the Basilica of Santa Croce, it offers elegantly furnished rooms that blend classic charm with modern amenities. The hotel's rooftop restaurant, Atenze, provides panoramic views of the city and serves contemporary Italian cuisine. Its central location makes it an ideal base for exploring Lecce's baroque architecture and taking part in local festivals.

Risorgimento Resort. Address: Via Augusto Imperatore, 19

Nestled within Lecce's historic district, 5-star Risorgimento Resort combines modern luxury with historical charm. The resort features spacious, elegantly designed rooms and a rooftop terrace offering views over the city. Guests can enjoy gourmet dining at the on-site restaurant and unwind at the spa. Its proximity to major attractions and event venues makes it convenient for festival attendees.

La Fiermontina Luxury Home Hotel. Address: Piazzetta Scipione De Summa, 4

In the historic center, 5-star La Fiermontina offers a unique blend of traditional architecture and contemporary design. Set in a restored 17th-century building, the hotel boasts an outdoor pool, a lush garden, and art installations throughout the property. The elegantly appointed rooms provide a serene retreat, while the on-site restaurant serves dishes inspired by local cuisine. Its central location ensures easy access to festival events and city landmarks.

CHAPTER TWENTY

Immersion Experience: Hands on Puglia

Mastering Orecchiette, Focaccia, and Local Flavors

Why Include a Cooking Class in Your Travels?

One of our favorite traditions when visiting a new region or country is taking a cooking class. Over the years, we have learned how to make empanadas in Argentina, arancini in Sicily, and cacio e pepe in Rome. Each experience has deepened our connection to the local culture, allowing us to bring a taste of our travels home. Cooking with locals is a unique way to engage with traditions, flavors, and history in an unforgettable and hands-on way.

Cooking is more than just a skill in Puglia; it is a tradition passed down through generations, deeply rooted in the flavors of the land. During our immersive cooking class and market tour with Cesarine, we not only learned how to make the iconic orecchiette pasta but also got a taste of the region's warm hospitality and vibrant culinary culture.

Brindisi Market Tour to Start

Our experience began with a guided stroll through a local market, where we admired the colorful displays of fresh produce, fragrant herbs, and artisanal cheeses. The market was a feast for the senses, buzzing with vendors passionately explaining their goods. Our host guided us through selecting the best seasonal ingredients, sharing insights into Puglia's rich culinary traditions.

Learning the Art of Orecchiette

Upon arriving at our host's welcoming home, we stepped into the kitchen, eager to learn. The star of the class was orecchiette, the signature "little ear" pasta of Puglia. Our host patiently demonstrated how to shape the pasta using just a knife and our fingertips, an artful technique perfected over centuries. Rolling and pressing the dough felt like a meditative ritual, and soon we were forming pasta pieces with surprising ease.

Orecchiette

Focaccia and the Joy of Sharing

Though we didn't prepare the focaccia barese from scratch, its enticing aroma filled the kitchen as it had been left to rise before our arrival. Topped with plump cherry tomatoes and fragrant oregano, it emerged from the oven with a crispy golden crust and a soft, airy center. We sampled it while our pasta was cooking, savoring every bite.

A Meal Among New Friends

Once the pasta was ready, we gathered around the table with our host and fellow travelers. We enjoyed our freshly made orecchiette, coated in a simple yet flavorful sauce that highlighted the region's olive oil, tomatoes, and Pecorino cheese. Conversation flowed effortlessly as we shared travel stories and toasted to a day well spent.

A Taste of Puglian Hospitality

Our cooking class was more than a lesson in pasta-making; it was an immersion into the heart of Puglian culture. The warmth of our host, the camaraderie with fellow travelers, and the flavors of the dishes we prepared made for an unforgettable experience. Whether you are an experienced cook or a novice in the kitchen, a hands-on class like this is a perfect way to connect with Italy's culinary heritage and bring home a piece of Puglia to recreate in your own kitchen.

CHAPTER TWENTY-ONE

Riding Through Time in Ostuni

The Cavalcade of Sant'Oronzo

La Cavalcata di Sant'Oronzo

Where: Ostuni

When: August 25-27

Average Festival Temperatures: High 30°C (86°F). Low 26°C (79°F).

Ostuni: A Town Shaped by Time

Rising above the olive-dotted plains of Puglia like a vision in white, Ostuni is a town whose history is deeply intertwined with its striking geography. Perched atop a hill, eight kilometers (5 miles) from the Adriatic Sea, its labyrinth of whitewashed houses and fortified walls speaks of centuries of resilience, conquest, and cultural fusion.

Ostuni's history begins in the Paleolithic period, when the first human settlements took refuge in the natural caves of the region, drawn by the nearby coastal plains and freshwater sources. Archaeological discoveries, such as the remains of Delia, a 25,000-year-old pregnant woman found in a cave near Ostuni, reveal a prehistoric society that flourished long before written records.

With the Roman conquest of Puglia in the 3rd century BC, Ostuni became part of the vast Roman network, benefitting from the empire's road systems and trade routes that connected it to major cities like Brindisi and Bari. The fertile plains surrounding the town became a hub for grain and olive oil production, a legacy that continues today.

The fall of Rome in the 5th century plunged Ostuni, like much of southern Italy, into a period of instability. However, its hilltop location proved advantageous. During the Byzantine era (6th–11th centuries), the town became a Christian stronghold, as monks and refugees fleeing the turmoil of the mainland settled within its protective walls. The Byzantine influence is still visible in the remnants of ancient Christian churches and the use of the Greek language in religious practices.

With the arrival of the Normans in the 11th century, Ostuni was fortified further, and a feudal system took root. Medieval Ostuni was a walled citadel, encircled by imposing ramparts, with a layout designed for defensive warfare. Streets were narrow and winding, creating a maze that would confuse invaders. The town flourished under Swabian, Angevin, and Aragonese rule, each dynasty leaving its architectural and cultural imprint.

Fortifications of Ostuni

Renaissance Ostuni: The White City Emerges

The 15th and 16th centuries were a golden age for Ostuni. Under the rule of the Duchy of Bari, the town experienced a cultural and economic revival, with new churches, palaces, and public squares adorning the landscape. But the most defining feature of Ostuni's Renaissance era was its transformation into the "White City" (La Città Bianca).

Plagued by periodic outbreaks of disease, particularly the Black Death, the people of Ostuni turned to a practical and aesthetic solution: whitewashing their buildings with lime. Not only did this create the dazzling, sunlit appearance that still defines the town today, but the lime also had antibacterial properties, helping to protect against infections.

The Renaissance also brought economic prosperity, as Ostuni's proximity to the coast allowed it to benefit from maritime trade. The noble families of the period, such as the Zevallos and the Sforzas, commissioned elegant palaces and supported the arts, while the Cathedral of Ostuni, built during this era, stood as a magnificent blend of Gothic and Romanesque styles.

Today, Ostuni remains one of Puglia's most captivating destinations, home to a population of around 30,000 residents that swells significantly in the summer months as visitors are drawn to its historic charm and nearby beaches. Its strategic location, perched at 229 meters (751 feet) above sea level, offers breathtaking views of the Adriatic coastline and the sprawling olive groves that define the region.

Picture a summer evening in 1657, when death stalked the streets of southern Italy. As the plague ravaged town after town, Ostuni's whitewashed walls stood like a beacon of hope amidst the devastation. Watching neighboring communities fall to the epidemic, the people of this hilltop city turned to an unlikely protector: a 1st-century Christian martyr named Oronzo. Their desperate prayers gave birth to a tradition that still thunders through Ostuni's cobbled streets, the Cavalcata di Sant'Oronzo, a spectacular festival where faith, history, and pageantry collide.

Calvalcade of Saint Oronzo

This majestic celebration transforms Ostuni into a vision of Spanish courtly splendor. Riders dressed in crimson and gold uniforms, their feathered hats catching the sunlight, parade through the streets on equally adorned horses. The Cavalcata is more than just a religious procession; it is a centuries-old promise kept. Born in an era of darkness, it endures as a brilliant display of gratitude, resilience, and devotion.

Even today, as horses' hooves clatter against ancient stone, they echo the story of Ostuni's survival. The festival continues to unite past and present, fulfilling the vow made by generations before—a promise to honor the saint they believe saved them from the plague.

Who Is Saint Oronzo?

Saint Oronzo was not a native of Ostuni, but his influence shaped the town's destiny. According to tradition, he was the first bishop of Lecce, converted to Christianity by Saint Paul himself. He spent his life preaching the new faith in Puglia, spreading the Gospel in a region still under Roman rule. This defiance of imperial authority made him a target, and he was ultimately martyred, some say by beheading, others by being thrown to wild beasts, in the 1st century.

Despite his violent death, Oronzo's legacy endured, and centuries later, his name became entwined with Ostuni's fate. When the plague struck in the 17th century, the people turned to him in desperation, believing that his intercession spared their city while others perished. In gratitude, they declared him their patron saint, replacing their previous protector, Saint Blaise, and vowed to honor him with an annual celebration.

From that moment on, Saint Oronzo became the symbol of Ostuni's survival. His feast day, August 26th, remains a time of grand processions, fervent prayers, and the spectacular Cavalcata: a tradition that ensures his name and Ostuni's story are never forgotten.

Festival Events

August 25th: Opening Day

Evening: Blessing Ceremony

The festival commences with a benediction of the horses and riders participating in the cavalcade. This ceremony typically takes place at the Cathedral of Ostuni, where clergy members bless the participants, setting a reverent tone for the festivities.

August 26th: Main Procession Day

Morning: Religious Services

Devotees gather at the cathedral for special masses dedicated to Saint Oronzo, reflecting the deep spiritual significance of the festival.

Afternoon: Cavalcade Procession

The highlight of the festival features riders adorned in traditional red and gold costumes, escorting the silver statue of Saint Oronzo through the historic streets of Ostuni. The procession weaves through the town, allowing spectators to witness the rich pageantry and devotion.

August 27th: Closing Day

Evening

The last day often includes musical performances, local food stalls, and communal gatherings in the town's main squares, fostering a sense of community and celebration.

Fireworks Display

The festival traditionally concludes with a vibrant fireworks show, illuminating the night sky over Ostuni and symbolizing the town's enduring gratitude to its patron saint.

Ostuni Walking Tour

#1. Porta San Demetrio

This 15th-century portal, carved from ancient limestone, stands as one of the last sentinels of Ostuni's once-mighty walls. Its weathered facade bears silent witness to centuries of travelers, merchants, and pilgrims who passed beneath its protective gaze.

#2. Piazza della Libertà

The Colonna di Sant'Oronzo, this magnificent Baroque column, soaring skyward, commemorates the saint who saved the city from plague's dark grip. The transformed Palazzo San Francesco, once home to contemplative Franciscan monks, now hums with civic activity, while cafés spill onto the square, offering sweet espresso and sweeter views of the rolling Pugliese countryside.

#4. Concattedrale Santa Maria Assunta

Perched at the city's summit like a jeweled crown, Ostuni Cathedral dominates the skyline with its mix of Gothic and Romanesque architecture. The large rose window, featuring 24 finely carved rays, dates back to the Aragonese period. Inside, the Baroque-style decor includes gilded stucco, 18th-century frescoes, and a coffered wooden ceiling, adding to the cathedral's historic and artistic significance.

Cathedral of Santa Maria Assunta

#5. Perimeter of the City Walls

Consider a walk along the outer perimeter, particularly near Piazza della Libertà and the Cathedral, where the walls are best preserved.

Perimeter of the Ostuni Fortifications

Ostuni Festivals and Sagre Throughout the Year

Festa di San Biagio

February 3rd

Saint Blaise (San Biagio) is venerated in Ostuni with a religious celebration dedicated to his role as a protector of the throat and healer of ailments. The festival includes a special blessing of the throat, where priests touch the throats of the faithful with crossed candles. The event takes place at the ancient Chiesa di San Biagio, located in the countryside outside Ostuni, where a pilgrimage is held in his honor.

Feast of the Madonna della Nova

Sunday after Easter.

This religious feast is dedicated to the Madonna della Nova, an important Marian figure in Ostuni's history. Locals make a pilgrimage to the sanctuary just outside the town, taking part in a mass and procession in her honor. The event maintains a centuries-old tradition of devotion and communal gathering, reinforcing Ostuni's strong religious heritage.

La Sagra degli Altri Tempi (The Festival of Old Times)

August 15th

Held on Ferragosto, this festival transforms the historic center into a living museum, showcasing ancient traditions, costumes, and artisanal craftsmanship. Locals prepare traditional dishes, and visitors can watch artisans at work, recreating the daily life of Ostuni's past. This sagra is a celebration of history and culinary heritage, making it a favorite among both residents and tourists.

La Processione della Grata (The Procession of the Grata)

Second Sunday in August.

This striking candlelit procession is one of Ostuni's most visually stunning religious events. The faithful walk from the Sanctuary della Grata to the city center, carrying candles and illuminating the countryside with their soft glow. Over six thousand people take part, creating a breathtaking spectacle visible from Ostuni's hilltop vantage points.

Festa della Madonna della Nova

Late September.

The Festa della Madonna della Nova is a cherished religious celebration in Ostuni, honoring the Madonna della Nova, also known as the Madonna della Buona Novella. The festivities include solemn processions through the historic streets, accompanied by traditional music and vibrant parades. Local markets and food stalls offer regional delicacies, creating a festive atmosphere that draws both residents and visitors. The event culminates in a spectacular fireworks display, illuminating the "White City" in a celebration of faith and community spirit.

Nearby Sites, Cities, and Towns

Carovigno. 8 kilometers (5 miles) from Ostuni. Carovigno is a small town with a deep history tied to its medieval past and the Knights of Malta. Dominating the historic center is the Dentice di Frasso Castle, a well-preserved fortress that offers panoramic views of the surrounding countryside and coastline. The town's old streets are lined with whitewashed houses, similar to Ostuni, but with a quieter, more local feel.

Carovigno is also known for its devotion to Our Lady of Belvedere, celebrated with a unique procession featuring battitori, or flagellants, in a centuries-old tradition. A visit here isn't complete without exploring the town's excellent olive oil producers, as Carovigno is part of the "Città dell'Olio" network, known for some of Puglia's finest extra virgin olive oil.

Torre Santa Sabina. 14 kilometers (8.7 miles) from Ostuni. Torre Santa Sabina is a picturesque seaside hamlet that takes its name from the 16th-century watchtower built to defend the coast from pirate invasions. Today, it's a beloved summer destination, offering crystal-clear waters, rocky coves, and sandy beaches perfect for a relaxing day by the Adriatic.

The waterfront promenade is lined with seafood restaurants and cafés, making it an ideal spot for a leisurely lunch with sea views. Visitors can also take a walk along the coastline to discover small, hidden inlets, perfect for swimming and sunbathing. It's a glorious spot for those who want a blend of history and beach time in one trip.

Quarto di Monte Beach. 12 kilometers (7.5 miles) east of Ostuni. Quarto di Monte is a serene and lesser-known beach between Torre Canne and Torre Santa Sabina. Unlike the more crowded beaches in the area, Quarto di Monte offers a mix of soft sand and rocky stretches, with shallow, clear waters that are perfect for swimming.

The surrounding landscape features Mediterranean maquis, adding to its wild and untouched appeal. This beach is ideal for those looking to escape the crowds and enjoy a peaceful day by the sea, surrounded by nature. Nearby, you'll find traditional beach clubs offering sunbed rentals and light meals, making it a comfortable spot for visitors seeking both relaxation and amenities.

Logistics

Train: The Ostuni train station is about 2.5 kilometers (1.5 miles) from the historic center. It is on the Lecce–Bari railway line, with regular Trenitalia services connecting it to major cities like Bari, Brindisi, and Lecce. From the station, visitors can take a local bus, taxi, or walk (uphill) to reach the town center.

Bus: Bus services to Ostuni are offered by several regional companies, including STP Brindisi, which connects Ostuni to Brindisi, Lecce, and other towns in Puglia. There are also seasonal bus routes catering to tourists, linking Ostuni with nearby beaches and towns during the summer months.

Car: To arrive in Ostuni from Bari (85 kilometers / 53 miles), take the SS16 (E55) highway south towards Brindisi, then exit at Ostuni/Pilone and follow the SP21 road inland to the town. From Brindisi (35 kilometers / 22 miles), follow the SS379 (E55) north and take the same exit. The final stretch into Ostuni is winding and uphill, offering scenic views of the "White City."

Parking: In Ostuni, the best parking options to avoid the ZTL (Limited Traffic Zone) are Parcheggio Via Specchia (near the historic center), Parcheggio Ostuni Foro Boario, and Parcheggio Ostuni Santa Maria delle Grazie. These parking areas are paid lots, but they offer easy access to the town center, with shuttle buses or a short walk leading to the historic district.

Restaurant Recommendations

Osteria Pizzeria Sant'Oronzo. Address: Via□Alfonso□Giovine□21

When we visited with friends, the pizza was nothing short of amazing. The crust struck the perfect balance of crisp and chewy, topped with the freshest ingredients. Alongside the pizza, the restaurant serves authentic southern Italian dishes, highlighted by fresh seafood preparations, and pours local wine in a convivial atmosphere that feels both informal and inviting.

Osteria del Tempo Perso. Address: Via Gaetano Tanzarella Vitale, 47

In a charming 16th-century cave-like setting, Osteria del Tempo Perso is one of Ostuni's most renowned restaurants. It offers an authentic Apulian dining experience, featuring dishes like orecchiette with turnip greens, slow-cooked lamb, and fresh burrata. The atmosphere is cozy and intimate, with stone walls and vaulted ceilings adding to the old-world charm. Reservations are recommended, especially in high season.

Ristorante Taverna della Gelosia. Address: Vicolo Tommaso Andriola, 26

Nestled in a quiet corner of Ostuni's old town, Taverna della Gelosia offers an enchanting outdoor terrace surrounded by lush greenery, perfect for a romantic meal. The menu highlights seasonal and locally sourced ingredients, with specialties such as homemade pasta, seafood risotto, and grilled meats. The wine list focuses on Puglian wines, making it a great place to savor the region's flavors.

Cielo – Relais La Sommità. Address: Via Scipione Petrarolo, 7

For a fine dining experience in Ostuni, Cielo is the Michelin-starred restaurant of Relais La Sommità, housed in a historic palazzo. The restaurant blends modern creativity with traditional Apulian flavors, offering dishes such as cuttlefish ink pasta, Adriatic fish carpaccio, and suckling pig with local herbs. The elegant courtyard setting, paired with impeccable service, makes it ideal for a special occasion or an unforgettable culinary experience.

Accommodation

For the Calvacade of Sant'Oronzo, I recommend three nights in town.

Hotel Relais La Sommita. Address: Via Scipione Petrarolo, 7

A luxurious 5-star hotel housed in a 16th-century historic residence, offering elegant rooms, a tranquil spa, and a gourmet restaurant. Guests can enjoy panoramic views of Ostuni and the Adriatic Sea from its prime location atop the White City.

Hotel La Terra. Address: Via Gaspare Petrarolo, 20

In a restored 13th-century building, this charming hotel combines historic architecture with modern comforts. It provides easy access to local attractions and offers cozy rooms along with a restaurant serving traditional Apulian cuisine.

CHAPTER TWENTY-TWO

Uggiano la Chiesa & the Art of the Frisella

Timeless Baking Traditions

S agra della Frisella

Where: Uggiano la Chiesa

When: Last Sunday in August or First Sunday in September.

Average Festival Temperatures: High 31°C (88°F). Low 20°C (68°F).

Uggiano la Chiesa: A Town of Ancient Roots and Monastic Traditions

Uggiano la Chiesa, nestled in southern Puglia's sun-drenched landscape, captivates with its timeless charm and rich culinary heritage. This enchanting town of 4,000 residents seamlessly blends history with vibrant local life, evident in its Baroque churches, whitewashed streets, and bustling piazzas.

Long before its medieval monastic heritage shaped its identity, Uggiano la Chiesa was part of the greater network of settlements that thrived under the influence of the Roman Empire. The area's proximity to Porto Badisco, a small natural harbor just a few kilometers away, suggests early strategic importance some believe this is the very landing site of Aeneas, the legendary Trojan hero, as described in Virgil's *Aeneid*.

Medieval Monastic Origins and the Meaning of 'La Chiesa' (The Church)

The name "Uggiano la Chiesa" directly reflects its medieval religious heritage, stemming from the presence of an important Basilian monastic settlement. In the early Middle Ages, following the decline of the Western Roman Empire, Puglia experienced waves of influence from Byzantine Greeks. Many Basilian monks, fleeing persecution in the East, arrived in southern Italy and established monasteries and rock-hewn churches in remote areas, including the lands surrounding Uggiano.

The Monestary played a pivotal role in the area's cultural and agricultural development. These monks not only preserved religious traditions but also introduced innovative farming techniques, including the cultivation of olive groves and cereals, which remain central to the town's economy today. The legacy of these monastic communities endures in the name "la Chiesa", marking Uggiano as a historic center of religious life.

Medieval Growth and Strategic Importance

During the Norman and Swabian periods (11th–13th centuries), Uggiano la Chiesa flourished as a small but strategically positioned town. With the consolidation of Norman rule over southern Italy, Lecce became a vital administrative center, and towns like Uggiano were fortified or incorporated into local fiefdoms.

The town's churches, some dating back to this era, showcase elements of Romanesque and early Baroque architecture, blending influences from Norman, Byzantine, and local Apulian styles.

As the Middle Ages progressed, Uggiano's fertile lands and proximity to the Adriatic made it an essential agricultural hub supplying grain and olive oil to the broader region. By the Renaissance and Baroque periods, the town's identity was further shaped by its rural economy and deep-rooted culinary traditions, including the enduring production of friselle, the twice-baked bread that remains a symbol of local heritage.

The Sagra della Frisella

The frisella (frisa or friseddha in dialect) exemplifies cucina povera, the art of creating extraordinary flavors from simple ingredients. This twice-baked durum wheat or barley bread ring transforms from stone-hard to sublime with a splash of water. Crowned with extra virgin olive oil, sea salt, sun-ripened tomatoes, and aromatics like garlic, capers, and oregano, it embodies centuries of Pugliese wisdom.

Friselle Ready for the Oven

Born as sustenance for sailors and farmers who needed preserved food, the frisella has evolved into a cherished culinary tradition.

Uggiano la Chiesa's reputation for exceptional friselle stems from its perfect storm of advantages: premium durum wheat fields, prized olive groves, and generations of master bakers preserving time-honored techniques. Here, each family's frisella recipe carries stories of summer evenings spent sharing wine and conversation.

What began as an intimate celebration has blossomed into a full-scale showcase of Apulian culture. Today's Sagra features local bakers demonstrating traditional methods alongside innovative preparations. Under star-filled skies, visitors discover both classic combinations and creative interpretations featuring burrata, seafood, or even sweet variations with honey and ricotta.

Festival Events (Both Sundays)

7:00 p.m.

Opening Ceremony: The festival starts in the early evening with speeches by local dignitaries and organizers.

Food Stalls and Tastings: Numerous stalls offer freshly prepared friselle with various toppings, operating throughout the evening.

Live Music and Performances: Local musicians and folk groups perform traditional Puglian music, including the energetic pizzica dance.

Throughout the Festival: Cultural Exhibitions: Exhibitions showcasing local crafts, historical artifacts, or art displays.

Cooking Demonstrations: Live demonstrations by local chefs or artisans showcasing traditional preparation methods.

Family-friendly activities: Workshops or games for younger attendees.

Uggiano la Chiesa Walking Tour

#1. Chiesa di Santa Maria Maddalena (Church of Saint Mary Magdalene)

Begin your journey at this magnificent Baroque church, the spiritual heart of Uggiano la Chiesa. Completed in 1775, the church showcases the elegant Salentine Baroque style with its ornate limestone façade and commanding bell tower. Inside, you'll be struck by the harmonious play of light across cream-colored walls and the detailed frescoes depicting scenes from Mary Magdalene's life. Don't miss the 18th-century organ and the gilded wooden altar, masterpieces of local craftsmanship.

#2. Torre dell'Angelo (Tower of the Angel)

Walking northeast from the church, you'll encounter this medieval watchtower, a testament to the town's strategic importance. Dating back to the 16th century, the tower stands as one of the best-preserved examples of coastal defense architecture in Salento. Its distinctive octagonal design and arrow slits offer insights into historical military engineering. From its position, guards could spot approaching pirates and signal to neighboring towns using smoke signals during day and fire at night.

#3. Cripta Bizantina di Sant'Angelo (Byzantine Crypt of Sant'Angelo)

Step back in time as you descend into this mystical Byzantine crypt, tucked away just beyond the town's bustling center. Hewn from living rock, this underground sanctuary still bears the ghostly traces of centuries-old frescoes on its walls. As you move through the cool, hushed space, you'll find yourself transported to an era when early Christians gathered in secret to worship, their faith preserved in every chisel mark and painted figure.

#4. Frantoio Ipogeo Mulino a Vento (Underground Oil Mill)

Cap off your journey with an extraordinary glimpse into Puglia's "green gold" heritage at this remarkable underground oil mill. Carved deep beneath the streets, this architectural marvel tells the story of generations of olive oil artisans who once worked in these chambered depths. On guided tours, you'll discover how the massive millstones once turned, crushing olives into liquid gold, while learning fascinating details about how this ancient industry shaped both the economy and daily life of countless families throughout the centuries.

Uggiano la Chiesa Festivals and Sagre Throughout the Year

Tavole di San Giuseppe (Tables of Saint Joseph)

March 18–19

Uggiano's homes and squares become a vibrant display of faith and food during this significant celebration. Following centuries-old traditions, thirteen tables are meticulously prepared to represent the Holy Family and saints. Each table becomes an artistic display of traditional Salentine cuisine, laden with symbolic foods and decorated with intricate bread sculptures called "cuccìa."

The centerpiece of the feast is "lu cranu stumpatu", a hearty dish of wheat berries slow-cooked with bay leaves and wild fennel, symbolizing abundance and renewal. Alongside it, you'll find "pasta culli ciciri" (handmade pasta with chickpeas) seasoned with local olive oil and wild herbs. The vermiceddhri, thin hand-rolled pasta strands resembling little worms, are served in a rich chickpea sauce fragrant with bay leaves and crushed red pepper.

Local families spend days preparing these tables, with recipes passed down through generations. Visitors are welcomed as honored guests, participating in the ritual of the "visit to the tables" where three children, representing Jesus, Mary, and Joseph, are served first. The air fills with the aroma of fresh herbs, warm bread, and the murmur of ancient prayers.

Festa Patronale di Santa Maria Maddalena (Patronal Feast of Saint Mary Magdalene)

July 21–23

This three-day celebration marks the high point of Uggiano's cultural calendar, transforming the town into a tapestry of light, sound, and devotion. The festivities begin at dawn on July 21st with the "Diana," when the local band marches through torch-lit streets, awakening the town with traditional marches.

The religious heart of the festival is the solemn procession on July 22nd, where the statue of Mary Magdalene, adorned with precious ex-votos, is carried through flower-strewn streets. Local women dress in traditional costume, carrying candles and singing ancient hymns passed down through generations.

The evenings culminate in spectacular fireworks displays, where modern pyrotechnics dance above baroque architecture, creating a magical fusion of past and present. The festival closes with the traditional "Processione della Cera," where faithful carry elaborate wax offerings to the church.

Festa Patronale di San Gaetano (Patronal Feast of Saint Cajetan)

August 6–7

In the cool evening air, the town's historic center transforms into an open-air festival, with strings of luminarie (traditional Pugliese light displays) creating ethereal archways above the ancient streets. Local musicians perform traditional Salentine folk music, while the aroma of street food fills the air - from freshly grilled bombette (meat rolls filled with cheese and herbs) to cartellate (honey-soaked pastries) made by local grandmothers.

The highlight is the evening procession, where the statue is carried through narrow streets lined with baroque balconies. Devotees follow with candles, their voices rising in traditional hymns that echo off the limestone walls. The celebration concludes with a spectacular fireworks display over the Chiesa Madre, accompanied by the town band playing time-honored marches.

Sagra dei Santi Medici (Festival of the Holy Doctors)

September 26-27

This autumn festival honors Saints Cosmas and Damian, the patron saints of physicians, with a unique celebration that blends spiritual devotion with traditional healing practices. The festival's timing coincides with the harvest of medicinal herbs in the Salento region, connecting ancient folk medicine with religious tradition.

The celebration begins with the blessing of healing herbs and traditional remedies in the church square. As evening falls, the festivities take on a more celebratory tone with traditional tarantella and pizzica performances, dances historically associated with healing, while street performers recreate medieval healing practices throughout the town. Theatrical representations of the saints' lives unfold as performers bring their stories to life, and the night culminates in a candlelit procession winding through the historic center.

Day Trips: Nearby Sites, Cities, and Towns

Giurdignano. 5 kilometers (3 miles) northwest of Uggiano la Chiesa. Giurdignano is renowned for its remarkable concentration of megalithic structures, ancient stone monuments such as dolmens and menhirs built during the prehistoric era, earning it the title "Megalithic Garden of Italy." Beyond its prehistoric heritage, Giurdignano boasts the Crypt of San Salvatore, an underground Byzantine church from the 8th to 10th centuries, carved entirely out of rock. Inside, visitors can admire well-preserved frescoes that provide insight into early Christian worship in the region.

Punta Palascìa Lighthouse. 15 kilometers (9 miles) east of Uggiano la Chiesa. At Capo d'Otranto, the easternmost point of Italy, the Punta Palascìa Lighthouse stands as a sentinel where the Adriatic and Ionian seas converge. Built in 1867, this 32-meter (105-foot) white stone tower has guided mariners for over a century. After a period of deactivation in the 1970s, it was restored and reopened in 2008.

Santa Cesarea Terme. 12 kilometers (7.5 miles) south of Uggiano la Chiesa. Perched along the Adriatic coast, Santa Cesarea Terme is celebrated for its therapeutic thermal springs and distinctive Moorish architecture. Since Roman times, visitors have sought the healing properties of its sulfur-rich waters, which are believed to benefit various ailments. The town's elegant villas, such as Villa Sticchi, showcase intricate designs that reflect a blend of cultural influences.

Logistics

Train: Uggiano la Chiesa does not have its own train station. The nearest major train station is in Lecce, approximately 44 kilometers (27 miles) away. From Lecce, travelers can continue to Uggiano la Chiesa by bus or car.

Bus: Several bus companies operate routes connecting Lecce to Uggiano la Chiesa. Notable services include Bus Line 202.1: Connects Lecce to Uggiano la Chiesa.

Car: From Lecce, take the SS16 highway towards Maglie. Exit onto the SP363 towards Otranto, then follow signs for Uggiano la Chiesa. The journey covers approximately 44 kilometers (27 miles).

Parking: Uggiano la Chiesa offers several public parking areas, especially near the town center and principal attractions. During peak tourist seasons or local festivals, it's advisable to arrive early to secure a spot. Always observe local parking regulations to avoid fines.

Restaurant Recommendations

Lu Passatiempu. Address: Piazza Umberto I, 25

A cozy spot offering a variety of delicious Italian dishes in a welcoming atmosphere. Perfect for a relaxed meal with friends and family.

Il Calzone Salentino. Address: Via Roma 92

Known for its authentic Salento cuisine, this restaurant serves traditional dishes like calzone, orecchiette, and more, made with fresh, local ingredients.

Accommodation

It is unnecessary to stay overnight for a sagra, but if you choose to say in the area, here are some accommodations. Like in many small towns, there are not hotels but these are good options nearby.

Agriturismo Le Tagliate. Address: Via Porto Badisco 135

Set within 2.9 kilometers (one mile) of Porto Badisco Beach, this farm stay offers rooms with air conditioning and private bathrooms. It features a pool with a view, a garden, and barbecue facilities. Guests can enjoy buffet breakfast options with local specialties and fresh pastries.

Agriturismo Agrodolce. Address: Sp358, 125

This charming agriturismo offers a delightful dining experience with a focus on authentic local cuisine. The property includes a restaurant that serves traditional Salento dishes, and guests can enjoy the beautiful countryside surroundings.

Fall Celebrations

September through October

CHAPTER TWENTY-THREE

Barletta's Legendary Duel

The Knightly Challenge and Triumph of 1503

Disfada di Barletta

Where: Barletta

When: 2nd weekend in September (with a secondary festival February 13).

Average Festival Temperatures: High 25°C (77°F). Low 20°C (68°F).

Barletta's: Where Kings and Culture Collide

Picture a place where medieval knights once clashed swords beneath a blazing Mediterranean sun, where ancient stone walls still whisper tales of crusaders and kings, and where the crystalline waters of the Adriatic lap gently against shores that have witnessed over two thousand years of history. This is Barletta, a jewel of Italy's sun-drenched Puglia region, where every cobblestone and corner has a story to tell.

Just 60 kilometers (37 miles) northwest of Bari, Barletta has been a crossroads of civilizations since antiquity. Roman merchants once filled its streets, trading goods that passed through its vital port. The city flourished under the Roman

Empire, its strategic position making it a key hub for commerce and military movements. Today, remnants of this ancient past still linger in its architecture and archaeological sites, where the echoes of togas and chariots can still be imagined.

Barletta's medieval past is written in its fortifications and grand architecture. The Normans arrived and left their mark with imposing castles, like the Castello Svevo di Barletta, which still dominates the cityscape today. Crusader knights passed through its streets on their way to the Holy Land, and Aragonese rulers shaped the city's identity, constructing elegant palaces and churches. The city's long history of resilience against invaders and foreign rule forged a strong local identity that persists to this day.

We visited Barletta for an afternoon and found it to be one of the most enchanting towns in all of Puglia. With a palm tree-lined seaside promenade, easy parking, and remarkably few tourists, the town felt like a delightful secret. The historic center is compact and easy to navigate on foot, making it perfect for a relaxing stroll. We explored the Cathedral of Santa Maria Maggiore, wandered through the halls of the Castello Svevo, enjoyed some gelato, and simply soaked in the charm of the winding streets and local life.

Barletta offers a striking mix of eras: Norman castles stand shoulder to shoulder with elegant Baroque churches, while bustling markets fill ancient squares with the aromas of sun-ripened tomatoes, fresh-caught seafood, and locally pressed olive oil. Along its coast, golden beaches stretch as far as the eye can see, backed by breezy promenades where locals continue the age-old tradition of the evening passeggiata.

This is a town where history isn't just preserved, it's lived, every day, in the rhythm of Barletta's sunlit streets.

The Disfida (Battle): When Honor and Steel Shaped History

It's February 13, 1503. The air crackles with tension as 26 of Europe's finest knights face each other on a field outside Barletta. At stake? Not just their lives, but the very honor of Italy.

The spark that lit this powder keg was a French captain's careless words. Charles de la Motte had publicly mocked Italian courage, claiming French superiority in battle. For the proud Italian knights, led by the charismatic Ettore Fieramosca, this insult demanded satisfaction. Thirteen champions from each nation would meet in combat to settle the matter. When the dust settled that day, the Italian knights stood victorious. What could have been a footnote in history instead became a powerful symbol of Italian pride and prowess that resonates to this day.

Today, Barletta transforms this medieval drama into one of Italy's most spectacular historical festivals. The narrow streets come alive with the pageantry of the 16th century: knights in gleaming armor parade through torch lit squares, while merchants in period costume sell their wares in recreated medieval markets. The air fills with the sound of drummers, the clash of practice swords, and the cheers of spectators.

The festival's culmination is the breathtaking reenactment of the duel itself. Skilled performers, trained in historical combat techniques, bring the famous battle to life with stunning accuracy.

For visitors, the Disfida festival offers a unique window into both Italy's proud past and its vibrant present. Whether you're watching skilled artisans demonstrate medieval crafts, sampling traditional foods prepared according to historical recipes, or cheering on your favorite knight during the grand reenactment, you'll find yourself transported to a time when honor was everything and legends were made with steel.

September Festival Events

Friday

5:30 p.m.

The Disfida in Play: Children's Entertainment

Within the ancient walls of the Castle Gardens Amphitheater, children step back in time as medieval games and storytelling bring the legendary Disfida to life for young imaginations. Here, against the backdrop of centuries-old stone, the next generation discovers the values of chivalry and honor through interactive performances and playful reenactments.

7:00 p.m.

A Night of Medieval Spectacle / The Historic Race

As twilight descends over Barletta, the Historic Challenge Race ignites the cobblestone streets with the spirit of 1503. Beginning on Via Cialdini, participants weave through the medieval heart of the city like threads through time. Their path takes them past the magnificent 12th-century Duomo Cathedral, where Gothic spires pierce the evening sky, and along Via Fieramosca, named for the legendary champion whose courage still echoes through these streets.

9:00 p.m.

The Dream of Ettore

As night embraces Castle Rivellino, "The Dream of Ettore" unfolds in a breathtaking fusion of history and artistry. Dancing fountains and ethereal mist create watery battlefields where ancient conflicts play out anew. Controlled flames leap and dance, their heat bringing to life the passion and fury of medieval combat. Above, aerial performers soar through the castle's ancient spaces, their graceful movements embodying the soaring spirit of victory, while on the ground, masterfully choreographed performers recreate the raw intensity of knight-to-knight combat.

Saturday

5:00 p.m.

Renaissance Games Theater Show

In the golden light of late afternoon, the ancient square in front of the castle transforms into a living Renaissance fairground. Performers recreate the boisterous games and martial spectacles that once delighted both noble and commoner in 1503's Barletta. Watch as skilled artisans demonstrate the deadly grace of swordplay, the thunderous impact of jousting, and the delicate art of court games. Musicians fill the air with period melodies while jugglers and acrobats display the same skills that once entertained dukes and peasants alike.

8:30 p.m.

Renaissance Encampment

As dusk settles over the castle gardens, they spring to life with the sights, sounds, and smells of a 16th-century military encampment. The flicker of torchlight illuminates authentically crafted tents where armored knights polish their weapons and discuss battle strategies. Armorers demonstrate their craft at portable forges, small open-air furnaces used for heating and shaping metal, while servants prepare evening meals over open fires using traditional recipes. Visitors wander through this living tableau, where every detail, from the hand-stitched banners to the carefully recreated camp furniture, transports them back to the eve of the famous challenge.

9:00 p.m.

The Offense

Within the torch-lit walls of Castle Rivellino, tension crackles through the air as actors recreate the pivotal moment that sparked the legendary duel. The dramatic performance captures the raw emotion of the French captain's fateful insult against Italian honor, bringing to life the pride, anger, and determination that would lead to one of history's most famous contests of arms. Each word of the insult rings through the ancient stones, echoing with the same power that stirred Italian hearts over five centuries ago.

9:30 p.m.

The Challenge

In a spectacular procession that begins at the Castle's massive gates, heralds dressed in richly detailed period costumes step forth into the torch-lit night. Their path weaves through Barletta's medieval heart, from the soaring spires of the Cathedral on Via Duomo to the ancient stones of Via Cialdini, finally reaching Piazza Mons. Damato.

At each stop, trumpet calls pierce the evening air before the heralds proclaim the terms of combat in ringing tones, just as their predecessors did in 1503. The crowd follows this mobile drama through streets where every stone and shadow seems to whisper tales of that legendary challenge, creating an immersive experience that dissolves the barriers between past and present.

Sunday

9:00 a.m.–12:45 p.m.

The Story Train

As morning light bathes Barletta's ancient stones, the Story Train beckons visitors on an enchanting journey through time. Every hour, from the ornate steps of Palazzo di Città, expert storytellers lead intimate groups through the city's medieval narrative. The highlight comes at the historic Cantina della Sfida, where visitors can stand in the very space where Italian honor was challenged in 1503, its centuries-old walls still seeming to echo with heated words exchanged between knights.

The journey continues to the majestic 12th-century Cathedral, where soaring Gothic arches frame tales of faith and valor. Each 45-minute tour weaves history and legend into an unforgettable tapestry of Barletta's golden age. This popular experience requires advance booking through +39 0883 331 331, as groups are kept small to ensure an intimate connection with the past.

7:30 p.m.

Investiture and Oath

As evening shadows lengthen across Piazza Marina, an ancient ritual unfolds. In a ceremony that bridges centuries, knights gather to receive their blessed arms and swear solemn oaths of honor. The air grows thick with tradition as each warrior pledges fealty and courage, their words echoing off the weathered stones of the ancient sea walls. The ceremony culminates in a solemn procession from the castle, where torchlight dances off polished armor and the evening breeze carries whispers of ancient vows.

8:00 p.m.

Triumphal Procession

The Grand Procession erupts through Barletta's twilight streets in a kaleidoscope of medieval splendor. Nobles stride forth in sumptuous period costumes, their silk and velvet shimmering in the evening light. Renaissance melodies soar above the crowds as musicians play ancient tunes on period instruments. The air itself seems to dance as flag throwers launch their banners skyward in precisely choreographed displays, creating a ballet of color against the darkening sky.

10:30 p.m.

Festival Finale

The festival reaches its crescendo as the night sky above the castle erupts in a carefully orchestrated symphony of light and sound. Choreographed fireworks paint the darkness in Renaissance colors while period music fills the air, creating a multi-sensory celebration of the Italian victory. The castle's ancient walls serve as both canvas and stage for this spectacular finale, its stones illuminated by cascading lights that seem to bring the very spirit of medieval Barletta to life one final time.

Barletta Walking Tour

#1. Castello Svevo di Barletta (Swabian Castle)

Castello Svevo di Barletta stands as a magnificent fusion of military engineering and royal grandeur, tracing its origins to Norman foundations in the 10th century before reaching its architectural apex under Frederick II's ambitious vision.

Castello Svevo

The castle's imposing limestone walls, punctuated by four commanding cylindrical towers, encompass a grand courtyard where medieval life once flourished. The fortress exhibits distinct architectural periods, from its Norman foundations to Angevin modifications and Aragonese additions, each layer telling its own story. Inside, vaulted halls and intricate stone staircases lead to panoramic ramparts offering sweeping views of the Adriatic.

#2. Cattedrale di Santa Maria Maggiore (St. Mary Major)

Cattedrale di Santa Maria Maggiore emerges as a stunning testament to medieval architectural evolution, where Romanesque solidity meets Gothic aspiration. Its facade harmoniously blends both styles, featuring robust Norman arches supporting delicate Gothic tracery and pointed windows. The cathedral's commanding bell tower rises in diminishing tiers, each level showcasing increasingly elaborate architectural detail.

The interior unfolds in three naves separated by ancient columns, their capitals carved with intricate biblical scenes and fantastic creatures. Beneath the main altar, an atmospheric crypt houses early Christian tombs and precious relics, while the upper walls display remarkably preserved frescoes depicting biblical narratives and saints' lives. The building's most striking feature remains its rose window, a masterpiece of medieval stonework that floods the interior with dappled light, creating an ever-changing play of shadows across the centuries-old stone.

#3. Cantina della Sfida

In this atmospheric cellar, honor and history intersect. Here, amidst stone walls and barrel-vaulted ceilings, thirteen Italian knights accepted the challenge that would become legend. The space preserves the spirit of that fateful 1503 confrontation, with period artifacts and displays, bringing the dramatic story to life.

#4. Colosso di Barletta

Standing 5 meters (16 feet) tall, this mysterious bronze giant has watched over Barletta since the late Roman Empire. Theories about its identity range from Emperor Theodosius to Valentinian I, while tales of its arrival via shipwreck add to its mystique.

Colossus of Barletta

#5. Basilica del Santo Sepolcro (Holy Sepulchre)

This 12th-century sanctuary bridges East and West in stone and spirit. Its Romanesque façade bears subtle touches of Byzantine artistry, while its interior housed countless pilgrims bound for Jerusalem. The basilica's architecture mirrors the Holy Sepulchre in Jerusalem (the location of the tomb of Jesus), creating a symbolic connection to Christianity's holiest sites.

Barletta Festivals and Sagre Throughout the Year

Festa dei Santi Patroni (Feast of the Patron Saints)

July 22

Barletta honors its patron saints, Saint Ruggiero and the Madonna dello Sterpeto, with religious processions, music, and communal festivities. The celebrations include a mix of devotion and entertainment, reflecting the city's deep-rooted traditions.

Piano Festival of Barletta

Late Summer: Dates vary annually

This festival celebrates classical music, featuring performances by renowned pianists in historic venues across Barletta. It aims to promote musical culture and appreciation within the community.

Day Trips: Nearby Sites, Cities, and Towns

Castel del Monte. 50 kilometers (31 miles) southwest of Barletta. This UNESCO World Heritage Site is a 13th-century citadel and castle commissioned by Emperor Frederick II. Notable for its unique octagonal shape and architectural precision, Castel del Monte is considered a masterpiece of medieval military architecture. Its purpose remains a subject of debate among historians, adding an element of mystery to its allure.

Lido di Ponente (Western Beach). 2 kilometers (1.2 miles) west of the city center. Lido di Ponente is the most extensive beach in Barletta, featuring fine, light-colored sand. The area offers many equipped beach resorts that cater to both fun and sports activities, including kite surfing. The promenade is adorned with tall palm trees, creating a picturesque setting.

Bisceglie. 20 kilometers (12 miles) southeast of Barletta. Bisceglie features a charming historic center with narrow streets and historic buildings. The town is known for its beautiful beaches, such as Salsello Beach, which boasts crystal-clear waters and well-equipped facilities.

Logistics

Train: Barletta is well-connected by rail, with the main Barletta Railway Station at Piazza Francesco Conteduca 1. The station serves several lines, including the Adriatic Railway (Ancona–Lecce), the Barletta–Spinazzola railway, and the Bari–Barletta railway operated by Ferrotramviaria.

Bus: Barletta's bus services are operated by companies including FlixBus, Itabus, Sais Autolinee, and Marino Autolinee. The primary bus stop is on Via Andria. Buses connect Barletta to various destinations, offering both regional and long-distance routes.

Car: Traveling by car provides flexibility to explore Barletta and its surroundings. The city is accessible via the A14 motorway (exiting at Andria-Barletta or Canosa) and the SS16 highway. Car rentals are available in Barletta and nearby cities.

Parking: Parking in Barletta can be challenging, especially near popular attractions. It's recommended to use designated parking areas outside the ZTL zones and explore the city center on foot or via public transportation.

Restaurant Recommendations

Antica Cucina 1983. Address: Piazza Marina 4/5

Antica Cucina 1983 offers a modern take on Apulian cuisine, emphasizing fresh, local ingredients. The elegant ambiance and attentive service make it a favorite among both locals and visitors.

Ristorante Al Tettuccio. Address: Via Nazareth 40

In the heart of Barletta's historic center, Ristorante Al Tettuccio boasts medieval-themed architecture, creating a unique dining atmosphere. The menu features creatively prepared dishes, with specialties like their signature pizzas and linguine.

Accommodation

For the Disfada, I would recommend three nights in town.

Nicotel Barletta. Address: Viale Regina Elena

Along the seafront, Nicotel Barletta, a 4-star hotel, provides guests with scenic views of the Adriatic Sea. The hotel offers well-appointed rooms, a bar, and easy access to nearby beaches, making it an ideal choice for those looking to enjoy the coastal charm of Barletta.

Hotel La Terrazza. Address: Via Trani 57

3-star Hotel La Terrazza is located close to the beach and offers a range of amenities, including an outdoor pool, restaurant, and private parking. Guests appreciate its proximity to both the sea and the historic center, providing a balanced experience of relaxation and cultural exploration.

CHAPTER TWENTY-FOUR

Faith and Miracles in San Giovanni Rotondo

Honoring Padre Pio

Festa di San Pio da Pietrelcina

Where: San Giovanni Rotondo

When: September 23

Average Festival Temperatures: High 26°C (79°F). Low 13°C (55°F).

San Giovanni Rotondo

San Giovanni Rotondo sits on a limestone plateau in the Gargano mountains of Puglia, southern Italy. The town overlooks the broad plains of the Tavoliere delle Puglie, with the Adriatic Sea visible in the distance. This strategic position at roughly 565 meters (1855 feet) above sea level has influenced its development throughout history.

The area around modern San Giovanni Rotondo was sparsely populated during Roman times, primarily serving as a rest stop along the route between the important ports of Siponto and Larino. Archaeological findings suggest small settlements existed here, with evidence of a temple dedicated to Janus, the Roman god of transitions and doorways.

The town proper was founded in the 11th century around a rotunda-shaped church dedicated to Saint John the Baptist, from which the town derives its name ("rotondo" meaning "round" in Italian). During this period, the settlement grew as a stop for pilgrims traveling to Monte Sant'Angelo and the Holy Land. The town's defensive walls and castle were constructed during this time to protect against Saracen raids.

During the Renaissance, San Giovanni Rotondo experienced modest growth as part of the Kingdom of Naples. The town suffered significantly during the earthquake of 1646, which destroyed many medieval structures. However, this led to a period of rebuilding and expansion, including the construction of new churches and noble palaces that still stand today.

Today, San Giovanni Rotondo has a population of 27,000 residents. The town's economy is primarily driven by religious tourism, with millions of visitors coming annually to visit the shrine of Padre Pio and the modern church designed by architect Renzo Piano.

Feast of St. Pio

San Giovanni Rotondo is deeply connected to San Pio da Pietrelcina, commonly known as Padre Pio, a Capuchin friar whose presence transformed this small Apulian town into a major pilgrimage site. The town celebrates the Festa di San Pio da Pietrelcina to honor his life, miracles, and enduring spiritual legacy.

Before Padre Pio's arrival in 1916, San Giovanni Rotondo was a modest rural town in the Gargano region of Puglia. It was his presence, teachings, and reported miraculous healings that turned it into an international religious center. Padre Pio spent more than 50 years in the town, first as a humble friar and later as a beloved spiritual guide, drawing thousands of devotees. His stigmata, which he bore for half a century, his ability to read souls, and his unwavering commitment to prayer and the sacraments led to his veneration even before his canonization.

The Festa di San Pio is a time for both spiritual reflection and public celebration, commemorating his life and works. It marks his passing on September 23, 1968, a date that continues to draw pilgrims from across the world. His presence in San Giovanni Rotondo shaped its modern identity, leading to the construction of important religious sites, including the Sanctuary of Saint Pio and the Casa Sollievo della Sofferenza, the hospital he founded as an act of faith and charity.

Who is San Pio?

Born Francesco Forgione in Pietrelcina (Campania) in 1887, Padre Pio entered the Capuchin Order at a young age, dedicating his life to prayer and service. He became known for his deep spirituality, mystical experiences, and extraordinary gifts, including the stigmata, wounds similar to those of Christ's crucifixion. Despite skepticism and investigations by the Church, his reputation as a healer and confessor spread widely. He spent countless hours in the confessional, guiding thousands of people in their faith.

Padre Pio, a modern saint.

Padre Pio's mission extended beyond spiritual healing. He envisioned and helped build the Casa Sollievo della Sofferenza, now one of the most advanced hospitals in Southern Italy. His teachings emphasized prayer, humility, suffering, and love for Christ, attracting a global following. In 2002, Pope John Paul II canonized him, cementing his status as one of the most venerated modern saints.

San Giovanni Rotondo remains the heart of Padre Pio's legacy, making the Festa di San Pio da Pietrelcina one of the town's most significant religious events.

Festival Events

Novena (September 14–22)

A nine-day period of spiritual preparation, including daily recitations of the Rosary and special Masses held in the Church of San Pio da Pietrelcina. Each day focuses on different themes related to Padre Pio's life and teachings.

Vigil (Evening of September 22)

On the evening before the feast day, a vigil is conducted, beginning with a welcoming ceremony on the church's forecourt. The vigil includes the celebration of Vespers (evening prayers), Eucharistic Adoration, and other devotions. The vigil also often features readings, hymns, and moments of silent prayer, creating a contemplative atmosphere.

A candlelight procession takes place, creating a powerful and emotional atmosphere.

Feast Day (September 23)

The main day of the celebration, the Feast Day, starts with a solemn Mass in honor of Saint Pio. The Mass is held in the Church of San Pio da Pietrelcina and is attended by a large number of pilgrims.

Procession

Following the Mass, there are processions through the streets of San Giovanni Rotondo, where a statue of Padre Pio is carried by the faithful. These processions are accompanied by music, prayers, and hymns, creating a vibrant and spiritual atmosphere.

During the celebration, devotees have the opportunity to venerate relics of Padre Pio, such as his gloves, habit, and other personal items. This act of veneration allows the faithful to feel a closer connection to the saint and seek his intercession.

Fireworks and Cultural Events

Although the event is primarily religious, in the evening, fireworks and local celebrations take place, lighting up the sky over San Giovanni Rotondo.

Some years include concerts or theatrical performances dedicated to Padre Pio's life.

The festival is an intensely spiritual experience, combining deep religious devotion with a celebration of Padre Pio's faith, miracles, and mission of healing.

San Giovanni Rotondo Walking Tour

#1. Chiesa di Santa Maria delle Grazie (Church of St. Mary of Grace)

This historic church was Padre Pio's spiritual home from 1916 until his death in 1968. Originally a 16th-century Franciscan chapel, it was expanded in the 1950s to accommodate the growing number of pilgrims.

Church of Santa Maria delle Grazie

Here, Padre Pio celebrated Mass, heard confessions, and received the stigmata in 1918. Inside, visitors can see the wooden confessional where he spent hours listening to penitents and the old choir loft where he had mystical experiences.

#2. Padre Pio's Cell and Convent of the Capuchins

Connected to Santa Maria delle Grazie, this humble convent was where Padre Pio lived for over 50 years. His monastic cell (Cell No. 5), preserved as it was on the day of his death, contains his simple bed, desk, and religious artifacts. The convent also houses a small museum with his robes, gloves used to cover his stigmata, and personal items.

Cell of Padre Pio

#3. Basilica di San Pio (Church of Saint Pio of Pietrelcina)

This modern basilica, designed by Renzo Piano, was inaugurated in 2004 to accommodate the growing number of pilgrims. It is one of the largest churches in Italy, with a striking contemporary design featuring curved stone arches and vast open spaces. Padre Pio's tomb and incorrupt body rest in the lower crypt, where pilgrims can pay their respects in a quiet and solemn atmosphere. The church's mosaics and artworks depict key moments of Padre Pio's life.

#4. Via Crucis Monumentale (Way of the Cross)

This scenic path winds up Monte Castellano and features life-sized bronze statues depicting the Stations of the Cross. The Via Crucis was designed to reflect Padre Pio's deep devotion to Christ's Passion. It offers a place for prayer and reflection, as well as panoramic views over San Giovanni Rotondo and the Gargano region.

#5. Casa Sollievo della Sofferenza (House for the Relief of Suffering)

Founded by Padre Pio in 1956, this hospital was his greatest charitable work, envisioned as a place where both medical treatment and spiritual care would be provided to the sick. Today, it is one of the most advanced hospitals in Southern Italy, offering cutting-edge medical research and treatments. Visitors can see a small museum dedicated to its foundation, as well as a chapel for patients and families.

#6. Piazza Europa and Padre Pio Monument

At the heart of San Giovanni Rotondo, Piazza Europa is a gathering place for visitors and locals alike. The square features a bronze statue of Padre Pio, where pilgrims often stop to pray or take photos. The surrounding streets have cafés, souvenir shops, and bookstores dedicated to the saint.

San Giovanni Rotondo Festivals and Sagre Throughout the Year

Festa di San Giuseppe (Feast of Saint Joseph)

March 19

Celebrated with traditional bonfires known as "fanoje," this festival honors Saint Joseph, reflecting the town's deep-rooted religious traditions.

Holy Week Observances

Varies

The week leading up to Easter features solemn processions and rituals, including the "Ufficio delle tenebre" on Holy Thursday and the procession of the Madonna dei Sette Dolori and the Cristo Morto on Good Friday.

Festa di San Giovanni Battista (Feast of Saint John the Baptist)

June 23–25

Honoring the town's patron saint, this festival includes religious processions, a traditional fair, amusement rides, concerts, and various cultural events.

Vestizione delle Madonne (Vestition of the Madonnas)

August 15

A unique tradition during which precious images of the Madonna dei Sette Veli are adorned and displayed for veneration, reflecting the community's deep Marian devotion.

Feast of Santa Maria delle Grazie

September 8–10

Centered around the venerated image of the Madonna delle Grazie, this festival features processions, a fair, amusement rides, and concludes with a concert on the evening of September 10.

Day Trips: Nearby Sites, Cities, and Towns

Villa Rosa. 10 kilometers (6 miles) southeast of San Giovanni Rotondo. Villa Rosa is a peaceful rural area located in the rolling hills surrounding San Giovanni Rotondo. While it is not widely known as a major tourist destination, it provides a glimpse into the agricultural traditions and pastoral beauty of the Gargano region. The area is dotted with small farms, vineyards, and olive groves, making it a pleasant stop for those seeking a tranquil escape from the bustling pilgrimage town.

Visitors can explore local agriturismi, where they can taste authentic Puglian cuisine and regional products such as fresh cheese, homemade pasta, and olive oil. The scenic landscapes also make Villa Rosa an excellent place for a leisurely walk or a countryside picnic.

Sanctuary of Santa Maria delle Grazie. 2 kilometers (1.2 miles) southwest of San Giovanni Rotondo. The Sanctuary of Santa Maria delle Grazie is an important religious site closely tied to Padre Pio, one of the most venerated saints of modern Catholicism. Built in 1959 to accommodate the growing number of pilgrims visiting San Giovanni Rotondo, the sanctuary was constructed next to the older Church of Santa Maria delle Grazie, where Padre Pio lived and celebrated Mass for many years.

Inside, visitors can see the small choir loft where Padre Pio often prayed, along with a preserved confessional box where he heard the confessions of thousands of pilgrims. The sanctuary's modern architecture contrasts with the historic church, but both are essential stops for those interested in the life and legacy of Padre Pio.

A visit here is deeply moving, as the location played a central role in the saint's spiritual mission.

Siponto. 25 kilometers (15.5 miles) southwest of San Giovanni Rotondo. Siponto, an ancient Roman port and early Christian settlement, is now a quiet coastal area near Manfredonia. Once a thriving city in antiquity, it was later abandoned due to earthquakes and pirate raids. Today, it is best known for the Basilica of Santa Maria Maggiore di Siponto, a magnificent Romanesque church built in the 11th century.

One of the most intriguing aspects of Siponto is the modern wire mesh installation by artist Edoardo Tresoldi, which recreates the lost early Christian basilica that once stood here. This ethereal structure, made entirely of metallic mesh, gives visitors a ghostly vision of the ancient church, seamlessly blending history with contemporary art.

Logistics

Train: The closest train station to San Giovanni Rotondo is Foggia Railway Station, approximately 40 kilometers (25 miles) southwest of the town. Foggia is a major transportation hub in Puglia, with frequent train services connecting it to Rome, Naples, and Bari. From Foggia, travelers can reach San Giovanni Rotondo by bus or taxi, as there is no direct train to the town.

Bus: Several bus companies operate routes to San Giovanni Rotondo from various cities in Italy. Ferrovie del Gargano offers regular bus connections from Foggia, Bari, and other towns in Puglia. Marino Bus and FlixBus also provide long-distance services from major cities like Rome, Naples, and Milan. The bus terminal in San Giovanni Rotondo is conveniently located near the town center and the Sanctuary of Padre Pio, making it an easy option for visitors.

Car: If driving from Foggia, take SS89 towards Manfredonia and follow the signs for San Giovanni Rotondo. The journey is approximately 40 kilometers (25 miles) and takes around 40–50 minutes, depending on traffic. The route winds through the scenic landscapes of the Gargano region, offering beautiful views of the surrounding hills and countryside.

Parking: San Giovanni Rotondo has several parking options, especially near the Sanctuary of Padre Pio, which attracts thousands of pilgrims each year. There are free and paid parking lots close to the sanctuary, with designated spaces for buses and private vehicles. During peak pilgrimage seasons, parking near the sanctuary can fill up quickly, so arriving early or using shuttle services from larger parking areas is recommended. There are also underground parking facilities for those looking for secure parking options.

Restaurant Recommendations

Trattoria Chiazza Ranna. Address: Via Pirgiano, 78

This cozy trattoria offers an authentic taste of Puglian cuisine in a warm, family-run setting. Known for its generous antipasti and traditional pasta dishes, Trattoria Chiazza Ranna provides a genuine local dining experience.

Fil & Max Ristorante. Address: Via Vaglio Fortuna, 10

Fil & Max Ristorante is celebrated for its diverse menu and friendly atmosphere. The restaurant offers a range of Italian and Mediterranean dishes, with an emphasis on fresh, local ingredients.

Osteria Antica Piazzetta. Address: Viale Aldo Moro, 161

In the heart of the town, Osteria Antica Piazzetta specializes in seafood and traditional Italian fare. The restaurant is noted for its inviting ambiance and attentive staff, making it a popular choice for both locals and visitors seeking a memorable dining experience.

Accommodation

For the festival, I recommend two to three nights in town.

Hotel Vittoria. Address: Via Santa Vittoria, 4

Opened in 2010, Hotel Vittoria is centrally located, less than a 5-minute walk from the Sanctuary of Padre Pio. The hotel offers modern, air-conditioned rooms and a buffet breakfast.

Hotel Valle Rossa. Address: Via San Filippo Neri, 28

Situated in the city center, Hotel Valle Rossa is a 20-minute walk from the Padre Pio Shrine. The hotel provides free parking, a restaurant, and air-conditioned rooms.

Hotel Fini. Address: Viale Cappuccini, 108

Located near the center of San Giovanni Rotondo, Hotel Fini offers a restaurant, bar, and air-conditioned rooms. The hotel is known for its excellent service, with amenities such as room service, breakfast, and pet-friendly accommodations. Its proximity to the city center makes it a convenient choice for travelers.

CHAPTER TWENTY-FIVE

Alberobello's Pillars of Faith

From Medicine to Martyrdom

Festa di San Cosma e Damiano

Where: Alberobello

When: September 25-28

Average Festival Temperatures: High 13°C (55°F). Low 5°C (41°F).

Festival Website:

https://www.comune.alberobello.ba.it/novita/le-celebrazioni-dei-santi-me dici/

Alberobello: A Fairytale Town in the Heart of Puglia

Step into Alberobello, and you might think you've wandered onto a storybook page. Rising from the sun-drenched hills of Puglia, thousands of cone-topped trulli houses dot the landscape like a village built by mythical creatures. These enchanting structures, with their whitewashed walls and mysterious symbols painted on their pointed roofs, have earned this magical town its coveted place as a UNESCO World Heritage Site.

Trulli of Alberobello

But behind this fairytale facade lies a fascinating tale of human ingenuity and rebellion. In the 14th century, when the crafty Counts of Conversano received these lands from the King of Naples, they devised a brilliant scheme to dodge royal taxes. Their solution? Order the locals to build homes that could vanish overnight. Using nothing but limestone slabs stacked without mortar, residents created the first trulli, ingenious structures that could be dismantled at a moment's notice when tax inspectors came knocking.

What began as an act of clever defiance developed into an architectural art form. The people of Alberobello perfected their stone-stacking skills across generations, transforming these "temporary" dwellings into sturdy homes that have stood for centuries. By the 1700s, the town was flourishing, though still under the heavy thumb of feudal rule. In 1797, after years of secret meetings and bold petitions, the citizens finally won their freedom when King Ferdinand IV declared Alberobello a royal town.

Today, nestled in the heart of Puglia's Itria Valley at 420 meters (1380 feet) above sea level, Alberobello stands as a living museum. While its 10,500 residents go about their daily lives, the town's narrow streets buzz with visitors from around the world, all drawn to its otherworldly charm. Between the trulli, you'll find locals tending to ancient olive groves or crafting wine from generations-old vineyards, keeping alive the authentic spirit of this remarkable corner of Italy.

The Feast of Cosmas and Damian

Each September, the ancient trulli of Alberobello become beacons of faith as the Festival of Saints Cosmas and Damian transforms this village into a living testament of devotion. Since the 17th century, when the Counts of Conversano built the first humble chapel to these healing saints, this celebration has grown from a simple act of worship into one of Puglia's most captivating spiritual gatherings.

Who Are Saints Cosmas and Damian?

Saints Cosmas and Damian were twin brothers born in Cilicia (modern-day Turkey) in the 3rd century AD. They were early Christian martyrs who became renowned for their skill as physicians. Known as the "Unmercenaries" (Anargyroi in Greek), they provided medical care without charging fees, offering their services freely to the poor as an expression of their Christian faith.

Their reputation as healers spread far and wide, and they became symbols of both physical and spiritual healing. They were arrested and executed during the persecution of Christians under the Roman Emperor Diocletian, but their legacy as saints of compassion and selflessness endured. Their feast day, September 27, is celebrated in many parts of Italy and the world, especially in communities with agricultural or medical traditions.

The centerpiece of the festival is the solemn procession on September 27, during which the statues of Saints Cosmas and Damian are carried through the streets of Alberobello. Pilgrims often walk barefoot as an act of devotion, and the procession is accompanied by prayers, hymns, and a sense of spiritual reverence. Many devotees arrive on foot from neighboring towns and villages, continuing a centuries-old tradition of honoring the saints with a journey of faith. Today, the festival also includes concerts, street performances, fireworks, and a vibrant market offering local foods, crafts, and souvenirs.

Festival Events

September 25th: Opening of the Celebrations

Morning: Cattle Fair

As dawn breaks over Alberobello's iconic trulli, the ancient tradition of the Cattle Fair springs to life, a custom that has echoed through these streets for centuries.

The Cattle Fair: A historical element of the festival, the Fiera del Bestiame (Cattle Fair), was established in the early 19th century by King Ferdinand I of Bourbon. This event was both a practical market for livestock and an integral part of the celebration, reflecting Alberobello's agricultural heritage. The grand Martellotta street, now the town's elegant "parlor," transforms as it recalls the days when hundreds of cattle and their handlers would converge here from every corner of Puglia and beyond. Though the fair has evolved from its agricultural roots, it still pulses with the same spirit of community and commerce that has drawn people to the foot of Alberobello's monumental area for over two centuries.

September 26th: Day of the Pilgrims

8:00 a.m.

The peaceful morning air suddenly erupts with the crackling symphony of "diane" - traditional firecrackers that have announced the festival's awakening for generations. Their echoes bounce off the limestone walls of the trulli, a wake-up call that has stirred festival-goers for countless celebrations.

Throughout the Day

Street bands weave through the narrow lanes between the trulli, their melodies dancing off the conical roofs and filling every corner of the town with music. The streets themselves become works of art as residents adorn their homes with intricate decorations, while strings of lights create constellations between the ancient buildings, transforming the town into a glittering wonderland.

Evening

As shadows lengthen, pilgrims begin arriving from neighboring towns, many maintaining the age-old tradition of traveling on foot. Their journey, a testament of devotion that spans generations, leads them to Alberobello for the first Mass of September 27th. The town keeps its vigil through the night, streets alive with the warmth of hospitality and anticipation.

In Piazza del Popolo, the "madonnari" - masters of an art form as old as the pilgrimage itself - kneel on the ancient stones, their chalk-stained hands bringing religious scenes to life on the pavement. These ephemeral masterpieces, created beneath the glow of festival lights, transform the square into an open-air cathedral of art, where sacred stories emerge from the very ground beneath visitors' feet. The square buzzes with energy as locals and pilgrims alike gather to watch these artists work, their temporary creations a poignant reminder of the festival's fleeting beauty and enduring spirit.

September 27th: Feast of the Pilgrims

4:00 a.m.

First Mass

In the hushed darkness before dawn, the basilica's bells pierce the night air, calling the most devoted pilgrims to the first Mass. Inside the candlelit church, centuries-old stones echo with ancient hymns as those who have walked through the night gather to pay homage to the healing saints. The air is thick with incense and anticipation as the earliest celebration begins, continuing a tradition that has marked this hour for generations.

6:00 a.m., 7:00 a.m., 8:30 a.m.

Traditional Fair of the Pilgrims

As the sun gradually illuminates Alberobello's distinctive skyline, waves of pilgrims flow into the church for successive Masses. Each service brings its own character: the 6 a.m. Mass welcomes early risers and traders preparing for the day's fair; the 7 a.m. gathering sees local families joining the celebration; and by 8:30, the church swells with visitors from across Puglia, their different dialects mixing in prayer and song.

Morning: Procession

The solemn procession emerges from the church like a river of faith flowing through Alberobello's ancient streets. The statues of Saints Cosmas and Damian, lovingly restored and adorned with offerings from the faithful, seem to float above the crowd on their ornate platforms. The "Knights of the Medic Saints," their ceremonial robes catching the morning light, lead the way with dignified steps. This brotherhood, comprising both local citizens and dedicated pilgrims, carries centuries of tradition in their measured pace. Their presence transforms the procession from a mere religious ceremony into a living link with the past, as many current members follow in the footsteps of their fathers and grandfathers before them.

Evening: Food, Fun and Fireworks

As day mellows into dusk, the celebration takes on a more festive air while maintaining its sacred undertones. The streets fill with the enticing aromas of traditional festival foods, each recipe passed down through generations of Alberobello families. Local bands play traditional songs that have accompanied this feast for centuries, their music weaving between the trulli and drawing people together in celebration. Food stalls serve age-old festival specialties, while families share meals at communal tables, continuing the tradition of breaking bread together on this sacred day.

Alberobello's one-of-a-kind skyline is dramatically lit by a breathtaking fireworks show, marking the night's peak. The trulli's distinctive silhouettes become dramatic backdrops as bursts of color paint the sky, their conical roofs seemingly reaching up to touch the sparkling display. A magical finale of choreographed light and color, celebrating medical saints, unites the sacred and celebratory in this ancient festival, showcasing the enduring power of faith and community.

September 28th: Feast of the Villagers

Evening: Grand Gala Procession

As twilight embraces Alberobello's trulli-crowned hills, the grand gala procession unfolds like a living tapestry of civic pride and sacred tradition. Local dignitaries in ceremonial attire walk alongside representatives from neighboring cities, their presence a testament to the deep regional bonds this festival has fostered through centuries. The statues of Saints Cosmas and Damian make their final procession through streets steeped in devotion, their gilded forms catching the last rays of sunlight. Each step of this parade writes another line in Alberobello's ongoing story of faith and community.

Night: Fireworks

The festival reaches its magnificent conclusion as the night sky above the trulli erupts in a symphony of light and color. From the prime vantage points along Viale Einaudi and Viale Aldo Moro, spectators gather to watch as bursts of light dance between the conical rooftops, creating a magical interplay between man-made spectacle and architectural wonder.

Throughout these sacred days, Alberobello transforms into a realm of enchantment. Illuminations trace the unique architecture of the town, strings of lights draped between trulli creating rivers of stars above the streets. The main thoroughfares buzz with life as vendors display their wares in stalls that seem to stretch endlessly, offering everything from traditional crafts to modern treasures.

Alberobello Walking Tour

#1. Rione Monti (Monti Neighborhood)

Step into a fairytale world in Rione Monti, where over 1,000 trulli create a mesmerizing landscape of limestone and light. These iconic dwellings, their conical roofs piercing the sky like ancient stone guardians, rise in captivating clusters along serpentine streets that seem designed by whimsy itself. Each trullo, constructed without a single drop of mortar, stands as a testament to the brilliant ingenuity of Pugliese craftsmen who developed this unique architectural style.

#2. Trullo Sovrano

Rising majestically above Piazza Sacramento, the Trullo Sovrano commands attention as Alberobello's architectural crown jewel. This extraordinary 18th-century structure, the only two-story trullo in existence, tells the story of the wealthy Perta family's ambition and artistry. Its soaring cones and spacious interior chambers challenge everything you thought you knew about trulli construction.

#3. Chiesa Madre dei Santi Medici Cosma e Damiano (Mother Church of Cosmas and Damian)

Against Alberobello's sea of conical trulli roofs, the neoclassical splendor of the Chiesa Madre rises like a spiritual beacon. Its twin bell towers reach skyward, while inside, breathtaking frescoes dance with light filtering through ancient windows.

#4. Casa d'Amore (House of Love)

The Casa d'Amore may appear modest, but its walls tell an epic tale of liberation. Built in 1797, this revolutionary structure – the first in Alberobello to defy tradition by using mortar – stands as a symbol of freedom from feudal oppression. When Francesco d'Amore dared to build this permanent home, he wasn't just laying stones; he was laying the foundation for Alberobello's independence from the Counts of Conversano.

#5. Rione Aia Piccola

The Rione Aia Piccola district offers a quieter, more authentic experience compared to the bustling Rione Monti. This area is still residential, with narrow streets and hundreds of well-preserved trulli.

It provides a glimpse into daily life in Alberobello and is perfect for those seeking a more tranquil, less commercialized experience. The charm of this district lies in its authenticity.

#6. Museo del Territorio (Territory Museum)

Housed in a cluster of interconnected trulli, the Museo del Territorio offers an in-depth look at Alberobello's history, traditions, and the techniques behind trulli construction. Exhibits include tools, photographs, and artifacts from the region's agricultural past.

#7. Belvedere Santa Lucia

Conclude your walking tour at the Belvedere Santa Lucia, a panoramic viewpoint located near the Chiesa di Santa Lucia. From here, you'll enjoy breathtaking views of the Rione Monti and its sea of trulli rooftops.

It's the perfect spot for photographs, offering a sweeping perspective of Alberobello's iconic architecture. Sunset is particularly magical here, as the warm light bathes the trulli in a golden glow.

Alberobello Festivals Throughout the Year

Carnevale di Alberobello (Carnival of Alberobello)

Held annually during winter, leading up to Lent.

This colorful carnival brings the town to life with parades, elaborate costumes, music, and dance. The streets come alive with vibrant processions, showcasing the rich cultural heritage of the Puglian region. Locals and tourists alike revel in the festive atmosphere, enjoying traditional cuisine and various activities.

Sagra dei Tarallucci e Vino

Late April

The Sagra dei Tarallucci e Vino is a beloved annual food and wine festival held in Alberobello, the UNESCO-listed town renowned for its iconic trulli. Typically taking place in late April, the festival celebrates two of Puglia's most cherished culinary staples: taralli, ring-shaped baked snacks that can be sweet or savory, and local wines, especially the robust Primitivo.

Alberobello Light Festival

Typically held during the last week of July.

As part of the UN's Year of Light and in celebration of the 125th anniversary of Van Gogh's death, Alberobello's old trulli town center is illuminated with hundreds of star images evoking the Dutch artist's masterpiece "Starry Night." This festival transforms the town into a luminous open-air gallery, attracting visitors to experience the unique interplay of art and architecture.

Day Trips: Nearby Sites, Cities, and Towns

Grottaglie. Located 40 kilometers (25 miles) from Alberobello. Perched on the edge of an ancient ravine, Grottaglie whispers stories of clay and creativity through its medieval streets. This enchanting Puglian town, whose very name springs from the mysterious grottoes that honeycomb its foundations, has been a sanctuary for master potters since the Middle Ages.

In the atmospheric Quartiere delle Ceramiche, the rhythmic hum of pottery wheels fills narrow alleyways as artisans transform humble clay into works of art, just as their ancestors did centuries ago. Curious visitors can peek into workshop doors to witness these craftsmen at work, their skilled hands coaxing elegant forms from spinning wheels or delicately painting traditional patterns passed down through generations.

Logistics

Train: Alberobello has a train station connected to Putignano.

Bus: Local buses run to Bari (1 hour) and Monopoli (50 minutes). Several bus companies operate routes to and from Alberobello, including FlixBus (connections to Rome and Naples), Itabus (routes from Naples and Rome), MarinoBus (services from northern Italy and Lazio), and Ferrovie del Sud Est (regional buses to Bari), with the main bus stop located at Via Cavour 14/16.

Car: From Bari you will take the SS16 towards Brindisi, follow signs for Monopoli, then continue on the SP113 to Alberobello.

Parking: Finding parking in Alberobello can be challenging, especially during major holidays. The town has implemented paid or limited-time public parking stalls, making free parking scarce. However, several secure private parking areas are available. Parking at the train station is at Viale Margherita, 70011 Alberobello.

Restaurant Recommendations

Ristorante L'Aratro. Address: Via Monte San Michele, 25/27

In the heart of Alberobello, Ristorante L'Aratro offers an authentic Apulian dining experience within a traditional trullo setting. The restaurant is renowned for its commitment to local cuisine, featuring dishes such as orecchiette with turnip tops and lamb chops. The rustic ambiance, characterized by exposed brick walls and dark-wood beams, provides a cozy atmosphere for guests.

Trattoria Terra Madre. Address: Piazza Sacramento, 17

Located just steps from Piazza Sacramento, Trattoria Terra Madre emphasizes a farm-to-table approach, utilizing fresh, locally sourced ingredients. The restaurant is known for its vegetable degustazione and handmade pasta dishes, all prepared with seasonal produce from their own garden. The setting is both picturesque and serene, offering diners a genuine taste of regional flavors.

Ristorante Casa Nova. Address: Via Monte San Marco, 13

Housed in a historic 1700s olive-oil mill with stone-vaulted ceilings, Ristorante Casa Nova serves traditional Italian fare with a modern twist. The menu features specialties like seafood risotto and tiramisu, all served in a charming and historic atmosphere.

Accommodation

For the festival, I recommend two or three nights in town.

Trulli and Puglia Resort. Address: Piazza Gabriele D'Annunzio, 2

A charming 3-star resort, Trulli and Puglia Resort offers old-world accommodations in traditional trulli homes, complete with modern amenities. Guests enjoy spacious rooms, a tranquil atmosphere, and an included breakfast. This resort is well-rated for its central location, friendly staff, and the unique opportunity to experience staying in a historic trullo.

Trulli Holiday Resort. Address: Piazza XXVII Maggio, 38

Rated 3 stars, Trulli Holiday Resort features beautifully restored trulli houses spread across the town. Each unit is uniquely designed, blending traditional architecture with modern comforts. Guests can enjoy a spa, free breakfast, and exceptional service. It's a perfect base for exploring Alberobello while staying immersed in its iconic trulli heritage.

Trulli Resort. Address: Via Monte Olimpo, 7/a

This 3-star hotel offers a luxurious stay in traditional trulli-style accommodations. Known for its spa area, pool, and modern amenities, Trulli Resort combines comfort with a unique, picturesque setting. It's ideal for guests seeking relaxation in a historic and charming atmosphere.

CHAPTER TWENTY-SIX

Bitonto's Olive Harvest Festival

Local Liquid Gold

G ala dell'Olio

Where: Bitonto

When: Third Weekend in September.

Average Festival Temperatures: High 18°C (64°F). Low 12°C (53°F).

Event Website: https://galadellolio.it/

Bitonto: The Olive Capital with a Timeless Soul

Nestled in the sun-drenched landscapes of Puglia, just 10 kilometers (6 miles) west of Bari, Bitonto is a town where history unfolds like the groves of ancient olive trees that define its landscape. With a population of approximately 50,000 residents, Bitonto has long been known as the "City of Olive Oil," a legacy rooted in centuries of agricultural and cultural prosperity. But beneath its reputation for producing some of Italy's finest extra virgin olive oil, Bitonto holds a deeper, richer history that dates back thousands of years.

Before Rome cast its shadow over the Mediterranean, Bitonto was a thriving settlement of the Peucetians, an ancient Italic people who flourished in this region of Puglia. Archaeological finds, including tombs, pottery, and defensive walls, reveal that Bitonto was a significant center of trade and culture as early as the 6th century BC. The town's proximity to the Adriatic Sea and its fertile plains made it an ideal hub for commerce, linking inland settlements to coastal markets.

With the expansion of the Roman Republic, Bitonto became an important stop along the Via Traiana, the strategic road connecting Benevento to Brindisi. This route cemented Bitonto's role as a vital trading post, enhancing its wealth and influence. Under Roman rule, the town saw the construction of amphorae workshops, public baths, and grand villas, many of which still whisper their stories through scattered ruins and underground archaeological sites. Olive oil production flourished, becoming a major export that traveled across the empire, from the markets of Rome to the farthest reaches of Britannia.

As the Roman Empire crumbled, Lombards took control of Bitonto in the 6th century, fortifying its defenses and shaping its early medieval identity. The town's strategic location made it a coveted prize, changing hands between Byzantines, Saracens, and eventually, the Normans. Under Norman rule in the 11th century, Bitonto thrived as part of the Kingdom of Sicily, and its most iconic landmark was born, the Bitonto Cathedral (Cattedrale di San Valentino), a stunning example of Apulian Romanesque architecture inspired by the cathedrals of Bari and Trani. The medieval walls, still partially visible today, protected a town that was growing in both religious and economic significance.

Medieval Bitonto

By the 15th and 16th centuries, Bitonto had become a flourishing Renaissance town under the influence of the Aragonese rulers of Naples. The town's aristocracy built palaces, churches, and elegant piazzas, many of which still grace its historic center. During this time, olive oil production reached new heights, establishing Bitonto as Puglia's premier oil-producing hub, a title it proudly holds to this day.

As the centuries passed, Bitonto weathered the tides of history, from Bourbon rule to Italian unification, all while remaining steadfast in its agricultural and artistic traditions. Today, this timeless town blends its rich heritage with modern life, inviting visitors to walk its narrow stone streets, admire its historic cathedrals, and savor the golden liquid that has been its lifeblood for millennia.

Olive Oil Festival

The event in Bitonto is a cherished annual celebration held every September, marking the commencement of the olive harvest and the production of the season's first extra virgin olive oil. This festival offers locals and visitors an opportunity to sample freshly pressed olive oil and engage in various cultural activities that highlight Bitonto's rich olive-growing heritage.

Bitonto's association with olive cultivation dates back to ancient times. The region's favorable Mediterranean climate and fertile soil have long made it ideal for olive tree cultivation. Historical records indicate that by the 13th century, Bitonto's olive oil was highly esteemed, particularly by the Republic of Venice, which valued it at three times the price of other Italian oils. This longstanding tradition underscores the town's pivotal role in olive oil production.

The festival not only celebrates the new oil but also serves as a testament to the community's enduring commitment to preserving and promoting their olive-growing traditions. While the exact inception date of the celebration is not specified, it has become an integral part of Bitonto's cultural calendar, reflecting centuries of agricultural heritage and communal pride.

Festival Events

Olive Oil Tastings: Visitors can sample freshly pressed olive oil, often accompanied by traditional local bread.

Guided Tours: Many festivals offer tours of local olive mills, providing insights into the production process.

Workshops and Seminars: Educational sessions on topics like olive oil tasting techniques, culinary uses, and health benefits.

Cultural Performances: Live music, dance, and art exhibitions that celebrate local traditions.

Food Stands: Vendors offering regional specialties that pair well with olive oil.

Bitono Walking Tour

#1. Porta Baresana (Bari Gate)

Start your tour at this impressive 18th-century triumphal arch, the historic gateway to Bitonto. It was built to honor King Charles III of Bourbon and features intricate Baroque decorations. This symbolic entrance sets the stage for your journey through Bitonto's storied past.

#2. Piazza Cavour & The Olivo Monumentale

Just inside the gate, Piazza Cavour is a lively square featuring the Monumental Olive Tree, a tribute to Bitonto's status as Puglia's "City of Olive Oil." The surrounding cafés and small shops make it a perfect spot to absorb the town's atmosphere.

#3. Cattedrale di San Valentino (Bitonto Cathedral)

This magnificent 12th-century Romanesque cathedral stands as Bitonto's architectural masterpiece. Meticulously modeled after the celebrated cathedrals of Bari and Trani, its imposing limestone façade captivates visitors with an exquisitely carved central portal flanked by ornate entrances depicting biblical scenes and mythical creatures. The cathedral's crowning glory is its intricate rose window, a mesmerizing circular masterpiece of stone tracery that filters sunlight into dancing patterns across the nave below.

The interior reveals breathtaking harmonies of space, with soaring columns supporting elegant arched vaults that draw the eye heavenward. The extraordinary medieval mosaic floor, partially visible through glass panels, displays intricate geometric patterns and symbolic imagery preserved from an earlier 5th-century paleochristian church that once occupied this sacred site.

Bitonto Cathedral

Descend into the atmospheric crypt, supported by 26 ancient columns with uniquely carved capitals, where you'll discover remnants of early Christian frescoes and the venerated relics of Saint Valentine, the cathedral's patron saint. Art enthusiasts will appreciate the collection of Byzantine-influenced religious paintings, the ornately carved wooden choir stalls, and the cathedral's prized possession, a 12th-century ambo (pulpit) adorned with remarkable sculptural elements, including an eagle lectern of exceptional artistic quality.

#4. Torrione Angioino (Angevin Tower) & Ancient Walls

A short walk leads you to this 14th-century defensive tower, part of Bitonto's medieval fortifications. The walls here once protected the city from invasions and played a role in the historic Battle of Bitonto (1734), when Spanish forces defeated the Austrians to reclaim southern Italy.

#5. Museo Archeologico De Palo-Ungaro

Housed in a former convent, this archaeological museum showcases artifacts from Bitonto's Peucetian, Roman, and medieval past. Highlights include ancient pottery, burial sites, and relics from the town's earliest settlements.

#6. Chiesa di San Francesco d'Assisi

This Baroque-era church is one of the town's most striking religious buildings. Its lavishly decorated interior features intricate stuccoes, gilded altars, and paintings by local Puglian artists.

#7. Galleria Nazionale della Puglia (Devanna Art Gallery)

Located inside a former noble palace, this national art gallery houses an impressive collection of Italian and European paintings, including works by Luca Giordano, Artemisia Gentileschi, and Francesco Solimena.

#8. Palazzo Sylos-Calò

A Renaissance gem, this noble palace once belonged to one of Bitonto's most powerful families. Today, it serves as a cultural center, often hosting art exhibitions and musical performances. The courtyard's elegant loggia and stone columns are a must-see.

#9. Piazza Aldo Moro & The Olive Oil Experience

End your tour in Piazza Aldo Moro, a vibrant square where you can relax with an Aperol Spritz or a local espresso. Nearby, visit one of the town's historic olive oil mills (frantoi), where you can learn about Bitonto's centuries-old olive oil production and sample some of the finest extra virgin olive oil in Italy.

Bitono Festivals Throughout the Year

Carnival (Carnevale)

February

Bitonto's Carnival features parades with colorful floats, masked groups, and traditional music, marking the festive season before Lent.

Holy Week (Settimana Santa)

March or April

Bitonto observes Holy Week with solemn processions, including the 'Processione dei Misteri' on Good Friday, showcasing religious devotion and local traditions.

Festa di San Leone

April 6

This traditional fair in Bitonto features historical reenactments, exhibitions, and local activities spread across various city locations, including Piazza Aldo Moro and Corso Vittorio Emanuele II.

Festa di San Michaele Archangelo

May 26

The Festa Patronale in Bitonto celebrates the city's patron saint, San Michele Arcangelo. The festivities include solemn religious ceremonies, a grand procession carrying the statue of the saint through the historic streets, and the participation of local confraternities dressed in traditional garments. The event also features elaborate street illuminations, live band performances, and a festive atmosphere throughout the city. Vendors set up stalls offering local food, sweets, and artisanal crafts. In the evening, spectacular fireworks light up the sky, concluding a day that blends devotion, tradition, and community celebration.

Patron Saint Festival of Saints Cosmas and Damian (Festa dei Santi Medici)

3rd Sunday in October

This significant event features the 'Intorciata' procession, where devotees carry statues of the saints through the city, accompanied by music and traditional rituals.

Beat Onto Jazz Festival

Last weekend in July

This jazz festival transforms the main piazza into a vibrant music venue, attracting jazz enthusiasts with performances by renowned artists. https://www.beatontojazz.com/

Traetta Opera Festival

October and November

This festival honors composer Tommaso Traetta with opera performances, concerts, and cultural events, celebrating Bitonto's musical heritage. https://www.traettafestival.it/sito/

Day Trips: Nearby Sites, Cities, and Towns

Altamura. 30 kilometers (18.6 miles) east of Bitono. Famous for its medieval architecture and its traditional Altamura bread, Altamura is a town steeped in history. You can visit the stunning Altamura Cathedral, a fine example of Apulian Romanesque architecture, and the archaeological site of the Lamalunga Cave, where the remains of "The Man of Altamura" were found.

Corato. 20 kilometers (12.4 miles) north. Corato is a charming town in the Murge region, rich in olive groves and famous for its olive oil production. The town's historic center offers a mix of Baroque and medieval buildings, including the impressive Cathedral of Santa Maria Maggiore.

Giovinazzo. 15 kilometers (9.3 miles) northwest of town. Giovinazzo is a beautiful coastal town known for its medieval center and stunning seaside views. Visit the ancient Norman Castle, the Cathedral of Santa Maria Assunta, and the charming harbor. The town offers a peaceful atmosphere, perfect for a leisurely walk along its historic streets or enjoying a seaside meal in one of the town's many restaurants offering fresh seafood.

Logistics

Train: Bitonto has its own train station, Bitonto Railway Station. The station is connected to Bari and other nearby towns, including Corato and Mola di Bari. Trains run frequently, and the journey to Bari takes around 20-30 minutes.

Bus: The main bus companies that service Bitonto are Autolinee FSE (Ferrovie del Sud Est), which operates regional routes connecting Bitonto with Bari and other towns in the Puglia region; STP Bari (Società Trasporti Pubblici di Bari), providing bus services to and from

Car: Bitonto is easily accessible by car. The town is just 15 kilometers (9.3 miles) from Bari, making it a short drive along the SS16 highway. The drive from Bari to Bitonto takes around 20-25 minutes.

Parking: The town offers several parking options, both free and paid, near the city center and the historic district. There are parking lots around Piazza Cavour and Piazza XX Settembre. There are also several street parking spaces available but be mindful of ZTL (limited traffic zones) in the city center.

Restaurant Recommendations

Il Quarto Storto -Trattoria. Address: Via Beccherie Lisi, 14

A charming osteria serving traditional Apulian cuisine with a focus on local meats, pasta, and regional wines. The rustic yet modern setting provides a delightful dining experience, and the attentive service adds to its appeal.

Pietrantica - Sapori e Tradizioni. Address: Via Bonifacio Nicola Logroscino, 12

Family-owned restaurant in a traditional location in Bitonto. Chef and owner offer delicious local specialities including pasta and seafood.

Accommodation

For the festival, I recommend two nights in town.

San Marco Antico Relais - B&B. Address: Via Altone, S.N.

Providing inner courtyard views, San Marco Antico Relais - B&B in Bitonto features accommodations and a garden. With garden views, this accommodation offers a patio. The property itself is lovely, and breakfast is very good.

Tenuta Gurgo. Address: Via Patierno

A wonderful family-run accommodation nestled among their own olive groves but within 12 minutes of the Bari airport. A tenuta is a large estate, often dedicated to wine production, olive oil, farming, or livestock, sometimes featuring a historic villa or event space.

CHAPTER TWENTY-SEVEN

Monte Sant'Angelo's Festival of San Michaele

Echoes of the Archangel

Festa di San Michele Arcangelo

Where: Monte Sant'Angelo

When: September 29 (with secondary festival May 8).

Average Festival Temperatures: High 20°C (69°F). Low 14°C (57°F).

From Grotto to Glory: Monte's Mountain Miracle

Perched dramatically on a limestone mountain at about 800 meters (2624 feet) above sea level in Italy's Gargano peninsula, Monte Sant'Angelo's story begins well before its official founding. During Roman times, the area was sparsely populated, with small settlements taking advantage of the defensive position offered by Monte Gargano's heights. The mountains were covered in dense forests that the Romans used for timber.

The medieval period marked the true beginning of Monte Sant'Angelo's significance, catalyzed by a series of reported apparitions of the Archangel

Michael in a cave between 490 and 493 AD. A town developed around a sacred grotto, eventually becoming a major Christian pilgrimage destination in medieval Europe. The Lombards were particularly devoted to the sanctuary and made Monte Sant'Angelo their national sanctuary. They built fortifications and the first iteration of the castle that still dominates the townscape.

The town's position along the Via Sacra Langobardorum and other pilgrim routes to Jerusalem helped it flourish. Monte Sant'Angelo became not only a vital stop for countless medieval pilgrims but also a spiritual waypoint for Crusaders departing from the Adriatic ports of Puglia to the Holy Land. Knights and soldiers paused at the Sanctuary of San Michele Arcangelo to seek the archangel's protection before embarking on their perilous journeys. This connection brought both prestige and prosperity to the town, fostering the growth of churches, monasteries, and hospices for travelers.

Its steep, narrow streets and clustered stone houses, still visible today, were built during this period, adapting to the challenging mountainous terrain.

During the Renaissance, Monte Sant'Angelo continued to prosper under various noble families, particularly the Aragonese, who expanded the castle into an impressive fortress. The town's architecture reflects this period with several palazzi and elegant buildings added to the medieval core. The unique geography continued to influence development, with buildings terraced into the mountainside and connected by elaborate systems of steps and passages.

Monte Sant'Angelo faced challenges and changes in the modern era. The 19th and 20th centuries saw periods of decline as pilgrimage became less central to European life, though the town's religious significance never completely faded. Its secluded location, once a defensive strength, has become a barrier to economic development in the area. However, this same isolation helped preserve its historic character. In 1996, the Sanctuary of San Michele Arcangelo was designated a UNESCO World Heritage Site as part of a group of Longobard sites in Italy.

Today, Monte Sant'Angelo has a population of 12,000 inhabitants. The town continues to balance its rich religious heritage with modern development, particularly in tourism, while maintaining its characteristic medieval urban layout that so distinctively marks the mountaintop.

Feast of Saint Michael Archangel

The festival of St. Michael has been celebrated in Monte Sant'Angelo since as early as the 5th century, immediately following the reported apparitions. The principal feast day is September 29th, which is celebrated throughout the Christian world as Michaelmas, but Monte Sant'Angelo also celebrates May 8th, commemorating the archangel's second appearance.

The festival involves both religious and cultural celebrations. Religious processions carry the statue of St. Michael through the town's ancient streets, while Mass celebrations take place in the sacred cave-sanctuary. Pilgrims from around the world receive special blessings, having journeyed to this remote mountaintop sanctuary just as their medieval predecessors did. Traditional music and folk performances fill the narrow medieval streets, while local food festivals showcase regional specialties that have been prepared for generations during this sacred time.

Historical reenactments bring the apparition stories to life, connecting modern visitors with the spiritual experiences that have drawn the faithful for millennia. The festival remains particularly significant because Monte Sant'Angelo is considered St. Michael's chosen sanctuary on earth, the only church he is said to have consecrated himself. This direct divine connection transformed what was once a remote mountain town into one of Christianity's most important pilgrimage sites, a status it has maintained for over 1,500 years.

Who is Saint Michael?

St. Michael the Archangel is one of the principal angels in Christian, Jewish, and Islamic traditions. In Christian theology, he is the leader of the heavenly armies against evil forces, often depicted as a warrior angel with a sword and armor. His name in Hebrew means "Who is like God?" and he is considered the defender of the Church and the protector of the faithful. He appears in various biblical passages, most notably in the Book of Revelation, where he leads God's armies against Satan.

The link between St. Michael and Monte Sant'Angelo began in 490 AD with the first of three reported apparitions of the Archangel in a cave on Mount Gargano. According to tradition, a wealthy landowner named Gargano lost his prized bull, which was later found kneeling at the entrance of a cave. When an arrow was shot into the cave, it mysteriously turned back and struck the archer. Troubled by this event, the local bishop, Lorenzo Maiorano, ordered three days of prayer and fasting. During this time, St. Michael appeared to the bishop, declaring the cave a sacred place and his earthly sanctuary.

11th Century Ex Voto
of St. Michael

The cave became known as the Sanctuary of Monte Sant'Angelo, and it is unique among Christian shrines as the only one not consecrated by human hands. This made it extraordinarily special in medieval Christianity, becoming one of the most important pilgrimage sites in Europe, alongside Santiago de Compostela and Jerusalem.

Festival Events

September 27: Opening of the Festival of St. Michael

5:30 p.m.

Children's Festival

7:30 p.m.

Evening Procession

As dusk settles over Monte Sant'Angelo, the streets come alive with a joyful family parade that captures the festive spirit of the feast day. Local families stream into the ancient thoroughfares, many wearing coordinated outfits that add splashes of color to the twilight, while others carry handmade lanterns that cast dancing shadows on the stone walls. The parade transforms the medieval town into a magical pageant of light and movement, with beloved local character "Michele the Little Angel" leading the way, his white robes and golden wings glowing softly in the gathering darkness.

Folk groups perform traditional Pugliese dances, their steps in sync with the rhythms of the past. Street performers dressed as historical figures from Monte Sant'Angelo engage with onlookers, adding a theatrical touch to the celebration.

The sound of the organetto and tamburello fills the air, blending with laughter and song. Towering stilt-walkers move through the streets, their illuminated umbrellas casting soft halos of light against the night.

Young people proudly carry elaborate paper lanterns they've crafted, each one telling a different scene from St. Michael's story through intricate cutouts and colored paper. The procession winds its way through the narrow medieval streets like a river of light, passing under strings of illumination that already drape the ancient buildings.

As darkness falls completely, the combination of handmade lanterns, official lighting, and thousands of smaller lights creates an otherworldly atmosphere that transforms the historic center into a scene of wonder and celebration.

8:30 p.m.

Light Displays

As evening falls, Piazza Duca d'Aosta becomes the dazzling heart of Monte Sant'Angelo's festival, where the official illumination ceremony transforms the square into a breathtaking spectacle of light. Elaborate archways of multicolored lights stretch overhead, while large illuminated angels seem to hover between the buildings, casting a celestial glow.

At the center of it all, a radiant light display of the Basilica of St. Michael stands as a tribute to the town's patron saint. Cascading curtains of LED lights shimmer like a starry night, and traditional luminarie, wooden frameworks adorned with thousands of twinkling bulbs, form intricate tunnels and grand architectural designs.

The Mayor, alongside religious and civic leaders, initiates the lighting sequence, which begins at the center of the square and radiates outward through the city's streets in a choreographed display. Each section lights up in sequence, accompanied by musical fanfares, until the entire historic center glows with festive illumination that will remain throughout the celebration period.

11:30 p.m.

Concert at Piazza Beneficenza

September 28: Day of Community Celebrations

10:00 a.m.

Morning Parade

The town's historic musical band emerges in the crisp morning air, their traditional uniforms with gleaming gold braiding and ceremonial caps cutting striking figures against the ancient stone buildings. Their appearance marks the beginning of a cherished parade that rouses the community from sleep with joyful melodies. The ensemble creates an impressive sight as brass instruments catch and reflect the morning sunlight, their polished surfaces throwing golden sparkles across the cobblestones. Traditional drums and percussion provide a steady heartbeat to the procession, their rhythms echoing off the medieval walls of Monte Sant'Angelo.

Flag bearers move with practiced grace, their arms steady as they carry the town's historic standards, each banner telling stories of the community's rich heritage through carefully preserved symbols and heraldry. Adding a touching dimension to the spectacle, young apprentice musicians march alongside the veterans, their presence bridging generations of musical tradition. These students, some as young as twelve, match their mentors step for step, their faces showing both concentration and pride as they take part in this time-honored celebration.

5:20 p.m.

Traditional Candle Offering Ceremony

A solemn procession begins at the Town Hall, where the Municipal Administration and Festival Committee members gather in a solemn procession to carry ornate candles to the Basilica, each piece a masterwork of local craftsmanship and devotion. The collection includes magnificent ceremonial candles towering over three feet tall, their surfaces adorned with intricate decorations that catch the light. Alongside these stand exquisitely hand-painted candles featuring detailed images of St. Michael, each one carefully crafted to honor the archangel. Local artisans contribute their finest traditional beeswax candles, made using techniques passed down through generations, while special votives bearing heartfelt prayers from community members complete the offering.

The procession makes its way into the basilica with measured steps, where the ceremony unfolds in an atmosphere of deep reverence. The clergy receives each candle with care, blessing them individually as the scent of incense fills the air. Traditional prayers echo through the ancient stone walls, voiced in both Latin and Italian, connecting present-day devotees to centuries of faithful who came before them. With impressive ceremony, the candles are carefully placed throughout the sanctuary, each position chosen to maximize both symbolic significance and practical illumination. The ritual concludes as representatives step forward to speak about the community's hopes and intentions for the coming year, their words reflecting the collective spirit of Monte Sant'Angelo's people.

6:00 p.m.

Traditional Games Festival

Piazza Maria di Leo bursts into life as traditional games passed down through generations of Monte Sant'Angelo families take center stage. The air fills with laughter as children and adults alike compete in the Corsa nei sacchi, hopping awkwardly in burlap sacks across the ancient stones. Neighborhood pride is on full display during the spirited Tiro alla fune matches, where teams strain and heave against the rope while supporters cheer from the sidelines.

9:30 p.m.

Concert in the Piazza

September 29: Feast of St. Michael the Archangel

8:00 a.m.

Daylight Fireworks

The festival begins with a spectacular display of daylight fireworks echoing through the ancient streets of Monte Sant'Angelo. Local families gather in the main square, dressed in their finest clothes, as church bells ring out across the town. Traditional musicians play tarantellas and local folk tunes, creating a festive atmosphere that marks the beginning of this sacred day.

4:30 p.m.

Rite of the Sacred Sword

Inside the ancient cave sanctuary and basilica, priests and religious officials gather for this centuries-old ceremony. The sacred sword, a masterfully crafted medieval weapon symbolizing St. Michael's divine protection, is carefully removed from its reliquary. Incense perfumes the sacred grotto as the Archbishop leads prayers in both Latin and Italian. The sword is blessed with holy water and presented to the faithful for veneration, accompanied by Gregorian chants that echo through the cave basilica.

5:00 p.m.

Procession of the Sacred Sword

The sacred sword is carried through Monte Sant'Angelo's medieval streets on an ornate silver platform decorated with white lilies, St. Michael's traditional flower. The procession is led by the Archbishop, followed by priests, religious orders, and confraternities in traditional dress. Local children scatter rose petals along the route, while devotees carry large candles and sing traditional hymns to St. Michael.

The procession winds through the historic center, passing under decorated balconies where residents display precious family tapestries and throw flower petals. Traditional bands play solemn marches as the sword makes its way through the city's most significant places. The sword is then returned to the Basilica as the sun sets over the Gargano peninsula, concluding this central part of the feast day celebrations.

7:00 p.m.

Fireworks Display

7:45 p.m.

Musical Tribute to St. Michael

Inside the illuminated basilica, the prestigious Police Band Association performs a special concert honoring St. Michael, patron saint of police officers. The acoustics of the ancient cave sanctuary enhance the resonant brass and woodwind instruments as they perform a carefully curated program.

8:00 p.m.

Fallen Soldier Procession

Following the concert, the Police Band, in their formal dress uniforms, leads a torch lit procession through the heart of Monte Sant'Angelo. The route extends from Via Reale Basilica to Corso Vittorio Emanuele, with local police officers in ceremonial dress joining the procession. The band performs solemn marches as they proceed through streets lined with residents holding candles.

The procession reaches its most poignant moment as it arrives at the Monument of the Fallen (Monumento ai Caduti), where years of history and sacrifice converge in a solemn ceremony. The Police Band moves with practiced precision to form a ceremonial semi-circle around the monument, their polished instruments reflecting the evening lights as they take their positions. A hush falls over the gathered crowd as they observe a moment of silence, the weight of remembrance settling over the square like a mantle.

The stillness breaks with the first haunting notes of "Il Silenzio" echoing through the air, the solo trumpet's clear tones carrying across the gathered crowd and down the ancient streets. As the last note fades, officials step forward with measured steps to place a ceremonial wreath at the monument's base, its ribbons bearing the vibrant green, white, and red of the Italian flag. The band then begins the stirring melody of the Italian national anthem, as officials and citizens alike stand in respectful silence, many with hands over their hearts.

11:30 p.m.

Party in the Castle Area

The event ends with a celebration in the area in front of the castle.

Monte Sant'Angelo Walking Tour

#1. Santuario di San Michele Arcangelo (Sanctuary of St. Michael the Archangel)

This UNESCO treasure marks the spot where St. Michael himself appeared in 490 AD, leaving his footprint in stone. Marvel at the massive bronze doors crafted in Constantinople, their panels telling biblical stories that have welcomed pilgrims since 1076. The 15th-century bell tower soars above the ancient grotto shrine, where countless prayers have echoed through the centuries.

Sanctuary of St. Michael Archangel

#2. Chiesa di Santa Maria Maggiore (Church of St. Mary Major)

This Romanesque church dates back to the 11th century and reflects the artistic influence of the Lombards. Inside, well-preserved Byzantine-style frescoes cover the walls, showcasing vibrant colors and detailed religious scenes. The architecture combines northern European and Mediterranean elements, making it an important example of Monte Sant'Angelo's historical and cultural heritage.

#3. Castello Normanno-Svevo-Aragonese (Norman Castle)

The Castello is a powerful reminder of the town's strategic importance over the centuries. Originally built by the Normans in the 11th century, it was later expanded and reinforced by the Swabians under Emperor Frederick II in the 13th century, and further modified by the Aragonese in the 15th century. Each ruling dynasty left its mark, transforming the fortress from a simple military outpost into a symbol of power and defense.

Castle in Monte Sant'Angelo

Key Features of the Castle:

Towers and Defensive Walls: The castle's most prominent features include its imposing towers, such as the Torre dei Giganti (Tower of Giants), an 18-meter-high structure with walls nearly 4 meters thick, designed to withstand siege warfare. Other towers added by later rulers enhanced the fortress's ability to defend against invasions.

Swabian Influence – Frederick II's Additions: Emperor Frederick II, known for his architectural prowess, reinforced the structure, adding elegant yet practical defensive elements, including fortified walls and arrow slits that allowed archers to repel attackers.

Aragonese Expansion: During the Aragonese rule, further modifications included additional bastions and courtyards, turning the castle into a more comfortable residence while maintaining its defensive strength.

Dungeons and Prison Cells: The lower levels house dark, atmospheric dungeons where prisoners were once held. Some legends suggest secret passages and hidden escape routes.

Panoramic Views: Climbing the castle's walls and towers offers breathtaking views of the Gargano National Park, the surrounding coastline, and the Adriatic Sea on clear days.

Inner Courtyards: These open spaces, bathed in sunlight, once served as gathering places for nobility and military leaders. They still echo with the history of royal processions, diplomatic meetings, and daily life within the fortress.

#4. Tomba di Rotari (Rotari's Tomb)

Don't let the name fool you this enigmatic 12th-century structure was never a tomb at all, but a baptistery where new Christians began their spiritual journey. Look up when you enter to admire the perfectly preserved barrel-vaulted ceiling, then trace your fingers along the intricate stone carvings that medieval artisans left behind.

#5. Museo Tancredi (Tancredi Ethnographic Museum)

Step into the everyday lives of Monte Sant'Angelo's ancestors. This intimate museum brings the past to life through tools, textiles, and treasures of rural life. Discover the ancient traditions of shepherds who guided their flocks through these mountains, following paths worn by centuries of seasonal migration.

#6. Belvedere Panorama Viewpoint

Save your breath for a final "wow" moment. This stunning viewpoint rewards your journey with a vast canvas of nature's glory. The rolling Gargano mountains cascade down to meet the glittering Adriatic Sea.

Monte Sant'Angelo Festivals Throughout the Year

Fanoje Fire of San Giuseppe

March 18

This ancestral ritual marks the end of winter and the beginning of the festival season in Monte Sant'Angelo. On the evening of March 18th, large bonfires, known locally as "fanoje," are lit throughout the town, especially in the historic center. These fires symbolize rebirth and community unity, bringing residents together to celebrate with music, food, and local wine. The tradition involves burning old wooden items, signifying a fresh start and the welcoming of warmer seasons.

Holy Week Celebrations

Varies (March or April, depending on the liturgical calendar)

Traditional rites and processions, culminating in the evocative procession on Good Friday, reflecting the town's deep-rooted religious traditions.

International "Michael" Festival

May 3–9

The International "Michael" Festival is an annual celebration that honors the cultural, spiritual, and natural heritage of Monte Sant'Angelo. This festival coincides with the Feast of the Apparition of St. Michael the Archangel on May 8, commemorating his appearance on Monte Gargano in 492. The festival features a variety of events, including religious processions, cultural exhibitions, musical performances, and the European Assembly of the Via Micaelica, emphasizing intercultural dialogue and shared values.

Monte Sant'Angelo Summer Festival

Throughout the summer months

During the summer, Monte Sant'Angelo hosts a series of cultural and environmental festivals collectively known as the Monte Sant'Angelo Summer Festival. This festival offers a diverse array of events, including concerts, theatrical performances, and art exhibitions, showcasing both local and international talents. The town's historic sites, such as the Sanctuary of San Michele Arcangelo and the medieval quarter of Rione Junno, often serve as picturesque backdrops for these events.

Festambiente Sud

Summer months

Festambiente Sud is the southern edition of Legambiente's national festival, focusing on environmental awareness, sustainability, and the relationship between nature and culture. Held annually in Monte Sant'Angelo since 2004, the festival features workshops, discussions, and performances aimed at promoting eco-friendly practices and celebrating the region's natural beauty.

Gathering of Tarantella Players

Summer months

The Gathering of Tarantella Players is a vibrant celebration of traditional music and dance, highlighting the tarantella—a folk dance integral to the region's cultural identity. During this event, musicians and dancers from various backgrounds come together to perform in the town's squares and streets, creating an atmosphere of communal joy and cultural pride.

Day Trips: Nearby Sites, Cities, and Towns

Manfredonia. 17 kilometers (10.5 miles) from Monte Sant'Angelo. Where medieval dreams meet Mediterranean shores, Manfredonia rises from the Adriatic coast with stories etched in every stone. Born from the vision of King Manfred of Sicily in 1256, this seaside gem still carries the romantic spirit of its royal founder.

The commanding Castello Svevo-Angioino stands guard over the harbor, its weathered walls now protecting treasures of a different kind. Inside, the National Archaeological Museum showcases mysterious Daunian steles - haunting pre-Roman stone sculptures that seem to whisper secrets from Italy's ancient past.

At the heart of the old town, the Cathedral of San Lorenzo Maiorano reaches skyward, honoring the city's beloved patron saint. Its bells have marked time for centuries, calling faithful and visitors alike to admire its sacred art and architecture.

As evening approaches, locals and tourists mingle along the lively lungomare (seafood promenade), where the day's catch becomes tonight's feast in charming restaurants overlooking the sparkling Adriatic. The air fills with the scent of grilled fish and sound of clinking glasses as families share meals and stories under the stars.

Just outside town, an artistic marvel awaits at Siponto Archaeological Park. Here, ancient meets contemporary as artist Edoardo Tresoldi's breathtaking wire-mesh installation rises ghost-like above the ruins of a paleochristian basilica. This ethereal structure seems to float above the archaeological site, bringing the past to life through modern eyes - a perfect metaphor for Manfredonia itself, where history dances eternally with the present.

Mattinatella Beach (Fontana delle Rose). 29 kilometers (18 miles) from Monte. Nestled between dramatic limestone cliffs that plunge into the Adriatic, Fontana delle Rose is a slice of Mediterranean paradise that takes your breath away. The beach reveals itself like a secret treasure, where crystal-clear waters shift from turquoise to deep sapphire as they stretch toward the horizon.

Nature has carved a series of intimate coves along this stunning shoreline, each one offering its own private retreat. The beach itself is a beautiful mix of smooth pebbles and golden sand, creating perfect perches for sunbathers and dreamers alike. Hidden among the rocks, lucky visitors might discover the ancient freshwater spring that gave this magical spot its romantic name - "Fountain of Roses."

The pristine waters here are a snorkeler's dream, with underwater visibility that makes every swim an adventure. Schools of fish dart through the rocky outcrops, while the clear depths reveal a mesmerizing seabed. As the sun moves across the sky, the cliffs cast ever-changing shadows on the water, creating a natural light show that makes every visit unique.

Grotta di San Michele (Cagnano Varano). 42 kilometers (26 miles) from Monte Sant'Angelo. Hidden away in the hills near Cagnano Varano lies a sacred cave that time seems to have forgotten. This mystical sanctuary, dedicated to St. Michael the Archangel, offers a rare glimpse into centuries of faith and devotion, untouched by modern tourism. Unlike its famous cousin in Monte Sant'Angelo, here you can experience the raw spirituality of an ancient pilgrimage site in peaceful solitude.

Step into this natural cathedral, where stalactites hang like nature's chandeliers and 8th-century frescoes tell their faded stories on the cave walls. The air itself feels charged with centuries of prayers and pilgrim footsteps, creating an atmosphere that speaks to both believer and explorer alike. Ancient light filters through natural openings, creating an ever-shifting play of shadows that adds to the cave's otherworldly ambiance.

The cave-church rests near the charming village of Cagnano Varano, which offers its own remarkable treasure - Lake Varano, Italy's largest coastal lake. This massive freshwater mirror stretches toward the Adriatic, creating a unique ecosystem where fishermen still practice their ancient trade against a backdrop of stunning natural beauty.

Logistics

Train: The closest train station is Manfredonia (17 kilometers / 10.5 miles away). There is no direct train to Monte Sant'Angelo, so travelers arriving by train must take a bus or taxi from Manfredonia to reach the town. The nearest major railway hub is Foggia, which has connections to the rest of Italy.

Bus: Monte Sant'Angelo is well-connected to the surrounding region through a network of reliable bus services. Ferrovie del Gargano provides regular connections from the transport hub of Foggia and the coastal city of Manfredonia, making day trips easily accessible. Sita Sud operates an extensive regional service that links the mountain town to various destinations throughout Puglia, while Cotrap runs convenient routes from major cities in the region.

Car: From Foggia (58 kilometers / 36 miles). Take the SS89 highway toward Manfredonia, then follow signs for SP55 up the mountain to Monte Sant'Angelo. The drive is scenic, with winding roads offering views of the Gargano National Park.

Parking: Monte Sant'Angelo has several public parking areas around the historic center, including near the Sanctuary of St. Michael and Castello Normanno-Svevo. Street parking is available but limited, especially during festivals. Parking lots outside the principal center provide access with a short walk into town.

Restaurant Recommendations

Osteria del Corso. Address: Via Belvedere, 11

This family-owned restaurant is known for its delicious homemade dishes and generous portions. The menu features a variety of antipasti and primi piatti, making it a must-visit for anyone looking to experience authentic Italian cuisine.

Ristorante Medioevo. Address: Via Castello, 21

Ristorante Medioevo offers a cozy atmosphere, and a menu filled with traditional Italian and Mediterranean dishes. It's a glorious spot for a lovely dinner with wonderful hosts and a warm ambiance.

Profumo | Osteria Del Gargano. Address: Via Giuseppe Verdi, 97

This restaurant is part of a superior entrepreneurial project and offers a mix of Italian and seafood dishes.

Accommodation

For the festival, I recommend three to four nights in town.

Palace Hotel San Michele. Address: Via Madonna degli Angeli

This elegant 4-star hotel, housed in a restored historic building, offers breathtaking views of the Gulf of Manfredonia. Guests can enjoy luxurious amenities, including a wellness center and fine dining options.

Santangelo Hotel. Address: Via per Pulsano Km 1

Nestled in the heart of Gargano National Park, this 3-star hotel boasts panoramic terraces and an outdoor pool. Its cozy rooms and proximity to Monte Sant'Angelo make it a perfect retreat.

Hotel Relais dei Normanni. Address: Via Raffaele Ciuffreda

This 4-star hotel features beautiful, spacious rooms and a lovely garden area. It's a great option for those seeking a bit more luxury and relaxation during their stay.

CHAPTER TWENTY-EIGHT

Casamassima: The Blue Jewel of Puglia

The Historic Parade

Corteo Storico Corrado IV di Svevia

Where: Casamassima

When: Second Weekend of October.

Average Festival Temperatures: High 26°C (79°F). Low 19°C (67°F).

Discover Casamassima: Italy's Hidden Blue Jewel

Step into a fairytale where an entire town is painted in mesmerizing shades of azure. Just 20 kilometers (12 miles) from Bari, in Casamassima every corner tells a story tinted in blue, where medieval charm meets a color palette that would make artists swoon. The population stands at around 17,400 residents.

The origins of Casamassima are believed to trace back to the Roman era. One theory suggests that the settlement was established by Quintus Fabius Maximus Verrucosus during the Punic Wars, with its name deriving from the

Roman family name "Massimi," indicating a "house of the Maximus family." Alternatively, the name could mean "the largest house."

The earliest documented reference to Casamassima dates to 962 AD, found in a record preserved in the archive of Bari Cathedral. This document details a transaction involving a vineyard, indicating the presence of an organized community during the 10th century. Throughout the Middle Ages, Casamassima was governed by various Apulian lordships and was often under the influence of neighboring feudal territories such as Conversano and Acquaviva delle Fonti. The medieval village developed around a Norman tower from the 8th century, which was later expanded into a castle, remnants of which still stand in the historic center.

In 1609, the Acquaviva family sold the fiefdom of Casamassima to the Portuguese Vaaz family, who were of Jewish origin. During the plague epidemic of 1658, which severely affected nearby Bari, Duke Odoardo Vaaz ordered the town's buildings, monuments, and churches to be painted with a mixture containing blue pigment, possibly copper sulfate, added to quicklime. This act was both a protective measure and a votive offering to the Madonna of Constantinople, to whom a small church was later dedicated in gratitude for sparing the town from the epidemic. This tradition gave rise to Casamassima's distinctive blue-painted architecture, earning it the nickname "Paese Azzurro."

The Corteo Storico Corrado IV di Svevia

The Corteo Storico Corrado IV di Svevia transforms this blue-painted town into a living medieval pageant, recreating a pivotal moment from 1252 that changed the course of local history forever.

Picture a spring day in 1252: Conrad IV of Germany, son of the mighty Emperor Frederick II, rode through Casamassima's lands on a mission of justice. The young king carried with him the power to right an old wrong, the return of lands to Roberto da Casamaxima, whose father Giovanni had seen them stripped away by Frederick II. This wasn't just any royal passage; it was a moment of redemption preserved forever in a precious parchment that still rests in the Historical Archive of the Library of Bari, a tangible link to this dramatic chapter of medieval politics.

Today, this historical moment explodes into vibrant life as over 400 costumed participants flood the streets with medieval splendor. The air fills with the haunting melodies of period instruments as musicians in authentic dress lead the procession. Flag wavers send their banners spinning against the blue-washed walls, creating a kaleidoscope of color and movement. Fire eaters paint the twilight with arcs of flame, while jugglers keep the ancient arts of entertainment alive.

Knights in gleaming armor parade through the narrow streets, their horses' hooves striking ancient stones that heard the same sounds centuries ago. Dancers twirl in elaborate period costumes, and theatrical performers bring medieval court life into sharp focus.

Festival Events

Friday: Festival Opening & Medieval Market

5:00 p.m.

Official opening of the festival in Piazza Aldo Moro with a welcome speech from local officials and festival organizers.

5:30 p.m.

The Medieval Market: Where Ancient Crafts Come Alive

As twilight descends on Casamassima's azure streets, the Medieval Market springs to life like a scene from an illuminated manuscript. Wooden stalls, constructed following ancient designs, line the cobblestone pathways where medieval merchants once haggled and traded. The air fills with an intoxicating blend of smoky forge fires, fresh leather, and aromatic herbs from the apothecary's stand.

At the heart of the market, blacksmiths demonstrate their ancient craft, their hammers ringing against hot iron in a rhythm that echoes through centuries. Sparks dance in the gathering dusk as they shape gleaming blades and intricate metalwork, just as their predecessors did in the time of Conrad IV. Nearby, leather workers tools their wares with practiced precision, creating everything from ornate pouches to sturdy belts, while explaining the medieval techniques that have been passed down through generations.

Artisans work their magic at every turn: glassblowers shape molten crystal into delicate forms; potters throw clay on wooden wheels; and woodcarvers transform local olive wood into beautiful utensils and decorative pieces. The scent of beeswax fills the air as candle-makers dip their wicks, while herbalists blend mysterious concoctions from dried flowers and leaves, sharing ancient remedies and folk wisdom.

On traditional looms, local weavers artfully craft textiles; the rhythmic clicking of shuttles transforms threads into intricate designs. Nearby, scribes practice the nearly lost art of calligraphy, their quills scratching gracefully across parchment as they create illuminated letters in rich jewel tones.

Food vendors recreate medieval flavors with historical accuracy: freshly baked bread emerges from stone ovens, while spiced meats roast over open fires. The air is rich with the aroma of herbs and spices that were once worth their weight in gold along medieval trade routes. Wine flows from leather bottles into ceramic cups, while storytellers weave tales of knights and nobles who once walked these very streets.

As night falls, torches illuminate the market square, casting dancing shadows on the blue-painted walls. The atmosphere grows more magical by the hour, as musicians playing period instruments fill the air with medieval melodies, and wandering performers entertain crowds with acts that would have delighted audiences centuries ago.

6:00 p.m.

Live Demonstrations

Traditional Puglian weaving, calligraphy, and medieval armor crafting.

7:30 p.m.

Knights' Training Exhibition: Steel, Skill, and Spectacle

As night falls in Casamassima, the square becomes a training ground for medieval warriors. Skilled reenactors demonstrate the techniques of knightly combat, from swordplay to the use of shields and maces.

Watch as they showcase the footwork and precision required in battle, explaining how plate armor was designed for agility rather than restriction. The event also offers insight into the training knights underwent from childhood and the code of chivalry that shaped their lives.

The sound of clashing steel fills the air as fighters engage in choreographed duels, illustrating historical combat techniques with accuracy.

8:30 p.m.

Music & Dance Performance

Traditional medieval music with minstrels and folk dancers.

9:30 p.m

Lords of the Sky: The Ancient Art of Falconry

As night falls over Casamassima, master falconers take the stage to showcase the medieval art of falconry. Dressed in period attire, they introduce hawks, falcons, and eagles, demonstrating their speed, agility, and precision in flight.

Learn how different birds were used for hunting, goshawks for forests, peregrines for open fields, and how falconers trained them with specialized techniques. The demonstration highlights the deep bond between handler and bird, with falcons diving at incredible speeds and responding to precise commands.

Beyond the spectacle, experts explain falconry's historical role in medieval society, from the strict rules governing ownership to the terminology it introduced into everyday language. This is a glimpse into a noble tradition that shaped European history.

10:30 p.m.

Fire and Flair: A Night of Medieval Spectacle

Casamassima's main square comes alive with fire and movement as medieval performers take the stage. Fire-eaters manipulate flames with precision, recreating the dramatic displays once seen at medieval fairs. Their fiery tricks light up the night, casting flickering shadows against the town's blue walls.

Between fire acts, jugglers showcase their skills with wooden clubs, metal rings, and flaming torches, performing tricks that once entertained nobles and commoners alike. Mixing comedy with danger, they engage the crowd just as medieval entertainers did while traveling from castle to village.

The evening builds to a thrilling finale, blending fire-eating and juggling into a breathtaking display that lights up the square, an unforgettable nod to the spectacle of medieval entertainment.

Saturday: Tournament & Historical Reenactments

10:00 a.m.

Medieval Village Opens (see description above).

11:00 a.m.

Children's Activities

Medieval games, storytelling, and hands-on crafts for kids.

12:30 p.m.

The Grand Feast: A Medieval Banquet in the Blue City

As the bells of Casamassima toll half-past noon, the historic center transforms into a medieval feast hall under the azure-painted walls.

Long wooden tables stretch through the winding streets, dressed with hand-woven linens and decorated with fresh herbs and flickering beeswax candles. The feast begins with the ceremonial blessing of the bread, a tradition that dates back to the time of Conrad IV. Servers in period attire present dishes on wooden trenchers and pewter plates, while wandering musicians fill the air with medieval melodies.

The menu recreates authentic flavors from the 13th century: succulent roasted meats seasoned with exotic spices that once traveled the Silk Road, hearty grain porridges enriched with local vegetables, and fresh-baked breads still warm from stone ovens. Sample porchetta prepared according to ancient Puglian recipes, its crispy skin perfumed with wild fennel and local herbs. Taste wines made from indigenous grapes, served in traditional earthenware cups, while jesters entertain diners with historical tales and tricks.

Local experts have meticulously researched each dish, ensuring historical accuracy while satisfying modern palates. Watch as master cooks demonstrate medieval cooking techniques over open fires, explaining how spices weren't just for flavor, they were symbols of wealth and sophistication in medieval society.

2:00 p.m. and 5:00 p.m.

Weapons of the Age: A Medieval Arsenal Comes to Life

In the sun-drenched piazza, master-at-arms and seasoned knights unveil the deadly artistry of medieval warfare. This isn't just a display of weapons, it's a journey through the evolution of combat. Expert demonstrators reveal the devastating power of the longsword, showing how these weapons were truly "hand-and-a-half" swords, capable of both one and two-handed techniques. Witness the precision of English longbows as archers demonstrate the training that once required royal decree. Every English yeoman was legally bound to practice archery on Sundays. Marvel as knights explain how different shields were used not just for defense but as weapons themselves, from the massive kite shields of the Norman era to the agile bucklers of later periods.

6:30 p.m.

The Grand Joust

As the day reaches its crescendo, Piazza Aldo Moro transforms into a medieval tournament ground. Colorful pavilions snap in the evening breeze as armored knights prepare their mounts for the ultimate test of skill and courage. The air grows thick with anticipation as trumpets announce the beginning of the joust. Watch as knights thunder down the lists, lances leveled, in heart-stopping passes that demonstrate the same skills their predecessors used centuries ago.

Each run is accompanied by expert commentary explaining the complex rules and scoring of medieval tournaments, how a broken lance scored higher than a solid hit, and how knights aimed for specific points on their opponent's shield or armor. The crowd roars with each pass, as the knights show both martial skill and horsemanship in their quest for victory. Between rounds, heralds entertain the crowd with tales of historical jousts, while squires demonstrate the intricate process of arming a knight for combat.

8:00 p.m.

Theater Under the Stars: Conrad IV Returns

As night embraces Casamassima's, the town square transforms into an open-air theater where history breathes again. Professional actors, adorned in meticulously researched 13th-century costumes, bring to life the pivotal moment when Conrad IV restored justice to these ancient streets. The performance unfolds against the authentic backdrop of medieval architecture, where every stone could tell tales of that fateful day in 1252.

Watch as the drama reveals the political intrigue behind Conrad's arrival: the story of Roberto da Casamaxima, whose family lands were stripped away by Frederick II, only to be restored by his son in an act of justice that would echo through centuries. The actors move through torch-lit scenes, their voices carrying across the hushed crowd as they recreate the tension, hope, and ultimate triumph of this historic moment. Original music, performed on period instruments, underscores the action while authentic props and carefully choreographed sword fights bring medieval Casamassima vividly to life.

9:30 p.m.

Fire and Light: A Medieval Night Sky Ignites

As the final echoes of the theatrical performance fade, the azure streets come alive with dancing flames and shimmering lights. Fire performers, dressed in medieval garb, spin wheels of flame that paint bright arcs against the darkened sky. Watch as they manipulate fire staffs and chains in hypnotic patterns, their performances choreographed to the haunting melodies of medieval musicians.

The show builds to a crescendo with demonstrations of historical pyrotechnic arts, the same techniques that once lit medieval celebrations and tournaments.

Greek fire demonstrations cast eerie green flames into the night, while master artificers recreate period-accurate fire displays using techniques documented in medieval manuscripts. The evening reaches its peak with a spectacular finale that combines all elements: fire dancers weaving between illuminated fountains, torch-bearers creating patterns of light, and carefully controlled pyrotechnic effects that transform the blue city into a canvas of flame and shadow.

11:00 p.m.

Medieval Dance Party with live music in the main square.

Sunday: Grand Historical Parade & Closing Ceremony

9:30 a.m.

Holy Mass

Mass in honor of Conrad IV at Chiesa Madre di Casamassima.

11:00 a.m.

Sacred Steel: The Blessing of the Knights

Within the hushed stone walls of Casamassima's ancient church, morning light filters through stained glass to illuminate one of chivalry's most sacred rituals. The Blessing of the Knights recreates the solemn ceremony that transformed warriors into knights of the realm. Watch as candidates approach the altar in plain white tunics, symbolizing purity of purpose, while ecclesiastical re-enactors perform the authentic medieval blessing ritual.

Incense fills the air as hopeful knights kneel before the priest, their swords on the altar. The ceremony unfolds exactly as it would have in 1252: the ritual washing of hands, the blessing of the sword, and the sacred oaths of chivalry sworn upon holy relics. The climactic moment arrives with the dubbing, that iconic shoulder tap with the flat of the blessed sword, accompanied by the traditional Latin phrases that have echoed through centuries.

12:30 p.m.

Feast of the Noble Court: The Medieval Banquet

In Piazza's sun-drenched expanse, long tables groan under the weight of historically accurate medieval delicacies. Costumed servers present courses in traditional order, from subtle pottages to elaborate "subtleties" (decorative dishes that were both food and entertainment). Musicians play period instruments while jesters and storytellers weave between tables, sharing tales and jests authentic to the era.

Sample dishes recreated from medieval cookbooks: spiced peacock presented with its own fantastical plumage, lamprey pies, and honeyed fruits. Each course arrives with ceremony and flourish, while expert historians explain the social significance of medieval dining customs and the complex symbolism behind each dish.

2:00 p.m.

The Grand Preparation

Step behind the scenes of medieval pageantry as the festival participants prepare for the afternoon's grand parade. This intimate showcase allows visitors to examine the intricate details of historical costumes up close, from the hand-stitched embroidery on noble ladies' gowns to the authentic construction of knights' armor. Meet the dedicated actors who bring history to life as they explain the historical significance of each costume element and the research that goes into their accurate recreation.

Expert costuming historians demonstrate how medieval clothing was constructed and worn, from the complex layers of a noblewoman's dress to the padding required under a knight's armor. Photographers will find this the perfect opportunity to capture the stunning detail of medieval craftsmanship against the backdrop of Casamassima's distinctive blue walls.

4:00 p.m.

The Grand Historical Parade

Here, history unfolds in a spectacular procession that transforms the entire town into a living medieval tapestry. Trumpets herald the parade's approach as over 400 costumed participants bring 13th-century Italy blazing to life. Flag bearers lead the way, their banners snapping against the blue-painted buildings as they perform intricate choreographed displays. Knights in gleaming armor astride magnificently caparisoned horses follow, their heraldic devices catching the late afternoon sun.

Noble lords and ladies process in their finest silks and brocades, while merchants display their wares and artisans demonstrate their traditional skills on moving platforms. Musicians playing authentic medieval instruments fill the air with period melodies, while jesters and acrobats entertain the crowds. Each group in the parade represents a different facet of medieval life, from solemn monks carrying ancient manuscripts to humble peasants showing traditional crafts.

6:00 p.m.

The Final Tournament

As the sun begins its descent, the festival's greatest warriors gather for the ultimate test of martial skill. The Final Tournament transforms the main square into a battlefield where knights demonstrate the full array of medieval combat arts. This isn't just swordplay, it's a historically accurate recreation of medieval martial arts, drawing from surviving fighting manuals and historical documents.

Watch as knights battle with longsword, sword and shield, polearm, and other period weapons in carefully choreographed but intensely realistic combat. Each bout is judged according to historical tournament rules, with points awarded for clean strikes and proper technique. The crowds roar as champions emerge, their victories celebrated with the same pageantry that would have accompanied medieval tournaments.

8:00 p.m.

The Closing Ceremony

As night embraces Casamassima, hundreds of torches ignite to guide the festival's final procession through the town's winding streets. The Closing Ceremony begins with the crowning of the tournament champion, who leads the torch-lit parade through the historic center. Medieval musicians play solemn melodies as the procession winds its way past the blue-washed walls, their flames reflecting off windows and creating dancing shadows that seem to bridge past and present.

9:30 p.m.

Last Music & Dance Performance

Casamassima Walking Tour

#1. Piazza Aldo Moro

Watch as gentlemen debate politics from their favorite benches while children chase pigeons across ancient stones. The square comes alive with the gentle buzz of conversation floating from family-run cafes, their doors thrown open to release the intoxicating aroma of freshly ground coffee.

#2. Porta Orologio

Follow the slope of Via Roma toward one of Casamassima's most photographed landmarks, the Porta Orologio. The gate's weathered stones have witnessed centuries of comings and goings, its clock faithfully marking time for generations of Casamassimesi.

As you pass beneath its arch, notice how the light changes, marking your transition from the modern world into the azure-painted realm of the Borgo Antico. The tower's bell still rings out across the blue-washed rooftops, its sound unchanged since medieval times.

#3. Chiesa Matrice di Santa Croce (Mother Church of the Holy Cross)

The Chiesa Matrice di Santa Croce stands as one of Casamassima's most significant religious monuments, dating back to the 13th century. Originally constructed in the Romanesque style that was prevalent throughout Puglia during this period, the church has served as the town's primary place of worship for centuries.

The building underwent substantial renovation during the 17th century, when Baroque elements were incorporated into its structure, creating the architectural fusion visible today. This reconstruction occurred after damage sustained during the 1627 earthquake that affected much of Puglia. Local noble families, particularly the Vaaz family who controlled the fiefdom at that time, funded much of this restoration work.

The church's facade features a prominent rose window and a stone portal with intricate carvings depicting biblical scenes. The bell tower, added in the late 18th century, stands as one of the tallest structures in the historic center. The characteristic blue paint that adorns its exterior walls ties it to Casamassima's "Blue District" tradition, believed to have originated during a plague epidemic when the town was painted blue as a symbol of devotion to the Madonna.

Inside, the church follows a Latin cross plan with three naves. The interior houses several valuable artistic works, including a 16th-century wooden crucifix, frescoes depicting scenes from the life of Christ dating to the 15th century, and an 18th-century pipe organ that remains partially functional. The main altar, reconstructed during the Baroque period, features marble work and gilded decorations characteristic of the era.

#4. The Blue Streets of Casamassima

Leaving the church, start wandering the famous blue-painted streets of the old town. These striking blue walls, reminiscent of Chefchaouen in Morocco, have their origins in a medieval legend. It's said that locals painted their houses blue in honor of the Madonna di Costantinopoli, who protected the town from the plague.

Wander through Via San Giuseppe and Via Santa Chiara, where the narrow alleyways and picturesque balconies filled with flowers make for fantastic photos.

#5. Chiesa di Santa Chiara and the Monastery (St. Clair)

In a secluded spot, the Chiesa di Santa Chiara embodies quiet devotion. The former convent's walls have witnessed countless transformations, from sacred sanctuary to healing haven when it served as a hospital. Inside, sunlight streams through simple windows, illuminating modest frescoes that seem to glow against whitewashed walls.

#6. Palazzo Amenduni

Rising proudly from the medieval street plan, Palazzo Amenduni commands attention with its aristocratic bearing. This isn't just another noble residence, it's a masterpiece of regional baroque architecture where every carved detail tells a story of wealth, power, and artistic ambition.

Though its grand rooms may be closed to visitors, the palace's façade serves as an open-air museum of architectural detail. Look closely at the ornate balconies, where iron railings twist into intricate patterns, and stone masks peer down from above, their expressions frozen in eternal watchfulness over the blue-tinted streets below.

#7. Castello di Casamassima

The Castello di Casamassima was originally constructed in the 12th century during the Norman period, though its exact founding date remains somewhat unclear in historical records. The initial fortress was built as part of the Norman defensive network established throughout Puglia after their conquest of southern Italy.

The castle underwent significant expansions during the Swabian period (13th century) under Emperor Frederick II, who strengthened many fortifications throughout his kingdom. The Angevin dynasty (late 13th-14th centuries) later modified the structure, and further renovations occurred during the Aragonese rule of the region (15th century).

The fortress served multiple strategic purposes: military defense against potential invasions from the Adriatic Sea, control over local trade routes and agricultural lands, symbol of political authority over the surrounding territory, and administrative center for tax collection and governance. The castle changed hands multiple times throughout its history, being owned by various noble families including the Acquaviva family and later the Vaaz Counts. Each noble family modified the structure according to the architectural styles and defensive needs of their era.

#8. Chiesa del Purgatorio

A short walk from the castle takes you to the Church of Purgatorio, a lesser-known but fascinating site. The church was dedicated to souls in purgatory, and its interior features religious iconography depicting themes of the afterlife.

#9. Piazza Giuseppe Garibaldi

End your walk at Piazza Giuseppe Garibaldi, another small but pleasant square lined with traditional Puglian trattorias and bars. It's the perfect spot to sit down, enjoy a glass of local Primitivo wine, and taste regional dishes like orecchiette pasta or focaccia barese.

Casamassima Festivals and Sagre Throughout the Year

La Pentolaccia

First weekend of Lent (February or March)

Originating in 1977, La Pentolaccia is Casamassima's unique take on the traditional Italian carnival. Initially centered around the breaking of a pot ("pentolaccia"), the festival has evolved into a vibrant event featuring parades of floats, performances by dance schools, masked groups, and special guests.

Le Pupe della Quarantana

Throughout Lent (February to April, Easter day varies)

This unique tradition involves displaying seven dolls named Anna, Pagano, Rebecca, Susanna, Lazzaro, Palma, and Pasqua at the beginning of Lent. Each Sunday, one doll is removed, symbolizing the passage of time leading up to Easter. This custom reflects the town's blend of religious observance and cultural heritage, offering a visual countdown to the resurrection celebration.

Festa di Nostra Signora del Monte Carmelo

Last Sunday of July

This festival honors Our Lady of Mount Carmel, one of the patron saints of Casamassima. The celebration includes religious processions, where the statue of the Madonna is carried through the streets, accompanied by local bands and devotees. The town is adorned with lights and decorations, creating a festive atmosphere that reflects the deep-rooted faith and traditions of the community.

Festa di San Rocco

Second Sunday of September

Dedicated to Saint Rocco, the other patron saint of Casamassima, this festival is a significant event in the town's cultural calendar. The statue of Saint Rocco is paraded through the streets, draped in a silver mantle donated by emigrants and adorned with gold jewelry offered by devotees in gratitude for blessings received.

Sagra del Coniglio

Mid-September

The Sagra del Coniglio is a food festival celebrating the local culinary tradition of rabbit dishes. Held at venues like Cantina Lattavino, the event offers attendees the opportunity to savor various rabbit-based recipes, showcasing the rich flavors of Casamassima's cuisine. The festival fosters community spirit and attracts food enthusiasts eager to experience authentic regional specialties.

Corteo Storico Corrado IV di Svevia

Second Sunday of October

This historical reenactment commemorates an event from April 1252, when Conrad IV of Germany, son of Emperor Frederick II, passed through Casamassima and restored the fief to Roberto da Casamaxima. The procession features around 400 participants dressed in medieval attire, accompanied by street artists, flag bearers, musicians, dancers, fire eaters, knights, jugglers, and theatrical performances.

Day Trips: Nearby Sites, Cities, and Towns

Castello Normano-Svevo. The Norman-Swabian Castle of Sannicandro stands like a stone sentinel just 12 kilometers (7.5 miles) from Casamassima's blue-painted streets. This magnificent fortress tells a tale of three empires: born under Lombard hands, raised by Norman vision, and perfected through Swabian ingenuity under the great Frederick II himself. Behind its imposing medieval walls and across its still-standing drawbridge, visitors discover a world where nobility once walked. The central courtyard echoes with centuries of history, while the intimate Chapel of San Giovanni offers a glimpse into medieval spirituality.

Rutigliano. Just 9 kilometers (5.6 miles) from Casamassima, Rutigliano reveals its artistic soul through the unique art of fischietti, whimsical terracotta whistles that have become symbols of local craftsmanship. Wandering through its whitewashed old town feels like stepping into a living museum, where every corner tells a story.

Logistics

Train: Casamassima has a small train station on the Ferrovie del Sud Est (FSE) line. Trains connect Casamassima to Bari, Putignano, and Taranto, but service is limited compared to major stations.

Bus: Ferrovie del Sud Est (FSE) buses run between Casamassima and Bari, Rutigliano, Turi, and other nearby towns. STP Bari also operates services connecting Casamassima to Bari and surrounding areas.

Car: Casamassima is near SS100 (Strada Statale 100), which connects Bari to Taranto.

Parking: Free parking is available in residential areas and outskirts of the historic center.

Restaurant Recommendations

Da Angelo - Pizzeria Antipasteria. Address: Corso Giuseppe Garibaldi, 85

Known for its amazing pizza and antipasti, this restaurant offers a delightful dining experience with a variety of delicious dishes.

FraCristò. Address: Via Noicattaro 2

A beautifully decorated restaurant with superb food and a very welcoming atmosphere. It's a magnificent spot for seafood lovers.

Accommodations

For the festival, I recommend three to four nights in town.

L'ArChasetta Historic Aparments. Address: Via Paliodoro, 7

A charming 4-star hotel offering a unique blend of history and comfort, with beautifully decorated rooms and a welcoming atmosphere.

CHAPTER TWENTY-NINE

Calzone Chronicles in Acquaviva

A Folded Feast of Tradition and Flavor

Sagra del Calzone

Where: Acquaviva delle Fonti

When: Third weekend of October.

Average Festival Temperatures: High 22°C (72°F). Low 14°C (57°F).

Sagra Website: https://www.sagradelcalzone.it/

Acquaviva's Legacy

Archaeological treasures tell tales of pre-Roman tribes who first recognized this land's promise, building lives around its pure waters and fertile soils. Acquaviva thrived as a key agricultural center, supplying Rome's sprawling empire when Roman influence extended across the peninsula. Ancient roads and aqueducts, their stones still visible today, trace the arteries of this ancient civilization like lines on history's palm.

As Rome's light dimmed, Acquaviva became a prize fought over by successive waves of conquerors. Lombard warriors, Byzantine generals, and Norman knights all left their mark on these hills. The medieval town rose like a fortress from the landscape, its walls and castle standing defiant against the chaos of the age. Within these protective embraces, feudal lords held court while common folk carved out lives from the generous earth. Though plagues and wars took their toll, a resilient community of several hundred souls kept the town's heart beating through the darkest of times.

Acquaviva bloomed during the Renaissance. Wealthy patrons, inspired by the revival of classical learning, transformed the town into a canvas for artistic expression. Churches reached heavenward with elegant spires, while noble palazzi lined streets with their sophisticated facades. The Baroque period painted additional layers of grandeur onto this renaissance masterpiece, gifting the town with ornate decorations that still catch the eye and stir the soul. As beauty flourished, so did prosperity, with the population swelling beyond a thousand residents.

Medieval alleys and Renaissance piazzas are now home to artisan workshops and family restaurants blending ancient recipes with modern tastes. The town's 4,200 residents share their heritage with visitors who come seeking authentic Italian experiences among these storied streets.

The Calzone Festival

The origins of the calzone can be traced to the agricultural and pastoral traditions of Puglia. The town of Acquaviva, known for its natural springs and fertile land, provided the ideal conditions for growing wheat, producing cheese, and cultivating vegetables, key ingredients in this dish.

During the Middle Ages, shepherds and farmers needed a meal that was both hearty and portable. Bakers developed a folded dough filled with local ingredients, creating a convenient, self-contained meal that could be eaten on the go. Evolving from humble worker fare to a regional specialty, the calzone is now traditionally stone-baked and celebrated at family gatherings.

Today, the Sagra del Calzone honors this culinary tradition, offering visitors a taste of Acquaviva's history through its signature dish.

From Field to Festival: A Celebration's Genesis

As summer's last warmth kissed the harvested fields in 18th-century Acquaviva, something magical happened. Farmers and bakers, their work done for the season, gathered to celebrate nature's abundance. Their feasts, sparked by gratitude and community spirit, centered around the humble yet ingenious calzone. These gatherings, informal at first, grew like well-kneaded dough, expanding to embrace merchants, travelers, and neighboring towns, until the very streets of Acquaviva became an open-air celebration of culinary prowess.

In the 1950s, as Italy emerged from darkness into a new dawn, visionary locals recognized their heritage's value. The Sagra del Calzone was reborn, not just as a festival, but as a declaration of cultural identity. Like the dish itself, the celebration expanded, embracing new flavors while honoring ancient techniques.

Today's Sagra transforms Acquaviva into a theater of culinary delights. The air fills with the perfume of baking bread and bubbling cheese as master bakers demonstrate their art alongside eager apprentices. Traditional calzoni stuffed with ricotta and salami share space with innovative creations, each a chapter in an strengthening culinary story.

Thousands of visitors crowd medieval streets, drawn by the promise of authenticity in an age of mass production. Yet beyond the festivities lies something deeper, a town's unwavering commitment to preserving its soul, one perfectly folded calzone at a time.

Friday: Opening Day

6:00p.m.

The festival begins with the inauguration of food stands in Piazza Garibaldi, where visitors can savor the signature calzone and other local specialties.

Later Evening

Cultural or community events, such as award ceremonies or presentations by local organizations, often take place.

9:00p.m.

Live musical performances kick off the festivities.

Saturday

9:00 p.m.

Entertainment continues with dynamic shows.

Sunday: Family Fun and Grand Finale

Morning to Afternoon

Activities such as model car exhibitions or other family-friendly events are organized, entertaining all ages.

9:00 p.m.

The festival concludes with a major musical act.

Throughout the festival

- **Food Stands:** Offering a variety of local dishes, with the calzone as the star attraction.

- **Artisan Markets:** Featuring handcrafted goods, antiques, and local products, perfect for those seeking unique souvenirs.

- **Children's Attractions:** Including rides and games to keep younger visitors entertained.

Acquaviva Walking Tour

#1. Piazza Garibaldi

Begin your tour Piazza Garibaldi, Acquaviva's main square and the center of local life. Surrounded by elegant buildings, cafés, and historical landmarks, this lively square is a perfect introduction to the town.

#2. Cattedrale di Sant'Eustachio (Acquaviva Cathedral)

A short walk from Piazza Garibaldi, this 18th-century Baroque-style cathedral is dedicated to Saint Eustace, the town's patron saint. It houses stunning frescoes, intricate stuccoes, and a relic of the saint. The cathedral is a significant religious and artistic landmark, reflecting Acquaviva's deep-rooted faith and history.

#3. Torre dell'Orologio (Clock Tower)

One of the town's most recognizable landmarks, this historic clock tower stands as a reminder of Acquaviva's civic past. Originally part of medieval fortifications, it offers a great photo opportunity and a connection to the town's evolution over centuries.

#4. Palazzo de Mari

A 17th-century noble residence, this palazzo once housed the ruling De Mari family. Today, it serves as the town hall, but its elegant courtyard, historic façade, and architectural details remain intact. It is a prime example of aristocratic life in southern Italy during the Baroque period.

Palazzo de Mari

#5. Chiesa di San Domenico

The Chiesa di San Domenico represents one of the town's most significant religious monuments, established in the 16th century as part of the Dominican

Order's expansion throughout southern Italy. Construction began around 1530 under the patronage of the Acquaviva family, the powerful feudal lords who gave the town its name.

The church exemplifies the transition between Renaissance and Baroque architectural styles that characterized religious buildings in Puglia during this period. Its facade features a harmonious design with classical elements, including a central portal framed by stone columns and topped with a triangular pediment. The bell tower, added in the early 17th century, rises alongside the main structure and remains a distinctive landmark in the town's skyline.

The interior follows a Latin cross plan with a single nave and several side chapels that were funded by prominent local families. The church houses numerous artistic treasures, including a significant collection of 17th-century paintings by Neapolitan artists. Particularly noteworthy is the altarpiece depicting "The Mysteries of the Rosary" attributed to Carlo Rosa, a prominent painter from the Apulian school.

Adjacent to the church stands the monastery complex with its serene cloister, surrounded by elegant porticoes supported by stone columns. The cloister served as the heart of monastic life for the Dominican community until the suppression of religious orders in the 19th century.

#6. Piazza dei Martiri (Fountain & Market Area)

A charming open space featuring a historic fountain, this piazza is home to local markets where you can find fresh produce, cheeses, and baked goods. If visiting in the morning, stop by a local bakery to try pane di Altamura, a traditional bread from the region.

#7. The Underground Cisterns (Ipogei dell'Acquedotto)

Beneath the surface of Acquaviva lies a captivating legacy of ingenuity and resilience, the Underground Cisterns (Ipogei dell'Acquedotto). Named for its abundant natural fountains, Acquaviva earned the title delle Fonti, a nod to the life-giving waters that once nourished every corner of the town. These hidden reservoirs were ingeniously engineered to collect and store water, ensuring a vital supply during dry spells and sustaining both daily life and local agriculture.

Acquaviva Festivals and Sagra Throughout the Year

Sagra della Cipolla Rossa (Red Onion Festival)

Late July

This festival celebrates the renowned red onion of Acquaviva delle Fonti, known for its sweetness and unique flavor. The event features culinary stands offering dishes centered on the red onion, live music, and cultural activities.

Patronal Feast of Madonna di Costantinopoli

First Tuesday of September

A significant religious event honoring the Madonna of Constantinople, the town's patron saint. The celebration spans several days, featuring religious processions, historical reenactments, and the traditional launch of a large hot-air balloon.

Festival of Primitivo Wine and Black Chickpeas

November

This festival celebrates local specialities, focusing on Primitivo wine and black chickpeas, both integral to the region's culinary traditions. Attendees can enjoy tastings, culinary workshops, and cultural events.

Day Trip Options: Nearby Sites, Citiess and Towns

Altamura. 27 kilometers (17 miles) from Acquaviva. Rising proudly from the rugged Murge Plateau, Altamura beckons with aromas of its world-famous bread wafting through medieval streets. This isn't just any bread, it's DOP Altamura, born from ancient grains and centuries-old techniques.

Behind massive limestone walls, the city unfolds like a historical tapestry, crowned by the magnificent Cattedrale di Santa Maria Assunta, Emperor Frederick II's architectural masterpiece. Venture deeper to discover the Pulo, a massive karst sinkhole that splits the earth in a dramatic display of natural architecture.

Perhaps most intriguing is the cave where Altamura Man, one of Europe's oldest Neanderthal specimens, lay undisturbed for millennia, whispering secrets of humanity's distant past.

Castellaneta. 55 kilometers (34 miles) from Acquaviva. Perched dramatically above deep ravines, Castellaneta stands as a testament to nature's grandeur and human ambition. This birthplace of silent film icon Rudolph Valentino offers an intoxicating blend of natural and cultural wonders.

The Gravina di Castellaneta cuts through the landscape like nature's own amphitheater, its towering walls echoing with centuries of history. The town's 13th-century cathedral, adorned with breathtaking frescoes, keeps watch over winding medieval alleys that seem frozen in time. In summer, the allure of Castellaneta Marina's pristine Ionian beaches provides a perfect counterpoint to the town's historic charms, offering visitors a taste of both mountain and maritime Puglia.

Laterza. 43 kilometers (27 miles) west of Acquaviva. Where ancient craft meets raw nature, Laterza guards its treasures with quiet pride. The Gravina di Laterza, one of Italy's most impressive canyons, slices through the landscape like a primordial wound, creating a paradise for hikers and wildlife enthusiasts. But Laterza's soul truly shines in its ceramic traditions. Workshops buzz with activity as master artisans shape tiles into works of art, continuing a craft passed down through generations.

The Chiesa Matrice di San Lorenzo stands as a testament to faith and artistry, its frescoes telling stories of centuries past. For a truly authentic experience, visit the fornelli pronti, where local butchers transform fresh cuts into flame-kissed delicacies on demand—a tradition as old as the canyon itself.

Logistics

Train: The Acquaviva delle Fonti railway station lies on the Bari–Taranto line and is operated by Trenitalia. It offers regional services connecting Bari, Gioia del Colle, and Taranto. Local trains (Treno regionale) facilitate travel between these cities.

Bus: Public bus transportation is managed by Sita Sud.

Car: Acquaviva delle Fonti is accessible via several provincial roads, including SP 20: connects to Gioia-Santeramo, SP 48: connects to Cassano delle Murge.

Parking: Various parking areas are available in the city, both free and paid. During events or festivals, it's advisable to arrive early to secure a parking spot.

Restaurant Recommendations

La Sorgente. Address: Piazza Giuseppe Garibaldi, 9

Known for its authentic local food and wine, this spot offers a warm welcome and fast service. It's a brilliant spot for enjoying traditional Italian dishes with a modern twist.

Macelleria e Braceria al Viltello d'Oro di Ventura Vincenzo. Address: Via, Estramurale S. Pietro, 70

Macelleria e Braceria "Al Vitello d'Oro" di Ventura Vincenzo is a well-known butcher shop and steakhouse that combines traditional Italian butchery with a grill experience. Customers can select premium cuts of meat directly from the counter and have them expertly cooked on-site, ensuring freshness, flavor, and quality.

Accommodation

There are no hotels in town. With the sagre it is unnecessary to stay overnight.

See Casamassima: The Blue Jewel of Puglia Chapter for a nearby hotel option if needed.

Winter Celebrations

November through January

CHAPTER THIRTY

Festa Fusion Martina Franca

Saints and Sweets

Fiera di San Martino e Sagra delle Frittelle

Where: Martina Franca

When: November 11 is St Martin's Feast Day. Events occur on the days and weekend around this feast day celebration.

Average Festival Temperatures: High 18°C (64°F). Low 11°C (52°F).

#1. Festa di San Martino: A celebration of Saint Martin marked by wine tastings, roasted chestnuts, and lively gatherings, symbolizing the transition from autumn to winter in Martina Franca.

#2. Sagra delle Frittelle: A food festival dedicated to frittelle (savory and sweet fried dough treats), where locals and visitors enjoy traditional flavors and festive street performances.

#FestaFusion: Two or more festivals in the same town around the same time allowing visitors to enjoy more than one event.

Martina Franca Through the Ages

Nestled in the picturesque Itria Valley of Puglia, Martina Franca is a town of Baroque elegance, whitewashed alleys, and a rich historical legacy that dates back thousands of years. Sitting at an elevation of approximately 431 meters (1414 feet) above sea level, the town offers sweeping views of the surrounding countryside, dotted with the region's iconic trulli houses. Today, with a population of 49,000, Martina Franca is one of the larger towns in inland Puglia, thriving as a cultural and economic hub while retaining its historic charm.

Martina Franca's origins trace back to pre-Roman times, when the indigenous Messapians inhabited the area, establishing early agricultural settlements. As the Roman Empire expanded, the region became part of the larger Roman infrastructure, benefiting from trade and road networks that connected it to Tarentum (modern-day Taranto) and Brundisium (Brindisi). However, with the fall of Rome in the 5th century, Martina Franca, like much of southern Italy, entered a period of decline as successive waves of Byzantines, Lombards, and Saracens fought for control over Puglia.

The official founding of Martina Franca, with its namesake and patron St. Martin, is attributed to the early 14th century, when Prince Philip I of Anjou granted the area to a group of settlers seeking refuge from invasions and economic hardship.

In 1310, Prince Philip of Taranto (a member of the House of Anjou) officially recognized the town's autonomy and offered it certain privileges, including tax exemptions, hence the name Franca (meaning "free" in medieval Latin). During this period, fortified walls and gates were constructed to protect the burgeoning settlement from bandit raids and outside threats.

By the 16th and 17th centuries, Martina Franca had grown into a thriving town, benefiting from the wealth and influence of local aristocratic families. The Duchy of Martina Franca, under Spanish rule, saw an era of economic prosperity driven by agriculture, wool production, and trade. Many of the grand Baroque palaces and churches that define the town today were constructed during this time, including the opulent Basilica di San Martino, dedicated to the town's patron saint, St. Martin of Tours.

Martina Franca's Palazzo Ducale, built in the 17th century, became a seat of power and administration, symbolizing the town's growing political significance. Its intricate frescoes and grand halls reflected the artistic and architectural flourishing of the period. The town's unique urban fabric, with its maze-like alleys and elegant piazzas, was shaped by this Baroque influence, distinguishing it from other Apulian towns dominated by medieval or Norman styles.

Entering the 19th and 20th centuries, Martina Franca experienced modernization while maintaining its historical identity. The unification of Italy in 1861 integrated it into the national framework, and the town gradually transitioned from an agricultural economy to a more diverse economic structure, including tourism, commerce, and cultural industries. The Itria Valley's increasing popularity as a travel destination has further elevated Martina Franca's significance in recent years.

#1. The Fair of St. Martin

Imagine wandering through the ancient streets of Martina Franca as the crisp November air carries the irresistible aroma of freshly fried dough and roasting chestnuts. For centuries, these same cobblestone paths have witnessed one of Puglia's most cherished fall celebrations: the Fiera di San Martino e Sagra delle Frittelle.

Who is St. Martin of Tours?

This vibrant festival honors Saint Martin of Tours, a Roman soldier turned humble priest who, legend says, cut his cloak in half to share with a freezing beggar, only to dream that night of Jesus wearing the gifted garment. This act of compassion made him one of Christianity's most beloved saints, and his feast day became synonymous with generosity and sharing.

As autumn paints the surrounding Valle d'Itria in golden hues, locals and visitors gather to honor Martin's legacy and an age-old Italian saying: "A San Martino ogni mosto diventa vino", on St. Martin's Day, all grape must becomes wine.

Festival Events

Late Morning to Afternoon

This period is filled with food stalls offering chestnuts, fried sweets, and wine tastings. There are also various entertainment activities, including music and games.

Afternoon

The festival continues with more food and drink offerings, as well as cultural events like book presentations, shows, and exhibitions.

Evening

The festival extends into the evening with live music, dance performances, and more food stalls.

Patronal Feast and Traditions on November 11

Mass and Procession: Honoring Saint Martin, with solemn mass in the Basilica di San Martino and blessed wheat seeds displayed alongside silver statues of the Patrons Martino and Comasia.

Animal Fair: Held in the Ortolini area, featuring Murgese horses, donkeys, farmyard animals, and horse harness dealers displaying bells, and saddles.

Local Products and Crafts: Stalls in Piazza XX Settembre and Corso Italia showcasing master coat makers, household goods, agricultural tools, and local delicacies.

Traditional Foods: Butchers prepare meat broth, porchetta, and capocollo, a typical local product.

#2. Sagra of the Frittelle

The Sagra delle Frittelle in Martina Franca is a beloved food festival celebrating one of the region's most traditional fried delicacies: the frittella. The Fiera di San Martino e Sagra delle Frittelle stands as a reminder that some of life's most precious moments are found in the simple pleasures of good food, fine wine, and warm company, all set against the backdrop of Puglia's timeless beauty.

While the exact origins of the sagra are not officially documented, it is believed to have developed as a local food celebration about 100 years ago, when many Italian towns began organizing sagre to preserve and promote culinary traditions. However, frittelle themselves have a much older history, dating back to peasant food traditions that utilized simple, readily available ingredients, flour, water, yeast, and oil, to create savory or sweet fried dough treats.

Martina Franca was a natural place for such a festival because it is one of Puglia's most culturally vibrant Baroque towns, known for its agricultural traditions and excellent local products. The town has long been a gathering place for markets, feasts, and culinary events, and frittelle, often associated with winter festivities and wine tastings, became the ideal food to highlight during this seasonal festival.

Special Festival Food
Frittelle

The festival's signature treat, frittelle, are pillowy rounds of fried dough that emerge golden and crisp from bubbling oil, often dusted with sugar or drizzled with local honey. These simple yet addictive pastries have been a festival staple for generations, their warmth perfectly complementing the first sips of new wine.

The narrow streets come alive with the joyful chaos of market vendors, their stalls overflowing with artisanal treasures and local delicacies. The air fills with the melody of traditional Puglian music, while the tantalizing scent of frittelle wafts from busy food stalls. Wine flows freely as local vintners proudly share their newly crafted vino novello, continuing a tradition that has brought communities together for generations.

Sagra Events

Wine Tastings: Featuring local vintners presenting their novello wines.

Street Food Stalls: Offering frittelle, roasted chestnuts, and other seasonal specialties.

Folklore Performances: Including traditional Puglian music and dance.

Market Stalls: With artisanal crafts, regional products, and local delicacies.

Martina Franca Walking Tour

#1. Piazza Roma & Palazzo Ducale

Begin your journey at Piazza Roma, the grand entrance to the town's historical center. Standing tall with its ornate balconies, grand staircase, and opulent frescoes, Palazzo Ducale invites you into the world of Martina Franca's noble past. Step inside to admire the lavishly decorated rooms, including the stunning Hall of Mythology, painted with intricate allegorical scenes.

Outside, relax by the elegant Fountain of the Dolphins, a charming centerpiece of the piazza. Built in the 17th century by the Caracciolo family, the Palazzo Ducale stands as a symbol of Martina Franca's aristocratic past. It was once the seat of the town's ruling dukes and today houses municipal offices, art exhibitions, and historical archives.

#2. Porta di Santo Stefano (St. Stephen's Gate)

Standing beneath the weathered limestone arch of Porta di Santo Stefano feels like crossing a threshold in time. This majestic 14th-century gateway, with its time-smoothed stones and elegant proportions, marks more than just an entrance to Martina Franca's historic heart. It's a portal to another era. As sunlight plays across its ancient stonework, you can almost hear the echoes of centuries past: the clip-clop of merchant horses, the calls of street vendors, and the rustle of noble ladies' silk gowns.

#3. Basilica di San Martino: A Symphony in Stone and Light

Rising majestically above Piazza Plebiscito, the Basilica di San Martino commands attention with its soaring baroque facade that seems to dance in the shifting Mediterranean light. This 18th-century masterpiece, built atop the foundations of a medieval church, represents the pinnacle of Pugliese baroque architecture. Its elaborate exterior is a celebration of faith rendered in limestone, where master craftsmen transformed solid rock into delicate lace-like decorations, dynamic spiral columns, and expressive statuary that seems to come alive in the golden hour.

Step inside, and the basilica reveals its true magnificence. Soaring vaulted ceilings painted with celestial scenes draw the eye heavenward, while the play of light through tall windows creates an ever-changing atmosphere throughout the day.

In the Chapel of San Martino, the patron saint's statue tells the famous story of his charity, the Roman soldier who cut his cloak in half to share with a beggar. The chapel's rich marble work and gilded details create a fitting shrine to this beloved saint, while side chapels offer quiet spaces for reflection, each one a jewel box of artistic treasures.

#4. Piazza Maria Immacolata (Loggia del Cavaliere)

A short walk from the basilica leads you to the enchanting Piazza Maria Immacolata, often referred to as Loggia del Cavaliere (Knights). Surrounded by curving white arcades, the square exudes an old-world charm that invites you to pause, sip a local espresso, and take in the bustling yet serene atmosphere.

#5. Chiesa di San Domenico

Step inside San Domenico to admire the richly adorned ceiling, frescoes, and intricate altars. The façade's swirling stone designs and statuary details are a true testament to the artistry of the time. Inside, an elaborate wooden pulpit and stunning side chapels bring centuries of devotion to life. Built in 1746 by the Dominican Order, this church is a striking example of Martina Franca's exuberant Baroque architecture.

#6. Via Cavour & Hidden Alleys

Wander along Via Cavour, where time seems to slow. The maze of whitewashed alleys, punctuated with ornate doorways and wrought-iron balconies, invites you to explore at a leisurely pace. Take in the scent of freshly baked focaccia from hidden bakeries, peek into artisan workshops, and let yourself get delightfully lost in Martina Franca's timeless charm.

#7. Chiesa del Carmine

A serene retreat from the lively streets, Chiesa del Carmine welcomes you with its simple yet elegant façade. Inside, admire the beautifully carved wooden altars and a collection of historic religious paintings. The peaceful ambiance makes it an ideal spot for reflection before concluding your tour.

Church of the Carmine

#8. Piazza XX Settembre & Local Delicacies

End your walk at Piazza XX Settembre, the perfect place to rest and savor the town's culinary delights. Treat yourself to a panzerotto (a fried pocket of dough filled with tomato and mozzarella) or sample the famous Capocollo di Martina Franca, a delectable local cured meat.

Martina Franca Festivals and Sagre Throughout the Year

Festival della Valle d'Itria

July

When July's golden light bathes the Valle d'Itria, Martina Franca transforms into an enchanted realm of forgotten melodies and rediscovered musical treasures. Since 1975, the Festival della Valle d'Itria has been more than just a summer opera festival. It's a passionate quest to breathe new life into opera's lost jewels. Within the grand halls of the Palazzo Ducale, where baroque frescoes dance overhead, long-forgotten arias soar once again. The festival's unique charm lies in its dedication to musical archaeology, unearthing rare scores and presenting them as they were first imagined by their composers. https://www.festivaldellavalleditria.it/il-festival

Ghironda Festival: A Global Symphony in Ancient Streets

August

Each August, the Ghironda Festival turns Martina Franca into a vibrant crossroads of world culture, where the pulse of African drums might mingle with Asian silk dancers and European street performers. Since its inception in 1995, this festival has woven a colorful tapestry of global arts through the town's historic fabric. The name "Ghironda" comes from the hurdy-gurdy, a medieval instrument that wandering musicians once carried through Europe, a fitting symbol for this nomadic celebration of arts. https://www.laghironda.it/

Festival dei Sensi

3rd weekend in August

In August, the Itria Valley transforms into a living celebration of sensory delights, where ancient masserie (fortified farmhouses) and sun-drenched olive groves become stages for an extraordinary cultural feast. The Festival dei Sensi isn't just an event, it's a journey through the five senses that defines Puglia's soul. Each year brings a new theme that weaves together the valley's treasures: perhaps the music of olive oil pressing, the perfume of wild herbs crushed underfoot, or the play of light on centuries-old stone walls. https://www.festivaldeisensi.it/w/

Festival del Cabaret

August

The Festival del Cabaret transforms the city into Italy's capital of comedy. For over 15 years, this festival has brought warmth and wit to the baroque streets, where medieval walls amplify waves of laughter into the starlit sky. Beyond a comedy competition, it serves as a springboard for Italy's future comedic stars, uniting newcomers with celebrated veterans of Italian television and theater. https://www.festivaldelcabaret.com/

Le Nove Lampade (The Nine Lamps)

December 16th to 24th

Le Nove Lampade, the Nine Lamps, transform the Church of San Domenico into a beacon of anticipation for Christmas. Each morning from December

16th to 24th, while the rest of the town still sleeps, devotees gather in the pre-dawn darkness. The ritual begins as the first hints of light touch the church's ancient stones, with traditional songs that have echoed through these walls for generations.

Day Trips: Nearby Sites, Cities, and Towns

Ceglie Messapica. Just 20 kilometers (12 miles) southeast of Martina Franca, Ceglie Messapica rises from ancient Messapian roots to present a town where culinary artistry and medieval majesty intertwine. In its historic heart, the Borgo Medievale unfolds like a stonemason's dream, where weathered limestone walls hold centuries of stories, and narrow vicoli (alleys) lead to unexpected piazzas perfumed with the aromas of local kitchens. The imposing Castello Ducale stands sentinel over the town, its robust walls softened by time and Mediterranean sun.

Noci. Venture 30 kilometers (19 miles) northwest of Martina Franca to discover Noci, a town that guards its architectural treasures like precious gems. Here, the mysterious gnostre – intimate courtyards enclosed by ancient stone – create a honeycomb of private worlds within the urban fabric. Each courtyard tells its own story through worn doorways and time-smoothed steps, while the serene Abbazia Madonna della Scala offers spiritual respite on the town's outskirts.

Logistics

Train: Martina Franca is on the Ferrovie del Sud Est (FSE) regional train network. Direct trains run from Bari Centrale (~2 hours).

Bus: The Marozzi and Miccolis bus companies operate routes connecting Martina Franca to Bari, Brindisi, Taranto, and Lecce.

Car: From Bari take SS100 to Gioia del Colle, then SS172.

Parking: The historic center is mostly a ZTL (Limited Traffic Zone). If you're staying overnight, check if your hotel provides a permit or parking recommendations. Parking options include: Parcheggio Piazzale Crispi (near the train station), Via Guglielmi Parking Lot, Parcheggio Viale Europa. Blue-lined (paid) and white-lined (free) parking outside the ZTL.

Restaurant Recommendations

Osteria del Coco Pazzo. Address: Via Arco Mastrovito, 18/19

A charming trattoria offering a delightful selection of antipasti, pasta dishes, and meat-based specialties. Known for its warm atmosphere and authentic Italian cuisine, it's a favorite among locals and visitors alike.

La Pasteria. Address: Viale Dei Lecci, 31

Famous for its freshly made pasta dishes, La Pasteria provides a wonderful dining experience with a menu that highlights the flavors of Puglia. The restaurant is known for its friendly service and cozy ambiance.

Braceria Granaldi. Address: Via Vincenzo Bellini, 108

A popular butcher-grill restaurant, Braceria Granaldi offers a variety of grilled meats and traditional Puglian dishes. It's a glorious spot for meat lovers looking to enjoy hearty and flavorful meals.

Accommodation

For the festival, I recommend three to four nights in town.

Park Hotel San Michele. Address: Viale Domenico Carella, 9

The Park Hotel is a 4-star property set within its own beautifully manicured park, creating a peaceful retreat despite being only a short walk from the historic center of Martina Franca. Its public areas exude a refined atmosphere, with grand interiors and traditional décor that pay homage to the region's history. Rooms tend to be classically furnished, featuring large windows or balconies overlooking the lush gardens or the inviting swimming pool.

Relais Casabella. Address: Via Tiro a Segno 6

This charming 4.5-star hotel presents a more intimate option in a tranquil residential neighborhood, just a leisurely stroll from the town's center. With fewer rooms than a larger hotel, this boutique-style accommodation puts a strong emphasis on personalized service.

Monopoli's Maritime Miracle

Mary's Arrival by Sea

Festa della Madonna della Madia

Where: Monopoli

When: December 15-16

Average Festival Temperatures: High 14°C (57°F). 10°C (50°F).

Monopoli: Where Stone Meets Sea

Nestled along the Adriatic coast, Monopoli stands as a testament to millennia of Mediterranean history. The city's origins can be traced to the 5th century BC, when Greek settlers first established a permanent settlement on this strategic stretch of coastline. The name "Monopoli" derives from the Greek "monos polis," meaning a unique city, though some scholars argue it refers to the city's historical role as a significant trading port.

The ancient settlement flourished under successive civilizations, each leaving an indelible mark on its character. During the Roman period, Monopoli served as a crucial maritime link between the Empire's eastern and western territories. The Romans developed the natural harbor, constructing facilities that would form the foundation of the city's maritime tradition for centuries to come.

The Medieval period brought dramatic changes to Monopoli's landscape. Following the fall of the Western Roman Empire, the city faced recurring invasions from various powers seeking control of the Adriatic. The Byzantines fortified the settlement in the 6th century AD, constructing defensive walls that still partially stand today.

The Norman conquest in the 11th century ushered in a period of relative stability and cultural flowering, during which many of the city's most notable religious buildings were constructed, including the magnificent Cathedral of Maria Santissima della Madia.

In the modern era, Monopoli has evolved while maintaining strong connections to its historical roots. Medieval walls enclose the old town's (centro storico's) maze of narrow streets and picturesque squares. The Porto Vecchio (Old Port) continues to shelter fishing boats, though today they share space with pleasure craft. Coastal and inland residential areas have expanded the city's limits beyond its historical footprint. Monopoli has a population of 49,000 inhabitants.

Festa della Madonna della Madia: A Maritime Miracle

Deep in the heart of winter, as December's chill sweeps across the Adriatic, the city of Monopoli awakens to its most cherished celebration. More than just a religious event, the annual Festa della Madonna della Madia embodies this historic maritime community's spirit, blending faith, history, and civic identity into a culturally significant tradition lasting nearly nine centuries.

The festival's origins trace back to a miraculous event in 1117, during a time of profound crisis in Monopoli's history. The city's cathedral, then under construction, had stalled because of a critical shortage of wooden beams needed to complete the roof. According to historical accounts and cherished local tradition, on the night of December 16, fishermen witnessed an extraordinary sight: a large wooden raft, known as a "madia," floating toward Monopoli's harbor. Upon this humble vessel rested a Byzantine icon of the Madonna and Child, its presence illuminating the dark waters of the Adriatic.

The discovery proved doubly miraculous. Not only had the city received a sacred icon of remarkable beauty and spiritual significance, but the wooden raft itself provided exactly the materials needed to complete the cathedral's roof. This convergence of practical necessity and divine intervention has remained central to the festival's narrative, reflecting the intimate connection between the sacred and the everyday in medieval Mediterranean life.

Monopoli Cathedral

The icon itself, painted in the Byzantine style, depicts the Madonna and Child with characteristic spiritual gravity and grace. Art historians date its creation to the 11th or early 12th century, suggesting it may have originated in the workshops of Constantinople or another major center of Byzantine art.

Festival Events

December 12–14: Triduum of Preparation

5:45 p.m. Mass

Meditative Holy Rosary recitation at the Cathedral and mass.

December 15: Vigil of the Feast

7:30 a.m., 10:00 a.m., 11:30 a.m Mass

Holy Masses at the Cathedral and Rosary.

December 16: Feast Day of the Madonna della Madia

4:00 a.m. Band Procession

The Jubilee Band of Monopoli performs a musical procession through the city, awakening residents for the forthcoming ceremonies.

5:00 a.m. Prayer Vigil

Prayer vigil at Cala Batteria, the historic landing site of the Madonna's icon.

The celebration begins in the pre-dawn hours, as fishing boats adorned with lights gather in the harbor. The centerpiece of these maritime preparations is a meticulously crafted replica of the original raft, bearing a copy of the miraculous icon. Local fishermen, many from families who have taken part in the ceremony for generations, guide the raft through the waters of the old port, recreating the icon's legendary arrival.

5:30 a.m. Procession of the Madonna

Solemn procession from Cala Batteria to the Cathedral, retracing the path taken during the icon's legendary arrival.

Thousands of devout followers take part in the early morning procession, marking a festival of deep religious significance.. The city's streets are adorned with festive decorations, and the atmosphere is imbued with a deep sense of community. The festive decorations adorn the city streets, fostering a strong sense of community and spirituality.

The reenactment also draws thousands of spectators who line the harbor walls and crowd the narrow streets of the old city. As the raft approaches the shore, the atmosphere grows increasingly charged with emotion. The moment of the icon's landing represents a powerful confluence of past and present, as modern Monopolitani connect directly with their medieval ancestors through shared ritual and remembrance.

8:30 a.m. Mass

A solemn Mass commemorates the miracle, followed by a grand procession through the city's streets.

8:00 p.m. Concert and Fireworks

Concert in the Cathedral and fireworks light up the sky as the events grand finale.

Monopoli Walking Tour

#1. Porta Vecchia

The Porta Vecchia's limestone walls, softened by sea breezes and time, lead you to a discovery of your own. Climb the adjacent bastions, where defensive cannons once stood ready, and you'll be rewarded with a breathtaking panorama that pirates once coveted.

#2. Cattedrale di Maria Santissima della Madia

We truly enjoyed our visit to the Cathedral, an awe-inspiring space filled with centuries of devotion and artistry. The intricate marble decoration, soaring ceiling, and richly adorned chapels reflect the town's deep-rooted faith and baroque grandeur.

Cathedral Interior

#3. Piazza Giuseppe Garibaldi

A short walk from the cathedral, this lively square serves as the heart of Monopoli's old town. Surrounded by charming cafes, shops, and historic buildings, the square is perfect for a quick break. Historically, it has been a central meeting point for locals and visitors alike. The nearby clock tower adds to its picturesque appeal.

#4. Castello Carlo V

Make your way to the Castle of Charles V, a 16th-century fortress built by the Spanish to protect Monopoli from pirate attacks and Ottoman invasions. On the edge of the sea, the castle now hosts exhibitions and cultural events. Its pentagonal design and defensive structures, including a moat, reflect its military purpose. The views of the harbor from the castle walls are spectacular.

#5. Chiesa di Santa Maria degli Amalfitani

This small Romanesque church, just a few steps from the castle, was founded in the 12th century by merchants from Amalfi. Its simple exterior contrasts with its beautifully frescoed interior. The church is a testament to Monopoli's maritime connections and its role as a thriving trade hub in the Middle Ages.

#6. Palazzo Palmieri

Walk towards Palazzo Palmieri, a grand 18th-century Baroque palace in a quaint square. Once the residence of the influential Palmieri family, the palace features an elegant façade and is surrounded by narrow cobblestone streets that exude old-world charm. It is one of the most photographed spots in the city.

#7. Lungomare Santa Maria

Stroll along the scenic Lungomare Santa Maria, the seaside promenade that offers breathtaking views of the Adriatic. This walk connects the old harbor with the newer parts of the city. Along the way, you'll pass picturesque fishing boats and historic buildings, perfect for photography.

Monopoli Castle and City View

#8. Cala Porta Vecchia Beach

End your tour at Cala Porta Vecchia, a small sandy beach at the base of Monopoli's ancient walls. This beach is both a tranquil retreat and a symbol of the city's harmonious relationship with the sea. Locals and visitors enjoy its crystal-clear waters and the scenic backdrop of historic architecture.

Monopoli Feste and Sagre Throughout the Year

Corteo dei Re Magi (Arrival of the Three Kings)

January 6

Historical reenactment of the arrival of the three kings.

Palm Sunday (Domenica delle Palme)

Sunday before Easter

The Holy Week begins with the blessing of palm branches and a procession through the streets of Monopoli.

Maundy Thursday (Giovedì Santo) – Sepolcri Visits

Thursday before Easter

After the evening Mass, locals visit the "Sepolcri," altars of repose decorated with flowers in various churches. Tradition holds that visitors should stop at an odd number of altars.

Festival Food
Focaccia con Spunzèle
Traditionally prepared on Maundy Thursday and eaten on Good Friday. A focaccia topped with spring onions, blending religious observance with local culinary tradition.

Good Friday (Venerdì Santo) – Processione dei Misteri

Friday before Easter

The solemn nighttime Processione dei Misteri reenacts the Passion of Christ. Six papier-mâché statues from the 18th century, depicting scenes from the Passion, are carried from the Church of San Francesco d'Assisi through the streets, accompanied by confraternities and the somber beat of wooden instruments called *trènele*.

Monopolele-Mediterranean Ukulele Fest

May 30 – June 2

Mediterranean Ukulele Fest was launched in 2022. This festival aims to promote the ukulele as a tool for cultural exchange. It features concerts, workshops, jam sessions, and parades, transforming Monopoli into a hub for ukulele enthusiasts from around the world.

Prospero Fest

June and November

Held at the old fort of Monopoli, this festival celebrates literature and culture with author meetings, book presentations, and discussions on various topics. It's a vibrant event that brings together writers, journalists, and intellectuals. https://prosperofest.events/edizioni/

Ritratti Festival

July 17-21

Since 2005, this music festival has been held in Monopoli, featuring concerts in charming locations throughout the city. It showcases international and Italian artists, promoting kindness and cultural exchange through music. https://www.ensemble05.it/

PhEST, the International Photography and Art Festival

September 1 – November 1

This festival, held in Monopoli, focuses on photography and visual arts. It features exhibitions, workshops, and events that explore various aspects of contemporary photography and art. https://www.phest.info/

Gozzovigliando

Every Sunday in October

The festival Gozzovigliando is a celebration in Monopoli, Italy, that honors the traditional Apulian fishing boat known as the "gozzo." The name "Gozzovigliando" is a clever blend of "gozzo" and the Italian word "gozzovigliare," which means "to feast" or "to revel." This play on words reflects the festival's focus on both maritime heritage and communal festivities.

The event features markets selling handicrafts and local products, workshops for children, guided tours of the historic center, art exhibitions, performances, and musical entertainment with traditional folk songs and dances. A highlight of the festival is the free gozzo excursions and the Palio dei Gozzi, an exhibition on board the historic boats of the local navy.

Monopoli Christmas Home

December 7 - January 6

This festive event transforms Monopoli into a winter wonderland with immersive installations, shows, and events that celebrate the holiday season. It includes Christmas markets, concerts, and family-friendly activities.

Nearby Sites, Cities, and Towns

Castellana Grotte. 18 kilometers (11 miles) from Monopoli. Castellana Grotte is famous for its spectacular cave system, considered one of the most impressive in Italy. The Grotte di Castellana extends for over three kilometers and features an extraordinary series of underground chambers, tunnels, stalactites, stalagmites and dramatic formations created by water erosion over millions of years. Guided tours take visitors through highlights such as the Grave, the vast main cavern, and the White Cave, renowned for its dazzling alabaster formations.

Above ground, the historic center of Castellana Grotte offers charming streets and the Church of San Leone Magno, which features a beautiful facade and richly decorated interior. The town also hosts seasonal festivals and markets that showcase local traditions and Puglian cuisine.

Logistics

Train: Monopoli is well-connected to Bari and other major cities in Puglia via Trenitalia. The Monopoli train station is located just a 10-minute walk from the historic center. Regional trains (Regionale and Regionale Veloce) run frequently between Bari Centrale and Monopoli, with travel times of about 30 minutes.

Bus: Several bus services connect Monopoli to nearby towns and cities. The Marozzi and Miccolis bus companies operate longer routes, while local buses, like those managed by STP (Società Trasporti Provinciali), provide connections to smaller villages and the surrounding countryside.

Car: Monopoli is located approximately 40 kilometers (25 miles) southeast of Bari. By car, the journey takes about 35-40 minutes via the SS16 Adriatica highway. This scenic coastal route makes for an enjoyable drive.

Parking; Monopoli's historic center has a ZTL (Zona a Traffico Limitato), meaning driving is restricted in the old town. Visitors arriving by car can park in designated areas outside the ZTL, such as Piazza Sant'Antonio Parking Lot: Conveniently located and just a short walk from the old town. Porta Vecchia Parking Lot: Close to the historic center and the waterfront. Or Viale Aldo Moro Parking: A larger lot offering more spaces.

Restaurant Recommendations

Il Guazzetto. Address: Via Dell'Erba, 39/41

Il Guazzetto is a charming restaurant known for its seafood dishes and traditional Italian cuisine. The ambiance is cozy and inviting, making it a perfect spot for a romantic dinner or a family gathering. The menu features a variety of fresh seafood, including pasta with clams, grilled fish, and delicious tiramisu for dessert.

La Locanda dei Mercanti. Address: Via Giuseppe Garibaldi 44

La Locanda dei Mercanti offers a delightful dining experience with a focus on local ingredients and seafood. The restaurant has a rustic yet elegant atmosphere, and the menu includes a wide range of seafood dishes, such as seafood pasta, grilled octopus, and fresh oysters. The house wine and desserts are also highly recommended.

Le Cucine di Masseria Spina. Address: Viale Aldo Moro 27

Le Cucine di Masseria Spina is a fine dining restaurant that offers a sophisticated dining experience. The restaurant is known for its creative and innovative dishes, using the finest local ingredients. The menu features a variety of seafood and Mediterranean dishes, and the service is impeccable. It's a splendid choice for special occasions or a memorable dining experience.

Accommodation

For the festival of the Madonna della Madia, I recommend three nights in town.

Masseria Il Melograno. Address: Contrada Torricella, 345

Masseria Il Melograno is a luxurious hotel set in a beautiful countryside location surrounded by olive trees. The hotel features elegant rooms with air conditioning, minibars, and satellite TV. Guests can enjoy the outdoor swimming pool, wellness center with a gym and sauna, and a paid private beach. The hotel also offers a delightful breakfast served in the garden.

Hotel Don Ferrante - Dimore di Charme. Address: Via San Vito, 27

Once an ancient fortress, Hotel Don Ferrante offers luxury accommodation with a panoramic view of the Mediterranean Sea. Guests can relax in the sunbathing area, enjoy a buffet-style breakfast, and take advantage of the hydro massage jets in the small pool.

Masseria Torrepietra. Address: Contrada Grotta dell'Acqua, 338/a

Masseria Torrepietra is a charming hotel located just 3 kilometers (one mile) from Monopoli. The hotel offers comfortable rooms with flat-screen TVs, seating areas, and private bathrooms.

CHAPTER THIRTY-TWO

The Timeless Carnevale of Putignano

Art, Tradition, and Fantasy in Europe's Oldest Carnival

Carnivale di Putignano

Where: Putignano

When: Weekends December 26 through Marti Gras.

Average Festival Temperatures: High 13°C (55°F). Low 4°C (39°F).

Festival Website: https://www.carnevalediputignano.it/

Putignano Unmasked: A Town Steeped in History and Carnival Magic

Nestled in the heart of Puglia, the town of Putignano rises gracefully from the Murge Plateau, its historic silhouette etched against the backdrop of rolling hills, ancient olive groves, and verdant vineyards. Located 40 kilometers (25 miles) southeast of Bari, this charming settlement sits at an elevation of 372 meters (1220 feet) above sea level, offering spectacular views of the surrounding countryside that has sustained its people for generations.

The story of Putignano begins in the mists of the Iron Age (pre-550 BC), when the Peucetians, an ancient tribe native to this region, first established settlements among these hills.

The medieval era marked a turning point in Putignano's history, as Benedictine monks established their presence and shaped the town's spiritual and cultural landscape. A pivotal moment came in 1394 when the relics of Saint Stephen were transported from nearby Monopoli to Putignano, an event that would profoundly influence the town's cultural identity. The monks' influence can still be seen today in the town's architecture and religious traditions.

As the Renaissance dawned, Putignano flourished. The Chiesa Madre di San Pietro Apostolo stands as a testament to this golden age, its baroque architecture reflecting the town's prosperity and artistic sophistication. The historic center, with its network of narrow streets and elegant buildings, preserves the architectural heritage of these prosperous centuries.

Today, Putignano is home to 27,000 residents, who maintain a delicate balance between preserving their rich heritage and embracing modern life. The Mediterranean climate that blessed their ancestors continues to nurture the olive groves and vineyards that have long been the backbone of the local economy. The town's strategic location and agricultural abundance helped it develop into a significant hub for olive oil and wine production during the 19th and 20th centuries, industries that remain vital to the local economy.

Carnival in Putignano

Born in 1394, the Carnival of Putignano stands as Europe's most enduring celebration of its kind, strengthening from humble medieval origins into a spectacular display of artistry, satire, and communal joy that captivates visitors from around the world.

The carnival's birth is intertwined with a sacred moment in Putignano's history and the arrival of Saint Stephen's relics. As the story goes, local farmers paused their fieldwork to accompany these holy remains to their new sanctuary, breaking into spontaneous celebration along the way. This impromptu festivity planted the seeds for what would become one of Europe's most remarkable carnival traditions, demonstrating how sacred reverence and joyous celebration could coexist in perfect harmony.

The Dawn of Modern Spectacle

The early 1900s marked a transformative period for the carnival when the introduction of allegorical floats revolutionized the celebration. These massive, intricately crafted papier mâché creations brought an additional dimension to the festival, turning Putignano's artisans whose skills have been passed down through generations.

These artisans begin their work long before the carnival season, laboring in vast workshops where imagination takes physical form. Their creations are far more than mere parade floats; they are sophisticated works of art that combine traditional craftsmanship with contemporary themes. Political satire mingles with cultural criticism, while whimsical fantasy dances with social commentary, all brought to life through the delicate medium of papier mâché.

Delightful Floats of Carnivale Putignano

The Artistry and Mechanics of Putignano's Carnival

The massive floats that define today's carnival are engineering marvels, typically reaching heights of 15-18 meters (approximately 50-60 feet). Each year, anywhere from 8 to 12 of these colossal structures parade through Putignano's streets, with the exact number varying based on participation and the year's artistic vision. These aren't static displays - many feature moving parts, elaborate mechanical systems, and interactive elements that bring their satirical messages to life.

Every float is a unique creation, never to be repeated. While certain skilled artisans, the maestri cartapestai, may work on multiple floats over the years, each carnival demands entirely fresh designs. Local artisan workshops become bustling hives of activity months before the carnival, with teams of sculptors, painters, engineers, and papier mâché specialists working collaboratively. These teams often include both veteran artisans and apprentices, ensuring the traditional techniques are passed down to new generations.

The parades themselves are a community-wide effort. Alongside the floats march hundreds of costumed performers, dancers, and musicians. Local schools often participate with their own themed groups, while professional performance troupes add their artistic flair. Each float typically requires 20-30 people for operation and performance, including operators managing the mechanical elements and performers who interact with the crowd.

After each carnival, these massive structures are typically dismantled because of the ephemeral nature of papier mâché, with some structural elements recycled for future creations. The Carnival Foundation maintains extensive photographic and video archives, and some local museums display scale models and preserved pieces from particularly memorable floats of the past.

The Rhythm of Celebration

The carnival calendar follows a unique rhythm, making it one of Italy's longest-running festivals. The celebration begins on December 26th with the ancient Propaggini rite, a deeply rooted traditional ceremony that sets the stage for months of festivities. Propaggini is a poetic and satirical performance in which local poets, dressed in traditional costumes, take the stage to recite rhyming verses, often humorous and critical of current events, politicians, or social issues. This centuries-old tradition is a form of artistic and cultural expression unique to the region, blending wit, local dialect, and storytelling to entertain and engage the community.

As winter progresses, the town transforms into a theater of joy, with each Sunday bringing new parades, performances, and festivities that build toward the grand finale on Shrove Tuesday. The combination of satire, spectacle, and community participation makes this carnival one of the most distinctive and enduring in Italy.

During these parade days, Putignano's medieval streets burst with energy. Masked performers weave through the crowds, their costumes a riot of color against the town's weathered stone buildings. Musicians fill the air with traditional melodies, while dancers move to age-old rhythms that echo through the narrow alleys. The massive floats, towering above the spectators, process through the streets like magnificent ships sailing on a sea of celebration. Between official parade days, the floats remain securely stored in their construction hangars, maintaining the surprise and spectacle of each performance.

The Art of Organization

Behind this spectacular display stands the Fondazione Carnevale di Putignano, an organization that carries the weighty responsibility of preserving and developing this centuries-old tradition. Their work begins almost as soon as one carnival ends, planning themes, coordinating with artisans, and organizing the complex logistics that such a massive celebration demands.

Each year, the Foundation selects an overarching theme that guides the artistic direction of the floats and performances. This theme often reflects current events or societal issues, ensuring that while the carnival honors its ancient roots, it remains a vibrant commentary on contemporary life. The result is a celebration that feels both timeless and thoroughly modern, where centuries-old traditions find new relevance in each generation.

The Legacy of Joy

What makes Putignano's carnival truly special is not just its longevity or spectacular displays, but how it embodies the spirit of its community. Local families pass down carnival traditions like precious heirlooms, with children learning the art of papier mâché or the steps of traditional dances from their grandparents. Each year's celebration adds another layer to this rich cultural tapestry, creating memories that will be shared for generations to come.

Larger than Life, the Floats of Carnivale

Today's carnival, while grander in scale than its medieval origins, remains true to its essential spirit - a celebration of life, creativity, and community that transforms the winter months into a season of joy. Whether you're watching master artisans shape delicate papier mâché into towering works of art, joining the masked revelry in the streets, or simply soaking in the atmosphere of celebration, the Carnival of Putignano offers a window into a tradition that has captivated hearts for over six centuries.

Carnival Events (see program on the website above for additional information.)

December 26, 2024 (Opening Day)

Propaggini Rite and St. Stephen's Feast Day

The Propaggini Rite marks the official opening of Putignano's Carnival on December 26th, representing one of the oldest and most distinctive traditions of the celebration. Dating back to the 14th century, this unique ceremony features local poets known as "propagginisti" who perform satirical verses in Putignano's distinctive dialect.

The poets gather in the main square, taking turns to deliver their "propaggini", witty, often biting commentaries on local politics, social issues, and community events from the past year. These performances follow strict traditional rules: verses must be composed in octaves (eight-line stanzas), delivered in the local dialect, and performed from memory with no written aids. The propagginisti often incorporate theatrical elements, using gestures and vocal variations to enhance their delivery.

The term "propaggini" itself comes from the agricultural practice of propagation, where vine shoots are buried to create new growth, symbolically representing how old years give birth to new ones. The performers traditionally dress in peasant attire, honoring the rural origins of this custom. A panel of judges evaluates each performance based on linguistic accuracy, satirical wit, and adherence to traditional metrical forms, with the best propagginista being crowned champion of the year.

Major Parade Days (Giornate Principali)

Sunday Week One: First Grand Parade

1:00 p.m. First Parade

The "Itinerant Performers" (Propagginanti Itineranti) kick off the first parade day by roaming through Putignano's historic center. These skilled performers, dressed in traditional carnival costumes, bring the medieval streets to life with impromptu shows, music, and interactive performances. Groups of musicians, acrobats, and street artists weave through the crowds, creating intimate moments of entertainment and drawing spectators into the carnival spirit.

3:30p.m. Parade of Floats

The main event begins with the parade of allegorical floats (Carri Allegorici), a spectacular display that showcases Putignano's master papier-mâché artisans. These massive floats, some reaching heights of 16 meters (52 feet), are the result of months of meticulous work in the town's carnival workshops. Each float represents a different theme, often incorporating satirical commentary on current events, politics, or social issues.

The procession follows a circular route through the historic center, passing key landmarks like the Church of San Pietro and Palazzo del Balì, with each float making several passes to ensure all spectators can appreciate the detailed craftsmanship. The event typically lasts about four hours, with judges noting their evaluations for the final carnival competition.

Saturday Week Two: Second Grand Parade

7:00 p.m. Parade of Floats

Nighttime elevates the carnival to a magical spectacle. The allegorical floats are specially illuminated for evening viewing, with LED systems and lighting effects highlighting their intricate details and bringing their mechanical animations to life in dramatic new ways. Dramatic shadows and striking visual effects are created by the lighting design, adding a new dimension to the papier-mâché artistry.

The masked performers adapt their costumes with luminous and reflective elements, while street lighting is dimmed along the parade route to enhance the theatrical atmosphere. Musical performances become more energetic, with additional light shows synchronized to the music. The cooler evening temperatures also draw larger crowds, creating a more festive street party atmosphere as local cafes and restaurants extend their service onto the parade route.

The parade route remains the same as the first week, but the nighttime setting offers visitors a completely different perspective on both the artistry of the floats and the historic center of Putignano itself.

Sunday of weekend before Fat Tuesday

11:00 a.m. Third Grand Parade

The third parade brings a unique morning energy to Putignano, traditionally drawing the largest family crowds of the carnival season. This timing was specifically chosen to accommodate visitors from neighboring regions, as the earlier start allows families with children and day-trippers to fully experience the carnival before returning home.

The morning light offers the best natural illumination for appreciating the detailed craftsmanship of the papier-mâché floats, revealing colors and artistic details that might be missed in evening performances. Float creators often save special mechanical features or new elements for this parade, adding fresh details or modifications to keep the displays exciting for returning visitors.

This parade is significant as it's one of the last chances for judges to evaluate the floats and performances before the final Fat Tuesday celebration, leading to especially energetic and polished presentations from all participants.

Fat Tuesday (Martedì Grasso): Final Day

10:00 p.m. Funeral of the Carnival

The "Funeral of Carnival" (Campana dei Maccheroni) marks the grand finale of Putignano's Carnival with a uniquely theatrical ceremony. This traditional mock funeral procession sees carnival participants dressed in black, carrying candles, and dramatically mourning the "death" of Carnival. At the heart of the ritual is the ringing of the Bell of Macaroni, a historical symbol that once signaled the beginning of Lent, as a symbolic carnival puppet is carried through the streets on a decorated funeral bier.

The procession is filled with dramatic and humorous elements, featuring professional mourners performing exaggerated lamentations, musicians playing somber versions of carnival tunes, and the beloved carnival mascot, Farinella, dressed in mourning attire. Traditional characters carry symbolic items representing the indulgence and excess of the carnival season, adding to the playful yet reflective atmosphere. As the final farewell, all carnival performers take part in a last parade, wearing subdued versions of their vibrant costumes, signaling the transition from revelry to the solemnity of Lent.

11:00 p.m. Awards Ceremony

Following the funeral ceremony, the mood shifts dramatically for the prestigious awards ceremony, held in Putignano's main square. This event celebrates the extraordinary artistry and effort invested in the carnival, bringing together participants and spectators to honor the festival's most outstanding contributions.

The most coveted prize is for Best Float, judged on artistic merit, technical innovation, thematic interpretation, and crowd response across all four parades. Other awards highlight different aspects of the spectacle, including recognition for the best choreography, the most innovative mechanical features, and excellence in papier-mâché craftsmanship. Additionally, prizes are awarded for the best musical performance and the most outstanding masked group, ensuring that every element of creativity and dedication is acknowledged in this grand celebration of tradition and artistry.

The evening concludes with a spectacular fireworks display, marking the end of carnival and the beginning of Lent, while participants and spectators share one final feast before the traditional fasting period begins.

Special Festival Foods
Carnival in Putignano

A signature dish of the day is maccheroni al sugo con salsiccia: macaroni served with a rich tomato sauce and sausage. This hearty meal is traditionally enjoyed during the Campana dei Maccheroni ceremony, where 365 chimes mark the end of Carnival and the beginning of Lent. The dish is often accompanied by local red wine, fostering a communal atmosphere as residents and visitors gather to share in the celebration.

Another staple is farinella, a finely ground mixture of roasted barley and chickpeas. Once a humble peasant food, farinella has become emblematic of Putignano's Carnival, even lending its name to the festival's iconic jester mascot. It is typically enjoyed sprinkled over pasta, mixed with sauces, or paired with fresh figs.

For those with a sweet tooth, chiacchiere, crispy, fried pastry strips dusted with powdered sugar, are a beloved treat during Carnival. Known by various names across Italy, chiacchiere are a festive indulgence that adds a sweet note to the day's celebrations.

Recurring Events

- Corteo dei Giovedì: Weekly Thursday processions with themes such as widows (Vedove), crazies (Pazzi), and married women (Donne Sposate).

- Live Music: Performances at three main stages (Palco del Boom, Palco del Folle, and Palco delle Onde) featuring DJs, local bands, and themed music nights.

Float Information

- Viewing Times: Floats are primarily showcased during parades, but workshops and displays might allow for viewings outside parade times. Check specific schedules for open viewing opportunities.

- Previous Year's Floats: Typically, previous floats are dismantled or repurposed, so they are not on public display.

Other Highlights

- Workshops: Papier-mâché crafting sessions, cultural talks, and interactive events for all ages.

- Food and Markets: Stalls offering traditional Puglian delicacies and Carnival-themed treats.

- Children's Area: Family-friendly activities for kids aged 0-5.

Putignano Walking Tour

#1. Porta Barsento

Begin your tour at Porta Barsento, an ancient gateway to the town. This stone archway dates back to the medieval period and served as one of the main entrances to Putignano. It is named after the nearby Barsento Abbey, emphasizing Putignano's historical ties to the surrounding area. The gateway marks the transition into the town's historic center.

#2. Piazza Plebiscito and Chiesa Madre di San Pietro Apostolo

The center of Putignano's old town, Piazza Plebiscito, is a bustling square surrounded by cafes and historic buildings. Dominating the square is the Chiesa Madre di San Pietro Apostolo, a stunning 12th-century Romanesque church. The interior features intricate frescoes, marble altars, and a beautiful wooden crucifix. The church highlights the town's deep religious roots and architectural evolution over centuries.

The Piazza serves as both the geographical and social center of Putignano's historic district. Its distinctive limestone paving, worn smooth by centuries of foot traffic, tells the story of countless festivals, markets, and gatherings. The square is framed by elegant noble palaces, including the 18th-century Palazzo Romanazzi-Carducci with its ornate baroque balconies and the former Sedile dei Nobili, where the town's aristocracy once gathered.

The Chiesa Madre stands as a masterpiece of Pugliese Romanesque architecture, its facade featuring a magnificent rose window and intricate stone carvings. The church underwent significant modifications in the 17th century, adding baroque elements while preserving its Romanesque core. Inside, visitors find a treasure trove of art, including a precious 16th-century wooden crucifix attributed to Venetian craftsmen, the Chapel of the Holy Sacrament with its gilded baroque altar, and a series of 18th-century frescoes depicting scenes from the life of St. Peter. The church's pride is a 13th-century stone baptismal font decorated with religious symbols. An impressive pipe organ dating to 1740, still used for concerts today, completes the church's remarkable collection.

During carnival season, the piazza transforms into the festival's center, with the church steps serving as a natural stage for performances and the square hosting many of the carnival's key ceremonies. The space between church and square creates a perfect theatrical setting, as the historic architecture provides an atmospheric backdrop for both religious processions and carnival celebrations.

#3. Palazzo Romanazzi Carducci

This elegant Baroque-style palace, once home to the noble Romanazzi Carducci family, showcases the wealth and influence of Putignano's aristocracy in the 17th century. Its façade features ornate balconies and intricate stone carvings. Though private, its exterior is a fine example of Baroque architecture in Puglia.

#4. Museo Civico "Principe Guglielmo Romanazzi Carducci di Santo Mauro"

Housed in a historic building, this civic museum offers a fascinating glimpse into Putignano's history, culture, and Carnival traditions. Exhibits include archaeological finds, artifacts from the town's past, and a dedicated section on the Carnival of Putignano, featuring costumes, photographs, and float designs from past celebrations.

#5. Chiesa di Santa Maria la Greca

This charming church, built in the 15th century, is renowned for its stunning Renaissance architecture and delicate stonework. Inside, you'll find the relics of Saint Stephen, which were brought to Putignano in 1394 and are integral to the town's Carnival traditions. The church is a place of pilgrimage and a symbol of the town's spiritual heritage.

#6. Teatro Comunale di Putignano

This 19th-century theater is a cultural gem and an active venue for plays, concerts, and performances. Its neoclassical façade and beautifully preserved interior reflect the town's dedication to the arts. The theater plays an essential role in community life, hosting events during the Carnival and throughout the year.

#7. Centro Storico (Historic Center)

Wander through the narrow, winding streets of the historic center. Adorned with whitewashed buildings, flower-filled balconies, and small piazzas, this area is a quintessential example of a Puglian old town. Look for artisan shops selling local crafts and traditional bakeries offering focaccia and taralli.

#8. Church of San Domenico and Convent

Conclude your tour at the Church of San Domenico, a beautiful 17th-century structure with an adjoining convent. The church features Baroque altars and a serene courtyard. It is also tied to the town's religious festivals, including processions during Carnival.

Putignano Festivals and Sagre Throughout the Year

Festa di Sant'Antonio Abate

January 17

Celebrated in honor of Saint Anthony the Abbot, this day signifies the deeper immersion into the carnival festivities. It features the blessing of animals, reflecting the saint's status as their patron. The day also marks the beginning of the traditional "Giovedì" celebrations, weekly events leading up to Lent, each Thursday dedicated to different societal groups, fostering community participation and reflection.

Festa di San Giovanni

June 23

The Festa di San Giovanni in Putignano celebrates the Nativity of Saint John the Baptist with a lively mix of history, folklore, and community spirit. The highlight of the celebration is a historical parade where locals dress in medieval and renaissance costumes, reenacting scenes from the town's rich past. Traditional music fills the streets as groups perform age-old dances and songs. The festival also includes street performances, craft markets, and food stalls offering local specialties.

As night falls, bonfires are lit in honor of Saint John, continuing a centuries-old tradition believed to ward off evil and bring good fortune. The event draws both residents and visitors who come to enjoy the vibrant atmosphere and participate in one of Putignano's most cherished early summer festivities.

Festa di Santo Stefano Protomartire

August 3

This festival venerates Saint Stephen, the patron saint of Putignano. The day's events include religious ceremonies, processions through the town's historic center, and various cultural activities, reflecting the community's deep-rooted devotion and cultural heritage.

Sagra del Fungo e dei Sapori di Bosco (Mushroom and Taste of the Forest Festival)

Third weekend in October.

The Sagra del Fungo e dei Sapori di Bosco in Putignano, Italy, is an annual autumn festival that began in the mid-1990s to celebrate the town's rich mushroom-growing tradition and forest cuisine. Organized by local associations, it highlights regional flavors, especially wild mushrooms like porcini and cardoncelli, through food stalls, live music, folk performances, and educational workshops. Held in the historic center each late October or November, the festival promotes sustainable tourism and offers visitors a cultural experience beyond Putignano's famous Carnival, strengthening community ties and supporting the local economy.

Day Trips: Nearby Sites, Cities, and Towns

Castellaneta. 50 kilometers (31 miles) from Putignano, Castellaneta presents itself as a hidden gem of the region, perhaps best known as the birthplace of silent film legend Rudolph Valentino. The town's dramatic ravines, known as gravine, rival the famous Sassi of Matera in their impressive scale and historical significance. Castellaneta's roots stretch back to the Byzantine era, when it served as a fortified settlement and refuge during invasions, later evolving into an important agricultural center.

Logistics

Train: Putignano has a train station and is located one hour from Bari Centrale.

Bus: Local buses are operated by FSE, connecting Putignano to nearby towns like Alberobello, Castellana Grotte, and Monopoli.

Car: From Bari you would take SS100 for 45 minutes, towards Gioia del Colle and then follow the SP106 to Putignano.

Parking: There is a ZTL (limited traffic zone) in the city center. These parking options are available. Via Matteotti Parking is a large lot near the town center.

Street Parking is available on roads leading into the center, marked by blue lines indicating paid parking.

Restaurant Recommendations

Scinuà. Address: Via Santa Lucia 18

A highly acclaimed restaurant offering traditional Puglian cuisine with a modern twist. Known for its use of local ingredients and creative presentations, Scinuà provides an intimate dining experience in the heart of Putignano's historic center.

Dal Mollusco. Address: Via Conversano 78

Specializing in fresh seafood dishes, Dal Mollusco is praised for its high-quality ingredients and attentive service. The menu features a variety of seafood options, prepared with a Mediterranean flair.

Premiata Pizzeria. Address: San Lorenzo, 1

Renowned for its extensive selection of gourmet pizzas, Premiata Pizzeria combines traditional techniques with innovative toppings. The cozy atmosphere and friendly staff make it a popular choice among locals and visitors alike.

Osteria Botteghe Antiche. Address: Piazza Plebiscito 8

Offering a genuine taste of Puglian cuisine, Botteghe Antiche serves a variety of regional dishes in a rustic setting. The restaurant emphasizes local flavors and traditional recipes, providing an authentic dining experience.

Pescheria Friggitoria San Domenico. Address: Piazza San Domenico 8

A go-to spot for seafood lovers, this eatery offers a range of fried and grilled seafood options. Known for its casual ambiance and delicious offerings, it's perfect for a laid-back meal.

Accommodation

For the carnival celebration in Putignano, I recommend three to four nights in town.

Porta Nuova. Address: Via Estramurale a Levante, 167

A 3-star hotel offering modern accommodations with comfortable amenities. Porta Nuova is known for its stylish rooms, attentive staff, and central location, making it ideal for exploring the historic center.

Dimora Bianche Santa Lucia 17. Address: Vico II Santa Lucia, 17

A beautifully restored historic property offering charming accommodations in the heart of Putignano. Guests enjoy its blend of traditional architecture and modern comforts, along with its proximity to local attractions and the historic center.

CHAPTER THIRTY-THREE

Otranto: Where Dawn Meets Destiny

A Crossroads of Empires and Cultures

Alba dei Popoli

Where: Otranto

When: December 31 and January 1.

Average Festival Temperatures: High 14°C (57°F). Low 7°C (45°F).

Event Website: https://comune.otranto.le.it/novita/alba-dei-popoli-9/

Otranto: Italy's Eastern Sentinel-A Crossroads of Civilizations

Otranto, the easternmost town in Italy, has long stood as a beacon of history, trade, and cultural exchange. This picturesque town, overlooking the turquoise waters of the Adriatic, has been a meeting point for ancient civilizations, medieval rulers, and Renaissance influences, shaping its unique identity.

While Otranto is not traditionally counted among the major Greek colonies of Magna Graecia, its coastal position made it an essential point of contact between Greek traders and the indigenous Messapian people. By the 3rd century BC, the town had become part of the expanding Roman Republic, eventually serving as a crucial port city connecting Italy to the eastern provinces. Otranto's strategic location made it a vital gateway for military campaigns and commerce, with ships departing for Greece, the Balkans, and beyond. The Romans recognized its importance and built roads, fortifications, and harbors to facilitate trade and defense.

With the fall of Rome, Otranto became a battleground for successive powers. During the early medieval period, it came under Byzantine control and flourished as part of the Eastern Roman Empire, further strengthening its connection to the Greek world. Byzantine influences are still visible in Otranto's Romanesque architecture and intricate mosaics, particularly in the famed Otranto Cathedral.

However, in 1071, the Normans, led by the Hauteville dynasty, seized Otranto, integrating it into their expanding kingdom in southern Italy. Under Norman and later Angevin rule, the town developed its fortifications, including the imposing Castello Aragonese, which still stands today. While Otranto's importance increased due to its defense against Ottoman attacks, its pivotal historical event was the 1480 siege and capture by the Ottoman Turks, resulting in the massacre of its citizens, among whom were the 813 Martyrs of Otranto, later recognized as saints.

After its liberation from the Ottomans in 1481, Otranto underwent a period of rebuilding. The Spanish rulers of Naples, particularly the Aragonese and later the Bourbons, reinforced its fortifications, fearing further Turkish invasions. During the Renaissance and Baroque periods, Otranto saw the construction of elegant palaces, churches, and public buildings, blending Gothic, Romanesque, and Baroque elements.

Otranto's population is relatively small, with around 5,500 residents, swelling in the summer months when visitors flock to its beaches and historical sites.

Alba dei Popoli / Dawn of the People

The Alba dei Popoli festival began in 1999 and has evolved into a month-long celebration from early December through early January. Beyond the signature New Year's dawn event, the festival features Christmas markets, musical performances, art exhibitions, and cultural workshops throughout Otranto's historic center.

The festival takes place at multiple venues, with the highlight occurring at Punta Palascia for the first sunrise. It draws thousands of visitors who come specifically to celebrate New Year's in Otranto, making it one of Puglia's premier winter events.

The celebration embraces Otranto's historical role as a bridge between East and West, promoting a message of peace and unity among peoples. While the tradition of celebrating the first dawn has older roots, the modern festival has transformed into a significant cultural event that celebrates both local heritage and international connection.

Festival Events

December 31: New Year's Eve Celebrations

Starting in the late evening, the historic center of Otranto comes alive with musical performances. Multiple stages are set up, featuring a mix of traditional and contemporary artists.

The town often features artistic displays, including light projections on historic buildings, art installations, and interactive exhibits that celebrate Otranto's cultural heritage.

Local vendors set up stalls offering traditional Puglian cuisine, allowing attendees to savor regional specialties as they enjoy the festivities.

January 1: The First Dawn Gathering

5:00 a.m.

In the early hours, attendees gather at Punta Palascia, Italy's easternmost point, located approximately 5 kilometers (3 miles) southeast of Otranto's center.

As the crowd awaits the sunrise, there are live acoustic performances or ambient music to set a reflective and anticipatory mood.

At the moment of dawn, participants witness the first sunrise over the Adriatic Sea. This experience is accompanied by symbolic gestures, such as releasing lanterns or communal toasts, celebrating renewal and unity.

Otranto Walking Tour

#1. Porta Alfonsina (Alfonso's Gate)

Rising from Otranto's 15th-century streets, the Porta Terra (Land Gate) stands as both sentinel and storyteller. Built in the aftermath of the devastating 1480 Ottoman siege, this imposing entrance marked King Alfonso of Aragon's reclamation and fortification of the city. Its weathered stones have witnessed centuries of history, from desperate battles to peaceful commerce.

Today, this gateway ushers visitors through Otranto's defensive walls into a maze of narrow streets, where whitewashed buildings and medieval architecture tell tales of the city's rich past.

#2. Castello Aragonese (Aragonese Castle)

Sitting majestically from Otranto's coastline, the Aragonese Castle is a masterpiece of 15th-century military architecture. Built in 1495 by Ferdinand I of Aragon, this fortress answered the city's need for defense after the Ottoman siege. Its imposing cylindrical towers, deep moat, and strategic position created an impregnable barrier against both land and sea attacks.

The castle's design reflects the era's most advanced military engineering, with walls engineered to withstand artillery fire and towers positioned for maximum defensive coverage. Today, while its mighty walls no longer ward off invaders, the castle serves as Otranto's cultural center, hosting exhibitions and events within its historic chambers.

#3. Cattedrale di Otranto (Otranto Cathedral) & The Martyrs' Chapel

The Otranto Cathedral, constructed by the Normans in 1088, crowns the city's highest point as a testament to medieval artistry. While its Romanesque exterior commands attention, the cathedral's true marvel lies within a vast 12th-century floor mosaic that stretches through the nave, aisles, and presbytery. Created by the monk Pantaleone between 1163-1165, this masterpiece depicts the Tree of Life rising through scenes of biblical history, mythological creatures, and medieval daily life.

The cathedral gained additional historical significance during the Ottoman siege of 1480. When invaders converted the cathedral into a mosque, a good deal of townspeople sought refuge within its walls. Today, the Martyrs' Chapel houses the remains of 800 martyrs who refused to renounce their faith during this invasion, their story forever intertwined with the cathedral's sacred stones.

#4. Chiesa di San Pietro (Church of Saint Peter)

This small Byzantine-style church dates back to the 9th–10th centuries, when Otranto was under Byzantine rule. It was once the town's principal place of worship before the construction of the cathedral. The interior is adorned with well-preserved frescoes depicting scenes from the life of Christ, showcasing the city's Greek influence.

#5. Lungomare degli Eroi (Seafront Promenade of Heroes)

This scenic waterfront promenade is dedicated to the Martyrs of Otranto and offers a stunning view of the Adriatic Sea. It's an ideal place to pause, admire the coastline, and reflect on the town's history. Statues and plaques commemorate Otranto's resilience, while nearby cafés and restaurants provide a relaxing spot for a break.

#6. Bastione dei Pelasgi (Bastion of the Pelasgians)

Named after the ancient Pelasgians, an ancient people believed to have inhabited the region, this fortified bastion provides panoramic views of the old town and harbor. It was part of Otranto's medieval defensive system, playing a key role in protecting the city from invaders.

#7. Punta Palascia (Optional Sunrise Spot – 5 kilometers (3 miles) from Town)

While slightly outside the town, Punta Palascia is Italy's easternmost point and the location of the first sunrise of the year during Alba dei Popoli. The historic lighthouse here is one of the most famous in Italy, standing as a symbol of Otranto's role as the Gateway to the East.

Otranto Festivals and Sagre Throughout the Year

Feast of Saints Peter and Paul (Festa di San Pietro e Paolo)

June 28–29

This festival marks the beginning of Otranto's summer season, featuring religious processions, local food stalls, and traditional Salento folklore performances.

Otranto Jazz Festival

Typically held over a weekend in mid to late July

Established in 2009, this festival showcases both local talents and international jazz artists. Concerts are often held in historic venues, offering a blend of music and culture.

Feast of the Martyrs of Otranto (Festa dei Martiri Idruntini)

August 13–15

Commemorating the 800 martyrs who died in 1480, the event includes solemn processions, cultural activities, and concludes with a vibrant firework display.

Day Trips: Nearby Sites, Cities, and Towns

Carpignano Salentino. Carpignano Salentino is 15 kilometers (9 miles) west of Otranto. This charming town is nestled in the Grecia Salentina region, an area known for its Griko-speaking communities, a dialect that traces back to ancient Greek settlers. Carpignano Salentino has a rich history influenced by the Byzantine Empire and the Norman Kingdom of Sicily.

One of its main attractions is the Crypt of Santa Cristina, a fascinating underground church dating back to the 9th century, adorned with well-preserved

Byzantine frescoes depicting saints and biblical scenes. The town's historic center features narrow stone alleys, old whitewashed houses, and elegant palazzi, showcasing a mix of medieval and Baroque influences.

The Madonna della Grotta Sanctuary, a pilgrimage site located just outside the town, offers visitors a peaceful retreat. Carpignano Salentino is also known for its Sagra te lu Paniri in September, a festival celebrating local bread and olive oil, reflecting the town's deep agricultural roots.

Martano. Martano is 18 kilometers (11 miles) west of Otranto. Martano is one of the largest towns in Grecìa Salentina, a region with Greek cultural heritage, reflected in its traditions, language, and religious customs. The town has a long history dating back to pre-Roman times, and it flourished under the Byzantine and Norman rules.

The town's centerpiece is the Mother Church of the Assumption (Chiesa Matrice Santa Maria Assunta), a grand Baroque-style structure with intricate stucco decorations. Nearby, the Monastery of the Cistercian Monks, founded in the 12th century, is a significant religious landmark. Its peaceful cloisters and beautifully maintained gardens offer a tranquil escape.

Palmariggi. Palmariggi is 8 kilometers (5 miles) northwest of Otranto. A small yet historically rich town, Palmariggi's name is said to derive from the Latin phrase "Palma Regis" (Palm of the King), referring to a victory of King Charles I of Anjou against the Byzantines in the 13th century.

The town's chief attraction is the Sanctuary of Montevergine, perched on a hill offering panoramic views of the surrounding olive groves and countryside. This site has been a place of worship for centuries, with legends linking it to Marian apparitions.

Palmariggi is also home to the Castello di Palmariggi, a medieval fortress that once played a defensive role against Ottoman incursions. Though much of it has been modified over time, some of its original stone towers and walls still stand, preserving its medieval character.

Logistics

Train: Otranto is served by the Otranto Railway Station, located a short distance from the town center. The station is part of the Lecce–Otranto railway line, operated by Ferrovie del Sud Est (FSE).

Bus: Several bus companies provide transportation to and from Otranto. FlixBus connects the city to major Italian destinations, while Marino Autolinee and Itabus offer intercity routes throughout the region. For local travel, Miccolis S.P.A. operates regular services within Puglia.

Car: Otranto is approximately 45 kilometers (28 miles) southeast of Lecce. To reach Otranto by car from Lecce, take the SS16 highway towards Maglie, then continue on the SS16 following signs to Otranto.

Parking: Otranto offers several parking options for visitors: Parcheggio Porto (Port Parking): Near the harbor, this parking area provides convenient access to the historic center. Parcheggio Via Rocamatura: Situated a short walk from the old town, offering ample spaces. Parcheggio Piazza dell'Unità d'Italia: Close to the city center, ideal for visitors planning to explore the principal attractions.

Restaurant Recommendations

Icon Restaurant Otranto. Address: Via Bastione Pelasgi, 13

Near Otranto Castle, this restaurant is widely renowned as one of the city's top dining establishments. It offers a popular tasting menu and an excellent value, a la carte selection featuring upscale dishes crafted from local ingredients. Guests can expect exceptional service and a delightful culinary experience with well-composed plates bursting with carefully chosen flavors.

Riva 21. Address: Via Immacolata, 1

This restaurant offers a variety of Italian, seafood, and Mediterranean dishes. It is known for its cozy atmosphere and delicious food, making it a glorious spot for both locals and visitors.

Marinero Ristorante. Address: Via Papa Costantino I, 3

A must-visit in Otranto, Marinero Ristorante is praised for its unique dining experience and fresh seafood dishes. The restaurant offers a charming ambiance and is highly recommended by both locals and tourists.

Accommodation

For the Dawn Festival you will want to stay in Otranto for at least two nights.

Hotel Miramare. Address: Via Giovanni Paolo II

This hotel is set in the heart of Otranto, just a few feet from the golden sandy beach. It offers a balcony view across the promenade, and the staff are known for their exceptional service and helpfulness.

Hotel Palazzo Papaleo. Address: Via Rondachi, 1

Next to the Otranto Cathedral, this hotel features a rooftop terrace with a hot tub. The staff are friendly and helpful, and it offers a peaceful oasis in the bustling town.

Vittoria Resort Pool & SPA. Address: Via Catona

This stylish resort features a luxury wellness center, gym, and summer swimming pool. Rooms come with private terraces, and the hotel is a quick walk to the beach and castle.

CHAPTER THIRTY-FOUR

Sant'Antonio Abate in Novoli

A Blaze of Tradition in Puglia's Heartland

F esta di Sant'Antonio Abate

Where: Novoli

When: January 16-17

Average Festival Temperatures: High 14°C (57°F). Low 4°C (39°F).

Novoli: A Town Ablaze with Heritage

Nestled in the Salento region of Puglia, Novoli is a charming town steeped in tradition, with a history as vibrant as its fiery festivals. Known as the "Town of Fire," Novoli is celebrated for its annual Fòcara di Sant'Antonio, a festival that attracts visitors from across Italy and beyond.

Novoli's origins date back to the Middle Ages, when the area was developed by settlers looking to cultivate its fertile lands. Over the centuries, it became a significant agricultural hub, particularly known for its vineyards and olive groves. The town's name likely derives from the Latin word novus, meaning "new," reflecting its status as a burgeoning settlement during its early days.

Situated 15 kilometers (9 miles) northwest of Lecce, Novoli is part of the Salento peninsula, an area renowned for its stunning coastline, rolling vineyards, and ancient olive trees. The town lies on a plain surrounded by gently undulating terrain, with fertile soils that support its robust agricultural economy. With a population of 7,500 residents, Novoli is a small but vibrant community.

The Fòcara di Sant'Antonio Abate: A Festival Forged in Fire

As winter's grip holds tight to Novoli, an ancient rhythm stirs the town to life. Here, in the heart of Puglia, the Fòcara di Sant'Antonio Abate rises like a monumental torch, a masterpiece of faith and fire that has burned since the 17th century.

Picture a tower of carefully woven vine branches soaring 25 meters (82 feet) into the sky, its massive 20-meter (65 foot) diameter base anchoring what seems impossible, a structure born from the humble vineyards that surround this modest Italian town. This is no ordinary bonfire; it's a masterpiece of devotion that has burned brightly since the 17th century, when the townspeople first gathered to honor their beloved patron, Sant'Antonio Abate, protector of animals, guardian of farmers, and master of sacred flame.

While January 17 marks the saint's feast day, Novoli's celebration has evolved into a magnificent multi-day festival where ancient and modern converge. The traditional processions and prayers now dance alongside contemporary concerts and art exhibitions, creating a vibrant tapestry of culture that draws visitors from across the globe. Yet at its heart, the Fòcara remains unchanged, a towering symbol of gratitude for harvests past and hope for blessings to come. The moment of ignition is pure magic: as prayers rise with the smoke and fireworks paint the sky, thousands gather in awe. Here, in this timeless instant, Novoli reveals its soul, a place where every vine branch, every prayer, and every spark tells a story of a community united by faith, fire, and the enduring power of tradition.

Who Is Sant'Antonio Abate?

Sant'Antonio Abate, also known as Saint Anthony the Abbot or Saint Anthony the Great, is one of the most venerated saints in Christian tradition, particularly in rural communities. Born in Egypt around 251 AD, he is considered the founder of Christian monasticism and is often depicted as a hermit living in the desert. His life was characterized by prayer, asceticism, and battles against temptations, which earned him the title "Father of Monks."

Sant'Antonio is especially revered as the patron saint of animals, farmers, and fire. His feast day marks the traditional blessing of animals in many towns and villages. This connection to animals is rooted in stories of his kindness toward them and the legend that he healed sick animals through prayer.

The association with fire comes from his role as the protector against the fiery disease erysipelas, once referred to as "St. Anthony's Fire." He is often depicted with a flaming torch or fire at his feet, symbolizing this protective power.

Festival Events

January 16: Eve of the Feast, Lighting the Fòcara

Morning

Preparations for the grand bonfire take center stage. Locals and workers arrange thousands of vine branches into the towering Fòcara, which serves as both a religious offering and a spectacular centerpiece.

Afternoon

A religious procession carries the statue of Sant'Antonio Abate through the streets of Novoli, accompanied by prayers, hymns, and traditional music. Participants wear historical costumes, creating a solemn yet festive atmosphere.

Evening

The lighting of the Fòcara is the highlight of the day. As night falls, the bonfire is ignited with a torch, often blessed during the religious ceremonies. This dramatic moment is accompanied by a fireworks display, symbolizing the victory of light over darkness. Thousands of onlookers gather to witness this spectacle, which is followed by live music, dancing, and food stalls offering local delicacies.

January 17: Feast Day of St. Anthony

Morning: Mass & Blessing of the Animals

The feast day itself begins in reverent solemnity with Mass, but it's the blessing of the animals that truly captures the heart of Sant'Antonio's legacy as patron saint of these creatures. The town square transforms into a magnificent menagerie, where the lines between the sacred and the everyday blur in the most extraordinary way.

Having witnessed this blessed chaos, I can attest to the remarkable sight: tiny turtles peering curiously from shoe boxes, roosters announcing the hour from their cages, and horses standing proud alongside their owners. Dogs of every size and temperament, cats maintaining their dignified aloofness, and an array of farm animals create a symphony of sounds that echo through the square. Each creature, from the humblest to the most majestic, awaits the priest's blessing, a tradition that speaks to the deep connection between faith, nature, and community that defines this festival.

Afternoon Procession

The afternoon procession on the feast day represents the pinnacle of religious observance. The statue of Sant'Antonio Abate, adorned in elaborate garments and surrounded by flowers, makes its way through Novoli's narrow streets on a carefully decorated platform. Clergy members lead the way, followed by local dignitaries and townspeople in traditional dress, their voices rising in prayer and song. The brass band's music fills the air with solemn yet uplifting melodies, creating a soundtrack for this moving display of devotion.

Evening

Each evening, as the Fòcara continues its slow burn, casting its warm light over the gathered community, one can't help but feel connected to the generations who have celebrated this feast before. Elegant illuminated chandeliers suspended across the medieval alleyways create a glittering canopy overhead, their warm glow complementing the bonfire's radiance and transforming the historic center into a magical tableau of light and shadow. The festival's rhythm flows naturally from morning's sacred observances through afternoon's communal gatherings to evening's joyous celebrations, creating a seamless blend of the sacred and the festive that defines the spirit of Novoli's beloved tradition.

Special Festival Food
Pittule

No celebration in Puglia, including the Fòcara di Sant'Antonio Abate in Novoli, is complete without pittule. These delightful, bite-sized fried dough balls are a quintessential festival food, enjoyed by locals and visitors alike for their simplicity and versatility. Light, fluffy, and golden brown, pittule are the ultimate comfort food, perfectly suited to the festive atmosphere of Novoli's celebrations.

At their core, pittule are made from a simple dough composed of flour, water, yeast, and salt. The dough is mixed into a sticky, soft consistency and left to rise for several hours. Once ready, small portions are pinched off by hand or with a spoon and dropped into hot oil, where they puff up and turn a rich golden color. The result is a tender, airy interior encased in a slightly crisp exterior. Served warm, they are a treat that everyone looks forward to during the festival.

While plain pittule are beloved for their simplicity, they can also be made with a variety of fillings or flavors. Traditional savory options include anchovies, capers, olives, or onions, which add bursts of Mediterranean flavor. For a touch of sweetness, raisins, sugar, or honey are sometimes added to the dough, transforming pittule into a delightful dessert. Vendors and home cooks alike often experiment with regional ingredients such as pumpkin, zucchini, or even chunks of cheese that melt deliciously into the dough during frying. These variations reflect the creativity and pride of Puglian culinary traditions.

Novoli Walking Tour

#1. Piazza Regina Margherita (Queen Margherita Square)

Begin your walking tour in Piazza Regina Margherita, the heart of Novoli and the principal gathering place during the Fòcara festival. This charming square is lined with historic buildings, cafes, and shops, offering a glimpse into the town's everyday life. During the festival, it transforms into a vibrant hub, hosting food stalls, live music, and cultural events.

Named after Queen Margherita of Savoy, the piazza has been a focal point of Novoli's social life for centuries. It's an ideal spot to observe the local community and feel the pulse of the town. Be sure to check out the elegant Fontana dell'Unità (Fountain of Unity), a modern symbol of Novoli's communal spirit.

#2. Chiesa di Sant'Antonio Abate (Church of Saint Anthony Abbot)

Dating back to the 17th century, this church is dedicated to the town's patron saint. Its simple yet elegant facade belies a richly adorned interior, featuring frescoes, a gilded altar, and statues of Sant'Antonio Abate. During the festival, the church is beautifully decorated, and the statue of Sant'Antonio is carried through the streets in a grand procession. Visitors can light a candle or offer a prayer, immersing themselves in the town's deep devotion.

The church underwent significant renovation in the late 18th century, which added its distinctive baroque elements, including the ornate marble altar and the striking ceiling frescoes depicting scenes from Saint Anthony's life. Of particular note is the church's bell tower, which stands as one of Novoli's most recognizable landmarks.

The interior houses several important artworks, including a valuable 17th-century painting of Saint Anthony blessing the animals, reflecting his role as protector of livestock and domestic animals. A small museum within the church complex displays historic religious artifacts, including ancient vestments, sacred vessels, and documents that trace the history of both the church and Novoli's religious traditions. During the Fòcara festival, the church becomes significant as thousands of pilgrims arrive to seek the saint's blessing and take part in special masses.

#3. Museo della Civiltà Contadina (Museum of Rural Life)

Housed in a restored historic building, the museum offers an engaging collection of tools, photographs, and artifacts that tell the story of rural life in the area. Exhibits highlight traditional winemaking and olive oil production, industries that have shaped Novoli's identity. This stop provides valuable context for the Fòcara festival's ties to the land and agriculture.

#4. I Vigneti di Novoli (The Vineyards of Novoli)

These sprawling vineyards are the source of the vine branches used to build the Fòcara bonfire. Many vineyards offer guided tours and tastings of Salento's renowned wines, including Primitivo and Negroamaro. Strolling among the vines provides a tranquil contrast to the festival's lively energy and deepens your appreciation for the region's agricultural roots.

#5. Palazzo Baronale (Baronial Palace)

This grand building dates back to the late medieval period and reflects the architectural styles of its time, with an imposing facade and intricate stonework. Today, it serves as a cultural space, hosting art exhibitions and community events. During the Fòcara festival, the palazzo often becomes a hub for cultural programming, offering visitors a glimpse into Novoli's artistic and historical heritage.

#6. Via Fòcara (Fòcara Street)

This road comes alive during the festival, bustling with food stalls, street performers, and vendors selling artisanal goods. Even outside the festival period, Via Fòcara is steeped in history, as it has long been a route for processions and gatherings. At the end of the street, you'll find the Monumento alla Fòcara (Fòcara Monument), a tribute to Novoli's iconic tradition and a glorious spot for a photo to commemorate your visit.

Novoli Festivals Througout the Year

Festa di Sant'Antonio di Padova (Feast of Saint Anthony of Padua)

June 13th

This religious festival celebrates Saint Anthony of Padua with a series of events, including a solemn Mass, a procession through the streets of Novoli, and various cultural activities. The faithful take part in the procession, carrying the statue of Saint Anthony, accompanied by prayers and hymns. The festival fosters a sense of community and devotion among the residents.

Festa della Madonna Assunta (Feast of Our Lady of the Assumption)

August 15th

Celebrated on Ferragosto, this festival honors the Assumption of the Virgin Mary. Festivities include religious ceremonies, a procession featuring the statue of the Madonna, and communal gatherings. The event is marked by traditional music, local cuisine, and a festive atmosphere, reflecting the deep-rooted Marian devotion in the community.

Day Trips: Nearby Sites, Cities, and Towns

Gallipoli. 40 kilometers (25 miles) west of Novoli. Nestled along the Ionian coast, Gallipoli (meaning "Beautiful City" in Greek) is a charming seaside town known for its historic old town, stunning beaches, and fresh seafood. Gallipoli's unique layout, with the old town on an island connected to the mainland by a 17th-century bridge, makes it a picturesque destination for a day trip. Gallipoli's strategic coastal location has made it a significant port since ancient times, with influences from Greek, Roman, and Byzantine civilizations. The town flourished during the Renaissance and Baroque periods, leaving behind a legacy of exquisite churches and palazzi. Main sites include the Castello di Gallipoli, the Cathedral di Sant'Agata and the waterfront promenade.

Logistics

Train: Novoli has a train station with a connection to Lecce in 15 minutes.

Bus: Bus services offered by FSE and STP bus companies. Tickets can be purchased at the bus station or authorized retailers.

Car: From Lecce you take the SS7ter or SP4, a straightforward 15-minute drive.

Parking: The town has a ZTL (limited traffic zone) so pay attention to not enter it. Parking in Novoli is relatively easy outside of peak festival times, but can become more challenging during major events. During festivals, designated parking areas are set up on the outskirts of town, with shuttles running to the main event areas.

Restaurant Recommendations

Pizzeria La Capricciosa. Address: Via Sant'Antonio, 120/F

This cozy, family-run restaurant is known for its warm atmosphere and dedication to preserving traditional Salento flavors. The menu highlights homemade pasta, locally sourced meats, and seasonal vegetables. Signature dishes include orecchiette with cime di rapa (a Puglian classic) and hearty braciole al sugo (beef rolls in tomato sauce).

Pizzeria Da Antonio di Giannini Antonio. Address: Via Madonna del Pane, 59

In the heart of Novoli, this elegant yet welcoming restaurant offers a refined take on traditional Puglian cuisine and wood fired pizza.

Trattoria Lu Cardillu. Address: Piazza Regina Margherita

For a casual and authentic dining experience, Trattoria Lu Cardillu is a local favorite. Known for its generous portions and affordable prices, this trattoria focuses on comfort food prepared with love. The daily specials often feature seasonal ingredients, and the house wine is a great accompaniment to any meal.

Accommodation

For the festival, I recommend a minimum of two nights in Novoli.

Tenuta San Nicola. Address: SP4

A charming countryside hotel rated 4 stars, offering a serene atmosphere with lush gardens and two fabulous swimming pools.

Il Vecchio Arco. Address: Via Pendino, 35

This cozy 3-star bed-and-breakfast provides a warm and welcoming ambiance. Located conveniently near the town center, it offers comfortable accommodations with a touch of traditional Puglian charm.

Casa Salento. Address: Via Gaetano Salvemini, 18

A 3-star bed-and-breakfast, Casa Salento, is a recently renovated property featuring spacious rooms, a garden, and a terrace. Perfect for a peaceful stay, it has received glowing reviews for its modern amenities and friendly hosts.

Spring Celebrations

February through April

CHAPTER THIRTY-FIVE

San Valentino in Vico del Gargano

Love and Oranges

Festa di San Valentino

Where: Vico del Gargano

When: February 14

Average Festival Temperatures: High 14°C (57°F). Low 3°C (37°F).

Vico del Gargano: A Land Between Forest and Sea

Vico del Gargano is perched on a hillside in the dense Foresta Umbra of the Gargano peninsula, sitting at an elevation of 445 meters (1460 feet) above sea level. This location, approximately 6 kilometers (3.5 miles) from the Adriatic coast, provided both natural protection and access to maritime trade routes. The town is surrounded by ancient olive groves and citrus orchards, earning it the nickname "Village of Love" because of its traditional cultivation of oranges.

While the immediate area of Vico del Gargano shows little evidence of significant Roman settlement, archaeological findings suggest scattered rural settlements existed in the surrounding countryside. The region was part of the broader Roman territory, with nearby areas serving as agricultural production centers for the Empire.

The town's documented history begins in the 11th century, when it was founded by Slavic peoples who had settled in the region. The name "Vico" derives from the Latin "vicus" meaning village or settlement. Under Norman rule, the town grew significantly, with the construction of its castle and defensive walls. The Svevian period (13th century) saw further development, including the establishment of several churches and monasteries.

During the Renaissance, Vico del Gargano flourished as a feudal center under various noble families, including the Spinelli dynasty, who ruled from 1469. This period saw the construction of elegant palaces and the expansion of the town's religious buildings. The town became known for its agricultural production, particularly citrus fruits and olives, which formed the backbone of its economy.

The 19th century brought significant changes as feudalism ended, though the town maintained its agricultural character. Vico del Gargano faced challenges during World War II, when it served as a refuge for displaced persons from surrounding areas. The post-war period saw gradual modernization, though the historic center has preserved its medieval character.

Today, Vico del Gargano has 7,500 inhabitants and is recognized as one of "I Borghi più belli d'Italia" (The Most Beautiful Villages in Italy). The town maintains its traditional agricultural focus, particularly in citrus production, while developing its tourism sector. The historic center continues to be characterized by narrow medieval streets, historic churches, and traditional architecture.

Feast of St. Valentine / Valentine's Day

Who is San Valentino?

Saint Valentine (San Valentino) was a 3rd-century Roman saint who is widely recognized as the patron saint of lovers, betrothed couples, and happy marriages. According to Christian tradition, he was martyred on February 14, around 269 AD, during the persecution of Christians under Emperor Claudius II. While many legends surround his life, he is most commonly known for performing secret marriage ceremonies for young couples when marriage was forbidden for Roman soldiers. He is also said to have written letters signed "Your Valentine" to his jailer's daughter, whom he had befriended and allegedly healed from blindness.

His connection to Vico del Gargano dates back to 1618, when the town's residents chose him as their patron saint to protect their citrus groves, particularly the prized IGP oranges and Femminiello lemons, from harsh winters (see glossary definition of IGP). This tradition has been preserved for over 400 years, reinforcing a deep bond between the saint, the land, and its people. Today, his feast day in Vico del Gargano is not only a religious celebration but also a festival that blends faith, love, and agricultural heritage, turning the town into the "Borgo dell'Amore" (Village of Love).

The Citrus Connection

One of the most distinctive features of Vico del Gargano's San Valentino celebration is its connection to citrus fruits, particularly oranges. The town has been famous for its citrus groves since medieval times, with the local variety of oranges being particularly prized. During the festa, the statue of San Valentino is traditionally decorated with local citrus fruits, creating a unique blend of religious devotion and agricultural tradition.

The tradition of incorporating oranges into the celebration stems from the town's historical identity as a major citrus-producing center. The orange groves surrounding Vico del Gargano were not just economically important but were also considered symbolic of love and fertility. This connection led to the tradition of couples exchanging oranges as tokens of love during the festival.

Today, the Festa di San Valentino in Vico del Gargano is celebrated with a blend of religious ceremony and cultural festivities that typically span several days around February 14th. The celebration includes:

- The decoration of the Vicolo del Bacio (Kiss Alley), a narrow medieval street that has become a symbol of romance in the town.

- The procession of San Valentino's statue through the town's streets, adorned with citrus fruits.

- The blessing of oranges, which are then distributed to the faithful.

- Traditional music and dance performances.

- Local food festivals featuring citrus-based dishes and sweets.

- The exchange of oranges between lovers as a symbol of their affection.

What makes Vico del Gargano's celebration particularly notable is how it has maintained its authentic character while other Valentine's Day celebrations worldwide have become increasingly commercialized. The festa represents a perfect synthesis of religious devotion, agricultural heritage, and romantic tradition, making it unique among Valentine's Day celebrations globally.

The town's celebration has gained recognition beyond Italy's borders, attracting visitors from around the world who come to experience this authentic and unique expression of both religious devotion and romantic love. Unlike many modern Valentine's Day celebrations, Vico del Gargano's festa maintains its historical roots while evolving to include new traditions that still honor its original spirit.

Festival Events

Pre-dawn

Traditional decoration of the town with citrus fruits, particularly oranges and lemons from local groves. The historic center's streets, particularly the famous "Vicolo del Bacio" (Alley of the Kiss), are adorned with citrus garlands and fresh flowers.

9:00 a.m. Mass

Holy Mass in the Church of San Valentino, where the saint's relics are preserved. The church is specially decorated with oranges and flowers for the occasion.

10:30 a.m. Mass

Solemn High Mass presided over by the Archbishop, with the presence of religious, civil, and military authorities, confraternities, and all the faithful. The mass includes special prayers for lovers and engaged couples.

11:30 a.m. Procession of San Valentino

Solemn Procession through the streets of the town.

The statue of San Valentino is carried through the medieval streets. Local families throw flower petals from their balconies as the procession passes. The procession includes a special stop at Vicolo del Bacio, where couples traditionally exchange kisses for good luck.

Fireworks

Upon returning from the procession, a fireworks display.

Throughout the Day

Local vendors sell traditional "Paposcia" (a typical local flatbread) filled with local products.

Display of the "Parete degli Innamorati" (Wall of Lovers) where couples can leave love messages.

Distribution of "Arance di San Valentino" (Saint Valentine's Oranges), considered symbols of love and prosperity.

6:30 p.m. Mass

Holy Mass, sharing of blessed oranges, and Blessing of Engaged Couples preparing for marriage

- Couples receive a special blessing and an orange blessed by the priest

- Exchange of traditional love promises under the patronage of San Valentino

- Communal sharing of blessed citrus fruits, believed to bring good fortune in love

Evening

Traditional community gathering in the main square. Folk music and dance performances and of course food, food, food.

The festival uniquely combines religious devotion with local agricultural traditions, particularly celebrating the area's famous citrus fruits. Vico del

Gargano is known as the "Village of Love" and is one of the few places in Italy where Saint Valentine is the primary patron saint of the town.

Vico del Gargano Walking Tour

#1. Porta Nuova (New Gate)

A gateway to the past, this medieval entrance was one of the original access points to Vico del Gargano. Built in the 14th century, Porta Nuova stands as a silent guardian of history, leading you into a labyrinth of stone alleys and centuries-old traditions. Step through and begin your journey into one of Italy's most beautiful villages.

#2. Castello Normanno-Svevo

An imposing medieval fortress, the Castello Normanno-Svevo dates back to the 11th century, built by the Normans and later expanded by the Swabians and Aragonese. Towering over the town, its stone walls and watchtowers once defended against pirate raids and foreign invasions. Though not open to visitors, the castle remains a powerful symbol of Vico's past, perfect for admiring its rugged grandeur.

#3. Chiesa Matrice di Santa Maria Assunta (Holy Mary Assumption)

A blend of Romanesque and Gothic beauty, this 13th-century church has stood as Vico's spiritual heart for generations. Inside, its soaring arches, ornate wooden ceiling, and historic statues transport visitors to an era when faith and artistry were deeply intertwined.

#4. Vicolo del Bacio (Alley of the Kiss)

A passage so narrow and intimate that lovers must press close to pass, Vicolo del Bacio is more than just a charming alley; it's a symbol of romance in the "Village of Love." Legend has it that young couples strolling through received San Valentino's blessing for a lifetime of happiness. Step into the past and feel the whispers of old love stories.

#5. Chiesa di San Pietro (Church of St. Peter)

One of the oldest churches in Vico, Chiesa di San Pietro was built in the 11th century atop an ancient Lombard chapel. Modest in design but rich in history, it houses frescoed walls and centuries-old stone altars, reminders of a time when faith shaped every corner of life.

#6. Rione Terra (Neighborhood)

Wandering through Rione Terra is like stepping back 1,000 years in time. The medieval heart of Vico del Gargano is a maze of stone alleys, whitewashed houses, and hidden courtyards, where each carved doorway and weathered balcony tells a story. Lose yourself in its timeless charm.

#7. Chiesa di San Giuseppe (Church of St. Joseph)

Tucked away in the heart of the old town, Chiesa di San Giuseppe is a Baroque gem from the 18th century. Inside, soft candlelight dances across an exquisite wooden altar and delicate frescoes, creating a warm and peaceful retreat.

#8. Largo del Conte

A place where history and breathtaking views meet, Largo del Conte is the perfect spot to pause and soak in sweeping vistas of the Adriatic Sea and Gargano countryside. Whether bathed in golden sunset light or kissed by the morning breeze, this square offers a picture-perfect moment in Vico.

#9. Convento dei Cappuccini & Santuario di Santa Maria Pura (Capuchin Convent and Sanctuary of Holy Mary Pura)

A sanctuary of peace and devotion, the Convento dei Cappuccini & Santuario di Santa Maria Pura have been welcoming pilgrims since the 16th century. Nestled on the outskirts of town, this monastery is surrounded by a fragrant garden of orange trees, making it an oasis of serenity and reflection.

Vico del Gargano Festivals and Sagre Throughout the Year

Holy Week and Easter Celebrations

March or April (dates vary annually)

The processional events of Holy Week are among the most eagerly awaited moments in Vico del Gargano. Five ancient confraternities preserve a heritage of rites, chants, and traditions that find their most authentic expression during these days. The town's 12 churches are adorned for the occasion, and on Holy Thursday, it's customary to visit these churches in a tradition known as the "sepulchres."

Sagra delle Arance (Orange Festival)

April (specific dates may vary)

Celebrating the local orange harvest, this festival showcases the importance of citrus cultivation in Vico del Gargano. Festivities include tastings of various orange-based products, traditional music, and cultural events that highlight the town's agricultural heritage.

Christmas Celebrations

December 8-January 6

During the Christmas period, Vico del Gargano comes alive with various events and demonstrations. The streets are filled with entertainment, music, and iconic figures such as Santa Claus and elves. Traditional "zampognari" (bagpipers) from Monte Sant'Angelo perform, and there are displays of handcrafted nativity scenes throughout the town.

Day Trips: Nearby Sites, Cities, and Towns

Mattinata. 35 kilometers (22 miles) south of Vico del Gargano. Nestled along the Adriatic coast, Mattinata is renowned for its pristine beaches and charming town center. Visitors can explore the Baia di Vignanotica, a stunning beach framed by white limestone cliffs, perfect for relaxation and swimming.

Logistics

Train: Vico del Gargano is served by the Vico-San Menaio station on the Ferrovie del Gargano line. Regular regional trains connect from Foggia and San Severo to this station.

Bus: Several bus companies operate routes to Vico del Gargano, including Ferrovie del Gargano, which provides services connecting the town with nearby locations such as Foggia and San Severo.

Car: From Foggia, Vico del Gargano is 75 kilometers (47 miles) away.

Parking: In Vico del Gargano, parking options include both free and paid areas. The town center has limited parking spaces, so it's advisable to use designated parking lots on the outskirts and explore the historic center on foot.

Restaurant Recommendations

Braceria Il Baffo. Address: Via Sbrasile, 46

Specializing in grilled meats, Braceria Il Baffo is known for its quality cuts and traditional preparation methods. While the ambiance is modest, patrons appreciate the flavorful dishes.

Cantina Il Trappeto. Address: Via Casale, 168

Cantina Il Trappeto, also known as L'Orto del Conte, offers a rustic ambiance with a menu featuring local specialties. Patrons can enjoy a variety of traditional dishes prepared with fresh, regional ingredients.

Accommodation

One or two nights in town for the festival will be perfect.

Hotel Maremonti. Address: Via della Resistenza, 119

3-star hotel situated just a short walk (approximately 550 meters) from the historic town center. The hotel offers a peaceful retreat with convenient access to local attractions.

Besides the Hotel Maremonti there are some Bed and Breakfast options in the town center.

CHAPTER THIRTY-SIX

Foggia's Feast of Faith

The Legend of Foggia's Mysterious Madonna

Festa della **Madonna dei Sette Veli**

Where: Foggia

When: March 22

Average Festival Temperatures: High 16°C (60°F). Low 6°C (42°F).

Foggia through the Ages

Imagine a vast plain stretching as far as the eye can see, golden wheat fields swaying in the warm Apulian breeze. Long before it became the capital of its province, this land was home to the mighty city of Arpi, where Greeks and Romans once walked. But the real story of Foggia as we know it began in the shadows of those mysterious pits - "fovea" in Latin, where locals stored their precious grain. These humble beginnings would transform into something truly remarkable.

The 11th century marked a turning point when Foggia caught the eye of none other than Frederick II, the Holy Roman Emperor himself. Picture this powerful ruler, known as "Stupor Mundi" (Wonder of the World), choosing this spot on the Tavoliere delle Puglie plain as one of his favorite residences. Under his patronage, Foggia blossomed from a simple farming community into a city of significance.

But Foggia's story isn't just one of royal favor, it's a tale of resilience. When the earth shook in 1731, the city was rebuilt. When World War II left its scars, Foggia rose again, each time emerging stronger and more determined.

Today's Foggia, home to nearly 146,000 people, is a fascinating blend of old and new. The same fertile soil that attracted ancient settlers still produces some of Italy's finest wheat, olives, and grapes.

Madonna of the Seven Veils

In the misty marshlands of 11th century Foggia, a tale began that would captivate generations. Picture this: local farmers, going about their daily work, halted in their tracks. Above the wetlands, mysterious flames danced in the air, flickering like golden butterflies against the sky. This wasn't marsh gas or a trick of the light, something magical was calling.

Driven by curiosity and perhaps divine inspiration, the farmers dug where the flames had beckoned. What they uncovered would change Foggia forever: a Byzantine icon of the Virgin Mary, her serene face adorned with seven delicate veils, each one adding to her mystique.

This discovery marked the beginning of Foggia's love affair with the Madonna dei Sette Veli (Our Lady of the Seven Veils). Today, she resides in splendor in Foggia's cathedral, her seven veils the subject of endless fascinating interpretations. Some say they represent the seven sorrows of Mary, others see them as symbols of divine protection, but all agree on her power to work miracles.

On March 22nd each year, Foggia comes alive with devotion. The streets fill with the sweet scent of incense as solemn processions wind through the city. Thousands gather to honor their beloved patroness, their voices rising in prayer and song. It's a spectacle of faith where ancient tradition meets modern devotion, where the mysterious flames that once lit up a marsh continue to light up hearts.

Festival Events

9:00 a.m. Mass

The day begins with a special mass honoring the patron saints. The church is beautifully decorated, and the atmosphere is filled with reverence and community spirit.

10:30 a.m. Procession from Church of San Lorenzo

The first procession of the day starts at the Church of San Lorenzo, featuring a beautifully decorated float carrying the statue of the Madonna dei Sette Veli. The procession moves through the principal streets of Foggia, with participants singing hymns and carrying candles.

1:00 p.m. Parades begin at Piazza del Popolo

Colorful parades start at the main square, featuring traditional music, dance performances, and participants in historical costumes. The parade winds through the city, showcasing the rich cultural heritage of Foggia.

Street fairs open on Via Arpi

Local vendors set up stalls offering traditional foods, crafts, and souvenirs. Visitors can enjoy sampling local delicacies, purchasing handmade items, and experiencing the vibrant atmosphere of the street fair.

4:00 p.m. Second Procession from Piazza del Popolo

Another procession starts at the main square, this time featuring a different float and statue. The procession follows a different route, allowing more people to take part and enjoy the festivities.

8:00 p.m. Fireworks display at Piazza del Popolo

The day concludes with a grand fireworks display at the main square. The sky lights up with colorful explosions, and the crowd gathers to watch the spectacular show, marking the end of the festival.

Foggia Walking Tour

#1. Foggia Cathedral (Cattedrale della Madonna dei Sette Veli)

In the heart of Foggia stands the Cattedrale della Madonna dei Sette Veli, a monument with nearly a thousand years of history. The story of this cathedral begins in the 12th century, when Norman craftsmen laid its first stones. Though most of the original Norman walls are gone, they set the foundation for centuries of architectural evolution.

Step inside, and you'll be greeted by the cathedral's Baroque grandeur. The ceiling showcases heavenly frescoes that seem to come alive in the light filtering through ancient windows. The neoclassical façade, added later, provides an elegant face with clean lines and harmonious proportions that draw the eye upward.

The cathedral's true treasure is the Byzantine icon of the Madonna dei Sette Veli, the heart of Foggia's faith, discovered centuries ago under mysterious circumstances. Inside, the cathedral is a blend of Baroque and neoclassical art, creating spaces that are both grand and intimate. Side chapels offer quiet contemplation, while the main altar captivates with its artistry. Earthquakes have left their marks over the years, but each one provided a chance for renewal, shaping the architectural gem we see today.

#2. Chiesa di San Francesco Saverio (St. Francis Xavier)

Dating back to the early 18th century, this church was originally managed by the Congregation of the Brothers Insigniti of San Francesco Saverio.

Church of Saint Francis, Foggia

It showcases a neoclassical architectural style, featuring an entrance portico with Ionic columns. The interior is designed in a Greek cross layout, crowned by a central dome, with walls and vaults adorned with intricate stucco decorations.

Over the centuries, the church has undergone various modifications, including significant interior transformations in 1968.

#3. Piazza Umberto Giordano

Named after the famous composer Umberto Giordano, who was born in Foggia, this picturesque square is a cultural landmark. Statues of characters from Giordano's operas, including Fedora and Andrea Chénier, are displayed here. It's a magnificent spot for a coffee break while soaking in the city's artistic heritage.

#4. Chiesa delle Croci (Church of the Crosses)

Rising from Foggia's urban landscape, the Chiesa delle Croci is a unique 17th-century marvel where faith and architecture come together for an extraordinary pilgrimage.

#5. Via Arpi – Foggia's Historic Street

Step onto Via Arpi, and you're treading the same stones that have carried the footsteps of emperors, merchants, and nobles for nearly a millennium.

The magnificent Palazzo Dogana commands attention with its imposing presence, its halls once echoing with the footsteps of visiting royalty. Here, kings and queens found rest during their journeys through Puglia, leaving their mark on the palace's rich history. Further along, the Arco di Federico II stands as a testament to one of history's most fascinating rulers. Local legends say the Emperor Frederick II himself would pass through this arch on his way to his beloved hunting grounds, his retinue bringing color and pageantry to these ancient streets.

#6. Museo Civico di Foggia (Foggia Civic Museum)

Housed in a former Jesuit monastery, this small but fascinating museum covers Foggia's history from prehistoric times to the modern era. It has artifacts from the ancient city of Arpi, medieval sculptures, and a section dedicated to the city's devastation during World War II bombings. It's a great place to understand Foggia's past before continuing your walk.

#7. Parco Karol Wojtyla (Villa Comunale di Foggia)

Take a break in Foggia's largest public park, named after Pope John Paul II. This beautiful green space has walking paths, fountains, and a monument dedicated to Umberto Giordano. It's a peaceful retreat in the middle of the city, perfect for unwinding before heading to your next stop.

#8. Teatro Giordano

This 19th-century neoclassical theater is one of the cultural landmarks of Foggia. Named after composer Umberto Giordano, it has hosted operas, concerts, and theatrical performances since 1828. Even if you don't catch a show, admire the impressive façade and peek inside if the doors are open.

Palazzo in Foggia's Main Square

Foggia Festivals Throughout the Year

Festa dell'Incoronata

April 22-28

Foggia's significant religious event honors the Madonna dell'Incoronata with ceremonies at the Santuario dell'Incoronata and the Basilica della Madonna dell'Incoronata, including the traditional "Cavalcata degli Angeli" from April 26 to 28.

Feast of St. Alfonso Maria de Liguori

August 1

This vibrant festival celebrates St. Alfonso Maria de Liguori with solemn religious ceremonies, lively cultural activities, and bustling street fairs. The atmosphere is filled with devotion, music, and local flavors, making it a memorable event for both residents and visitors.

Foggia Film Festival

November (specific dates vary)

Attracting cinema enthusiasts from around the globe, the Foggia Film Festival showcases an impressive array of national and international films. This annual event is a haven for film lovers, featuring screenings, discussions, and opportunities to meet filmmakers and actors. https://www.foggiafilmfestival.com/

Day Trip Options: Nearby Sites, Cities, and Towns

Atessa. 120 kilometers (75 miles) from Foggia. Perched dramatically on a hilltop in Abruzzo, Atessa weaves together history, legend, and culinary tradition into an unforgettable experience. The medieval town center, with its winding cobblestone streets and ancient stone buildings, transports visitors back in time.

The Cathedral of San Leucio guards one of Italy's most unusual relics: what locals claim is a dragon's rib. According to legend, Saint Leucio himself slayed this fearsome beast, protecting the town's inhabitants. Whether you believe the tale or not, the massive bone displayed in the cathedral certainly sparks the imagination.

In August, the Sagra della Ventricina transforms Atessa into a food lover's paradise. This festival celebrates the local ventricina, a distinctive spicy cured meat that embodies the bold flavors of Abruzzese cuisine.

Campobasso. 120 kilometers (75 miles) from Foggia. Rising above Campobasso, the majestic Castello Monforte stands sentinel over the capital of Molise, just as it has since the 15th century. From its ramparts, visitors can enjoy breathtaking views of the city and surrounding mountains, understanding why this strategic location has been prized for centuries.

The Chiesa di San Giorgio, dating to the 11th century, represents one of Molise's oldest and most precious religious monuments. Its ancient stones tell the story of nearly a millennium of faith and artistry.

The Museum of the Mysteries offers a fascinating glimpse into one of Italy's most unique religious traditions. During the Corpus Domini Festival in June, the city comes alive with the famous "Misteri" parade, where participants appear to float through the streets on elaborate floats, creating an otherworldly spectacle that combines religious devotion with theatrical magic.

Logistics

Train: Foggia boasts a significant railway station at Piazza Vittorio Veneto, on the northeastern edge of the city center. The station accommodates high-speed services, including Frecciargento and Frecciabianca, connecting Foggia to major cities such as Rome, Milan, Bologna, and Bari. Regional services link Foggia to nearby destinations like Barletta, Potenza, and Lucera.

Bus: FlixBus offers routes connecting Foggia to many Italian cities, providing amenities like free Wi-Fi and power outlets on board. Itabus provides affordable travel options to and from Foggia. Ferrovie del Gargano is another bus company in the area.

Car: From Bari it is a 1.5-hour drive via the A14/E55 motorway northbound.

Parking: Foggia's historic center features Limited Traffic Zones (ZTL) to preserve its character and reduce congestion. Unauthorized vehicles are restricted during specific hours, and violations may incur fines. For parking options: Parcheggio Piazza Vittorio Veneto, Parcheggio Via Galliani: A multi-story car park within walking distance of central attractions. And finally Parcheggio Piazza Cavour.

Restaurant Recommendations

La Kucina. Address: Via G. de Petra, 67

A contemporary Italian restaurant focusing on fresh, local ingredients. La Kucina blends traditional flavors with modern culinary techniques in a stylish and inviting atmosphere.

Nenna Nè. Address: Via Cirillo Domenico 18

A family-run restaurant famous for its seafood and Mediterranean cuisine. Known for warm hospitality and dishes that highlight fresh, regional flavors.

Ambasciata Orsarese. Address: Via Iorio Tenente, 53

A traditional Apulian trattoria offering authentic local dishes. With a cozy ambiance and a commitment to quality regional cuisine, it's a must-visit for an immersive dining experience.

Accommodation

For the festival, I recommend three or four nights in town.

Hotel Up Wellness & Spa. Address: Via Trieste 14

4-star hotel offering accommodations with a bar and private parking. Guests have praised its cleanliness and modern amenities.

DEMSI Palace Hotel & Restaurant. Address: 40 Via Piave

4-star hotel featuring a terrace, private parking, a restaurant, and a bar. It has a modern design and central location.

Outside Boutique Hotel. Address: Piazza Caduti sul Lavoro 1

4-star hotel offering accommodations with a shared lounge, private parking, a terrace, and a bar. It is near the train station and city center.

CHAPTER THIRTY-SEVEN

Immersion Experience: Grotte Marine di Vieste

Discovering the Sea Caves of Vieste

Secrets Beneath the Gargano: The Mystical Sea Caves of Vieste

Where the Adriatic Sea meets ancient limestone, nature has carved a masterpiece along Puglia's Gargano Peninsula. The sea caves of Vieste stand as testament to time itself, each wave-worn chamber and crystalline grotto telling tales of millennia past. These natural cathedrals, sculpted by the patient hand of water and wind, create an underground realm where light dances on mineral-stained walls and the sea whispers ancient secrets.

A Legacy Written in Stone

What began as simple fishermen's havens has transformed into one of Italy's most captivating natural attractions. The caves' modern story intertwines with that of Michele Trimigno, a local fisherman whose curiosity in the 1950s led him beyond mere shelter-seeking. His pioneering spirit transformed these hidden grottos from maritime refuges into windows into Earth's artistry, laying the cornerstone for Vieste's evolution into a destination for wonder-seekers.

Nature's Gallery

Within these marine sanctuaries, nature displays her finest work. Sunlight filters through crystal-clear waters, painting the cave walls in an ever-changing palette of blues and greens. Massive stalactites reach down like nature's chandeliers, while expansive caverns open up like underground amphitheaters. Each formation tells its own geological story, from the dramatic collapse of Grotta Sfondata to the twin portals of Grotta dei Due Occhi, peering like ancient eyes toward the Mediterranean sky.

The intrigue deepens in caves like the Grotta dei Contrabbandieri, where hidden passages whisper tales of daring smugglers and clandestine operations. Meanwhile, the majestic Grotta Campana soars 70 meters upward, its bell-shaped chamber adorned with velvet-soft mosses that add subtle color to the limestone canvas.

Journeying to the Underworld

Access to these subterranean wonders comes primarily by sea, with options suited to every adventurer's spirit. Traditional boat tours depart regularly from Vieste's harbor, with experienced operators like Vieste Sea Adventure and Desirèe Coastal Trips guiding visitors through the maritime maze. For those seeking a more intimate encounter, private boat rentals offer the freedom to explore at will, while kayak expeditions allow adventurous souls to slip into narrow passages where larger vessels dare not venture.

Preparing for the Journey

Success in cave exploration demands thoughtful preparation. The seasoned traveler arrives equipped with quick-drying attire and non-slip footwear ready for slick surfaces. Essential gear includes sun protection for the approach journey and waterproof storage for valuables. Photography enthusiasts should prepare for the challenging light conditions that make these caves both a technical challenge and a rewarding subject.

Maximizing Your Cave Adventure

The caves reveal their secrets best during morning hours, when calm seas and gentle light create optimal conditions for exploration. In peak season, advance booking becomes essential for securing your preferred expedition time. As with all natural wonders, preservation remains paramount, visitors are encouraged to observe without touching, ensuring these geological masterpieces endure for future generations.

Here, in these chambers carved by time, visitors find themselves suspended between ancient past and present moment, surrounded by the raw beauty of nature's patient artistry. Each visit becomes not just an excursion, but an encounter with the sublime, a reminder of the endless wonders that await those willing to venture beneath the surface of the ordinary world.

Arch of Gargano, Vieste

Agencies providing tours:

Motobarca Desirèe grottemarinegargano.com

Valentina Tours. https://www.facebook.com/valentinamotorboat/

Holidoit.

https://www.holidoit.com/en/e/giro-in-barca-delle-grotte-marine-di-vieste

Get your Guide and **Trip Advisor** also have tour offerings.

CHAPTER THIRTY-EIGHT

Ruvo di Puglia: The Passion of Holy Week

Tradition, Faith, and Devotion

La Settimana Santa e La Pasqua

Where: Ruvo di Puglia

When: March/April (varies based on liturgical calendar).

Average Festival Temperatures: High 19°C (66°F). Low 7°C (45°F).

Event Website:

https://www.settimanasantainpuglia.it/content/citta.asp?lan=eng&id_citta=11

Ruvo di Puglia: A Tapestry of Time and Tradition

Perched gracefully on the eastern slopes of the Murge plateau, just 33 kilometers (20 miles) from Bari, Ruvo di Puglia tells a fascinating tale that spans millennia. This charming town of 25,000 citizens rises 240 meters (787 feet) above the Pugliese countryside, where ancient olive groves and vineyards paint the landscape in shades of silver and green.

Long before Rome's eagles flew over these hills, this was Rubi, the proud home of the Peucetii people. But it was under Greek influence that the town truly found its artistic voice. Between the 5th and 3rd centuries BC, local artisans created pottery that would make even Athenian artisans pause in admiration. Their masterpieces, including the legendary Vase of Talos, now rest in the Jatta National Archaeological Museum, whispering tales of ancient creativity to modern visitors.

Time has layered history like brushstrokes on a canvas here. The Romans recognized Rubi's strategic value, making it a key stop on their Via Traiana. Today, medieval splendor still crowns the town in the form of its magnificent cathedral, while the surrounding Alta Murgia National Park cradles this historic jewel in its natural embrace.

Holy Week and Easter in Ruvo di Puglia

The origins of Ruvo di Puglia's Holy Week rites trace back to the 16th and 17th centuries, a period marked by the establishment of various confraternities (religious brotherhoods) in the town. These confraternities played a pivotal role in organizing and perpetuating the Holy Week processions, each contributing unique elements to the celebrations.

The Confraternities and Their Roles

Confraternity Opera Pia San Rocco (Founded in 1576)

Initially composed of humble, often illiterate peasants, this confraternity was dedicated to Saint Roch. In 1920, they commissioned a simulacrum inspired by Antonio Ciseri's painting "The Transport of Christ to the Sepulcher," which became central to their Maundy Thursday procession.

Archconfraternity of Carmine (Founded in 1604)

Founded by clergymen and noblemen, this became one of the most influential confraternities in Ruvo. They are responsible for the Good Friday procession of the Mysteries, featuring wooden statues depicting scenes from Christ's Passion.

Confraternity of Purgatory under the title of "Mary Most Holy of the Suffrage" (Founded in 1678)

Associated with the ancient cult of Saint Cletus, this confraternity organizes the Holy Saturday procession of the Pietà, showcasing a revered statue of the Virgin Mary holding the lifeless body of Christ.

Confraternity Purification-Addolorata (Founded in 1777)

Emerging from earlier Jesuit influences, this confraternity venerates Our Lady of Sorrows. They lead the Procession of the Desolate on Passion Friday, featuring a poignant statue of the grieving Virgin.

Why Ruvo di Puglia is Renowned for Its Holy Week Celebrations

Step into Ruvo di Puglia during Holy Week, and you'll witness one of Italy's most spellbinding sacred spectacles. As twilight descends, ancient cobblestone streets come alive with solemn processions where life-sized statues seem to float through torch lit alleyways, carried by members of historic confraternities in their traditional robes. These ceremonies represent living history, carefully preserved through generations.

Each procession tells a chapter of the Passion story, but it's the way Ruvo tells it that captures hearts. Centuries old statues, masterfully crafted by local artisans, move through the medieval streets while haunting traditional hymns echo off stone walls. Local confraternities, some dating back hundreds of years, orchestrate every detail with passionate precision, from the placement of each candle to the timing of each step.

This celebration embodies Ruvo's soul laid bare: a mesmerizing blend of artistry, devotion, and tradition that draws visitors from across Italy and beyond to witness this uniquely Pugliese interpretation of Holy Week.

Holy Week Events

Venerdi di Passione (Passion Friday-Friday before Palm Sunday)

5:00 p.m. Processione della Desolata (Procession of Our Lady of Sorrows)

Church of San Domenico

In the heart of Holy Week, Ruvo di Puglia presents one of its most profound traditions: the Procession of the Desolata. In Italian religious tradition, "Desolata" refers to Our Lady of Sorrows (Maria Addolorata), portraying the Virgin Mary in her moment of deepest grief as she mourns the death of Christ. This solemn title captures her profound desolation at the foot of the Cross.

Mary in the Procession of the Desolata

As twilight approaches, the ancient streets of Ruvo di Puglia fall silent for this poignant ritual. The Confraternity of Purification-Addolorata leads a procession that embodies centuries of tradition and raw emotion. At its center stands a masterfully crafted statue of the Virgin Mary, draped in midnight black, her face bearing the weight of divine sorrow.

The air fills with haunting laments as local women, dressed in traditional mourning attire, raise their voices in songs passed down through generations. Their melodies echo off medieval stone walls, telling a mother's grief so powerfully that even first-time visitors find themselves deeply moved by this profound expression of faith and suffering.

Giovedì Santo (Holy Thursday)

2:00 a.m. (early morning hours of Holy Thursday). Processione degli Otto Santi (Procession of the Eight Saints) also called Procession of the Deposition.

Church of San Rocco

In the depths of night, when the medieval streets of Ruvo di Puglia are lit only by flickering flames, the Confraternity of San Rocco embarks on their solemn journey. Eight intricately carved statues emerge from the darkness, each illuminated by carefully positioned candlelight that creates dramatic shadows across their sacred faces. Each statue tells a part of Christ's final hours:

1. **The Agony in the Garden:** The first statue depicts Jesus praying in the Garden of Gethsemane, his face etched with the weight of what is to come. His expression conveys a mixture of sorrow and resolute acceptance.

2. **Christ Bound Before Pilate:** The second statue shows Christ bound and brought before Pilate, signifying the start of His suffering under Roman judgment. His hands are tied, symbolizing the beginning of His Passion.

3. **The Scourging at the Column:** The third statue captures the haunting image of Jesus at the column of flagellation, his body marked with the brutal lashes he endured. The detail of the wounds conveys the severity of His suffering.

4. **Ecce Homo:** The fourth statue is the Ecce Homo, where Jesus is presented to the crowd crowned with thorns, dressed in a purple robe, and mocked as the 'King of the Jews.' The agony and dignity in His eyes tell a poignant story.

5. **The Carrying of the Cross:** The fifth statue portrays Jesus carrying His cross along the Via Dolorosa, each step filled with pain and determination. The weight of the cross and His burden is evident in His posture.

6. **The Crucifixion:** The sixth statue captures the crucifixion itself, with Christ nailed to the cross, His face a mix of pain and forgiveness. The scene is solemn, representing the pinnacle of His sacrifice.

7. **The Deposition:** The seventh statue depicts the deposition from the cross, where Christ is gently taken down by His followers. The

expressions of sorrow and reverence on the faces of those present emphasize the gravity of the moment.

8. **The Sepulcher:** Finally, the eighth statue shows Christ laid in the sepulcher, His body prepared for burial. The scene conveys a sense of finality and somber reflection.

The procession weaves through the narrow alleys, each member of the confraternity in their traditional robes skillfully maneuvering the statues, creating a moving masterpiece that brings the story of Christ's passion. The air is filled with the sound of traditional funeral marches, their mournful notes echoing through the sleeping town. Local families watch from candlelit balconies, many having stayed awake specifically for this moment that their ancestors have witnessed for centuries.

This nocturnal procession, known to locals as "Otto Santi" (Eight Saints), creates an almost otherworldly atmosphere. The combination of darkness, candlelight, and sacred music transports participants and spectators alike to the very moments of Christ's sacrifice, just as it has done for generations of Ruvesi before them.

Venerdì Santo (Good Friday)

5:30 p.m. Procession of the Mysteries

Church of Carmine

As the sun begins its descent over Ruvo di Puglia, an extraordinary spectacle unfolds from the ancient doors of the Church of Carmine. The air grows thick with anticipation as the first notes of a funeral march echo through medieval streets. Then, emerging like figures from a Renaissance painting come to life, massive wooden statues begin their solemn journey through the town's historic heart.

Each life-sized statue, crafted by master artisans centuries ago, tells a chapter of Christ's final hours with stunning emotional power. All of Jesus' suffering is visible in The Flagellation. The Crowning with Thorns captures a moment of divine humility. The Ecce Homo presents Christ to an invisible crowd that, on this evening, becomes real as citizens and visitors line the ancient streets.

Watch closely as twelve bearers approach each statue. These men, members of the Archconfraternity of Carmine in their striking white robes and black hoods, have trained for months for this moment. With a precision born of devotion, they lift the massive structures onto their shoulders. Then comes the "nazzicata," a mesmerizing traditional "dance" where the bearers move in perfect synchronization, making these enormous statues appear to float through the air like visions from another world.

As twilight deepens into evening, hundreds of candles create a river of light flowing through Ruvo's narrow streets. Women in traditional black mantillas walk alongside, their voices rising in ancient laments sung in local dialect, passed down through generations. Each statue group pauses before the town's historic churches in a ritual greeting, the candlelight throwing dramatic shadows across centuries-old facades.

The procession moves with deliberate slowness, allowing onlookers to absorb every detail: the tears on the Virgin's face in the Pietà, the profound solitude of the Desolata, the peaceful repose of the Dead Christ. Local bands play funeral marches composed specifically for this occasion, their mournful notes echoing off stone walls that have witnessed this ceremony for hundreds of years.

As midnight approaches and the procession returns to the Church of Carmine, these sacred figures will remain on display until Easter Sunday, silent witnesses to centuries of faith and tradition in this corner of Puglia. The experience leaves visitors with an indelible impression of having stepped back in time, becoming part of a living tradition that connects past and present in an unbroken chain of devotion and community.

Sabato Santo (Holy Saturday)

4:30 p.m. Procession of the Pietà

Church of Purgatorio

In the golden light of late afternoon, when shadows begin to lengthen across Ruvo's ancient stones, the Confraternity of Purgatory emerges to present one of Holy Week's most emotionally charged moments. The air grows hushed as the first wisps of incense drift through the medieval streets, announcing the approach of something extraordinary.

The centerpiece of this sacred procession is a breathtaking statue of the Pietà, carved by master hands centuries ago. It captures, with heartrending detail, that most intimate moment when Mary cradles her son's lifeless body. Every fold of her robe, every line of grief on her face, every tender gesture speaks volumes about both divine sacrifice and human loss. As the statue moves through Ruvo's narrow streets, the shifting sunlight plays across its surface, revealing in stark detail the profound expressions of both heavenly purpose and earthly anguish.

Members of the confraternity, their traditional robes marking them as custodians of this ancient tradition, carry their precious burden with extraordinary gentleness. Their steps are measured and reverent, as if bearing a real body rather than carved wood. Around them, local women dressed in black sing traditional laments in the town's ancient dialect, their voices rising and falling in patterns of grief unchanged for generations.

The procession winds its way through streets where every stone holds centuries of memories, past windows where grandmothers stand with tears in their eyes, teaching their grandchildren the significance of this moment, just as their own grandmothers once taught them. This powerful representation of loss and love creates an atmosphere so thick with emotion that even casual observers find themselves drawn into its profound gravity.

As day fades into dusk, candles begin to flicker to life along the procession route, their gentle light adding yet another layer of solemnity to this ancient ritual. This is more than a religious ceremony; it's a moment when past and present merge, when ancient grief feels immediate and raw, when an entire community comes together to share in the universal experience of loss and the hope of resurrection that waits on Easter's dawn.

La Pasqua (Easter Sunday)

9:30 a.m. Procession of the Risen Christ & the Bursting of the Quarantanas

Church of San Domenico

As dawn breaks over Ruvo di Puglia, the somber atmosphere of Holy Week dissolves into an explosion of jubilation. The medieval streets, which days before echoed with laments, now pulse with anticipation. The morning air fills with the aroma of fresh Easter bread from local bakeries and the sweet scent of spring flowers adorning every church doorway.

The Procession of the Risen Christ bursts forth from San Domenico in a celebration that awakens every sense. The statue of Christ, radiant in gold and white, seems to glow with inner light as it moves through the thronged streets. Gone are the black-robed mourners; now the procession streams with colorful banners and flowers, while the confraternity members wear their finest ceremonial robes.

The air crackles with excitement as the beloved Quarantanas make their appearance. These whimsical cloth puppets, stuffed with treats and hanging above the streets throughout Lent, represent the forty days of sacrifice. At the height of celebration, they burst open in a spectacular shower of confetti, candies, and festive explosions. Children weave through the crowds like bright birds, snatching up scattered sweets and competing to collect the most treasures.

Church bells joyfully roll across the town, their triumphant sound echoing from the ancient stone walls. Families dressed in their Easter finest line the processional route, many holding traditional blessed olive branches. The afternoon will find them gathering for elaborate Easter feasts where tables groan under the weight of traditional dishes like lamb, blessed eggs, and the local specialty of scarcella, elaborately decorated Easter bread shaped into doves and crosses.

This ancient tradition marks not just the end of Holy Week but celebrates a jubilant release from the restrictions of Lent, combining profound spiritual significance with pure, unrestrained joy. In this moment, Ruvo di Puglia transforms from a town of solemn reflection into a festival of life renewed, where centuries of tradition merge with the simple pleasure of community celebration.

Holy Week in Puglia Beyond Ruvo

Ruvo di Puglia offers an unforgettable immersion into Holy Week traditions, but what makes Puglia truly remarkable is the tapestry of sacred experiences woven across its ancient towns.

#FestaFusion: The ability to witness multiple celebrations allows you to craft your own spiritual journey through the region, experiencing different interpretations of these sacred days.

Venerdì di Passione (Friday before Palm Sunday)

Noicattaro: Processione dei Misteri (Procession of the Mysteries). Starting Point: Church of Santa Maria della Pace.

Francavilla Fontana: Processione dei Pappamusci (Procession of the Pappamusci).

Sabato di Passione (Saturday before Palm Sunday)

Grottaglie: Passione Vivente (Living Passion)

Ginosa: Passione Vivente "Passio Christi" (Living Passion "Passio Christi"). Starting Point: Rione Casale.

Domenica delle Palme (Palm Sunday)

Molfetta: Processione della Benedizione delle Palme (Procession of the Blessing of the Palms)

Taranto: Processione dell'Addolorata (Procession of Our Lady of Sorrows). Starting Point: Church of San Domenico.

Giovedì Santo (Holy Thursday)

Noicattaro: Visita ai Sepolcri (Visit to the Sepulchers)

Francavilla Fontana: Processione dei Pappamusci cu li trai (Procession of the Pappamusci with the Crosses)

Venerdì Santo (Good Friday)

Bisceglie: Processione dei Misteri (Procession of the Mysteries). Starting Point: Church of Santa Margherita.

Taranto: Processione dell'Addolorata (Procession of Our Lady of Sorrows) and Processione dei Sacri Misteri (Procession of the Sacred Mysteries). Starting Point: Church of San Domenico (Addolorata); Church of Carmine (Sacri Misteri).

Bari: Processione dei Misteri (Procession of the Mysteries).

Sabato Santo (Holy Saturday)

Molfetta: Processione della Pietà e del Cristo Morto (Procession of the Pietà and Dead Christ). Starting Point: Church of Purgatorio

Bisceglie: Processione della Pietà (Procession of the Pietà). Starting Point: Church of Santa Margherita.

Taranto: Veglia Pasquale (Easter Vigil). Location: Church of San Domenico.

Domenica di Pasqua (Easter Sunday)

Conversano: Processione della Madonna della Croce (Procession of Our Lady of the Cross). Starting Point: Cathedral of Conversano.

Francavilla Fontana: Processione del Cristo Risorto (Procession of the Risen Christ). Starting Point: Church of San Francesco.

Bari: Processione del Cristo Risorto (Procession of the Risen Christ). Starting Point: Basilica of San Nicola.

Lecce: Processione della Resurrezione (Procession of the Resurrection). Starting Point: Cathedral of Lecce.

Each of these historic towns presents its own unique rituals and traditions, from solemn nocturnal processions to dramatic representations of the Passion. Some are known for their ancient statuary, others for their haunting musical traditions or the artistry of their sacred displays. By moving between these celebrations, you can experience the full richness of Puglian religious culture, where each community's interpretation has been shaped by centuries of local history and artisanship.

This mobility between celebrations allows you to create an intensely personal Holy Week experience - perhaps witnessing the nocturnal processions in one town on Holy Thursday before traveling to experience profound Passion rituals in another on Good Friday. Each location offers something unique to the spiritual traveler, creating opportunities for a deeply meaningful Holy Week journey through one of Italy's most evocative regions.

Ruvo Walking Tour

#1. Porta Noè

This ancient gateway marks the historic entrance to Ruvo di Puglia. Built as part of the town's medieval fortifications, it was one of the main access points to the old city. The gate is named after the noble Noè family and offers a picturesque starting point for exploring the centro storico.

#2. Cattedrale di Ruvo di Puglia (Ruvo Cathedral)

Standing majestically in the heart of the historic center, Ruvo's Cathedral rises as one of Puglia's finest examples of Romanesque architecture. Built between the 12th and 13th centuries, its limestone facade glows golden in the Mediterranean sun, telling stories in stone that span nearly a millennium.

The cathedral's western facade captivates visitors with its architectural harmony. Three distinct portals welcome the faithful, with the central doorway framed by elaborately carved columns and arches depicting biblical scenes and local medieval life. Above, a magnificent rose window dominates the facade: its intricate stone tracery creates patterns of light that dance across the nave at different times of day. Stone creatures and saints peer down from capitals and cornices, their weathered faces bearing witness to centuries of town life.

Inside, the soaring nave draws eyes heavenward, supported by two rows of ancient columns reportedly salvaged from Roman temples that once stood nearby. The cathedral's interior reveals layers of history: fragments of medieval frescoes peek through later baroque additions, while the floor preserves sections of an earlier mosaic pavement decorated with mysterious symbols and creatures.

Rose Window of the Cathedral

The crypt, accessible by twin staircases, holds some of the cathedral's most precious treasures. This atmospheric space, supported by forest of columns with uniquely carved capitals, contains remnants of earlier churches dating back to the 5th century. Archaeological finds displayed here connect visitors to Ruvo's ancient past, including artifacts from the town's Greek and Roman periods.

The cathedral plays a central role in Ruvo's Holy Week celebrations. Its bells mark the beginning of each procession, and its massive doors open to receive the sacred statues during their journey through town. The play of candlelight on the ancient stones during these nighttime ceremonies creates an atmosphere that transports participants back through centuries of faith and tradition.

#3. Museo Nazionale Jatta

Housed in a 19th-century neoclassical palace, this museum contains an extensive collection of ancient Greek and Apulian pottery, including the famous Vase of Talos, a 4th-century BC masterpiece. The collection was assembled by the Jatta family and remains one of Italy's finest private archaeological collections.

#4. Palazzo Caputi

This elegant Baroque palace, originally built in the 17th century, is an architectural highlight of Ruvo di Puglia. The building has been restored and now serves as a cultural center and library. Its ornate balconies and detailed stonework reflect the town's noble past.

#5. Chiesa del Purgatorio (Church of Purgatory)

The Chiesa del Purgatorio stands as an interesting testament to 17th-century religious artistry and baroque spirituality. Its distinctive facade immediately captures attention with its dramatic imagery: intricately carved skulls, crossbones, and other symbols of mortality remind visitors of life's transient nature. These aren't mere decorations but profound spiritual messages carved in local limestone, their details grown softer over centuries of sun and rain.

The church serves as the spiritual home of the Confraternity of Purgatory, whose traditions shape some of Holy Week's most moving moments. The confraternity's historical archives, preserved within, document centuries of processions, prayers, and community service. Their ceremonial robes and processional items, some dating to the church's founding, are still used in today's ceremonies.

Inside, the church reveals a treasure trove of baroque artistry. The main altar, crafted from precious polychrome marbles, demonstrates the skilled craftsmanship of 17th-century artisans. Six side chapels, each maintained by historic local families, house altars decorated with intricate inlaid stonework and paintings depicting souls in purgatory seeking salvation.

#6. Piazza Matteotti & Teatro Comunale

This charming central square is the heart of Ruvo's social life. The Teatro Comunale, built in the 19th century, was an important cultural center, hosting theatrical performances and concerts. Today, the square is a great place to pause and enjoy the local atmosphere.

#7. Chiesa di San Domenico (Saint Domenic)

Rising above Ruvo di Puglia's medieval quarter, the 15th-century Chiesa di San Domenico stands as a testament to both faith and artistic brilliance. Its limestone facade, weathered by centuries of sun and rain, glows golden in the morning light and takes on a ethereal pink hue at sunset. The church's prominent position along Via Vittorio Veneto makes it a natural gathering point for both religious ceremonies and daily life.

The church's architectural elements tell a story of evolving styles: its Gothic-influenced bell tower soars skyward, while Renaissance elements grace its main portal. The adjacent cloister, with its elegant arched walkways supported by slender columns, provides a peaceful retreat from the bustling streets. Here, ancient stone benches still bear the subtle wear marks of countless Dominican friars who once walked these corridors in contemplation.

Inside, the church reveals its spiritual and artistic treasures. The main altar, crafted from precious marbles, draws the eye immediately. Notable artworks include a striking 16th-century wooden crucifix and several important paintings depicting the life of Saint Dominic. The side chapels, each maintained by historic local families, showcase different periods of religious art from the 15th to the 18th centuries.

#8. Chiesa del Carmine (Carmelite Order of Monks)

Standing sentinel in Ruvo di Puglia's historic center, the Chiesa del Carmine embodies the spiritual heart of the city's Holy Week traditions. Founded by Carmelite monks in the 16th century, this church's austere limestone exterior belies the artistic treasures within. Its facade, with its distinctive rose window and carved portal, reflects the architectural style of Pugliese churches of the period.

The church serves as the spiritual home of the Archconfraternity of Carmine, one of Ruvo's most significant religious organizations. The confraternity's presence dates back centuries, and their carefully preserved ceremonial robes and artifacts tell the story of generations of devotion. Their historical archives, still maintained in the church, contain documents dating to the 1500s that detail the evolution of Holy Week traditions.

Inside, the church houses an extraordinary collection of life-sized wooden statues that bring the Passion of Christ to vivid life. The church's interior architecture creates a perfect setting for these sacred artworks. Soft light filters through ancient stained glass, illuminating the statues in ways that enhance their dramatic impact. The main altar, adorned with precious marbles and intricate carvings, provides a magnificent backdrop for religious ceremonies.

During Holy Week, the Chiesa del Carmine becomes the focal point of Ruvo's most solemn observations. The Procession of the Mysteries begins here on Good Friday, when the wooden statues are carefully carried through an elaborate ritual that has remained largely unchanged for centuries. The church's massive doors open to reveal each statue undefined creating a theatrical effect that transforms the piazza into an open-air cathedral.

#9. Torre dell'Orologio (Clock Tower)

Near Piazza Bovio, this historic clock tower was constructed in the 18th century. It has been a landmark of Ruvo for centuries, marking time for residents and providing a scenic focal point in the town.

#10. Chiesa di San Rocco (Saint Roch)

Anchoring its corner of Ruvo's historic center, the 16th-century Chiesa di San Rocco stands as a testament to both faith and community resilience. This beloved church, dedicated to Saint Roch, patron saint of plague victims and healers, holds special significance for the town's spiritual heritage.

The church's austere limestone facade tells stories through its architectural details. The main portal features delicate carvings of Saint Roch with his characteristic pilgrim's staff and faithful dog, while decorative elements incorporate symbols of healing and protection. A simple rose window above bathes the interior in gentle light, creating ever-changing patterns across the ancient stone floor.

Inside, the church showcases remarkable religious artistry. The most notable treasures are the Eight Saints: a collection of life-sized wooden statues depicting Christ's Passion. The Confraternity of San Rocco, custodians of these treasures, maintains their centuries-old traditions with passionate dedication.

The church reaches its greatest prominence during Holy Week, particularly in the predawn hours of Maundy Thursday, when the Eight Saints procession begins. The massive wooden doors open precisely at 2:00 a.m., revealing each statue dramatically illuminated by candlelight, creating an atmosphere that transports participants back through centuries of faith and tradition.

Ruvo Festivals and Sagre Throughout the Year

Talos Festival

Early September (typically September 1–10)

Named after the mythological giant Talos depicted on a Greek vase, the Talos Festival is an international jazz music festival that attracts artists and enthusiasts from around the world. The event features a series of concerts, workshops, and cultural activities, celebrating both traditional and contemporary jazz.

Sagra del Fungo Cardoncello (Cardoncello Mushroom Festival)

November

Dedicated to the Cardoncello mushroom, a delicacy in Apulian cuisine, this festival offers attendees the chance to savor various mushroom-based dishes. The event includes cooking demonstrations, tastings, and stalls selling local products, all set against a backdrop of music and entertainment.

Day Trip Options: Nearby Sites, Cities, and Towns

Terlizzi. 9 kilometers (5.6 miles) southeast. Terlizzi is known for its rich agricultural heritage, particularly in olive oil production. The town features the impressive Torre Normanna, a Norman tower that stands as a testament to its medieval past. The historic center boasts charming streets and the beautiful Cathedral of San Michele Arcangelo.

Corato. 12 kilometers (7.5 miles) west. Corato is a vibrant town celebrated for its olive oil and wine production. The historic center is characterized by narrow alleys, ancient churches, and the notable Palazzo Gioia. The town's cultural calendar includes traditional festivals that showcase its deep-rooted customs.

Molfetta. 20 kilometers (12.4 miles) northeast. Molfetta is a coastal city with a significant maritime history. The old harbor area is picturesque, featuring the Duomo di San Corrado, a stunning example of Romanesque architecture. The city also offers lively markets and seafront promenades.

Logistics

Train: Station: Ruvo di Puglia Train Station (Stazione di Ruvo di Puglia). Bari to Ruvo di Puglia (~35 minutes).

Bus: Bus services in Ruvo di Puglia are operated by two main companies: Ferrotramviaria Bus, which handles regional routes to nearby towns, and Cotrap, which operates longer-distance routes throughout Puglia.

Car: SP231 (Ex SS98) connects Ruvo di Puglia to Bari, Andria, and Foggia.

Parking: Parking options in Ruvo di Puglia include both free and paid facilities. Free parking can be found at the Via Scarlatti Parking Lot near the historic center and along Viale Madonna delle Grazie, which offers open-air parking spaces. For those preferring paid parking, Piazza Dante Parking provides a central location, while additional paid parking is available near the train station, suitable for longer stays.

Restaurant Recommendations

La Locanda di Ciacco. Address: Via Antonio Acquaviva 17

Near the cathedral, La Locanda di Ciacco offers a menu that highlights traditional Apulian dishes, emphasizing fresh, locally sourced ingredients. The ambiance is cozy and intimate, making it a favorite among both locals and visitors seeking an authentic dining experience.

U.P.E.P.I.D.D.E. RistorArte. Address: Vico Sant'Agnese 2

This establishment uniquely combines art and cuisine, offering diners a feast for both the palate and the eyes. The menu features a variety of Mediterranean and Apulian dishes, with an emphasis on grilled meats and seasonal produce. The interior showcases local artwork, creating a vibrant and eclectic atmosphere.

Accommodation

For Holy Week and Easter, I suggest a nine or ten night Puglia stay to explore local events.

Hotel Pineta Wellness & Spa. Address: Via Carlo Marx, 5

Polished 4-star hotel with a pool and spa, offering free parking, free breakfast, and wellness services. Near the historic center.

Rubis Relais & Spa. Address: Via Rogliosa, 27

A luxurious 5-star bed-and-breakfast featuring elegant decor, personalized services, and a spa. Perfect for an indulgent stay in the historic center.

Le Suites Al Torrione. Address: Vico San Carlo

Modern 4-star hotel with free breakfast, Wi-Fi, and air conditioning, in a charming area of the historic center.

Navigating Puglia

From Its Vibrant Past to Practical Travel Tips

CHAPTER THIRTY-NINE

Dining & Puglian Specialities

A Culinary Journey Through the Heel of Italy

P uglia's cuisine is a celebration of simple, high-quality ingredients, deeply rooted in the region's agricultural and coastal bounty. Known as "cucina povera" (peasant cuisine), it transforms humble ingredients into flavorful, satisfying dishes that showcase Puglia's traditions. Whether you're dining at a rustic trattoria, a seaside osteria, or a family-run masseria, you'll experience the essence of Puglian hospitality through its bread, pasta, olive oil, fresh seafood, and robust wines.

Puglian Specialties: What to Eat in Puglia

Bread & Baked Goods

Pane di Altamura: A DOP-protected bread from Altamura, made with durum wheat and baked in wood-fired ovens. Known for its thick crust and soft interior, it's best enjoyed with olive oil or local cheeses.

Puccia: A round, chewy bread, often stuffed with olives, cured meats, and cheese. Found in Salento.

Panzerotti: Deep-fried turnovers filled with tomato, mozzarella, and anchovies, similar to a small calzone.

Focaccia Barese: A crispy, olive oil-rich flatbread, topped with tomatoes, olives, and oregano, commonly eaten as a snack.

Pasta & First Courses

Orecchiette con cime di rapa: Puglia's signature dish, featuring ear-shaped pasta sautéed with turnip greens, garlic, anchovies, and chili flakes.

Strascinati al sugo: A rustic, hand-rolled pasta served with tomato sauce and ricotta forte (a tangy, aged ricotta cheese).

Pasta al forno alla pugliese: Baked pasta with meatballs, eggplant, mozzarella, and tomato sauce, a Sunday favorite.

Seafood & Second Courses

Riso, patate, e cozze: A layered dish of rice, potatoes, and mussels, baked with onions, tomatoes, and pecorino cheese.

Polpo alla pignata: Octopus slow-cooked in a clay pot with tomatoes, garlic, and local herbs, a specialty in Gallipoli.

Baccalà alla salentina: Salt cod cooked with tomatoes, capers, and olives, typical of Lecce.

Gamberi rossi di Gallipoli: Sweet red prawns, often served raw with a drizzle of olive oil.

Meat & Rustic Dishes

Bombette pugliesi: Grilled meat rolls (pork or beef) filled with cheese, herbs, and pancetta, popular in Cisternino.

Agnello al forno con patate: Roast lamb with potatoes, seasoned with rosemary and garlic.

Zampina di Sammichele: A spiraled sausage made with beef, pork, and cheese, grilled over an open flame.

Cheese & Dairy

Burrata di Andria: A rich, creamy cheese made from mozzarella and cream, best enjoyed fresh with bread or prosciutto.

Caciocavallo Podolico: A sharp, aged cheese made from Podolica cow's milk, often hung to mature in caves.

Ricotta forte: A fermented, pungent ricotta, spread on bread or mixed into pasta sauces.

Vegetable Dishes & Side Specialties

Fave e cicoria: A rustic dish of mashed fava beans and sautéed chicory, drizzled with olive oil.

Melanzane ripiene: Stuffed eggplants, baked with breadcrumbs, cheese, and herbs.

Pizzette pugliesi: Mini pizzas with onion, olives, and anchovies, eaten as street food.

Desserts & Sweets

Pasticciotto leccese: A golden pastry filled with custard cream, originally from Lecce.

Cartellate: Fried dough ribbons, coated in honey or vincotto (cooked wine syrup), popular at Christmas.

Mostaccioli pugliesi: Chocolate-spiced cookies, made with almonds, honey, and citrus zest.

Wines & Liqueurs

Primitivo di Manduria: A bold, full-bodied red wine, with flavors of dark berries, spice, and chocolate.

Negroamaro: A deep, earthy red wine, commonly found in Salento.

Bombino Bianco: A light, citrusy white wine, perfect for seafood dishes.

Rosato Salentino: A rosé wine made from Negroamaro grapes, ideal for hot summer days.

Limoncello del Gargano: A lemon-infused liqueur, traditionally made in Gargano.

Amaro del Salento: A herbal digestif, enjoyed after meals.

Where to Eat in Puglia

Puglia offers a wide variety of dining experiences, from local trattorias to gourmet restaurants. Here's what to look for:

Osteria & Trattoria: Casual, family-run restaurants with homemade pasta and rustic dishes.

Rosticceria: Street food spots serving panzerotti, focaccia, and fried delicacies.

Masseria Restaurants: Farmhouse restaurants specializing in farm-to-table Puglian cuisine.

Pescheria con Cucina: Seafood markets that cook the fresh catch of the day.

Pasticceria: Bakeries where you can find pasticciotti, cartellate, and biscotti.

Final Tips for Dining in Puglia

Try the street food! Focaccia, panzerotti, and seafood cones (paper cones filled with breaded and fried seafood) are must-eats.

Order local wines. Puglia's reds, whites, and rosés pair perfectly with regional dishes.

Look for agriturismo dining. Many masserie offer authentic, farm-fresh meals in a scenic countryside setting.

Book ahead in summer. Restaurants in Polignano a Mare, Alberobello, and Lecce fill up fast!

From creamy burrata to smoky bombette and fresh Adriatic seafood, Puglia's cuisine offers a true taste of Southern Italy's culinary traditions. Buon appetito!

CHAPTER FORTY

Transportation Detail

Arriving and Getting Around Puglia

Airports in Puglia

P uglia is served by two main international airports, connecting the region to the rest of Italy and major European cities. Additionally, smaller airports provide regional and seasonal flights.

Bari Karol Wojtyła Airport (BRI)

Location: 8 kilometers (5 miles) northwest of Bari

Also known as: Aeroporto di Bari-Palese. The busiest airport in Puglia, handling over 5 million passengers annually

Brindisi Salento Airport (BDS)

Location: 6 kilometers (3.7 miles) north of Brindisi

Also known as: Aeroporto del Salento. The gateway to southern Puglia, including Salento's beaches and historic cities

The Supporting Cast: Other Puglian Airports

While Bari and Brindisi handle most air traffic, Puglia has a few additional airports with seasonal and regional connections.

Foggia "Gino Lisa" Airport (FOG) – A small regional airport serving Gargano National Park and northern Puglia, recently reopened for commercial flights.

Taranto-Grottaglie Airport (TAR) – Primarily a cargo and aerospace hub, with occasional charter flights.

Choosing Your Landing Spot

When deciding which airport to fly into, consider:

Your itinerary: Are you exploring Bari & Gargano (fly into Bari) or Salento & Lecce (fly into Brindisi)?

Flight options: Bari has more international flights, while Brindisi is ideal for seasonal beach travelers.

Ground transportation: Both airports have train, bus, and car rental options.

Budget: Some low-cost carriers (Ryanair, EasyJet, Wizz Air) offer cheaper flights into Brindisi.

While Puglia is a long, narrow region, it is well-connected, and you are never too far from your destination, no matter where you land. Whether you're flying in over the Adriatic's turquoise waters or Puglia's sun-drenched olive groves, your journey starts the moment you touch down.

Navigating Puglia – Overview

Puglia's transportation network includes trains, buses, ferries, and car rentals, making it easy to explore the region's towns, coastlines, and countryside.

Trains: Puglia's Rail Network

Operated by Trenitalia, Puglia's train system connects major cities and coastal towns, with regional trains reaching smaller destinations. The main lines include:

- Bari to Lecce, with stops in Monopoli, Fasano, and Brindisi

- Bari to Foggia, connecting northern Puglia

- Lecce to Gallipoli, reaching the Salento coast

- Bari to Taranto, linking the Ionian and Adriatic coasts

For smaller towns, regional rail services like Ferrovie del Sud Est (FSE) operate slower trains through the Itria Valley and Salento.

Trains are great for coast-to-coast travel, but some inland destinations require buses or car rentals.

Bus Services: Reaching Small Towns

Buses in Puglia connect areas without train service, including rural towns and coastal villages. Several companies operate in the region:

- Ferrovie del Sud Est (FSE) serves Ostuni, Locorotondo, and Alberobello.

- Marozzi and FlixBus offer long-distance routes to Naples, Rome, and Milan.

- Miccolis and STP Brindisi provide regional bus routes around Lecce, Brindisi, and Taranto.

Buses are useful for reaching historic villages and countryside destinations that lack direct train connections.

Car Rentals: Exploring the Countryside

While Puglia's cities are walkable, renting a car is the best way to explore rural areas, masserie (farm stays), and hidden beaches.

- Best for exploring the Valle d'Itria, Gargano National Park, and Salento beaches

- Availability at airports, train stations, and major cities

- Challenges include narrow roads, ZTL zones (limited traffic areas), and limited parking in historic centers

- Avoid driving in historic centers like Lecce or Bari Vecchia—park outside and walk in.

Whether you are hopping on a scenic train, sailing to the Tremiti Islands, or road-tripping through olive groves, Puglia's transport options help you experience the region at your own pace.

Trains in Detail: Cities and Towns in Puglia with Trenitalia Stations

Puglia's rail network is primarily operated by Trenitalia, connecting major cities and coastal towns with regional routes reaching inland destinations. Trains are an efficient way to travel between Bari, Lecce, Brindisi, and Taranto, though some smaller towns require bus connections.

Website: Trenitalia

Main Cities with Trenitalia Stations

Bari: Bari Centrale

Brindisi: Brindisi Centrale

Lecce: Lecce Station

Taranto: Taranto Station

Foggia: Foggia Station

Barletta: Barletta Station

Andria: Andria Station

Trani: Trani Station

Bisceglie: Bisceglie Station

Molfetta: Molfetta Station

Smaller Towns with Trenitalia Stations

Polignano a Mare: Polignano a Mare Station

Monopoli: Monopoli Station

Fasano: Fasano Station

Ostuni: Ostuni Station

San Severo: San Severo Station

Manfredonia: Manfredonia Station

Cerignola: Cerignola Campagna Station

Orta Nova: Orta Nova Station

San Ferdinando di Puglia: San Ferdinando di Puglia Station

Margherita di Savoia: Trinitapoli-Salina Station

Gioia del Colle: Gioia del Colle Station

Putignano: Putignano Station

Castellaneta: Castellaneta Station

Carovigno: Carovigno Station

Latiano: Latiano Station

San Pietro Vernotico: San Pietro Vernotico Station

Ferries and Boats in Puglia – The Detail

Puglia's coastline and strategic location along the Adriatic and Ionian Seas make ferry travel an essential part of its transportation network. Whether you're crossing to Greece, Albania, or Croatia, or exploring the Tremiti Islands, Puglia offers a variety of ferry services for both short and long-distance trips.

Here are some websites for ferry companies that operate in Puglia:

International and Domestic Ferries

Grimaldi Lines

Operates ferry routes from Brindisi and Bari to Greece (Igoumenitsa, Patras, and Corfu), as well as connections to Albania and other Mediterranean destinations.

Website: https://www.grimaldi-lines.com/en/

Superfast Ferries & Anek Lines

Provides services from Bari to Greece (Patras, Igoumenitsa, and Corfu) with modern passenger ferries.

Website: https://www.superfast.com/en/

Website: https://www.anek.gr/en/

Adria Ferries

Specializes in ferry connections between Bari and Durres (Albania).

Website: https://www.adriaferries.com/en

Tremiti Islands Ferries

For those looking to explore the Tremiti Islands, ferries and hydrofoils operate from multiple coastal towns in northern Puglia.

Navi Tremiti

Offers ferry services from Termoli, Vieste, Peschici, and Rodi Garganico to the Tremiti Islands.

Website: https://www.navitremiti.it/

Gruppo Armatori Garganici

Runs ferry and hydrofoil connections between Gargano towns and the Tremiti Islands.

Website: https://www.garganoferries.com/

Seasonal & Local Boat Services

In addition to large ferry operators, smaller boats and hydrofoils provide seasonal services along the Puglian coast:

Vieste & Peschici to the Tremiti Islands – High-speed boats operate during the summer.

Gallipoli & Porto Cesareo – Small boats offer Ionian Sea excursions and transfers to nearby islands and beaches.

Polignano a Mare & Monopoli – Boat tours explore the dramatic coastal caves and sea cliffs.

Ferry schedules vary by season, so it is recommended to book in advance during peak summer months. Puglia's ferries offer not just transportation but a chance to experience stunning Adriatic and Ionian seascapes from the water.

Rental Car Options in Puglia – The Detail

Several well-known car rental agencies operate in Puglia, providing a range of vehicle options across major cities, airports, and tourist destinations.

International Car Rental Agencies

Hertz

Locations: Bari, Brindisi, Lecce, Taranto, Foggia, and major airports. Offers a wide selection of vehicles, including compact cars and SUVs.

Avis

Locations: Available at Bari and Brindisi airports, as well as in major cities. Known for reliability and a variety of rental options.

Europcar

Locations: Available at airports and in cities like Bari, Brindisi, Lecce, and Foggia. Provides economy, luxury, and electric vehicle options.

Sixt

Locations: Primarily at Bari and Brindisi airports. Offers a mix of budget-friendly rentals and premium vehicles.

Budget

Locations: Available in Bari, Brindisi, and Lecce. A good choice for affordable rentals with a range of vehicle sizes.

Enterprise

Locations: Found in major airports and select city locations. Offers a variety of cars, from economy to luxury.

Thrifty

Locations: Primarily available at Bari and Brindisi airports. Focuses on cost-effective rental options with basic services.

Local Car Rental Agencies

Noleggiare

Locations: Bari, Brindisi, Lecce, and other key cities. Well-rated for service and affordable rates.

Locauto

Locations: Available in major cities and airports. Known for a modern fleet and flexible rental options.

Maggiore

Locations: Found across all major airports and cities in Puglia. One of Italy's oldest car rental companies with excellent customer service.

Puglia Rent

Locations: Local offices in Bari and Brindisi. Offers competitive rates and personalized service.

Tips for Renting a Car in Puglia

Book in advance: Demand is high during peak travel seasons, especially in summer.

Check insurance options: Roads in the countryside can be narrow, and parking in historic centers is limited. Make sure your rental includes coverage for accidents and damages.

ZTL zones: Many towns (like Ostuni, Lecce, and Alberobello) have restricted traffic areas (Zona a Traffico Limitato). Park outside and walk into the historic centers.

Renting an automatic car: Manual transmissions are standard in Italy, so if you prefer an automatic, reserve early, availability is limited, and prices are higher.

CHAPTER FORTY-ONE

Accommodation Detail

A comprehensive guide to accommodation options in Puglia

P uglia offers a diverse range of accommodation options, whether you're looking for a seaside retreat, a countryside escape, or a charming stay in a historic town.

Hotels & Traditional Accommodations in Puglia

Hotels in Puglia are graded from one to five stars, reflecting their amenities and service levels. However, in Puglia, accommodations come in various local categories beyond just "hotel." Here are the types of hotels you'll find:

Types of Hotels in Puglia

Albergo: The general Italian word for a hotel, used for accommodations ranging from budget-friendly to luxury.

Hotel: The international term, often used for larger or chain-operated accommodations.

Resort: Typically a seaside or countryside all-inclusive stay, offering pools, private beaches, spas, and restaurants. Found in Savelletri, Monopoli, and Torre Canne.

Dimora Storico: A historic mansion or noble residence converted into a boutique hotel. Common in Lecce, Martina Franca, and Ostuni.

Palazzo: A former aristocratic palace transformed into a luxury boutique stay, often featuring Baroque or Renaissance architecture. Found in Bari, Lecce, and Gallipoli.

Relais: A small, upscale countryside retreat, often housed in historic villas or masserie. These offer a tranquil escape with fine dining and wellness facilities.

Boutique Hotel: A charming, uniquely designed hotel, usually with fewer rooms, focused on personalized service. Many are in Alberobello, Polignano a Mare, and Cisternino.

Hotel Star Ratings in Puglia

One-star hotels: Basic accommodations, often family-run, with minimal amenities and shared bathrooms.

Two-star hotels: Simple, budget-friendly rooms with private bathrooms, ideal for short stays.

Three-star hotels: Comfortable rooms with amenities like air conditioning, TV, and a mini-fridge, often with breakfast included.

Four-star hotels: Higher-end accommodations, often in historic palazzi or seafront resorts, with restaurants, pools, and spa services.

Five-star hotels: Luxury stays with full-service spas, rooftop terraces, private beaches, and Michelin-starred restaurants. Common in Bari, Lecce, Savelletri, and Otranto.

Popular Hotel Areas in Puglia

Seaside Resorts: Monopoli, Polignano a Mare, Torre Canne, Gallipoli

Luxury Palazzi: Lecce, Martina Franca, Bari

Countryside Retreats: Valle d'Itria, Salento, Gargano National Park

Websites: Booking.com, Hotels.com, Expedia and local websites.

This variety ensures that whether you're looking for a coastal resort, historic city boutique hotel, or countryside retreat, Puglia has something for every traveler.

Private Rooms and B&Bs

Puglia has a wealth of B&Bs and private guesthouses, often run by local families who provide homemade breakfasts featuring regional specialties like focaccia, orecchiette, and pasticciotto leccese. Many are in historic centers, offering authentic local charm.

Top Locations:

- Lecce and Otranto: Stay in Baroque townhouses with vaulted ceilings and original stone walls.

- Polignano a Mare and Monopoli: B&Bs with stunning sea views from cliffside balconies.

- Ostuni and Alberobello: Whitewashed trulli-style B&Bs in the heart of the Valle d'Itria.

Websites: Airbnb, Booking.com, BedandBreakfast.it

Holiday Apartments

Self-catering apartments are perfect for longer stays or for those who prefer more independence. You'll find charming stone apartments in Matera, modern beach rentals along the Salento coast, and elegant flats in Bari's old town.

Great for families needing extra space, groups traveling together and travelers wanting to cook with fresh Puglian ingredients from local markets.

Websites: Airbnb, Booking.com, VRBO

Rural Accommodations

For a more authentic experience, consider staying in Puglia's countryside, where massive olive groves, vineyards, and trulli-lined landscapes create a magical setting.

Masserie (Farmstays & Agriturismo)

Masserie are historic farmhouses, often beautifully restored, that offer farm-to-table dining, cooking classes, and olive oil tastings. Some of the best masserie have swimming pools and spa facilities, blending rustic charm with modern comfort.

Top Masseria Stays:

- Masseria Moroseta (Ostuni): A modern take on a traditional farmhouse.

- Masseria Cervarolo (Cisternino): A masseria with its own trulli houses and organic farm.

- Masseria San Domenico (Savelletri): A luxury masseria with a spa and private beach club.

Websites: Agriturismo.it, ItalyFarmStay

Trulli Stays

If you've ever dreamed of sleeping inside one of Puglia's iconic whitewashed trulli houses, you can book a trulli stay in Alberobello or the surrounding Itria Valley. Many trulli have been renovated into stylish accommodations with private pools and modern amenities.

Top Trulli Locations:

- Alberobello (UNESCO-listed trulli village)

- Locorotondo and Cisternino (rural trulli stays with olive groves and vineyards)

- Martina Franca (trulli with modern interiors and outdoor terraces)

Websites: TrulliHoliday.com, Airbnb

Wineries & Vineyard Stays

Puglia is famous for its Primitivo and Negroamaro wines, and some vineyards offer on-site accommodations where you can sip wine overlooking the rolling countryside.

Top Winery Stays:

- Masseria Li Veli (Salento) – Stay in an ancient vineyard estate with wine tastings.

- Tenuta Girolamo (Valle d'Itria) – Family-run vineyard with luxury suites.

- Antica Masseria Jorche (Manduria) – A wine resort in the heart of Primitivo country.

Websites: Agriturismo.it, Winerist

Hostels

While hostels in Puglia are not as common as in bigger cities like Rome or Milan, you can still find affordable options in Bari, Lecce, and Gallipoli. Many hostels cater to young travelers, digital nomads, and backpackers looking for a social atmosphere.

Campsites & Glamping

For outdoor lovers, Puglia offers coastal and countryside camping options, ranging from simple tent sites to luxury glamping with bungalows and pools.

Websites: Eurocampings and ACSI

References and Resources

Calendar, Alphabetical Index,
Glossary, Index, and Inspirations

CHAPTER FORTY-TWO

Festival Calendar

Dates, Cities, and Celebrations in Puglia

T hese are the primary festivals covered in this guide, but each chapter offers information on the other festivals that take place in each town throughout the year.

Date / City Name / Festival Name

For more information about these events, refer to each city's chapter detail.

January

January 6. Monopoli. Corteo dei Re Magi (Three Kings).

January 8-12. Castellana Grotte. Festa dei Falo (bonfires).

January 16-17. Novoli, Gallipoli, Giovinazzo, Latiano, Molfetta, Rutigliano, Arnesano, Biccari, Racale, Putignano, and Conversano. Feast of St. Anthony Abbot.

Sunday after January 17. San Severo. Feast of St. Anthony Abbot.

January 17. Massafra. Carnival di Massafra.

January 17th and every Thursday until Fat Tuesday (Shrove Tuesday). Putignano. I Giovedi del Carnevale (The Thursdays of Carnival).

Around January 20. Gallipoli, Galatone. Festa di San Sebastiano.

January 31. Grottaglie. Festa di San Ciro.

February

February 2-Fat Tuesday. Putignano. The Bear Festival (Spring Festival).

February 3. Ostuni, Cisternino. Feast of St. Biagio.

February 14. Vico del Gargano.□Festa di San Valentino.

February 19. Nardo. Festa di San Gregorio.

February 24. Deliceto. Falo di San Mattia. (Bonfires of San Mattia).

February with Dates that Vary

February/March: Easter date varies. Carnival Celebrations and Parades.

- Putignano

- Alberobello

- Bitono

- Massafra

February/March, first weekend of Lent. Casamassima. La Pentolaccia Festival.

February/March, throughout Lent. Casamassima. Le Pupe della Quaranta (The Puppets of Lent).

March / April

*I am putting March and April together because Easter changes date each year so these events can fall into March or April.

March 18. Monte Sant'Angelo. Fire of St. Joseph.

March 18-19. Uggiano La Chiesa, Lizzano, Cucmola, Giurdignano, San Marzano. Festival / Tables of St. Joseph.

March 19. Bari. Feast of St. Joseph.

March 22. Foggia. Festa della Madonna.

March/April with Dates that Vary

March/April, on Fat Tuesday (Shrove Tuesday). Putignano. La Campana dei Maccheroni (the Macaroni Festival).

March / April: Easter date varies. Ruvo di Puglia. La Settimana Santa and La Pasqua.

March/April: Holy Week varies. Holy Week Processions and Events.

- Turi

- Conversano

- Monte Sant'Angelo

- Bitono

- Vico del Gargano

March/April: Easter Monday. Cisternino. Pasquaredde, Easter Monday Festival.

March/April: Sunday after Easter. Ostuni. Feast of the Madonna della Nova.

March, early March. Lecce, Lizzano. Sagra della Pasta e Ceci. (Pasta and Chickpeas)

March, late March. Bari. Bari International Film Festival.

March, last weekend. Gravina in Puglia. La Primavera in Puglia (Spring Festival).

April 6. Bitonto. Fiera di San Leone.

April 22-28 Foggia. Festa dell'Incoronata.

April 23. Melpignano, Chieuti. Locorotondo. Feast of St. George.

April 23. Varano. Festa del SS. Crocifisso di Varano.

April 24–28. Ceglie Messapica. Ricotta Festival.

April 24-26. Castro. Festa dell'Annunziata.

April 25. Liberation Day. National Holiday. Italy commemorates the end of Nazi occupation during World War II with various events and ceremonies.

April 25. Turi. Festa del Passa Passa (Annunciation).

April 26–May 1. Valle d'Itria Festival: Ostuni, Cisternino, and Locorotondo (BR). A cultural festival featuring concerts and performances across multiple towns in the Valle d'Itria region.

April with dates that vary

April. Lecce. Lecce European Film Festival.

April. Vico del Gargano. Orange Festival.

May

May 1–4. Galatone. Festa del SS. Crocifisso.

May 2-5. Lecce.Fiera di San't Irene.

May 3. Trani. Festa del Crocifisso dei Colonna.

May 3-9. Monte Sant'Angelo. International Michael Festival.

May 7-9. Bari. Festa di San Nicola.

May 8-10. Taranto. FestaFusion Taranto.

May, 3rd Sunday and following Monday.□San Severo. Festa della Madonna del Soccorso.

May, 3rd Sunday. Conversano. Feast of Mary of the Well.

May 17–19. San Severo. Festa del Soccorso

May 17–18. Lizzano. Fiera di San Pasquale.

May 25-27. Parabita. Festa della Madonna della Coltura.

May 26. Bitonto. Festa Patronale.

May 30 to June 2. Monopoli. Monopolele-Mediterranean Ukulele Festival.

May 31. Andria. Infiorata.

May with dates that Vary

May. Taranto. Matrimonio di Maria d'Enghein.

May, second weekend. Novoli, Sagra della Puccia all'Ampa (Bread).

May, late May. Lecce. Lecce Cortili Aperti (Private Courtyard Tours).

May, first Saturday, fourth Sunday. Conversano. Festa della Madonna della Fonte.

May. Polignano a Mare. Kite Festival.

May. Otranto. Truffle Festival.

May/June. Brindisi. Procession of Corpus Christi.

June

June 1-21. Fasano. FestaFusion Fasano with La Scamiciata and Patron Saint Festival.

June, 1st or 2nd weekend. Turi. Sagra della Ciliegia Ferrovia.

June 1. Canosa di Puglia. Festa di Santa Maria Altomare.

June 13. Conversano and Novoli. St. Anthony of Padua.

June 15. San Vito dei Normanni. Festa di San Vito Martire.

June 14-16. Polignano a Mare. Feast of St. Vito.

June 16-21. Monopoli. Prospero Fest (Literature and Cultural Arts Festival).

June 17–August. Locus Festival in both Locorotondo (BA) and Bari (BA)

June 23. Putignano. Festa di San Giovanni.

June 24. Conversano. Infiorata di San Giovanni.

June 28-29. Otranto. Feast of St. Peter and St. Paul.

June 29. Conversano and Galatina. Feast of St. Peter and St. Paul.

June, throughout the month. Bari. Sagra delle Orecchiette.

June with dates that vary
June, early June. Brindisi. Negroamaro Wine Festival.

June, date varies. Polignano a Mare. Red Bull Cliff Diving Competition.

June. Polognano a Mare. The Book Festival (Il Libro Possible)

June. Conversano. Cherry Festival.

June. Cisternino. Sausage Festival.

June. Locorotondo. Locus Festival.

June. Throughout Summer. Monte Sant'Angelo. Monte Sant'Angelo Summer Festival, Gathering of Tarantella Players and Festambient Sud.

July

July, throughout the month. Bari. Bari in Jazz.

July, throughout the month. Martina Franca. Festival della Valle d'Itria (Opera and Music Festival)

July 2. San Severo. Feast of Our Lady of Grace.

July, first Sunday. Mola di Bari. Feast of our Lady of the Sea.

July 5–9. Scorrano. Notte delle Luci.

July 14–16. Porto Cesareo. Sagra del Pesce.

July 16. San Severo, Melpignano, and Conversano. Feast of Madonna del Carmine.

July 17-21. Monopoli. Ritratti Festival (Music Festival).

July 21-23. Uggiano La Chiesa. Feast of St. Mary Magdelene.

July 22. Barletta. Patron Saint Festival.

July, last week. Ostuni. Light Festival.

July, last Sunday. Casamassima. Feast of Our Lady of Mount Carmel.

July, last weekend. Mola di Bari□Sagra del Polpo (Octapus).

July with dates that vary

July. Polignano a Mare. Mareviglioso Festival (Sea Festival).

July. Locorotondo. Locus Festival.

July, weekend in mid July. Otranto. Otranto Jazz Festival.

July, late July. Acquaviva delle Fonte. Red Onion Festival.

August

August, throughout the month. Melpignano and throughout Puglia. La Notte della Taranta.

August, throughout the month. Martina Franca. Ghironda Festival (International Music and Global Arts Festival)

August 1. Foggia. Feast of Alfonso Maria de Liguori.

August 3. Putignano. Feast of St. Stephen.

August 1–4. Sammichele di Bari. Sagra della Zampina (sausage)

August, first weekend. Bitonto. Beat Onto Jazz Festival.

August, first weekend. Cisternino. Feast of St. Quirico and Giulitta.

August, first Sunday. Conversano. Feast of Maris Stella.

August 6-7. Uggiano La Chiesa. Festival of st. Cajetan.

Early August. Trani. Medieval Weekend.

August, second weekend. Cisternino. Sagra delle Orecchiette.

August, second Sunday. Ostuni. Procession of the Grata.

August 11–17. Lecce. Panorama Festival. https://www.panorama-festival.it/en/

August 13-15. Otranto. Feast of the Martyrs of Otranto.

August 15. Novoli. Feast of Our Lady of the Assumption.

August 15-17. Locorotondo, Conversano, and Taranto. Festa di San Rocco.

August 15. Ostuni. Festival of Old Times.

August 23. Melipgnano. La Notte della Taranta.

August 23-September 1. Brindisi. Festa Patronale dei Santi Teodoro d'Amasea e Lorenzo da Brindisi.

August 24-27. Lecce. Fiera di Sant'Oronzo.

August 24-28. Turi, Patron Saint Festival.

August, third weekend. Martina Franca. Festival dei Sensi (Festival of the Senses)

August, last Sunday or September, first Sunday. Uggiano la Chiesa. Sagra della Frisella.

August, last weekend. Martina Franca. Festival of Cabaret (Comedy Competitiion).

August with dates that vary

August, mid month. Melpignano. South East Independent Music Festival.

August. Locorotondo. Locus Festival.

August. Lecce. Festival del Cinema.

August. Grottaglie. Sagra dell'Orecchietta.

August. Taranto. Festa del Mare.

August. Martina Franca. Festival della Valle d'Itria.

Late August. Taranto. Festival of the Sea (Sagra del Mare).

Late summer. Barletta. Piano Festival.

September

September. Bari. Fiera del Levante.

September through November. Monopoli. PhEST, International Photography Festival.

September, weekends. Bitonto. Traetta Opera Festival.

September 7. Brindisi. Festa Patronale.

September 1-10. Ruvo di Puglia. Talos Festival (International Jazz Festival).

September, first Tuesday. Feast of the Madonna of Constantinopli.

September, second Sunday. Casamassima. Feast of St. Roch.

September, second weekend. Barletta. Disfada di Barletta.

September, second Sunday. Mola di Bari. Feast of Our Lady of Sorrows.

September 23. San Giovanni Rotondo. Festa di San Pio da Pietrelcina.

September 25-27. Ostuni. Calvacata di Sant'Oronzo.

September 25-28. Alberobello. Festa di San Cosma e Damiano.

September 25-28. Bari. European Jazz Conference.

September 29. Secondary festival May 8. Monte Sant'Angelo. Festa di San Michaele Archangelo.

September with dates that vary

September. Bitonto. Gala dell'Olio (Olive Oil Festival).

September, early. Castro. Sagra del Pesce Fritto (Fried Fish).

September, mid month. Trani. Trani Dialogues, Intellectual Festival.

September, mid month. Casamasima. Sagra del Coniglio (rabbit).

September 26-27. Uggiano La Chiesa. Festival of the Holy Doctors.

September, late. Locorotondo. Wine Festival.

September, late. Ostuni. Festa della Madonna della Nova.

September, late. Sammichele di Bari. Sagra della Zampina, del Boccino e del Buon Vino (sausage, cheese and wine)

October

October, every Sunday. Monopoli. Gozzovigliando (Fair and Fishing Festival).

October, first Sunday. Conversano. Feast of St. Cosmas and Damian and St. Rita.

October, second Sunday. Casamassima. Corteo Storico Corrado IV di Svevia (Historical Court Reenactment and Procession)

October, second weekend.□Casamassima. Corteo Storico Corrado IV di Svevia.

October, third weekend. Acquaviva. Sagra del Calzone.

October, third Sunday. San Severo. Feast of Mary of the Rosary.

October, third Sunday, Bitono. Patron Saint Festival St. Cosmas and St. Damian.

October, weekends. Bitonto. Traetta Opera Festival.

October with dates that vary

October. Turi. Primitivo Wine Festival.

October, early October. Polignano a Mare. Festival dei Balcone Fioriti (balconies in flower).

October, mid-October. Cisternino. Chestnut Festival.

October, mid-Otober. Cardoncello. Sagra del Fungo Cardoncello (Mushroom).

October, late October. Locorotondo. Festa dell'Uva. (Grape and Wine)

November

November 1. Osara di Puglia. Fuoc acost and Cocce Priatorje (All Saints Day)

November 11. Martina Franca. FestaFusion Martina Franca.

November 11. Taviano. La Fiera di San Martino.

November 22. Bari. Festa di Santa Cecilia.

November 24. Conversano. Feast of St. Flaviano.

November with dates that vary

November, dates vary.▫Bitonto. Festa dell'Olio Nuovo.

November, dates vary. Ruvo di Puglia. Cardoncello Mushroom Festival.

November, weekend in mid November. Foggia. Foggia Film Festival.

November, mid-November. Conversano. Novello sotto il Castello (Fall Festival).

November. Acquaviva delle Fonte. Festival of Wine and Black Chickpeas.

November. Polignano a mare. Pettole e fritelle in Sagre.

December

December 8. Bari, Conversano, and Taranto. Festa dell'Immacolata (Immaculate Conception of Mary).

December 8–January 6.

- Taranto. Christmas in Taranto Festival.

- Trani. Christmas in the Old Village.

- Brindisi. Nativity Scenes and Christmas Market.

- Monopoli. Christmas Home.

- Vico del Gargano. Christmas Market.

- Alberobello. Living Nativity Scenes.

December 13. Conversano, Locorotondo, Canosa di Puglia, Otranto, Monopoli. Festa di Santa Lucia. (Feast of St. Lucy).

December 15-16. Monopoli. Festa della Madonna della Madia.

December 16-24. Martina Franca. The Nine Lamps Festival.

December 23. Surano. Sagra della Pittula e Foccareddha. (Sweets and Bonfire).

December 26 through Marti Gras. Putignano. Carnevale of Putignano.

December 31/January 1. Otranto. Alba dei Popoli (Sunrise of the People, New Year's Day)

December with dates that vary

December. Fasano. Sagra delle Olive.

December, late in the month to early January. Trani. Festival of Musical Bands.

CHAPTER FORTY-THREE

Alphabetical Index of Locations

The Cities of Puglia with Chapters in this Guide

CHAPTER FORTY-FOUR

Glossary of Key Terms

A Bit of Italian & Key Words to Enhance Your Journey

Agriturismo: An agriturismo, or farm stay, is a type of accommodation in Italy that allows you to enjoy the peace and quiet of the countryside. Often functioning farms, these accommodations often include breakfast, a pool and spa, and luxurious rooms (4 and 5 star) or they an offer affordable accommodation with the family who enjoys having you. This type of stay helps to support farmers. The farm can be olive groves, orange groves, wineries, or farms with animals.

Albergo: Albergo is the Italian word for hotel. It refers to any type of lodging establishment that provides accommodation, ranging from budget hotels to luxury resorts. In Italy, an albergo can vary in size, amenities, and services, and they are typically classified by a star rating system (1 to 5 stars) based on quality and facilities.

Angevin Dynasty (Italy): A French royal house that ruled parts of southern Italy between 1266 and 1442. The Angevins gained control of the Kingdom of Sicily in 1266 when Charles I of Anjou defeated the last Hohenstaufen ruler. After the War of the Sicilian Vespers (1282), the kingdom was split: the Angevins retained the mainland territories (becoming the Kingdom of Naples), while Sicily passed to the Aragonese. The Angevin kings ruled Naples and its surrounding regions, including Campania, Calabria, Puglia, Basilicata, Abruzzo, and Molise, until 1442, when Alfonso V of Aragon conquered Naples and unified it with his Sicilian kingdom. The dynasty left a lasting impact on Gothic architecture, governance, and legal structures in southern Italy.

Aragonese Dynasty (Italy): A European royal house that ruled parts of Italy between 1282 and 1516. The Crown of Aragon gained control of Sicily in 1282 following the War of the Sicilian Vespers, ruling it separately from the Kingdom of Naples until 1442, when Alfonso V of Aragon unified both under his rule. The Aragonese ruled the Kingdom of Naples from 1442 to 1501 and regained control from 1504 to 1516, when the kingdom was absorbed into the Spanish Crown. Their rule covered present-day Sicily, Campania, Calabria, Puglia, Basilicata, Abruzzo, and Molise. The dynasty influenced administration, law, and architecture, leaving a legacy of fortified cities, Renaissance palaces, and Catalan-Gothic styles in southern Italy.

Basilica: A term derived from the official building of a Greek magistrate, Basileus. In antiquity, it was a roofed building with a double colonnade used for law courts, assemblies, or markets. In the Christian era, it meant a characteristic type of church building with a high nave and two or four aisles. Usually oriented to the west. basilicas usually have windows on the elevated part of the walls (clerestory) where the roof meets the wall. A basilica is the shape of Catholic churches since the 4th century. The Pope has given a Basilica special privileges as a major church.

Benedictines: St. Benedict of Nursia (c. 480-547) founded the oldest order of Western monks. 529AD. The Benedictine rules formed the basis of western monasticism. The primary task was to cultivate liturgy and prayer. Physical labor, scholarly and artistic work supplemented this.

Blue Flag Beaches: The Blue Flag is an international certification awarded to beaches, marinas, and sustainable boating tourism operators that meet high environmental and safety standards. It is granted by the Foundation for Environmental Education (FEE), a non-profit organization, and is recognized worldwide as a symbol of clean and well-managed beaches.

Bourbon Dynasty (Italy): A European royal house that ruled southern Italy from 1734 to 1861. The Bourbon branch of Spain gained control of the Kingdom of Naples and the Kingdom of Sicily in 1734 under Charles of Bourbon. In 1816, these kingdoms were formally merged into the Kingdom of the Two Sicilies, ruled by the Bourbon monarchs until 1861, when the kingdom was annexed into the newly unified Kingdom of Italy. Their rule covered present-day Campania, Calabria, Puglia, Basilicata, Abruzzo, Molise, and Sicily. Bourbon rulers left a lasting impact on architecture, administration, and cultural institutions in southern Italy.

Brotherhoods: The brotherhoods, or "confraternite" in Italian, are religious lay organizations that play a crucial role in preserving and celebrating local traditions of the region. These brotherhoods have deep historical roots, often dating back centuries, and are named after various saints or religious concepts.

Byzantine architecture: This style relates to the architecture developed in the Byzantine or Eastern Roman Empire. Characterized by enormous domes, mosaics, rounded arches, and spires.

Byzantine Rule in Italy: The Eastern Roman (Byzantine) Empire controlled various parts of Italy between 535 and 1071. Under Emperor Justinian I, the Byzantines launched the Gothic War (535–554), reclaiming the Italian Peninsula from the Ostrogoths and establishing the Exarchate of Ravenna (584–751) as their administrative center. Byzantine rule extended over Ravenna, Rome, Naples, Calabria, Apulia, Basilicata, Sicily, and Sardinia, though it weakened over time due to Lombard invasions. Sicily remained under Byzantine control until 878, when it fell to the Arabs, while southern Italy (Calabria, Apulia, and parts of Campania and Basilicata) remained Byzantine until the Norman conquest in 1071. The Byzantines left a lasting cultural and architectural influence, particularly in religious art, mosaics, and Orthodox traditions in southern Italy.

Campanile: A bell tower of an Italian church. Sometimes, a watchtower for the town, the bell tower, grew in importance during the Renaissance.

Centro Storico: The historic center of town.

Chiesa di: "Church of" followed usually by a saint's name.

Chiesa Madre: Mother church or the most important church in town. This is not a duomo or cathedral.

Cinquecento: A term shortened in Italian from mille-cinquecento. It means the 1500s or the 16th century.

Cistercians: The Cistercians are a monastic Catholic order that has its origins in the reformed Benedictine monastery of Citaeux founded in 1098. The new order set out to achieve fully the ideal from the Rule of St. Benedict.

Confraternite: Religious brotherhoods composed of laypeople dedicated to prayer, charity, and community service, especially within Catholic traditions. Confraternities in Italy, including those in Sicily, are often responsible for organizing and participating in religious processions during major festivals. During events such as the Festa di Santa Rosalia in Palermo, the confraternities don traditional garments—typically long tunics and capes—carrying banners and religious symbols. They play a key role in maintaining the solemnity and spiritual focus of the event, embodying centuries-old traditions of faith and devotion.

Consul: A Roman consul was one of the highest-ranking elected officials in the Roman Republic. After the overthrow of the Roman monarchy, the Romans introduced the office of consul around 509 BC. The Roman Republic elected two consuls each year to serve jointly for a one-year term. They held significant power and responsibilities.

Corpus Domini: Corpus Domini is the Latin term for the Solemnity of the Most Holy Body and Blood of Christ, a major feast in the Catholic Church. Commonly referred to as Corpus Christi in English, this celebration honors the real presence of Jesus Christ in the Eucharist. It is traditionally celebrated on the Thursday after Trinity Sunday or, in many places, moved to the following Sunday to encourage broader participation.

Corso & Via: Street.

DOC: DOC stands for Denominazione di Origine Controllata (Designation of Controlled Origin) in Italian. It is a quality assurance label for Italian wines, cheeses, and other agricultural products. This classification guarantees that the product meets strict production standards and comes from a specific geographic area.

DOP (Denominazione di Origine Protetta): A certification granted by the European Union to protect and guarantee the authenticity of traditional Italian food and agricultural products. DOP status ensures that a product is produced, processed, and prepared in a specific geographic area using traditional methods.

It applies to a wide range of Italian products, including cheese (Parmigiano Reggiano, Pecorino Romano), cured meats (Prosciutto di Parma), olive oils, and balsamic vinegar. Each DOP product undergoes strict quality control to preserve its regional identity and historical production methods.

Duchy: A duchy is a territory or domain ruled by a duke or duchess. It's similar to a kingdom, but typically smaller and ranked below a kingdom in historical European hierarchies.

Duomo or Cattedrale: These are all referred to as the town's Cathedral but they have different significance. Cathedral means the main church of the diocese where the bishop's seat is located. Duomo is the Italian word for Cathedral, but both Duomo and Cattedrale are used when seeking the bishop's seat in Italy.

Ex-voto: Ex-votos are devotional offerings such as jewelry, medals, or tokens left in gratitude for answered prayers or miracles.

IGP: Indicazione Geografica Protetta is a European Union quality certification that guarantees a product originates from a specific region in Italy and has at least one production phase (processing, preparation, or transformation) occurring there. It ensures authenticity, traditional methods, and a strong link between the product and its geographical area.

Lombard Rule in Italy: A Germanic people who ruled parts of Italy from 568 to 774. The Lombards invaded the Italian Peninsula in 568, establishing the Kingdom of the Lombards, which covered much of northern and central Italy, as well as parts of the south. Their rule extended over Lombardy, Veneto, Emilia-Romagna, Tuscany, and parts of Umbria, while in the south, semi-independent Lombard duchies controlled Benevento, Spoleto, Salerno, Capua, and parts of Apulia and Calabria. In 774, the Franks under Charlemagne conquered the kingdom, but Lombard rule persisted in Benevento and Salerno until the 11th century, when the Normans took control. The Lombards influenced Italian law, governance, and architecture, particularly in fortifications and religious buildings.

Masseria: A Masseria is a traditional farmhouse or rural estate in southern Italy, particularly in Puglia, Sicily, and Calabria. These large agricultural estates were historically self-sufficient, often fortified, and used for farming, livestock, and olive oil or wine production. Today, many Masserie have been restored and converted into luxury agriturismos, boutique hotels, or farm stays, offering visitors an immersive experience in Italian countryside life. They typically feature courtyards, stone walls, whitewashed buildings, and beautiful rural landscapes.

Medieval Italy (500–1500): The period between the fall of the Western Roman Empire (476) and the beginning of the Renaissance (circa 1300–1500). During this time, Italy was divided among various kingdoms, duchies, and city-states. Key phases include Byzantine rule (535–1071), Lombard rule (568–774), Carolingian rule (774–888), and the rise of the Holy Roman Empire (962–1806). The period also saw the emergence of powerful Maritime Republics (Venice, Genoa, Pisa, Amalfi), the rise of papal authority, and the development of communes and city-states such as Florence, Milan, and Siena. Feudalism, trade expansion, and conflicts between the Guelphs and Ghibellines (supporters of the pope and emperor) shaped the political landscape. Medieval Italy laid the foundation for the Renaissance through its rich cultural, economic, and architectural developments.

Municipio: Town hall or city hall.

Piazza: Square, as an element of urban layout.

Reformation: A major religious movement from within the Catholic Church that began in Germany in 1517 at the instigation of Martin Luther. His challenge of the practices and doctrines of the Roman Catholic Church ultimately led to the establishment of the Protestant churches.

Relais: Relais is a French term that has been adopted into Italian and English to describe an exclusive countryside hotel, luxury inn, or boutique accommodation, often in a historic building or scenic rural setting. In Italy, Relais hotels are typically elegant properties, offering high-end hospitality, fine dining, and a focus on relaxation and comfort. Many Relais establishments belong to prestigious hospitality groups, such as Relais & Châteaux, which is known for luxury accommodations with exceptional service, gourmet cuisine, and unique charm. These hotels are often found in historic villas, castles, or restored farmhouses in picturesque regions like Tuscany, Umbria, and the Amalfi Coast.

Renaissance (Italy): A cultural, artistic, and intellectual movement that began in Italy around 1300 and flourished between 1400 and 1600. It marked a revival of classical learning, humanism, and artistic innovation, influencing painting, architecture, literature, science, and philosophy. The movement originated in Florence and spread across Italy, impacting cities like Rome, Venice, and Milan. Key figures include Leonardo da Vinci, Michelangelo, Raphael, Brunelleschi, and Machiavelli. The Renaissance shaped Italy's identity, leading to masterpieces in art, architecture, and literature, with enduring influences on Western civilization.

Romanesque: A term used to describe forms of Roman architecture such as rounded arches, columns, capitals, and vaults that were used in buildings in the early Middle Ages. The term Romanesque covers the period from about 1000 to the point when Gothic began.

Savoy. House of Savoy (Italy): A European royal dynasty that ruled parts of Italy from 1720 to 1946. The Savoy gained control of the Kingdom of Sardinia in 1720, which included the island of Sardinia and territories in northern Italy, such as Piedmont, Liguria, and Savoy (now in France). In 1861, under King Victor Emmanuel II, the Savoy dynasty led the unification of Italy, becoming rulers of the newly formed Kingdom of Italy. They reigned until 1946, when Italy became a republic following a national referendum. The Savoy left a lasting legacy in military, political, and administrative reforms, as well as in architecture, particularly in Turin, which served as their capital.

Swabian (Hohenstaufen) Dynasty (Italy): A German royal house that ruled southern Italy and Sicily from 1194 to 1266. The Hohenstaufens, also known as the Swabians, gained control when Emperor Henry VI (son of Frederick Barbarossa) inherited the Kingdom of Sicily in 1194 through his marriage to Constance of Sicily. His son, Frederick II (r. 1198–1250), expanded imperial power and made Sicily a center of learning and administration. The dynasty ruled Sicily, Campania, Calabria, Apulia, Basilicata, Abruzzo, and Molise until the papacy-backed Angevins defeated Manfred of Sicily in 1266, marking the end of Hohenstaufen rule.

CHAPTER FORTY-FIVE

Editing and Photo Credits

Acknowledging the Editor and Those Who Made This Journey Brighter

A very special thank you to my editor, **Pamela Zale**

Pam, thank you for your sharp eye, steady guidance, and heartfelt enthusiasm throughout this journey. Your insight helped shape every page, and your belief in this Puglia project never wavered. I'm deeply grateful for your care, precision, and the joy you brought to the process. This book is all the better because of you.

Photo Credits

Appian way map. AlMare, Public domain, via Wikimedia Commons.

Map of Southern Italy, Public domain, by Ypsilon from Finland - Own work, CC0, https://commons.wikimedia.org/w/index.php?curid=41072155

San Severo Festa del Madonna del Soccorso. Astolinto, Public domain, via Wikimedia Commons.

Turi Cherries.Hans Braxmeier, CC0, via Wikimedia Commons. Public Domain.

Cherries in Basket. Hans Braxmeier, CC0, via Wikimedia Commons. Public Domain.

Foggia Chiesa di San Francesco. Francesco interman, Public domain, via Wikimedia Commons.

Acquaviva Palazzo. Driante70 at Italian Wikipedia, Public domain, via Wikimedia Commons.

Padre Pio Image. By The original uploader was Manfredonia at Italian Wikipedia. - Transferred from it.wikipedia to Commons.www.vatican.va, Public Domain, https://commons.wikimedia.org/w/index.php?curid=129862676.

Ruvo di Puglia (Holy Week) Cathedral. Sailko, CC BY 3.0 <https://creativecommons.org/licenses/by/3.0>, via Wikimedia Commons

Ruvo di Puglia (Holy Week). Procession della Dolorata. Forzaruvo94, CC BY 3.0 <https://creativecommons.org/licenses/by/3.0>, via Wikimedia Commons.

Immerson Experience Vieste. Arch. Carmen Fiano, Public domain, via Wikimedia Commons.

All Other Photos are my Own.

CHAPTER FORTY-SIX

Select Bibliography

Great Reads for those who Love Italy

Attlee, Helena. *The Land Where Lemons Grow: The Story of Italy and Its Citrus Fruit*. London: Penguin, 2015.

Burke, Peter. *The Italian Renaissance: Culture and Society in Italy.* Princeton: Princeton University Press, 1986.

Facaros, Dana, and Michael Pauls. *Puglia, Basilicata & Calabria*. Chalfont St. Peter, UK: Bradt Travel Guides, 2022.

Mueller von der Haegen, Anne. *The White Cities of Italy: The Architecture of Puglia*. Munich: Prestel, 2016.

Rowland, Robert J., Jr. *Italy's Southern Shore: Archaeological and Historical Landscapes of Magna Graecia*. New York: Routledge, 2018.

Simeti, Mary Taylor. *Bitter Chicory to Sweet Espresso: Survival and Revival in Southern Italy*. Totnes, UK: Prospect Books, 2019.

Lonely Planet Southern Italy. Lonely Planet Travel Writers. Dublin: Lonely Planet, 2023.

Thank You & Please Leave a Review

Reviews Enhance a Book's Discoverability

Thank you for reading this Ultimate Festival & Tavel Guide. It is the fourth in the Travel Italy Series.

If the guide enhanced your travel planning, I'd greatly appreciate it if you could leave a review on Amazon. Your feedback not only helps other travelers, but also supports this book's success.

Scan to Review on Amazon

I sincerely hope you have enjoyed this tour through Italy via its festivals. I would love to hear about your own festival adventures! Connect with me on Instagram, where I share hundreds of videos from the festivals of Rome and Italy, perfect for a sneak peek before your trip. @katerinaferraraauthor

Thank you for being part of this journey, and I look forward to hearing about yours!

Wishing you the safest and happiest travels!

Katerina Ferrara

Connect with Me

Free Italy Travel Resources and More

N ewsletter / Travel News

Sign up for my newsletter and stay updated with insider secrets about Italy's charming towns, vibrant festivals, and mouthwatering food, things you won't find in any travel guide. Stay updated with the latest on festivals, tours, podcasts, and special insights that go beyond the book!

KaterinaFerrara.com

Immersion Travel by Katerina Ferrara Blog

Looking for even more hidden gems in Italy? My blog is packed with insider tips, from secret beaches tucked away on Italy's lesser-known coastlines to self-guided walking tours that take you off the typical tourist path. Whether you're planning a relaxing escape or an adventurous exploration, you'll find everything you need to create unforgettable Italian journeys. Subscribe for exclusive travel insights and start uncovering Italy's best-kept secrets! www.katerinaferrara.com

Festival Enthusiasts - Immersion Travel Italy offers one-of-a-kind experiences for travelers seeking to connect deeply with Italy's culture. We organize small-group journeys to discover Italy's most vibrant festivals and sagre, explore charming towns, and embark on unforgettable adventures. Whether you're savoring local delicacies at a food festival or taking part in centuries-old traditions, our personalized trips allow you to experience the heart and soul of Italy like a local. Join us for an immersive travel experience you'll treasure forever!

Corrections / Updates / Suggestions Oops!

Even the best of us can make mistakes. I would appreciate your help to make my content better. Please visit the book page here: www.katerinaferrara.com and scroll down to the book feedback button.

About the Author: Katerina Ferrara

Festival Follower and Founder of Immersion Travel Italy

Katerina Ferrara is a published author and the founder of Immersion Travel Italy, a company dedicated to creating unforgettable travel experiences in Italy. With over 25 years of exploring Europe, Katerina has developed a deep love for immersing herself in the diverse cultures, traditions, and culinary delights of the places she visits. Fluent in Italian, she effortlessly connects with locals and travelers alike, bringing an insider's perspective to her travel writing.

Katerina jokes that she lives her life on a perpetual diet, not for vanity, but to prepare for the next irresistible festival in Italy. Her ultimate dream is to inspire **Festival Followers,** travelers who prioritize experiencing incredible festivals first and then explore the surrounding sites while immersing themselves in local traditions. She believes festivals offer a unique lens into a region's heart and culture, making them the perfect starting point for any adventure.

An avid hiker and fitness enthusiast, Katerina incorporates her passion for staying active into her travels, often seeking out scenic trails, walking tours, and outdoor adventures that connect her to the natural beauty of a destination (while making room for just a little more gelato).

When she's not exploring new destinations or writing, Katerina enjoys sharing her travel insights and tips with fellow adventurers, inspiring them to delve deeper into the cultural richness of the places they visi, —and maybe even discover their own favorite festival.

Visit: https://katerinaferrara.com/

Follow the Immersion Travel Podcast on Spotify

Also Available on Apple Itunes:

https://podcasts.apple.com/us/podcast/immersion-travel-italy/id1795327762

Katerina's YouTube Channel:

https://www.youtube.com/@ImmersionTravelItaly

Made in the USA
Las Vegas, NV
19 June 2025

23855487R00302